DIGITAL BAROQUE

ELECTRONIC MEDIATIONS

Katherine Hayles, Mark Poster, and Samuel Weber, Series Editors

For more books in the series, see page 311.

DIGITAL BAROQUE

New Media Art and Cinematic Folds

TIMOTHY MURRAY

Electronic Mediations, Volume 26

UNIVERSITY OF MINNESOTA PRESS

MINNEAPOLIS • LONDON

Published by the University of Minnesota Press
111 Third Avenue South, Suite 290
Minneapolis, MN 55401-2520
http://www.upress.umn.edu

Library of Congress Cataloging-in-Publication Data
Murray, Timothy.
Digital baroque : new media art and cinematic folds / Timothy Murray.
p. cm.—(Electronic mediations ; v. 26)
Includes bibliographical references and index.
ISBN 978-0-8166-3401-9 (hc : alk. paper)—ISBN 978-0-8166-3402-6 (pb : alk. paper)
1. Video recordings. 2. Digital video. 3. Installations (Art). 4. Civilization, Baroque. I. Title.
PN1992.945.M87 2008
791.4—dc22
2008030996

Printed in the United States of America on acid-free paper

The University of Minnesota is an equal-opportunity educator and employer.

15 14 13 12 11 10 09 08   10 9 8 7 6 5 4 3 2 1

For my life partners in the cinematic fold,
Renate, Ashley, and Erin

CONTENTS

PREFACE

Digital Baroque. What happens when two nouns, "the digital" and "the Baroque," are conjoined without articles to anchor them: digital/Baroque? Does the one, "digital," play the qualifying adjective to the weightier noun, "Baroque"? Does the adjective signify something of the digit, the deictic, the gestural, and the rhetorical nature of the Baroque, as in the baroque trope *faire voir?* Or might the terms without their articles also stand juxtaposed analogically in enigmatic difference: digital (,) Baroque or Baroque (,) digital—something like 1 (,) 0? Perhaps they thus stand figurally as if enfolded into one another, thereby signifying the paradox and enigma of analogy itself. Might not we understand analogy as something not simply transcended by digitality but as something deeply cryptic and disturbingly disjunctive that is deeply crucial to digitality's structure and representations? As for digitality, is it even possible to distinguish the digital / the deictic from the digital / the algebraic? Can we make a clean numerical break from the rhetorical tradition?

The conceit of Digital Baroque multiplies when we add to this titular mix the histories, thresholds, and memories of cinema, to which this book gives particular attention, as they have been enfolded into new media art. Does new media stand forth as the memento mori of cinema? Does the Baroque function as a marker of the death of cinema in the twenty-first century, as an energetic carrier of the figures of mourning, melancholia, and even ascesis so fundamental to the Baroque? And what is implied by cinema's frequent identification with the Baroque, particularly by pioneering

French theorists of cinema such as Roger Leenhardt and André Bazin? Has their fascination with cinematic forms associated with the Baroque, such as temporal and narrative ellipsis, anamorphosis, and light, simply become so naturalized into the language of cinema and culture that it seems rather predictable for Christine Buci-Glucksmann to claim the Baroque for the cinema of Raoul Ruiz, or for Sean Cubitt to give the trope a digital turn in his catalogue essay on new media artist Simon Biggs? Might cinema's conceptual and technical registration in the Baroque be deeply akin to the psychosocial properties of new media interactivity and immersion? These are the sorts of questions that motivate this book's analysis of the critical paradox of Digital Baroque through the close reading of film, video, cinematic installation, and new media art.

My conceptual blueprint for *Digital Baroque* has undergone significant shifts since I first conceived it in the midnineties. I initially set out to analyze the dialogue of recent video and digital installation art with Renaissance and Baroque visual sources and models. As a result of research and teaching in my two areas of academic specialty, interactive arts (video, cinema, performance, installation, electronic art) and early modern studies, I became intrigued by the extent of the interface between recent projects in the electronic arts and the public memory of early modern art, culture, and philosophy. A wide range of influential projects in eighties and nineties video art and electronic installation dialogued with Renaissance constructions of artistic form and social place as well as with early modern philosophical analyses of space, light, volume, passion, memory, and utopia. References to early modern painting, culture, and history provided the context for video and electronic installation projects by artists as diverse as Juan Downey, Thierry Kuntzel, Esther Parada, Gary Hill, Keith Piper, Bill Viola, Valie Export, Francesc Torres, Peter D'Agostino, and Steve Fagin. The majority of this work commented on historical material to forge a new understanding of the social, artistic, and theoretical imperatives confronting contemporary artistic culture. While Juan Downey reflected on the erotics of artistic form, the currency of artistic capital, and the politics of artistic criticism in his video *The Looking Glass* (1981), Keith Piper mused in his CD-ROM *Relocating the Remains* (1997) on the historical paradoxes of Christianity's investment in slavery and capitalism's continuous investment in the black athletic body. It is no mere coincidence that so many video and electronic artists turned their attention, at least momentarily in their careers, to consider the consequences of the new technologies of printing, science, art, and colonialism that developed rapidly during the early modern period.

In evaluating video's understanding of its links to the early modern past, I aimed to clarify the historical and ideological complexity of the "new" apparatuses of digitized electronic arts and to articulate the future promise of video's reconfiguration of historical methods, artistic icons, and cultural memories. In my proposal for a fellowship from the National Endowment for the Humanities, which helped to fund the initial research for this book, I delineated a threefold critical aim: (1) to complicate the extensive historical claims made by electronic artists and critics regarding this art's avant-garde and utopic break from early modern visual models and subject positions; (2) to evaluate the conceptual and historical links of projects in video and digital art to concepts of vision, utopia, space, and memory that were important to early modern culture; (3) to appreciate, in turn, how contemporary experiments in video and electronic discourse contribute to the retrospective understanding of artistic concepts, visions, and practices of the early modern past.

While readers of *Digital Baroque* will recognize traces of these goals throughout the book, it has taken a decidedly focused turn toward the cinematic and temporal conditions of new media art (not as exclusive conditions of digital information relay, certainly, but as significant elements of the artworks I discuss). What I argue to constitute the important legacy of this work is not simply the thematic corollaries between early modern history and contemporary art but how their engagement with baroque and early modern conceptual and artistic precedents provides the electronic arts with psychosocial paradigms that are significantly broader and more elastic than those framed merely by modernism, the avant-garde, or even the philosophical imperatives of cultural and subjective dialectics—these are the critical frameworks that seem to have dominated new media theory and criticism. Indeed, I will argue throughout *Digital Baroque* for the critical imperative of a psychophilosophical approach to new media art. This book's return to the charged, baroque psychosocial enigmas of analogical disjunction, temporal shifts, spatial simultaneities, and conceptual incompossibilities provides critical frameworks for understanding the contemporary subject's inscription in the accumulating flow of digital data, information, and imagery. *Digital Baroque* ironically reflects on the cultural shift enacted by the artistic turn of emphasis away from the centered subjectivity often associated with early modern precedent and cinematic viewing to the energized relay of information shared so curiously by Digital Baroque cultures, art practices, and archival communities.

I should add that my sensitivity to Digital Baroque is indebted to a number of writing projects that have helped to shape it. While working on my book *Like a Film: Ideological Fantasy on Screen, Camera, and Canvas* (1993), I investigated the deep influence of baroque art and thought on cinematic projects and studies by Derek Jarman and Roland Barthes. This is where I most fully articulate the layers of affect constitutive of melancholia and its subsequent theoretical appropriation by both Jarman and Barthes. Similarly, in my next book, *Drama Trauma* (1997), I studied televised Shakespeare, on the one hand, and the ambivalent attitude of contemporary African-American playwrights toward Shakespeare, on the other. The psychosocial weight of trauma articulated differently by both periods provides the critical framework of that project and informs this book's emphasis on a move away from the negative valences of discourses of loss and lack toward a more affirmative assertion of interiorized procedures of scansion, sublimation, and archivization. Equally influential to the thinking that went into this book are my two collections, *Mimesis, Masochism, and Mime: The Politics of Theatricality in Contemporary French Thought* and *Repossessions: Psychoanalysis and the Phantasms of Early Modern Culture* (which I coedited with Alan K. Smith) that reflect broadly on the processes of interiorization and aesthetics, which I understand to be structurally inherent in social and artistic practice.

Even more crucial to the critical evolution of this book has been my involvement in a number of curatorial projects whose role in the significant delay of the completion of this manuscript has worked to its benefit by expanding the range and scope of the project as well as my understanding of Digital Baroque. While writing the catalogue entries for the eighty artworks in the exhibition I toured from 1999 to 2004, *Contact Zones: The Art of CD-ROM,* I began to appreciate the extent to which the conceptual concerns of the artworks grouped under the rubric of "Baroque Interface" were crucial to a broader understanding of the theoretical, and sometimes formal, implications of artworks throughout the exhibition. *Flora Petrinsularis* (1993–94) by Jean-Louis Boissier, *Relic/relique* (1999) by Rae Davis, *Bits of Paper* (1998) by Douglas Holleley, *Red Iris Interactive* (1997) by Kate

Richards, and *Hortus Musicus* (2001) by Daniel Warner foreground interactive experiences with sounds, bodies, texts, and visual traces that provide
structural and theoretical support for many of the other pieces in the exhibition. Their emphasis on "digital cartography," "the fold," "analogy,"
"memory errors," "cinematic ghostings," and "contrasting chords" echoes
the structural and theoretical principles of a majority of the other pieces
in the exhibition. Since then, my enjoyable collaboration with Arthur and
Marilouise Kroker on *CTHEORY Multimedia* and my subsequent work as
founding curator of the Rose Goldsen Archive of New Media Art in the
Cornell Library have left me sensitive to the scope of the baroque depth
of the new media archive, as well as its important relation to the memories of cinema and video—the conceit with which I initially undertook
this project (one whose critical primacy to the theorization of new media
may now be more open to question but which nevertheless seems to per-
sist). At the core of *Digital Baroque* is an appreciation of the maturation
of the archival subject that has developed since early modern times in conjunction with the growth of new machineries in the social field. Concluding reflections on the thought of temporality in new media, via Gilles
Deleuze's cinema books, provide the critical framework for my current book
project on the immaterial archive in the new media age.

ACKNOWLEDGMENTS

A central feature of the Baroque is the accumulation of fragments of texts and bits of conversation whose proliferation provides the seeds of emergent discourse. I am particularly indebted to Tom Conley, Mitchell Greenberg, Patty Zimmermann, David Rodowick, Anne-Marie Duguet, Norie Neumark, Tim Corrigan, and Walter Moser, whose supportive friendship and ongoing conversations about digitality, the Baroque, and the memory of cinema have been key along the way.

I have been fortunate to count on the advice and support of a generous group of insightful friends and colleagues, particularly Jean-Louis Boissier, Verena Conley, Lynn Hershman, Maria Miranda, Arthur and Marilouise Kroker, Antonio Muntadas, Scott Durham, Sam Weber, Richard Herskowitz, Wendy Chun, Judith Mayne, Eliane dal Molin, Karen Ball, Marcia Ferguson, Jill Bennett, Roseanne Kennedy, Annette Barbier, Michelle Citron, Horit Herman-Peled, Maureen Turim, George Legrady, Reggie Woolery, Jim Drobnick, Jennifer Fisher, Christina McPhee, Tony Cokes, Georges Van Den Abbeele, Tom Lamarre, Rebecca Schneider, Manuela de Barros, Eliane dal Molin, and Paul Vanouse.

The recent deaths of two friends important to key elements of this book have heightened my sensitivity to the specters of death and melancholy that fill these pages. Thierry Kuntzel died before he could read the final version of chapter 3, which focuses on his forceful work in video, installation, and theory. Priamo Lozada, who suffered a tragic death while curating the Mexican Pavilion at the 2007 Venice Bienale, collaborated with me on the installation of *Contact Zones: The Art of CD-ROM* at the Centro de la Imagen in Mexico City and produced the invaluable Mexican catalogue. I also regret the passing of Jacques Derrida prior to my completion of this book; his Paris seminars in the late 1970s first pointed me in the direction of the philosophy of the fold.

It is difficult to put a value on the impact on my thinking that has come from my friendships at Cornell University. Although their influences on my thinking are too numerable to mention, particular thanks go to Neil Saccamano, Brett de Bary, Maria Fernandez, Naoki Sakai, Anette Schwartz, Marie-Claire Vallois, Jonathan Culler, Dominick LaCapra, Ellis Hanson, Phil Lewis, Buzz Speetor, Xiaowen Chen, Shelley Wong, Ellis Hanson, David Bathrick, Amy Villarejo, Natalie Melas, Salah Hassan, and Rayna Kalas. Much of the thinking in this book has taken place alongside my development of the Rose Goldsen Archive of New Media Art in the Cornell Library, whose artistic participants and resources have enriched these pages. I wish to extend particular thanks for this fusion to Mickey Reich Casad, Thomas Hickerson, Elaine Engst, Katherine Reagan, Sarah Thomas, and Danielle Mericle.

My graduate students, current and former, have been a constant source of inspiration when it comes to thinking the folds of cinema and new media. I am deeply grateful to Timothy Billings, Grace An, Shin-Yi Yang, Harvey Young, Mickey Reich Casad, James Way, Rebecca Egger, Katherine Groo, Lauren Beeley, Megan Shea, Ryan Platt, and Ricardo Arribas.

Research on this book has been aided by grants from the National Endowment for the Humanities, the Society for the Humanities at Cornell University, and the Faculty Advisory Board on Information Technology at Cornell University.

At the times I undertook and completed this manuscript, I was fortunate to be in residence at the Society for the Humanities. I am particularly indebted to Mary Ahl for her many personal and practical interventions as well as to others at Cornell who assisted me with research and travel: Lisa Patti, Linda Allen, Robin Doxtater, Sue Besemer, Vicky Brevetti, Darlene Flint.

At the University of Minnesota Press, I am grateful to Doug Armato for his unfailing commitment to this baroque project, as well as to Andrea Patch, Nancy Sauro, and Daniel Leary.

My family has tolerated the many stages of this book more than I can imagine, from lengthy absences from home to countless hours of inaccessibility. What's wonderful is how we all seemed to have crossed similar thresholds in recent years. Adequate gratitude cannot be expressed to my son, Erin Ferro-Murray, who is now setting his sights on video and art; to my daughter, Ashley Ferro-Murray, whose scholarly and artistic passion for choreography, visual studies, and feminism keeps me on my toes; and finally, to my collaborator in life and work, Renate Ferro, who never seems bothered by the many times that panic hits home and who is a constant source of inspiration, information, and aspiration for the many stages of this book.

Ithaca, July 2008

BAROQUE FOLDS AND DIGITAL
INCOMPOSSIBILITIES

The universe to the eye of the human understanding is framed like a labyrinth,
presenting as it does on every side so many ambiguities of way, such deceitful
resemblances of objects and signs, natures so irregular in their lines and so
knotted and entangled. And then the way is still to be made by the uncertain
light of the sense, sometimes shining out, sometimes clouded over, through
the woods of experience and particulars.

—FRANCIS BACON, *The Great Instauration*

A few years ago I helped to pen a grant for a U.S./UK initiative in digital
libraries. My charge was to articulate the digital transformation of the library
in terms of its impact on the humanities. For this purpose I turned to tropes
from visual studies to characterize the library's role in humanistic research
and contemplation. I chose to emphasize the trope of the "dark cabinet"
partly in response to a poster for a Cornell University Renaissance conference, "Making the Text," that featured Holbein's portrait of Erasmus hud-
dled over his writing in the privacy of his cell. Here we have the visual icon
of the rise of the Western author, isolated in his study for the purpose of
penning a text with which he "projects" his authoritative knowledge out
onto the world via the eye of human understanding. I argued that the traditional understanding of the collaboration between the humanist and the
university library remains loyal to this Renaissance model of the dark cabinet. Made infamous in engravings from Holbein to da Messina, the dark
cabinet of knowledge is replete with rare books and manuscripts with which
scholars seclude themselves for intensive research and private contemplation. Such a model of research has pivoted on a relatively fixed scholarly

canon centered on the Occidental classics in philosophy, literature, theater, history, and art, with additional attention paid to the peripheral areas of Oriental and Asian studies.

Although the international growth of the library and the university during the twentieth century has loosened the parameters of this model in a way that includes the public media of radio and cinema, while lending authority to the geographical periphery of texts and regions previously little considered, the humanistic paradigm of the dark cabinet has remained predominant until very recently: the Occidental humanist stands forth as the source of the projection of knowledge gained in the comforting confines of the library. This trope of projection has held less firm when extended outside of the library via the apparatuses of photography and cinema that have turned the walls of the library from protective enclosures to the alluring screens of the public intellectual mediascape. So it goes that Adriene Jenik recently transformed the facade of the Martin Luther King Jr. Main Public Library in San Jose into the multi-site screen surface of her "distributed cinema" performance, *SPECFLIC 2.0* (2006). The facade of the library became the after-hours media skin for crowds that gathered during ISEA 2006 to watch Praba Pilar perform as the InfoSpherian (Figure 1), a 2030 virtualized information specialist, who answers questions via video distribution about books no longer available for direct consultation as a result of digitization and the computerized transformation of access and information control. Contributing to the multimedia adventure were two projections of the "ancient" stacks, mounted in horizontal windows on the second and third stories above the street-level screens that displayed the InfoSpherian's golden visage. One featured tracking shots of the ancient "stacker"; the other had sequences of the antiquarian "searchers" traversing the bookshelves in a hunt for the volumes requested by the InfoSpherian. Even though visitors were offered multiple points of view as well as the opportunity to ask the InfoSpherian reference questions via acoustic connection from outside the building, the extent of their interactive engagement depended on procedural conditions that hearkened back to the model of the dark cabinet. The digital age spectators seemed delighted when the InfoSpherian performed parodic, meditative trances in order to recall deeply embedded information, as if a theatricalization of the scholarly mind serving as the archival receptacle of historical knowledge. Those on the outside of the library (and mind) subsequently had to await reception of the informational results of the internal trance via the distribution of her response through projection of the InfoSpherian on the front and rear walls of the building. Her responses varied from amusing sociophilosophical aphorisms to her acknowledgment of "No Access" to either the context of the question or its informational response, very much in the playful spirit of Chris Marker's film *Level 5,* which I discuss in chapter 6. Most evident and amusing was how her info-communications carried with them the interference of mental pause and informational static that now highlights the inscription of the projection model in the far more complex webs and networks of the digital age. Since Jenik's televisual cabinet was no longer dark and not always dependable as a source of information, her cinematic display as the performative muse of the history of the printed book seemed to challenge

Figure 1. Adriene Jenik,
SPECFLIC 2.0, 2006.
Photograph by
Chris O'Neal.

with every technological relay the reliability of the humanistic model of the outward, public projection of interiorized, private knowledge.

Soon before my work on the digital libraries grant, which prompted my critical thinking about the role of the library in the age of the new media book, I had completed an essay that positioned the cinematic theories of Gilles Deleuze in relation to Peter Greenaway's *Prospero's Books*. Greenaway's film also frames its protagonist, Prospero, in the confines of a dark cabinet. It is noteworthy that Greenaway chose for his source not the rather sparse cabinet of Erasmus but the plentiful writing room of da Messina's St. Jerome. Greenaway encloses this cabinet in the deep recessive spaces of a baroque interior replete with arches, folds, recesses, conflicting sources of light and shadow, and centered by a bookcase overflowing with the competing ornaments of science, arts, and conquest. Crucial to Greenaway's appropriation of this study is its portability in the mise-en-scène as "a structure which can be dismantled and reconstructed—sometimes with other parts . . . sometimes in a different arrangement."[1] Greenaway appreciates how the irregularity and portability of the cabinet serves as a metaphor of Prospero's openness to what Bacon called "the woods of experience and particulars": Prospero "is not wholly a closeted academic," muses Greenaway, "for there is much which demonstrates his interest in the contemporary world. He has the enquiring, scholastic imagination which recognised no boundary between art and science or literature and natural history and, open-minded and unprejudiced, looked forward to the first century of science."[2] While still serving as the space of intellectual projection, Greenaway's cabinet is framed more like a material labyrinth than a mental closet, presenting as it does the "many ambiguities of way [and] natures so irregular in their lines," which are, as Bacon put it, "so knotted and entangled." In this film of excessive digital dazzle, corporeal mannerism, and moving, shaking, and fluttering texts, the composite presentation of shifting space and structure with the uncertainty of the light of sense (sometimes shining out, sometimes clouded over) confuses and challenges the centrality of ontological projection and its source in the dark cabinet. As I elaborate in chapter 4, the makings of text in *Prospero's Books* is as much a process of the fold as it is a standard of projection in how it enfolds on the screen the activity of writing, the deep memory of the archive, and the digital machineries on which we now rely for the production, retention, and dissemination of text and image.

FROM CINEMATIC PROJECTION TO DIGITAL FOLD

At issue in *Digital Baroque* is a deeply significant archaeological shift from *projection* to *fold* that is emphasized, if not wholly embodied, by the digital condition. While still often inscribed in models of knowledge and representation derived from single-point perspective and Euclidean systems of projection (whether the stuff of the cinematic apparatus or the variants of GPS tracking), the fold embodies the elasticity of seriality and the continuous labyrinth of single points (1's and 0's). These folds expand infinitely in all directions rather than definitively in the shape of a cone, line, or sight that culminates in a single, utopian point or subjectivity. Such a concept turns around the paradoxical inscription of novel procedures of accumulation, divergence, and fractal simultaneity in past paradigms of projection, dialectics, and philosophical teleology. The paradox of the Digital Baroque acknowledges while contesting the ultimate distinction made by Maurice Merleau-Ponty between the Hegelian notion of "a hole in Being" and the subject as "a fold that shapes and can unshape itself" in internal dialogue with "perceived spectacle."[3] While there is much in my book that lends itself to Merleau-Ponty's distinction between the perception of dialectical spectacle and the changing vicissitudes of folding subjectivities, it will be evident throughout that my critical turn to the fold derives much more from my ongoing intellectual dialogue with poststructural philosophy.

In the creative and insightful book *The Fold: Leibniz and the Baroque,* for instance, Gilles Deleuze recounts his fascination with Leibniz's interests in fluidity, elasticity, and spirit (passion). Deleuze's notion of the fold contrasts starkly with Cartesian investments in line as an analytical, punctual equation and in projection as the culmination or end point of reason (a legacy that finds its culmination in the Hegelian spectacle of mind). The fold appears to Deleuze as

a flexible or an elastic body [that] still has cohering parts that form a fold, such that they are not separated into parts of parts but are rather divided to infinity in smaller and smaller folds that always retain a certain cohesion. Thus a continuous labyrinth is not a line dissolving into independent points, as flowing sand might dissolve into grains, but resembles a sheet of paper divided into infinite folds or separated into bending movements, each one determined by the consistent or conspiring surroundings.[4]

The labyrinthine continuousness of the fold, in contrast to the deceptive cohesion of projection, also functions as the seminal figure of Jacques Derrida's reading of the machinic supplement in "The Double Session." Derrida seizes on Mallarmé's trope of the fold to articulate his understanding of supplementarity as the stuff of representation:

> What will always defy and baffle criticism is the effect of being a supplementary double. There is always one extra rejoinder, one recess or representation too many, which also means one too few. The "recess [le repli]": the Mallarmean fold will always have been not only a replication of the tissue but also a repetition-toward-itself of the text that is a re-folding, a re-playing, a supplementatary re-marking of the fold. "Re-presentation" . . . is less engaged in setting forth things or the image of things than it is in setting up the machine."[5]

Important to the analyses of *Digital Baroque* is not only the supplementarity of the fold and its infinite, machinic motion but also its influence on our understanding of subjectivity. As Derrida insists, "the fold is not a form of reflexivity," in the sense of a motion of consciousness or self-presence, since "reflexivity is but the effect of the fold as text."[6] For both Derrida and Deleuze (two philosophers often at odds), the fold is the machinery of intersubjectivity and inter-activity through which, as Derrida frequently repeats, "The fold multiplies (itself) but (is) not (one)."[7]

If *Digital Baroque* could be said to have an overarching conceptual aim, it would be to remain open to the multiple becomings and machinic eventfulness of the fold rather than to seek refuge in preconceived universals grounded in self-presence, such as the notions of "technoromanticism" or " digital dialectic" that have deeply influenced discussions of the theoretical parameters of new media art.[8] By providing close readings and analyses of films, videos, CD-ROMs, and installations attuned to the baroque nuances of the fold, I hope to shift our critical attention away from what Jay David Bolter and Richard Grusin term "the romantic and modernist strategies" that have dominated the criticism and creation of new media.[9] Key to this shift, I will argue throughout *Digital Baroque,* is a critical openness in our approach to films, videos, and artworks that screen the subject's inscription in the accumulating flow of digital data, archival information, and virtual imagery. Rather than position us simply in the pull of teleology's dialectical future or the romantic dazzle of technology's present, the Digital Baroque will be discussed as enfolding the user in the energetic present, as articulated in relation to the analog past while bearing on the digital future. This temporal fold positions the user and the critic within the force of time's flow through which the past and its divergent epistemologies call on the future for their inclusion, whether as haunting articulations of visions previously unmaterialized in the baroque past or as critical revisions of those dialectical and romantic new media paradigms on which modernism so confidently relies.

While new information systems enhance the intensity of this flow, their displacement of possessive individualism by the wonder of data accumulation evokes the very ideal of knowledge that Walter Benjamin argued to be characteristic of the Baroque: the process of storing and schemata to which the emergent libraries of the seventeenth century were a monument.[10] This is what Benjamin joyfully proclaimed as "the finest material in baroque creation. For it is common practice in the literature of the baroque to pile up fragments ceaselessly, without any strict idea of a goal, and in the unremitting expectation of a miracle, to take the repetition of stereotypes for a process of intensification."[11] If we turn briefly to a work by the pioneering British new media artist Simon Biggs, we can appreciate his visualization of the paradoxical legacy of the Baroque that sensitizes the user of new media art both to the intersubjective experience of the emergent network and, vice versa, to the contributions made by the digital framework to a keener sensitivity toward the early modern fascination with the extraneous remnants of serial accumulation. Thus it works in Biggs's piece *Solitary* (Figure 2) that the obscured figure of the portrayed, solitary subject appears on the screen only as the accumulative traces of fleeting corporeal shadows whose overlapping folds interpellate the user to interface with a surface of line and shadow. The looping repetitions that mime "solitary" with the figures of electronic shadow display the electronic verve of what Benjamin also calls the vital "transposition of the originally temporal data into a figurative spatial simultaneity."[12] Precisely the simultaneity of accumulation, whether of books, objects, traces, or shadows, works actively to temporalize the space of new media. This temporalization of space is, moreover, what Christine Buci-Glucksmann argues to be the baroque operation par excellence: "The baroque is characterized by development, by the capacity to create infinite operations of expression, by the active unity of a force and an artistic form

. . . The baroque continually transforms itself in an operation that tem-
poralizes space and brings about its own appearance-disappearance. This
is the form of time in its fluid continuity."[13]

Had Greenaway shot *Prospero's Books* just a couple of years later, he might
have profited from Biggs's more contemporary montage of the scholarly
cabinet for his material paradigm of baroque intellectual accumulation. This
is a space that is rendered visual, if not also textual, in Biggs's first-gener-
ation interactive installation, which he subsequently rendered into a CD-
ROM artwork, *Portrait of a Young Man* (1993). Here the artist's autopor-
trait time-travels back to the age of early modern portraiture, as we remember it so well from da Messina and Holbein's *The Ambassadors*.[14] In *Portrait of a Young Man* (Figure 3), we find the young scholar, now turned
gamer, framed like Holbein's diplomats by the objects of a brave new world
of discovery, amusement, and concentration: from computer discs, digital
clock, and toy robot, to appointment book, mood light, and even Paul Virilio's book *War and Cinema,* a text that traces the evolution of the projection
apparatus from the anamorphic lens adapted by cinema to the laser-guided
missile of contemporary colonial conquest and fantasy.[15] So that the users
of Biggs's interactive portrait do not forget that these familiar objects of

Figure 2. Simon Biggs, *Solitary,* 1992.

contemporary everyday life carry with them labyrinthine specters of history and representation, Biggs positions them somewhat paradoxically not only in the space of the conventional library, where the book frames the robot, but also in the interactive display of the Holbeinian conceit of anamorphosis itself. As the users roll the mouse over the robotic toy, the robot morphs into a telescope, just as the appointment book becomes a parcel, the disposable paperback becomes an archived book, the computer disk becomes parchment text, the digital timepiece becomes a historical analog clock, and the lamp of illuminated projection becomes a cartographical globe of projected conquest. While some critics might argue that Biggs's juxtapositions amount to no more than ludic appropriations of serious historical representations (much like Jenik's playful portrayal of analog library culture), others could just as well insist on the project's invitation to reflect on the complexity of digital art's analogical relation to the cultural past and the history of cultural politics. Indeed, Biggs's anamorphic objects enfolded in the present/past of morphing temporality stand out as the critically enigmatic figures of a prolegomena to *Digital Baroque.*

I aim in the pages that follow to reflect on the historical and ideological complexity of the "new" apparatuses of digitized electronic arts in relation to their critical and ideological reconfiguration of historical methods, literary authorship and authority, artistic icons, cinematic memories, and most of all, new world communities. While not setting out to provide a detailed overview of early modern precedents of the digital arts, as performed ably by books such as Angela Ndalianis's *Neo-Baroque Aesthetics and Contemporary Entertainment* (a book that remains loyal to rather conventional Cartesian notions of early modern subjectivity),[16] I wish to dwell on moments where experimental works in the contemporary screen arts solicit reflection on the enigmatic folds of analogy itself, particularly as expressed within the baroque context. As if taking the lead from Biggs, this book will dwell on the role played by the new screen arts in addressing the paradigm shift away from the remnants of humanist visions of subjectivity and projection toward reflections on a baroque model of the folds of intersubjective and cross-cultural knowledge. This is a model that will be shown to expand continually in the electronic and psychosocial webs and digital registrations that link text, film, and computer, all now institutionally and materially conjoined as charged phantasmatic carriers of cultural and historical interconnectivity. Crucial to this study is the critical benefit derived from playful

Figure 3. Simon Biggs, *Portrait of a Young Man,* 1993.

interactive artworks, like those of Biggs, whose parodic gestures link socio-historical representations and epistemology with the archive, the rise of technology, and the flow of colonialism. Such a conjunction of epistemology and politics is fundamental to the titular paradox of this book, *Digital Baroque,* from the particular importance of propriety and property in the age of Prospero and King Lear to the broader questions of race and sexuality posed by complex, global projects of contemporary digital art.

In many helpful ways, Biggs's use of software to encourage and permit users to actively traverse the space of still life with the touch of the hand, as well as with the look of the eye, simulates another loosely phenomenological procedure that Walter Benjamin suggests to be characteristic of the Baroque. "The term 'panoramatic' has been coined," writes Benjamin,

> to give an excellent description of the conception of history prevalent in the seventeenth century. "In this picturesque period the whole conception of history is determined by such a collection of everything memorable." If history is secularized in the setting, this is an expression of the same metaphysical tendency which simultaneously led, in the exact sciences, to the infinitesimal method. In both cases chronological movement is grasped and analysed in a spatial image.[17]

While the extent to which movement is so grasped in *Portrait of a Young Man* will vary, no doubt, according to the user's familiarity with the historical referents noted above, Biggs foregrounds the call to analysis by highlighting particular images in a sort of still time as items for artistic play and critical reflection. What I will argue in order to distinguish the new media panorama from its historical precedent is precisely its revision of how we understand simultaneity and its folds in something other than a meta-physical or dialectical manner. Regarding twentieth-century alternatives to the dialectical tradition, both Derrida and Deleuze recommend that we think of the fold in relation to the Heideggerian notion of "*Zweifalt*, not a fold in two—since every fold can only be thus—but a 'fold-of-two,' an *entre-deux*, something 'between' in the sense that a difference is being dif-ferentiated."[18] The two-fold, or the *entre-deux*, also is a conceit of the fold that embodies for Deleuze the most fundamental operation of time:

> Since the past is constituted not after the present that it was but at the same time, time has to split itself in two at each moment as present and past, which differ from each other in nature, or, what amounts to the same thing, it has to split the present in two heterogeneous directions, one of which is launched towards the future while the other falls into the past.[19]

To be "in" the machinic state of time, in this sense, is to be confronted with the touch, turn, vision, and thought of the interval, the in-between, as the recombinant turning of time.[20]

A reader who is drawn to this machinic legacy of labyrinthine vision might appreciate, for instance, the recombinant conceit of the capped bust in *Portrait of a Young Man* whose perspective shifts with the movement of the cursor. Resembling the prototypical Phrygian cap, this awkward object of curious perspective might well function precisely like the Holbeinian apparatus of the anamorphic skull that summons and thereby arrests the self-confident patriarchal gaze in the annihilation of subjectivity. The bust's enfolded beret points the user precisely in the historical direction of this kind of intersubjective arrestation that Lacan theorized in his reading of anamorphosis in Holbein's *The Ambassadors*.[21] *The Ambassadors* disturbs the realistic, frontal portraits of two ambassadors, Jean de Denteville and Georges de Selve, with a monstrously enigmatic image hovering curiously in the picture's low, frontal plane. When viewed from the side, this per-spectival phantasm appears clearly as the representation of a skull. The dynamics of this painting exemplified for Jacques Lacan the captivation and loss of visualization itself.[22] At the moment the viewers give up on de-ciphering the enigmatic form stretched across the bottom of an otherwise easily decipherable painting, they shift their glance to the next picture in the gallery only to be arrested by an oblique, side-glimpse of the anamorphic skull hovering on Holbein's canvas. Representing the subject's nothingness, so Lacan suggests, the skull conveys this annihilation just as the spectators seek to evade it. Through the ellipsis of anamorphic vision, the spectator is positioned in the masochistic split of an otherwise assuring representation of worldly wealth and power.[23]

The Phrygian cap is also what caught the fancy of Neil Hertz who, in *The End of the Line,* described its early modern iconological function as representing the inscription of patriarchy and the threat of its impotence or castration. While figuring the liberty of the French Revolution, the Phrygian cap also signifies the frailty of sovereignty and authorial legitimation.[24] But rather than marking a teleological passage from one cap to the other, Biggs's morphing bust can be said to enfold them together as a difference whose differentiation continues to play out and should not be overlooked. So what Biggs's *Portrait of a Young Man* contributes to my labyrinthine fantasy of Erasmus's dark cabinet in the age of the computer is its visualized citation of the fragile ideological framework of the young male artist as subject and source of projection.

Nowhere is the legacy of this vulnerable network more apparent than in a 2002 new media installation and publishing project sponsored by Vivaria.net and the Institute of Digital Art and Technology at Plymouth University, *Notes toward the Complete Works of Shakespeare,* 2002. When I discovered this carefully packaged early modern quarto in my mailbox at the Rose Goldsen Archive of New Media Art in the Cornell Library's Division of Rare and Special Collections, I imagined that a mistake might have been made when it was placed in my mailbox instead of that belonging to the curator responsible for early modern books and manuscripts. Upon marveling at the gold-embossed signature of Shakespeare gracing its cover, I fantasized that perhaps someone rummaging around an old attic had fallen upon this handsome tome full of the newly recovered notes by the heralded playwright regarding plans for his works (perhaps the notes of Greenaway's Prospero leading up to the penning of his *Tempest* or those of Godard's William Shakespeare Jr. the Fifth who sets out to re-create the text of his ancestor that had been lost in the wake of Chernobyl). But after handling the book, my fantasies gave way to the realization that I was fingering a digital simulation, in an edition of one hundred, whose title page identifies its source not as the playwright, Shakespeare, but as a group of collective authors named Elmo, Gum, Heather, Holly, Mistletoe, and Rowan. These turned out to be Salawesi Crested Macaques monkeys housed at the Paignton Zoo Environmental Park in Devon, England. Their collectivity revealed in endnotes demystifies Shakespearean authorship by calling attention to the collectivity of authorship, perhaps an indirect reference to critical debates over the extent of the collective penning of many of Shakespeare's foul papers (although the papers inside this quarto appear not to be soiled themselves).[25]

The monkeys' text, we discover, reproduces the results of an artistic installation in which a computer was placed in the monkeys' cage so they would have access to the seductive sight of the screen and the tactile touch of the keyboard. The project was based on the premise that if a monkey randomly hits the keys, it will type a recognized word over time. "Theoretically, given an infinite number of monkeys and an infinite number of time," claim the artists, "one of the monkeys would eventually type out the entire works of Shakespeare."[26] While we could anticipate a clever poetic play on Shakespeare's occasional identification of monkeys with jesters, whores, and equivocators, what we see in this published facsimile are the much plainer material results of these *Notes:* two *f*'s, seven *v*'s, three *p*'s, a few *s*'s, lines of *g*'s, a couple of pages of *s*'s, etc.

This text was produced as Vivaria.net's contribution on generative writing for the computer art exhibition "GENERATOR," in May and June 2002. Vivaria.net is a collective scientific and artistic research initiative aimed at the task of classifying and differentiating between animals, humans, and computational machines in the culture of late technocapitalism. This artistic project investigates the slippery historical slope of commodity exchange signaled perhaps no better than by Shylock when he exclaims that he would not have exchanged his prized turquoise ring, the sign of his bachelor conquest of Leah, "for a wilderness of monkeys" (III.i.123). Were he to revise his script in relation to the conditions of commodity and sign in the twenty-first century, Shylock would have realized that it now could be possible to exchange not just a ring but the creative production of its bearer for precisely such a troupe of monkeys. The interrelationships of animals, humans, and computational machines "are enduring ones," argues Vivaria.net on its Web page, "reactivated by changes in social and technological production, making the former distinction further complicated by the addition of artificial life-forms and biotechnologies—the merging of biological and computational forms."[27] The purpose of the "GENERATOR" project, then, was to reflect on the possibilities of linked writing and communicational procedures when the whole world has become literally a wired stage. The monkeys' activities were translated to a computer environment, producing live updates published on the Web alongside a webcam view of the production scene showing the creative activity in its fuller context. The context included not only the monkeys' gradual interest and facility in manipulating the keyboard but also their naturalization of the writing process in the corporeal procedures of everyday life as they alternately ate and defecated on the keyboard (foul papers now modernized into soiled keys).

As I understand this installation, which I didn't have the opportunity to experience, it was mirrored by word processing software that also generated *The Complete Works of Shakespeare*. An autogenerator endlessly produced random words ("as if performed by a monkey") and checked each word against a dictionary of terms gleaned from Shakespeare's texts. When a word was recognized, the computer highlighted it, and added it to the document in the lower portion of the screen. Over time, Shakespeare's words will combine to form a new work.

In response to critics who might challenge the seriousness of this playful exercise and its potential contribution to reflections on Digital Baroque, permit me to cite a rather lengthy explanation by the Vivaria.net collective:

> The project . . . aims to raise questions . . . as to the role of chance in evolution and the creative process. . . . . Political and creative processes in the most general sense contain unpredictable elements because they are complex by nature and open to outside influence. By extension, the individual success or failure of creative types (artists and writers, not least) is accounted for by luck and circumstance (and not simply good breeding). Contradiction between parts is required for the complex whole to adequately describe the ways in which these parts express both disorder and order (and is thus one of the essential functions of life itself).
>
> . . . [The project] appears to test the truth of the formula, in reality it emphasises the unreliability of human (scientific) hypotheses. Animals are not simply metaphors for human endeavour. The joke . . . must not be seen to be at the expense of the monkeys but on the popular interest in the idea—especially those in the computer science and mathematics community (interested

in chance, randomness, autonomous systems and artificial life). . . . The creative thinking subject as the site of consciousness, and the subject as a crucial part of a sentence and text—that which the action is determined by—remains a contested and contradictory set of ideas. Creativity is neither random nor entirely predetermined, in other words.

The project aims to address these ideas, to activate these contradictions, and demonstrate how these contradictions generate new ideas and possibilities, and in turn provide a much more acceptable political metaphor.[28]

Just such a political and philosophical metaphor that foregrounds the fraught contradictions between linguistic generation and cultural production has occupied the work of a wide number of philosophers and scholars committed to examining the uncanny links between digital and baroque cultures. Writers as diverse as myself, Gilles Deleuze, Tom Conley, Walter Moser, Christine Buci-Glucksmann, Sean Cubitt, Mieke Bal, Mario Perniola, and more recently, Angela Ndalianis, Anna Munster, Michele Barker, and Christina McPhee have been reflecting on the lingering status of early modern conceptions of subjectivity and property and their morphed traces in projects of contemporary cinema, video, and digital art (had they lived through the nineties, Louis Marin and Michel de Certeau certainly would have been leading proponents of such research).[29]

These artistic projects range in concept and form from Orlan's performance art sequence *Triumph of the Baroque* (2000), where she morphs herself through surgery and computer imaging into a verisimilar figure straight out of Bernini, to Mona Hatoum's *Testimonio, 1995–2002*, whose exhibition in Mexico City's former Convent of San Diego has prompted critics to confuse her close-up video of a rosy scrotum with the popular cult of the Virgin of Guadalupe. As I discuss in more detail throughout the pages that follow, the variety of contemporary artworks explicitly investigating the Digital Baroque extends further from Nam June Paik's *Baroque Laser* (1995), which was installed in the baroque parish church Mariae Himmelfahrt-Dyckburg, in Münster-St. Mauritz, to Peter Greenaway's extravagant *Prospero's Books* (1991) and Jean-Louis Boissier's CD-ROM catalogue of baroque visions *Globus Oculi* (2001) and his interactive adaptations of Jean-Jacques Rousseau (1993–2001). In response to the strength of CD-ROM artworks that follow Boissier's lead, I developed a selection of such work, "Baroque Interface," as part of my touring art exhibition "Contact Zones: The Art of CD-ROM" (1999–2004).[30] "Baroque Interface" includes Boissier's *Flora Petrinsularis* (1993–94), which I discuss in chapter 8, with the CD-ROMs *Relic/Relique* (1999) by Rae Davis, *Bits of Paper* (1998) by Douglas Holleley, *Red Iris Interactive* (1997) by Kate Richards, and *Hortus Musicus* (2001) by Daniel Warner. My curatorial goal in grouping these works was to highlight the surprisingly wide range of CD-ROM artwork that appropriates early modern constructions of artistic form, space, light, volume, passion, memory, and utopia. The artists in "Baroque Interface" reflect on the electronic apparitions of Rousseau, Velasquez, early music, the textural folds of relics and bits of paper, as well as the excessive traces of baroque space, rhetoric, performance, and corporeality. Also important to the curatorial vision of this program is the uncanny coincidence that today's paradoxical attraction and resistance to electronic art occurs, like that of the early modern artistic sources, in an age of the crisis of rapid global transformation, mistrust of the passions, pervasive epidemic and death, ambivalent attraction to the cultural other, revisionary philosophical investigation, and widespread cultural wars. In planning that exhibition, just as in shaping this book, I kept in mind Deleuze's assertion that "the Baroque is linked to a crisis of property," which, he argues in *The Fold*, is "a crisis that appears at once with the growth of new machines in the social field and the discovery of new living beings in the organism."[31] As with many of the films and artworks I analyze in *Digital Baroque*, the cross-historical CD-ROMs in "Baroque Interface" emphasize the degree to which the growth of artistic machines are subject to, interfaced with, complex historical and institutional modalities of race, sexuality, and political difference that emerge from the cultural residue of the new science, the old art, and the Gutenberg revolution.

Receiving particular attention in the wide-ranging new media works that dialogue with the Baroque is the memory of cinema. While new media art has extended far beyond the boundaries of the screen arts, I have chosen to limit the scope of this book to digital art's inscription in the memory of cinema because new media bears the heavy imprint of cinema's place in the twentieth century and the deeply engrained stains of the apparatus (from Gutenberg to Gates). Crucial to my consideration of Digital Baroque is cinema's evolution via the electronic arts, as well as its baroque inscription in the paradigm of its own passing into the digital age (in my book-in-progress "Immaterial Archives: Curatorial Instabilities @ New Media Art," I analyze the extensive shift from screen arts to broader experimentations in computing, bio- and data-art, the Web, and archivization that result from cinema's digital passage). Highlighted by readings of the experimental adaptations of Shakespeare by Godard and Greenaway, not to mention Thierry Kuntzel's subtle dialogue with Nicolas Poussin, my critical consideration of how cinema has served as a projection back into the early modern past contributes to our understanding of contemporary transformations of ontological projection and cultural property in relation to the functions and properties of the interactive apparatus. The Shakespearean backdrop of *King Lear* provides Godard, for instance, with a fraught platform for his reflections on the historical contributions and fragility of cinema, just as it paradoxically places his practice and theorizing on the threshold of new media, a genre that he has emphatically denounced as "la soupe informatique."[32] In providing an alternative to Godard's preference for cinematic "sense and direction," Greenaway and Chris Marker will be shown to join a variety of new media artists who articulate a sense and direction for the screen arts in the age of new media. My hope is that this book's consideration of a wide range of approaches to new media screen arts, from those of Mona Hatoum, Nam June Paik, Bill Viola and Keith Piper to Perry Hoberman, Norie Neumark, Renate Ferro, David Rokeby, and Jill Scott, will enliven the new media community's interest in and commitment to maintaining a critical engagement with the Digital Baroque. What I hope will become evident as the book progresses is that the new media screen arts, while not always dialoguing directly with the Baroque, consistently embody and display the tissue of baroque paradigms, from the dynamics of serial accumulation and the trauma of temporal folds to the cultural promise of what I will call digital incompossibility that makes quake the previously confident stature of single-centered subjectivity.

Throughout these critical endeavors, the paradoxical place of the authorial subject remains paramount. During the period when Greenaway was positioning Prospero in competition with Caliban as the keeper of cultural history and when Godard was making a cameo appearance in *King Lear* as the authoritative Professor Pluggy, the French performance artist Orlan relinquished her identity in her ongoing performance as St. Orlan in her piece *The Draped / The Baroque.* In her subsequent multimedia performance that combined cosmetic surgery and televisual simulcasting, *The Reincarnation of St. Orlan,* she subsequently extended the folds of her artistic body to the surgical construction of a composite computerized visage that permanently rendered her visage into a facial cartography of feminine features idealized by the history of art. The enigmatic hinge between artist, artwork, and network lies at the heart of *Digital Baroque* where the artist so frequently becomes the artwork, just as the networked spectator becomes the data of the new media environment.

A PSYCHOPHILOSOPHICAL APPROACH TO NEW MEDIA ART

The status of the producer of art in the brave newness of the computerized world is the subject of Sean Cubitt's catalogue essay "The Relevance of the Baroque," published in the 1996 booklet accompanying Biggs's CD-ROM *Book of Shadows* (which includes *Portrait of a Young Man*):

> The fact of individuality is not negotiable, but neither is it static. The Cartesian proprietor of individuality reconfigured as the homesteader of the electronic frontier is an exemplary attempt to hang on to and reuse a definitively outmoded form of self . . . and which, in the attempt to anchor the personal as discrete from the flux, has been rendered as the agonistic field of competition.[33]

While Cubitt permits the lineage of Cartesian individuality to hang around, however agonistically, the Italian philosopher Mario Perniola contests the premise of individuality in a cultural environment in which "the library, the archive, the mediatheque, the collection are situated in a horizon of the virtuality of moral intention."[34] In his 1990 book, *Enigmi: Il momento egizio nella società e nell'arte (Enigmas: The Egyptian Moment in Society and Art)*, Perniola theorizes thoughtfully and subtly his understanding of a revived contemporary culture of the Baroque in which the library, the computer, and the archive have teamed up to displace the centrality of the facile world order of mass media and commodity. The result of the effective return of the centrality of the library, he argues, is that "the humanist vision that had conferred to the subject an ontological meaning has since disappeared. . . . What's essential comes not from the depths of the soul, but from the extraneity of writing, the book, the computer. . . . The information society seems to propose a model of knowledge that is not answerable to the activity of the subject."[35] Perhaps the closest we now might come to heading toward the ontological depth of subjectivity through the extraneity of writing would be via that figure of the InfoSpherian who performs the role of a terrestrial information relay device in Jenik's production at the San Jose Public Library. "Projection-as-relay, -as-fold," is the operable term here. While this might sound particularly devastating to the authorial legacy of the young man and the older Prospero, Perniola invites us to lean on his baroque trope of the informational interconnectivity of networks, libraries, and archives in order to dislodge the making of text from its modernist dependence on strictly Cartesian and Hegelian paradigms. His argument positions the making of text and knowledge as an enigmatic activity of cross-culture. It is in something like the environment of the repertory, in something like the archive of Vivaria.net or the library mediascape of *SPEC-FLIC 2.0,* that "two crucial and seemingly opposed critical orientations become connected and enfolded: one directed toward the most advanced developments of technology, the technical reproducibility of the work of art, the videographic and the electronic; the other, in contrast, directed toward the most emotional dimensions of experience, toward the ethnology and the phenomena of possession."[36]

Such a cohabitation of seemingly incompatible possessions in artistic explorations of the Digital Baroque, from the technological to the emotive, from the political to the personal, result frequently in the expression of a dissimilarity of cultural and emotional positions that give rise to "agonistic tensions," the kind that Christine Buci-Glucksmann thinks to be constitutive of the "power of the Baroque."[37] It is here that caution to attend to the enfolding of seemingly opposed critical orientations becomes crucial to my approach to Digital Baroque. A logic of simple oppositions rendered forceful in the power of tension would likely result in the world-ordering promise of what Deleuze frequently described as Leibnizian compossibility. This concept, so important to the logic of *Difference and Repetition,* provides for the possibility of multiple series whose points of divergence and convergence are commonly shared by all monads. "In the continuum of a compossible world," adds Deleuze, "differential relations and distinctive points thus determine expressive centres (essences or individual substances) in which, at each moment, the entire world is contained from a certain point of view."[38] Rather than remain complacent with the compossible logic of simple oppositions and their containment in a common point of view, not to mention confidence in the teleological promise of "digital dialectics," the artistic manifestations of the Digital Baroque, at least as I read them in this book, call on their participants to remain critically open to the eventfulness of what Lyotard would call the playful agonism of "multiple co-present intensities"[39] or what Deleuze affirmatively embraces as the chaotic expression of artistic, cultural, and political "incompossibilities." Rather than reducing such intensities to contradictions or to real opposition in relation to the convergence of point of view, "the incompossibility of worlds" will be shown in a range of work, from video installation to cinema and interactive CD-ROM, to result in the juxtaposition of points, "the in-between" or "the fold-of-two," that make the resultant series diverge.[40] Inscribed in the simultaneity of juxtaposition that is rendered so forcefully by the digital platform, such divergence constitutes for Deleuze the very promise of artistic expression: "each series tells a story: not different points of view on the same story, like the different points of view on the town we find in Leibniz, but completely distinct stories that unfold simultaneously."[41]

How the *in-between* of seemingly opposed technologies, cultures, and philosophies combines with the *possession* of affect and material could end up being the key critical fold most indicative of the enigmatic, cultural promise of Digital Baroque. In weaving the in-betweens of a new world-memory and the future possession of affect, I will recommend the promise of a psychophilosophical approach to new media art, one that insistently conjoins epistemology and politics in the activities of artistic production and critical reflection. Given the critical distancing from the psychoanalytic and even the philosophical by many new media critics of more materialist, empiricist, or simply forward-looking bents, I dwell in the chapters that follow on the incompossible terms of the baroque screen arts to articulate the promise of an ideological paradigm of digital possession.

Possession, not simply in the sense of John Locke's "Of Property," but more akin to the enfolded remnants of asubjective mysticism, fetishism, cross-cultural identification, and paranoia. These are charged enigmatic signifiers of the extraneity of the book and the computer that enfolds the depths of the psyche in the wired network of psychosocial interconnectivity. Put succinctly by Perniola, "The information society seems to propose a model of knowledge deriving not from the activity of a subject but from fancy and possession."[42] In reflecting on baroque resurgence in contemporary art, Walter Moser takes the lead of Perniola by attributing such possession to the affective fervor at the core of the baroque. Faced with the excess of aesthetic intensity, the baroque spectator, reader, or listener is said by Moser to be enveloped in an emotional state of ecstasy or delirium well before being able to attribute to this intensity the sense of an attraction or repulsion.[43] I would add, moreover, that such a machinery of possession rekindles the early modern attraction to fantasy and fancy, which I have argued in *Repossessions: Psychoanalysis and the Phantasms of Early Modern Culture* to have been "repossessed" by the science of psychoanalysis and its kin in poststructural philosophy. There I suggest that possession is a phantasm positioned analogously in the contrasting machineries of philosophy, psychoanalysis, science, and literature as a liminal figure conjoining perversion and certainty, imagination and cognition, desire and mind, along with, I would now add, subject and archive.[44]

A crucial aspect of this shift from cinematic and ontological projection to the possessive informatics of the fold remains the affect of (cinematic) loss and its revisionary relation to baroque precedents of ascesis, rapture, and melancholia. It is important to note, however, that critical attention to affect in *Digital Baroque* will not lead us down the path of Ndalianis's analogy of baroque mysticism with the metaphysical transformations of New Age belief systems, "the states of euphoric transcendence, the spirituality and wonder that is evident in the baroque and the neo-baroque."[45] In contrast, consider how another of Biggs's screen works, *On Sight* (1991) puns on the artistic tradition of depictions of the Dead Christ that has been brought into precise critical perspective by two other influential theorists of the baroque, Julia Kristeva and Louis Marin, as well as by the video artist Thierry Kuntzel, who with Marin is the focus of chapter 2. Rather than dwell darkly on the baroque legacy of death and its concomitant authorial scene of the dark cabinet, what Kristeva calls the living tomb of the identification with death,[46] *On Sight* (Figure 4) presents a quivering nude figure lying on a clothed funereal altar that morphs in and out of male/female shape. In the vertical space above, the user views a translucent splayed cadaver whose veins and muscles pulsate in orangish luminosity, as if it were a haunting electric phantasm of the skinless anatomies of Valverdi's illustrated treatise *Anatomia del Corporo Humano* (1560). Adding to the virtual phantasmagoria that brings new life to the memento mori, user interaction triggers the transformation of this bodily vision into a series of corporeal specters, from a floating heart being shot through by cupids to parallel heads with pulsating eyes and mouths interconnected by some kind of neural material that embodies the networked stuff of the digital in-between. Here sight becomes something of an archival reception screen rather than a subjective perspective device. It shifts the scene of representation away from the deadening vision of the momento mori caught in a negative nexus of lack and loss toward something more luminous and vibrant, something akin to the paradoxically baroque tradition of light itself, "la lumière."

We need to think of "la lumière" not simply in the Enlightenment sense deriving from the tradition of Cartesian speculation but also in the more dynamic contradictory sense described by Louis Marin. Playing on his paradoxical reading of Philippe de Champaigne, Marin seizes on the affirmative legacy of "la lumière," one that signifies "less reflection than intensification . . . a figure-figura untenable to vision and sight, a figure which is in excess of every figure."[47] So it goes that Biggs's reclining figure of androgynous luminosity solicits the user to interact with an intense fold of psychosocial accumulation, one similar to the Deleuzian machinery, "insofar as a muscular conception of matter inspires force in all things by invoking the propagation of light and the 'expulsion into luminosity.'"[48] This fold exceeds the phenomenological frameworks of subjective sight and vision as much as it implicates its user, to return to Perniola, in "the most emotional dimensions of experience, toward the ethnology and the phenomena of possession."

Such phenomena take us right to the core of Digital Baroque in relation to Biggs's *Book of Shadows,* a composite book project of ink and light, both a traditional artist's book and an interactive piece on CD-ROM.

Figure 4. Simon Biggs, *On Sight,* 1991.

Here, the luminous figures of screened textual traces read more accessibly in the folds of the digitally created book. As they work together across the fields of the traditional and interactive book, they summon a baroque legacy of cross-cultural interaction, accumulation, and intensification, as expressed elegantly by poetic text:

> You read as many shadows as I, tracing space, speaking, unfolding ourselves.
> You here, in front of this image, with your shadow-cast of the common-voice.
> . . . Two shadow-clouds of breath speak within this space, within the rooms
>   we have entered.
> In memory's place the eyes look for you, in this space shaped shadow-bright.
> When I was not here. When you walked with me. To catch my eye, I was not
>   alone.

The time-traveling of memory's shadows and the extraneous lingerings of textual fragments and interpersonal substitutions here flicker by as if digital imprints of the decaying senses of feeble memory and the slippages of collective, cultural archives. If the inscription of *Book of Shadows* in the materialized procedures of Digital Baroque grounds it in something recognizably visible, it does so in a way that embraces and thus haunts Francis Bacon's detested, labyrinthine deceit of "resemblances of objects and signs, natures so irregular in their lines and so knotted and entangled."[49] The folds and entanglements of Biggs's artistic productions illuminate precisely the sort of baroque visual system that Benjamin so admired where "chronological movement is grasped and analysed in a spatial image." Crucial here is the continuous variation of movement itself and how such electronic possession carries on in memory's place without the aid of the fixed subject or self-centered monad.

Critical attentiveness to the intersubjective procedures of cinematic interiority, from historical trauma to the psychic and social wounds of cinematic projection, lead me to articulate in *Digital Baroque* the imperative of reconsidering the parameters of analogy in relation to its psychopolitical possessions. Crucial to this approach is sensitivity to the paradox guiding my reading of cinema's relation to new media. Rather than insisting that new media marks a complete break from the analogous procedures of cinema, one that creeps teleologically toward the promise of a new utopia, I argue that we attend to digitality's force as the analogue of analogy, particularly as we understand analogy within the energetic parameters of association rather than equation. Key is the fluid, shifting nature of analogy in our cultural imaginary that has become so dependent on cinema and its shifting signifiers. Building on prior emphasis on the analogous possessions of melancholy, trauma, and fantasy in my books *Like a Film: Ideological Fantasy on Screen, Camera, and Canvas* and *Drama Trauma: Specters of Race and Sexuality in Performance, Video, and Art,* I reflect in this study on the merits of calling on structures of scansion and sublimation to enhance our understanding of the practice, ontology, and temporality of new media art through which ocular projection gives way to the digital fold.

What I hope will become particularly apparent in the pages that follow is how these electronic variations usher us across the threshold of new political and cross-cultural metaphors and structures. Regarding the cultural implications of new baroque artistic practice, as evidenced in the discordant performances of electronic music, Deleuze suggests that new electronic music, as I claim for new media, offers alternative cultural paradigms that

> no longer pass through accords . . . we have a new Baroque and a neo-Leibnizianism. The same construction of the point of view over the city continues to be developed, but now it is neither the same point of view nor the same city, now that both the figure and the ground are in movement in space. Something has changed in the situation of monads. . . . To the degree that the world is now made up of divergent series (the chaosmos), or that crap-shooting replaces the game of Plenitude, the monad is now unable to contain the entire world as if in a closed circle that can be modified by projection.[50]

The political legacy of this shift is nowhere more apparent than in the installation and interactive projects of Keith Piper, whose work I analyze in chapter 5. A leading British figure in video and new media installation, still recognized for his invaluable contribution to the British Black Arts movement of the 1980s, Piper's CD-ROM *Relocating the Remains* takes its user on a journey of interactivity between the divergent series of the history of colonialism and its cultural folds, between the object of the technological interface (from slave ship to computer chip) and cultural collectivities representing racial, cultural, and national diversity. Piper mimics the colonial procedures of visual regulation by freeing memory from the holds of the slave ship of the early modern archive to unsettle the epistemological nature and cultural assumptions of the universal monad. In an interactive segment titled "An English Ship," for instance, Piper establishes a historical linkage between the colonial institutions of Christianity, British Empire, and slavery whose traces surface in other installations that comment on the cultural centrality of the black athlete, the infusion of black music into British culture, and the racialized paradox of the digital divide in which the hierarchies of digital access work to revive the figure of the slave ship, this time one riding the electronic waves of the informational superhighway. Overall, Piper's complex CD-ROM platform will be shown to generate a new medium of cultural capital out of the historical traces and memories of black residue that cast a lasting shadow on the purity of the Empire. Indeed, his juxtaposition of the complex legacy of the Baroque and the equally fraught conditions of the digital divide work to capitalize and comment on the informational extraneities of archive, library, and computer in a way that haunts earlier archival theorizations by the likes of Francis Bacon. What clearly distinguishes Piper's project from Bacon's is how Piper's panoramic organization of space loosens the archive from any vertical privilege of direction and permits the screen to become an interactive data bank through which information becomes repossessed by the perpetual thought and networked distribution of incompossible worlds.[51]

TEMPORAL FOLDS AND BAROQUE READINGS

Once loosened from the privilege of teleological direction, the new media archive presents a wide array of challenges to interactive creation, reception, and reading. Much like a dream or fantasy, video installations accustom their viewers to the eternal return of the loop rather than the unidirectional progression of cinematic sequence. The CD-ROM often drops its interactive user midstream into loops and links that contain no apparent structural referent, such as the cinematic flashback or establishing shot. Indeed, one of the enigmas posed by the baroque texture of the new media and its archival traces is the multidirectionality of temporal flow. Performing in the present only in relation to the past, as it bears on the technological and psychophilosophical orientations of the future, this continually developing archive solicits an equally fluid approach from its reader. The strategy of this book, for instance, is not to anchor new media art solely in the referents of the early modern past in order to argue a causal effect of old media on the new; rather, I aim to remain sensitive to how artistic dialogues with historical referents open us to the rhetorical, emotive, and social force of these referents while expanding the same referents' horizons in order to reflect on the consequence of their continual imprint on contemporary practice. Of course, it can work just as easily the other way around, when contemporary artistic practice, such as cinematic experimentation by Godard or Greenaway, works to sensitize the viewer to complex psychosocial structures perhaps inherent in early modern practice but not overtly self-evident in its representations, particularly when early modern culture lacked the technological/material apparatuses, such as graphic representations of the fractal, necessary for the exploration of notions as complex as the Leibnizian fold.

Indeed, the temporality of the fold, its overlappings and turnings back and forth in time, provides both a fundamental subject of this book's analysis as well as its structure. Much like the paradoxical conundrum of Digital Baroque, the four parts of this manuscript could easily be flipped to be read front to back, or to be read in the order preferred by the reader. In this case, the chapters of Part IV, "Scanning the Future," would provide the conceptual skeleton of structures and commentaries on incompossibility and temporality crucial to contemporary practice that is much more thematically self-evident in the early modern examples studied more explicitly in the first two parts of *Digital Baroque.* This book is designed, then, not to move merely in a teleological progression from front to back where futurity is the explicit issue, but to be folded and enfolded in the process of reading, in which each section or chapter could easily point to, refer deictically to, or provide the touchstone to something of a hyperlink to other chapters in the book enveloped in the same archival horizon.

It is for the purpose of isolating and clarifying the conceptual parameters of Digital Baroque, and to distinguish them from rather commonplace artistic and critical assumptions about electronic art's attraction to the Baroque, that I begin with two sections focusing on artistic adaptations of and dialogues with early modern authors, artists, and concepts. Part I moves "From Video Black to Digital Baroque" by opening with a chapter on performative passages through early modern space and epistemology by contemporary video installation artists. In order to challenge the pattern of embrace of mystical and religious referents by a wide range of electronic artists and their critics, from Daniel Reeves and Paul Chan to Mona

Hatoum, Paula Dawson, and Nam June Paik—exemplified by Bill Viola's promotion of mysticism's "via negativa," I read against the grain of much of this work to foreground the importance of its more energetic baroque characteristics: the performativity of analogical disjunction, divergent points of view, and digital incompossibility. This chapter ranges in study from consideration of architectural installations by Hatoum, Dawson, and Paik to a more detailed analysis of the prominence of Digital Baroque in the installations of Bill Viola. Important to the book as a whole is this chapter's articulation of how the new media subject becomes inscribed in the accumulating flow of digital data, information, and imagery. Chapter 2 focuses this broader analysis of electronic intensity in relation to the understanding of representational power shared by the philosopher of early modern representation, Louis Marin, and the theoretician of cinema and video artist, Thierry Kuntzel. Kuntzel's subtle video appropriation of Poussin's series of paintings *The Four Seasons* provides this chapter with a striking conceptual landscape for the consideration of paradigms of light, power, and corporeality, which I argue, in conclusion, to have important bearing on the contemporary politics of race and sexuality.

Part II brings together two rather incompossible bed partners in Gilles Deleuze and William Shakespeare, who together provide the textual and intellectual frameworks for cinematic statements on the Baroque by Jean-Luc Godard and Peter Greenaway. Godard's irreverent adaptation of Shakespeare's *King Lear* provides the backdrop in chapter 3 for a phantasmatic dialogue between Godard and Deleuze. At issue is the instauration of what I call a new baroque era in which Godardian cinema seems caught paradoxically within clashing systems of analog and digital representation. Godard's philosophical film essay on *King Lear* provides the occasion, I suggest, for a break from the mastery of analog sequence and centering point of view in a way that repositions the subject in the disjunctive gap of the cinematic machine, in the baroque space of the in-between. Chapter 4 shifts its attention from the tragic terrain of *King Lear* to the panoramic mise-en-scène of "collective memory" in *Prospero's Books*. Heeding the cinematic call of the Leibnizian formula so dear to Deleuze for its nomadism, "we're no longer seeing, we're reading," this chapter positions Greenaway's sensitivity to serialization, time, and trauma in dialogue with Deleuze's articulation of the philosophical promise of new cinema. As discussed earlier, it is in this chapter that the process of the cinematic fold is distinguished from projection as the textured event shared by writing, the deep memory of the archive, and the digital machineries on which we now rely for the production, retention, and dissemination of text and image. Greenaway's flamboyant experimentation with digital processing prompts him to consider the impact of his representation of the baroque crisis of property in the social field as a means of articulating novel lineages and folds of world-memory, which are positioned in what Deleuze calls the groundless future of the eternal return.

This groundlessness of temporality in the "present past" provides the conceptual trope of Part II, which concentrates on the memory of cinema in the digital age. Chapter 5 sketches the relation of melancholically baroque concerns with the death of cinema in the age of new media to narratives of loss and trauma as staged in a range of experimental projects in digital media, from tapes by Gary Hill and Daniel Reeves to CD-ROMs by Grace Quintanilla and Keith Piper. Rather than sharing the rather mournful perspective on the passing of cinema in the wake of televisual and digital apparatuses, voiced most loudly by Godard, my readings of new media works articulate the means by which the cinematic code might be understood to linger in digitality as something of a crypt or a carrier of the discourse of loss, mourning, and melancholia. In so doing, these same mournful procedures of interiorization provide a conceptual code that, I suggest, reanimates baroque memento mori in interactive works by Quintanilla and Piper. Energetic processes of cultural anxiety and the resurgence of loss and trauma function in their work as a kind of melancholia with affirmatively revolutionary consequences. These interactive works provide the users with intricate critical spaces where they can pause to examine the political legacies of our visual and intellectual cultures. I extend this notion of revolutionary melancholia in chapter 6 in a close reading of Chris Marker's film *Level 5,* a film that dialogues both with the critical legacy of Resnais and Duras's traumatic film *Hiroshima mon amour* and with the cultural and artistic promises of new technology and wired culture. The chapter recommends *Level 5* for embracing the artistic challenge of generating critical energy that emanates from the conjoined pathos of absence and loss, from the mnemonic interface of identification and incorporation that attests to the collusion of the personal and the social and even the fictional and the historical. It engages in a dialogue among Laplanche, Lyotard, and Horkheimer and Adorno that develops a cinematic theory of energetic sublimation.

Chapter 7's reading of interactive cinematic works by Toni Dove and Zoe Beloff follows up on the lessons drawn from Marker in the previous chapter to stage the elaboration of my call for a psychophilosophical approach to new media art. My readings of the artists' playful engagements with the legacies of philosophical toys and Freudian narratives clarify how the interface of interactivity and its digital conjunction of past and future cinematic time lend shape to the otherwise convenient metaphorical borrowings of psychoanalysis and philosophy from cinema. Beloff and Dove stage interactive works that, instead of serving as simply passive receptacles of theoretical assumptions about cinematic perspective, position the new media apparatus as a helpful means of extending the range of the visual and aural theories of libidinality and the dependence on prior codes of representation, resemblance, and analogy. The artworks considered in chapter 8, "Digital Incompossibility," open themselves in relation to their dedicated refashioning of past codes of similitude and resemblance while also refocusing our critical attention on the conceit of incompossibility so crucial to *Digital Baroque*. Particularly noteworthy in this regard is Jean-Louis Boissier's elaborate interactive project on Jean-Jacques Rousseau, which puts into practice "the sensorial cartography" of the interactive image, as well as Perry Hoberman's *The Sub-Division of the Electronic Light,* which rehearses the history of amateur cinema to position the user at the interface of vision and touch, light and machinery, sight and remembrance. Readings of CD-ROM works by Miroslaw Rogala and Norie Neumark frame my insistence that digital aesthetics is foremost *an interval of becoming*. It thus opens to the spectators an amoebic, fractal space of the temporality of becoming, one that envelops past, present, and future, one that foregrounds the creative enigmas of the many tensions driving modernism's ideological fantasy: being and non-being, resemblance and simulation, body and spirit, material and simulacrum. These experiments in new media art emphasize the critical valence of enfolded juxtapositions rather than dialectical oppositions. Particularly made evident by Neumark's *Shock in the Ear* and Reginald Woolery's inventive *world wide web/million man march (www/mmm)* is how the sometimes seemingly endless duration of digital repetition can be said to figure an ontological crisis through which the user is confronted by the dis-locations of perspective and projection. Woolery's project insistently returns us to the social promise of incompossibility as a logic of digital practice and culture through which divergent world cultures of race and sensibility share a common screen lacking common points of view.

The concluding part returns critical attention to the paradigms of the past as a means of reflecting on the artistic archive and its imprint on the future. In considering Marker's digital projects, particularly his inventive CD-ROM *Immemory* and his installation *Owls at Noon Prelude: The Hollow Men,* chapter 9 provides a more extensive reflection on the internalized memory of the archive as it works in art and subjectivity. But rather than remain confident in conventional notions of memory, as they have been passed down via baroque memory theaters and early modern philosophy (what Hobbes calls "decaying sense"), in this chapter we profit from the psychoanalytic discourse of art to distinguish procedures of digital and psychic "scansion" from subject-centered conventions of perspective and memory. In considering the applicability of psychoanalytic concepts of scansion and sublimation to new media criticism, the interactive strategies of *Immemory* enable us to appreciate how Marker's temporal overlapping of the "present past" transports a cinematic dialectic of past and present into the precipice of an interactive future, where the combination of digital code and cinematic content are appreciated by the artist only as an aftereffect of his digital creation and *Immemory's* repeated use. I conclude *Digital Baroque* by returning to one of its most explicit referents, the thought of time expressed by Deleuze in his cinema books, now some twenty years past. In keeping with my commitment throughout *Digital Baroque* to think digitality through interaction with the artworks themselves, not as ephemeral theorizations but as readings-in-folds-of-thought, I close by thinking about the status of "future cinema," both in terms of the instantiation of the future on the memory of cinema itself and in the sense of a concluding question: wherein lies the "future" in the art of new media? "Future cinema" constitutes the fundamental machinic constituent of new informatics itself as, I argue, the very replication of information in relation to its anchorage in the pull of the future and its morphings of subjective projection into archival event. To get there, I trace the digital vicissitudes of what Deleuze calls the "time-image" and the "irrational interval" in relation to a series of incompossible events: *archival intensities, interactivities, coded automatons,* and *the returns of the future.* Considering a wide range of works, from the video installations of Renate Ferro and Du Zhenjun to interactive pieces by Jill Scott, Boissier, Shu Leah Cheang, Mark Hansen and Ben Rubin, Lynn Hershman, and David Rokeby, the chapter traces the temporal folds of cinema's internal struggle with the temporality of informatics. Its end point is the now of the future, a now enacted by David Rokeby's *n-cha(n)t,* which depends on the future aural input of its interactive users to grow the archival database of its artificial intelligence. Rather than serving as the base of authorial projections and the source study of baroque culture, *n-cha(n)t* embodies the expansive panorama of the kind of baroque archive that so intrigued Walter Benjamin. This is an ongoing new media archive that awaits the data of the future for the sake of Rokeby's unfolding narrative of communication.

Rokeby's archive is something of a promise of the materialization of the archival event traced throughout *Digital Baroque.* The machinic archive itself now embodies the baroque fold of the continuous labyrinth put into play by Simon Biggs in simple interfaces, not, as Deleuze reminds us, of "a line dissolving into independent points, as flowing sand might dissolve into grains, but [resembling] a sheet of paper divided into infinite folds or separated into bending movements, each one determined by the consistent or conspiring surroundings" of future cinema.

I.
FROM VIDEO BLACK TO
DIGITAL BAROQUE

chapter 1

DIGITAL BAROQUE:
PERFORMATIVE PASSAGE FROM HATOUM
TO VIOLA

In fond memory of Priamo Lozada (1962–2007)

Solutions no longer pass through accords. It is because the conditions of the problem itself have changed: we have a new Baroque and a neo-Leibnizianism. The same construction of the point of view over the city continues to be developed, but now it is neither the same point of view nor the same city, now that both the figure and the ground are in movement in space. Something has changed in the situation of monads. . . . To the degree that the world is now made up of divergent series (the chaosmos), or that crapshooting replaces the game of Plenitude, the monad is now unable to contain the entire world as if in a closed circle that can be modified by projection.

—GILLES DELEUZE, *The Fold: Leibniz and the Baroque*

Consider the technological intensification of cinema as it moves into the twenty-first century. Advances in digital technology have spawned a sharp increase in the quantity and quality of multimedia production: video and digital installations, sound and light shows, multimedia dance, virtual reality performances, interactive CD/DVD-ROMs, Internet art. Enhanced by the dazzling images of computer wizardry and the magical resonance of digitized sound, the public appeal of spectacle might never have been stronger. As a result, the scene of performance now extends far afield from the theater of the movie palace to the fluid spaces of the museum, the gallery, the concert hall, and even the architectural facade and darkened public square. Rock concerts happen in environments of multimedia spectacle where sound mixes with the dazzle of visualized special effects and the electric dynamism of laser shows and digitized pyrotechnics. Both the figure and the ground of multimedia performance move in space, enveloping audiences in the electrobeat of VJ techno-vision. Visitors to art museums and galleries also find themselves bathed in electronic light, from the luminous three-dimensionality of James Turrell installations and the holographic spectacles of Lin Shu-Min or Paula Dawson to the digital video performances of Luc Courchesne, Antonio Muntadas, Marina Grzinic, Du Zhenjun, and Krzysztof Wodiczko, in which spectators move among representational imagery to become a vital part of the spectacle.

It is no exaggeration to suggest that new media provides performance with an energy and excitement perhaps unparalleled since the advent of silent cinema. Spectators faced with the morphing shapes of holographic form and virtual reality are confronted with an artistic spectacle strangely similar in effect to that of the silent cinematic image described in 1927 by Antonin Artaud: "The soul is roused beyond the limits of representation. A kind of virtual force of images opens up unrealized possibilities at the depth of spirit. . . . This is why cinema seems to me made above all to express the stuff of thought, the interior of consciousness, and not only by the play of imagery but by something more imponderable that confront us with interiority through direct matter, without interventions, without representations."[1] Today's audiences of multimedia spectacle delight once again in the virtual *display* ("without interventions") of the image; the difference is that it is now characterized not by the flatness of its "raw cinematic material" but by the transparency and three-dimensionality of digital figuration. What we know as the "cinematic surface" is now porous, electric, amoebic, fractal, and networked.

For traditional practitioners of performance and its theorization, however, the results of the digital revolution could be said to be somewhat mixed. Ironically, this return to the show and display of visual form contests the one humanistic remnant lingering in even the most radical of performance theory: the celebratory display of the actor's body as the foundation of dramatic realism, mimesis, and even its internalized masochism.[2] Even as forceful a choreographer as William Forsythe has developed a spectacular mise-en-scène that confounds the actor's body with the endless visions of the flat screen. *Kammer/Kammer,* performed in 2006 at the Brooklyn Academy of Music, is a dance-theater work that enacts the live shooting of a film onstage. Although the movements of the dancers are frequently concealed from the audience behind portable walls whose positions change abruptly, their actions are readily available to spectators throughout the performance via some fourteen wide-screen monitors hanging at different levels and angles throughout the opera house. Indeed, a large number of spectators would have had their visions of the dancers blocked by the screens as well as by the walls. In this case, performance happens screenically. Forsythe would no doubt disagree with his avant-garde predecessor, Herbert Blau, who writes elegantly about the force of corporeality in the face of its increasing immaterialization. "So as regards the power of a disappearing presence," writes Blau, "the theatre would appear to have the advantage [over cinema and its technological offspring], its very corporeality being the basis of its most powerful illusion, that something is substantially there, the thing itself, even as it vanishes."[3] In contrast, Forsythe and numerous other digital practitioners show the actor vanishing not in corporeality but in spectral illusion—as a video projection or a hologram. The actor's corporeal presence fades and vanishes on the electronic platform in a way that might be understood to foreground the illusions of substance and presence themselves.[4]

Yet, just the contrary of such a demystification of subjectivity fuels the artistic strategies behind many successful multimedia performances. Rather than mark the subject's complex constitution along the representational divide of the internal and external, the virtual and actual, such a spectralization of the performing body has been utilized by a wide variety of artists to transcend the theatrical otherness of the subject-object dichotomy and its encrustation in the critical narratives of the modernist/postmodernist era. A case in point is Daniel Reeves's videotape *Obsessive Becoming* (1995), which I analyze in chapter 5. Reeves offsets the trauma of the body's figuration as the visceral site of the wounds of war and the abuse of sexuality with an overbearing tone of spirituality, inward redemption, and accord— sensibilities that also inform Reeves's Zen-inflected video and digital installations *Eingang* (1990) and *Lines of Lamentation* (1997). Paul Chan's installation for the 2006 Whitney Biennial, *1st Light,* presents the viewer with a silent digital animation projected anamorphically onto the gallery floor through which the materiality of objects (automobiles, cell phones, bodies, sunglasses, power poles) are rendered spectral as but shadowy stains of light. However, what I appreciate as a virtuoso performance of what I'll describe at various points in this book as the digital stain—the murky imprint of digitality on the cinematic trace—is translated by Johanna Burton as "a post-9/11 version of the Rapture," one in which "Chan invokes religion as he speculates on the mechanisms of faith and belief."[5] Similarly, while Bill Viola insists that his video art brings the viewer more in touch with the body, his endgame is the spiritual negation of the body in the sense of mysticism's "via negativa."[6]

In the most sophisticated arenas of electronic spectacle, theatrical performance, and multimedia installation, new media artists frequently endorse a paradoxical return to primitivism, mysticism, and spiritualism. Particularly in the digitized arena of electronic installation and performance, artists as divergent in form and vision as Nam June Paik, Reeves, Dawson, and Viola have developed artworks that are often described, sometimes by the artists themselves, as soliciting a unifying, spiritualizing aesthetic in contrast to the shifting terrain of politics and identity. A public relations spin that frequently frames electronic art in the language of spirituality reflects a similar desire or nostalgia for simpler times and less complicated worldviews than those wrought by the divergent narratives of identity and difference prevalent in the theory of the past few decades. Indeed, the artistic call for a spectacle of comforting accord openly disavows the poststructural legacy of dissonance and divergence for the purpose of regaining something of a universalist point of view, whether of a chapel ceiling, a domestic interior, an urban panorama, or a singular body floating in virtual space. It is almost as if the allure of the clean lines and stark simplicity of much digital and laser spectacle hearkens back to a calming ideology of representational harmony, one prevalent in visual studies ever since the advent of Renaissance single-point perspective. Such a drive for the theatricality of accord, for the display of a new/old world order, depends on the anchoring of representation in the assumption of analogical certainty, in the metaphysics of point of view, and sometimes even in the via negativa of mysticism. The latter is what Bill Viola calls "video black," the artistic/mental fade to "the black of the annihilation of the self."[7]

To some degree, the mystical proclivity of many electronic artists is understandable in view of an avant-garde sensibility that aligns artists of the new media with the pioneers of early cinema. I refer not so much to comparative analyses of digital art with early work in collage and special effects[8] but more to the visionary drive of the cinematic avant-gardes who, in the words of the early French theoretician of cinema Roger Leenhardt, "discovered and baptized the seventh art, as a universal language of the image and a privileged expression of the modern world. The whole in a literary sense, effusive, passably baroque, which constitutes less a philosophy than a mystique."[9] The striking characteristic of the universal language of the image and its mystique, consistently emphasized by Leenhardt as what is "passably baroque," is perhaps the feature of early cinema that most drives digital representation. To Leenhardt, the fundamental feature of cinematic theatricality, its *faire voir*, was how it reintegrated "the baroque in the real." On one level, the Baroque characterized a certain simplicity of cinematic narrative time that could evoke mystical or universalistic sensibilities: "this taste of adventure, dream, the object, the baroque, myth, and of infancy."[10] On another level, Leenhardt turned to the legacy of the Baroque to understand the essence of cinematic styles: "because of this primordial realism, it is precisely not the cinematographic material . . . that constitutes the art, but only assemblage, rapprochement, ellipsis." "Ellipsis," he insists, constitutes the essence of cinema: "the figure which is the ground of rhythm (it already exists in the elementary phenomenon of the rapprochement of two different views)."[11]

The alignment of the rhythmic movement of much electronic and digital art with the doubled grounds of analogy and mysticism ushers in a paradox that typifies critical trends in digital studies. While situating new media experimentations in installation and performance on the very conceptual foundation of analogy per se—from which virtuality distances itself—the intensity of new electronic representation also sheds new light on the productive instability of analogy and its representational corollaries. Such a doubled folding of analogy within the digital field foregrounds incessant attempts to stabilize the image of representation, which so easily "fades to black."[12] While the following discussion will trace the desire of many artists to enshrine their artwork in the plenitude of spiritual accord, it will emphasize how their return to baroque models and paradigms foregrounds structural and representational elements of these same models that unsettle any sense of the comforting ground of unifying plenitude. It is in this sense that Leenhardt's notion of ellipsis calls to mind Deleuze's emphasis on the divergence of "new baroque" points of view, "now that both the figure and the ground are in movement in space."[13] By entwining lessons from the theory and practice of electronic installation, I will suggest that the promise of new media, from Mona Hatoum to Bill Viola, lies in its performativity of analogical disjunction, divergent points of view, and digital incompossibility.

ILLUMINATING BAROQUE SPACE:
HATOUM, DAWSON, PAIK

At the heart of this paradox stands an extensive array of recent projects in video and electronic installation that dialogue energetically with Renaissance and baroque constructions of space, light, passion, memory, and utopia.[14] While a good many electronic artists embrace earlier historical models of representation in order to frame their work in an unchallenged discourse of interiority, mysticism, spirituality, and utopia, others position their work in relation to the past as a means of foregrounding the prominence of representational disjunction in neobaroque paradigms of artistic place, subjective space, and political practice. While the differences between these two strategies are generally quite easy to discern, they often share conceptual strategies and artistic contexts that stage cultural miscegenation, or movements between conflicting cultures, methods, and ideologies, as the common artistic result of electronic interfaces with the baroque past. This somewhat "gray" area of "video black" is particularly evident in the work and writings of Bill Viola. The longstanding residue of Eastern mysticism in his work is frequently overshadowed by a psychophilosophical interface that heightens the disjunctive intervals of re-presentation as much as the holistic plenitude of their interiority. Just how video black can turn so readily to digital gray in Viola's work will become more apparent by initial discussions of works by two prominent laser artists, Paula Dawson and Nam June Paik, and by the multimedia artist Mona Hatoum, whose installations manifest the contrasting poles of the Digital Baroque.

An interesting point of departure is provided by Hatoum's 2002 exhibition at the Laboratorio Arte Alemeda in Mexico City, curated by Priamo Lozada (who died tragically at the Venice Biennale in June 2007). Lozada staged the work of this Palestinian artist from Lebanon in the spectacularly baroque space of his contemporary art center, which is situated in the renovated church of the former Convent of San Diego. The poignancy of the cultural paradox of Hatoum's postcolonial work in Mexico, hung on the architectural supports of the colonial legacy, was not lost on the artist who shaped her representations of photography, weaving, and video in dialogue both with the spiritual venue of the Laboratorio Arte Alemeda and with the popular Mexican devotion to the Virgin of Guadalupe. Two video installations are noteworthy in this context. Framed by the archway of the former Chapel of Dolores, *Vidéau* is projected from floor level at the rear of the chapel where the altar would have been. Its abstract close-up of falling water blends into the volatility of flame and smoke (as if a single-track montage of Viola's celebrated large-scale installation, *The Crossing,* which I discuss in detail later). The Mexican critic, Francisco Reyes Palma, understands Hatoum's abstraction of flame and smoke in the context of the heavy incense of Mexican ritual, while the misty video loop "can be perceived as the ungraspable persistence of the popular cult to the Virgin of Guadalupe."[15] While this piece seems to have elicited religious associations in tandem with the architectural context of its Mexican installation, Hatoum's exhibition actually worked to stage the disjunctions of such socio-historical analogies. This becomes particularly clear in Palma's account of the video installation *Testimonio, 1995–2002,* displayed in the space of the former vestibule (Figure 5). Here the viewers' eyes were embraced by an enigmatic image of complex texture whose oval shape and rose coloration signaled to Palma "the tondo, or circular painting of Renaissance religious iconography."[16] Yet, the video's surprising subject matter inverted the talismanic quality of this projection appearing on the walls of a colonial, religious edifice. It is actually a projection of a close-up image of a scrotum whose adjustment to changes in temperature results in the color variation understood as religious by Palma. Combining realistic footage screened in a convent setting with erotic fascination from the perspective of the feminist gaze, Hatoum's installation belied reverent testimony to the immediacy of mystical iconicity. If this piece evokes a sense of immediacy, it is less that of religious iconicity than of visceral corporcality. Hatoum's work summons the viewer to see feelingly, in the deepest, perhaps even mystical, sense of eroticism. As Palma notes, in referring to the complexity of his Mexican cultural heritage so ingrained in imaginary subservience to the culture of the Virgin and its patriarchal framework, *Testimonio, 1995–2002* provides "an ironic transcription of our ingrained *machismo*" while it "abandons us at the limit, at the point of internal fracture."[17]

Hatoum's installations provide somewhat of a sharp contrast to those of the pioneering Australian holograph artist Paula Dawson, whose technically sophisticated work is indifferent to Hatoum's more obvious postcolonial

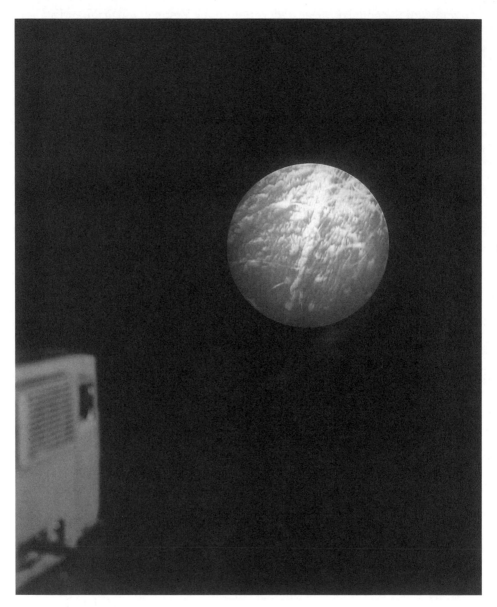

Figure 5. Mona Hatoum, *Testimonio, 1995–2002.*

and postmodernist agenda. Yet a similar divergence of seventeenth-century referents also provides the religious ground and figure for two significant works that have drawn praise to Dawson. Dawson's permanent holographic installation created for St. Bridget's Church in Coogee, Australia, *Shrine of the Sacred Heart* (installed in 1997), combines laser and camera obscura technology to project a mise-en-scène of spiritual illumination. The user of this piece activates a holographic light show at the center of the church by bending down on a kneeler as if to pray (the installation runs only on Sunday mornings, thus enhancing its inspirational value). In this kneeling position, the user activates a holograph screen that reflects a domed installation unit, which is illuminated to represent a hemisphere. The hologram portrays the intersecting flame and cross that mark the wounded heart of Christ in a way that also bathes the observer's chest with light shining through the holographic plate. Dawson describes her piece as being analogical to the seventeenth-century, mystical visions of Saint Mary Margaret:

> The hemisphere, which represents the aureole, is itself illuminated from above by five rays of light. The invisible, imagined origin of these five converging rays is the five wounds of the risen Christ. So it appears as if the Body of Christ hovers above the hemisphere. The Transfiguration suggests the aspirational aspect of Divine Love. The holographic images of light— the flame and the mandorla—can be seen because they are illuminated by a real light—the laser light shining through the holographic plate onto the viewer's chest. The laser light originates from the central point of the virtual hemisphere and bathes chest and praying hands in golden light. This light suggests the all-encompassing Holy Spirit. In this way, the location, direction and orientation of light sources within the hologram is used to suggest the Trinitarian states. . . . The simulation of the holographic image employs the metaphor of the Church as the body of Christ both by using parts of the existing church as elements of the model and by altering the orientation and translation of spatial elements of the Church. The elaborate relief casting on the surface of the inverted dome replicates decorative motifs of the marble sanctuary.[18]

As Dawson understands the religious significance of her installation, its visual motifs provide an artistic catalogue of the iconography of Saint Mary Margaret's visions and the spatial elements of the physical church. But it is light itself that constitutes both the figure and ground of its representation: "In this holographic artwork, the light associated with the Sacred Heart is the subject of the visual representation."[19] As is frequently the case with new media expressions of early modern concepts, this is a piece whose contemporary conceit of laser technology provides a materialization of a vision whose light could only have been fantasized in the seventeenth century. Much more poignantly than the analogical referents of religious iconography, the electric wonder of holographic science energizes and renews the deadened symbolism of religious tradition.

What Dawson's account of this recent installation fails to emphasize, however, is its structural relation to her earlier, 1984 piece, *Working Model One,* which was based on the seventeenth-century church of Sant' Agnese in Agone (Piazza Novona, Rome), designed by the lauded baroque architect Francesco Borromini. Dawson's installation, which consisted of six small plates presented in a sculptural frame forming a window on a pedestal, derives from Borromini's emphasis on repetitive structural elements, light, and receding perspective. As noted by John Rupert Martin, Borromini's interplay inside and outside the structure of convexity and concavity works, in baroque fashion, to enhance "the provocative mobility" of the organic "flow of space from within and without." For this 1984 holograph piece, quite early for such a sophisticated piece of laser installation, Dawson capitalized on a similar dynamics of "spatial advance and retreat."[20] The result, in the words of Rebecca Coyle and Philip Hayward, was "to create a visual model which alters according to different viewpoints."[21] While the holograph staged a three-dimensional arena for an approximation of the contemplative specularity of the baroque chapel, much like the mystical light of *Shrine of the Sacred Heart,* it did so in a way that staged the disjunctive planes of perspectival illusion at the expense of a passive reception of visual harmony. Dawson's evocation of historical materiality here haunts and disrupts the mystical sanctity of accord projected backward on the baroque by contemporary artistic analogy. As described in detail by Coyle and Hayward:

> The work also uses unstable images that seem to appear and disappear, thus challenging the notion of monocular perspective, that is, the centrality of the eye of the individual observer. The subject matter (or "object") of each holographic tile in the work is a picture frame made from plaster cornice. . . . Each frame has a curved piece of plaster that, from certain viewpoints, appears

solid and from others appears as a shadow coming out of the void. This appearance/reappearance element was calculated by exploiting the limited coherence of the helium-neon laser. . . . Dawson deliberately employed this phenomenon and calculated the recordings to coincide with the sections of the beam where the light fails (becomes incoherent) and hence where only a shadow of the image is recorded. As such, not only does the work remark upon phenomena of light and lasers, but also indirectly refers to the "black hole" element of holography, that is the fact that an object that moves more than a fraction of a wavelength while being exposed for holographic production will not be recorded as a 3-D object but instead turns black in the image.[22]

While the frame of *Working Model One* relies on its allusion to the perspectival systems of baroque religious architecture and spiritual iconography, its electronic pulse positions this system as one contingent on the performance of representational illusion, excess, and disjunction. From shadows coming out of the void to the failure of light, this holograph's gestures to perspectival and spiritual plentitude simultaneously stage its fade to black.[23] Just as the illumination of light constitutes both the figure and ground of *Shrine of the Sacred Heart,* shadow and the failure of light in *Working Model One* provide a contrasting pole from which to appreciate the shifting legacies of the Digital Baroque.

Two major light installations by Nam June Paik further confuse the analogical clarity of baroque theological referents by blending the form of electronic light and the performativity of spectatorial interface. In *Sistine Chapel before Restoration,* installed in the German Pavilion at the 1993 Venice Biennale, Paik presented a four-channel video installation of image and sound on a paneled ceiling displayed with forty-two video projectors. Gesturing to the contemplative aura of religious and museum display, one initially honed by Renaissance and baroque fresco artists, Paik flooded the ethereal space with morphed imagery combining the visual memory of pop culture, visual media, and Paik's own electric iconography. The flow of imagery functioned, on the one hand, to reroute the religiosity of iconography into the secular space of everyday visual communications and, on the other hand, to diminish the centrality of the viewer caught off balance by the upward tilt of electronic form and communication overload. The containment of iconography gave way to the excessive bleeding and overlap of

Paik's electronic colorations and figurations, thus loosening the traditional parameters of iconology and reception. Combining the synthesized bleeding of color and line of his single-track works, such as *Global Groove* (1973), with the excessive information flow of large-scale installations, such as the forty-seven channel *Electronic Superhighway* (1995), *Sistine Chapel before Restoration* performed similar shifts in both figure and ground by catapulting them into electronic movement in space. As Matzner points out, the "fixed architectural boundaries" of the installation space dissolved among the traces of "ever-changing pictorial cycles."[24] But while its structural links to the via negativa might lead critics such as Matzner to read in this dizzying experience the Renaissance inscription of "the human being in the center,"[25] this piece more likely positioned its viewer as the doubled screen of baroque, spatial simultaneity, as the relayer, transmitter, or receiver of imagistic flow rather than as the ultimate soul of perspective or the figural center and source of visual illumination.

This distinction is crucial since it shifts emphasis away from centered subjectivity to energized information relay as the core of the Digital Baroque. Paik's performative staging of a flow of accumulated imagery dialogues in a fascinating way with the theory of the baroque enigma articulated at the same moment by Perniola. In *Enigmas,* the first book to elaborate on the baroque aesthetics of information culture, Perniola argues that the linkage of new media art to baroque interiority depends on a model of knowledge that is grounded less in the centrality of the thinking subject than in the flow and energetics of mania and possession in all of its mystical intensity. "A world that takes its fundamental tonality from a psychic, subjective temporality without a solution of continuity succeeds a world whose principal characteristic is a fragmentation and spatialization of the psychic experience permitting only that calm, crystalline states follow or precede state of pure delirium."[26] Key to this shift is what I stress in the Introduction as the subject's inscription in the accumulating flow of digital data, information, and imagery. Just as digital information systems enhance the intensity of this flow, their displacement of thinking subjectivity by the wonder of data accumulation evokes the very ideal of information that Walter Benjamin argued to be fundamental to the Baroque: the processes of storing and schemata to which the emergent libraries of the seventeenth century were a monument.[27]

Key to such accumulation, I wish to reemphasize, is Benjamin's sense of how "chronological movement is grasped and analysed in a spatial image."[28] It is such an imagistic condensation of temporal flow, even more than the rather obvious dissolution of architectural boundaries, that lends electronic verve to Paik's site-specific installation *Baroque Laser,* his most explicit homage to analogical passage. This 1995 installation adapted the interior of the baroque parish church Mariae Himmelfahrt-Dyckburg, in Münster-St. Mauritz, to the needs of a complex laser and multimedia show. Paik designed the piece for an exhibition planned by the Westphalian Landsmuseum in Münster in celebration of the three-hundredth birthday of the influential eighteenth-century German architect Johan Conrad Schlaun. In keeping with notions of the baroque Gesamptkunstwerk as a synthesis of the arts,[29] Paik chose to combine a laser light show in the church's central chapel and a multimedia image extravaganza in the smaller tomb chapel off to the side. Embodying the mystical/ideological baroque fascination with light (important to Dawson and discussed in more detail in the following chapter), a flame in the central axis of the church was placed in front of a gauze curtain and filmed by a video camera. These video images were intermixed with his footage of Merce Cunningham dance movements (*Merce by Merce by Paik* [1975–78]) and projected alternately on the gauze screen. Both motifs of light and movement (laser and video) became unified, according to Matzner, into a highly contemplative, almost meditative game of images. This is said to have created a surprisingly tranquil spatial atmosphere in the site of the church: "through medial reproduction, the 'now' of the burning candle became the timeless 'now' of a sanctuary light, of a continually lived past."[30] At the heart of this high-tempo installation, then, lies something analogous to what Benjamin understood as being vital to baroque representation. Derivative of the mystical via negativa, an essential element of baroque life constitutes, returning to Benjamin, "the transposition of the originally temporal data into a figurative spatial simultaneity."[31]

Yet the dazzling "timeless 'now'" of the laser event remained inscribed in the provocative split of retrospective time and vision so characteristic of Paik's work. Paik used mirrors to multiply three additional lasers of blue, green, and red that "transported" the flame onto the screen, while a fourth red beam was projected onto the candle flame from high up and then splashed onto the walls of the church by an optical diffraction grating. Matzner notes that this technique "had already been discovered in the Baroque period by the Jesuit father Francesco Frimaldi (1613–63) and which Isaac

Newton later designated as 'inflection,' i.e., bending."[32] While *Baroque Laser*'s multilayered performance of diffracted light surely would have supplemented the contemplative aura of this church annually visited by pilgrims, it also rendered material the marvelous baroque transition from monocular to curious perspective, not to mention the sometimes tense interface linking theologically based inquiries, such as Frimaldi's, and the secular investigations of new scientists, such as Newton. Hubert Damisch suggests, in his book *The Origin of Perspective,* that the new science concerned itself not so much with the perspectival object as a predetermined symbolic locus (of grace or power, for example) as with unparalleled visual and emotive "after-effects" ("du *post*"), which could be materialized and recognized only "après-coup":

> There is a great danger of treating perspective as just one object among others, if not as a simple product or effect, whereas it interests us here primarily as something that is *productive* of effects, insofar as its capacity, its power to inform extends well beyond the limits of the era in which it was born.[33]

Perhaps it is no simple coincidence that Paik could turn to the adjacent chapel of the dead to foreground the paradoxical, baroque display of figurative spatial simultaneity and its emotive "après-coup." Here Paik returns to the play of the *Sistine Chapel before Restoration* to bathe the domed ceiling of this intimate chapel with projected virtual imagery and animations. Generated by computer in Paik's studio, the colorful iconic and three-dimensional imagery projected in the chapel of death, adjacent to the laser spectacle of light and movement, produced an "après-coup" effect of both the encrypted dead and the encrypted code that exceeded all evidence of the temporal limits engendering them.

This distinction between the constant flow of images and the mediatized spectacle of after-effects constitutes for Mieke Bal a core element of contemporary baroque aesthetics. Such an aesthetic explores "the possibilities of an alternative temporality in which the past is subsumed but *not* lost in the present, because the present itself, *its* pace and instantaneity, is called to a halt, slowed down, and made an object of reflection.[34] Put otherwise, instead of producing only the image flow of a "timeless now," Paik's articulation of spatial simultaneity in *Baroque Laser* lent figuration to the mediatized spectacle of electronic after-effects and their retrospective registration and interpretation. Nor must we remain within the confines of the baroque chapel to appreciate the importance of retrospective suspension to Paik's many artistic interventions in the culture of speed. Consider the implications of an installation such as the forty-seven channel *Electronic Superhighway: Continental U.S.* (1995) (which hangs adjacent to two single channel pieces, *Alaska* and *Hawaii*). This piece, whose colors and motions resonated out onto Soho's Houston Street from the large storefront window of the Holly Solomon Gallery, condensed the media motion of 313 monitors into a cartographic grid of the forty-eight states, delineated by colorful neon boundaries hanging adjacent to this piece. The speed of movement and the flow of media blend into something of a crystalline map of flickering sound bites and overlapping video grabs. Here motion and flow constitute the very materiality of the installation (just as neon flows through porous boundaries). Paik provided a stilled, cartographic snapshot of the allusiveness of televisual flow as a means of re-presenting the figurative spatial simultaneity of the culture of speed itself, as the movement through which the United States constitutes itself. Key to Paik's many projects is the paradox, to return to Benjamin, of "the transposition of the originally temporal data into a figurative spatial simultaneity,"[35] a paradox also inscribing the affective subject in the accumulating flow of information, imagery, and digital data.

VIA VIOLA

As I have argued in a variety of other contexts, and will develop throughout this book, similar analogical stagings of baroque representational precedents might readily foreground the divergence, fissure, and variation of the space, movement, temporality, and texture of the very same machineries and theories of performativity that sustain the utopic discourse of interiority.[36] Through the mediating procedures of electronic and digital presentation, these installations not only "show" the reconfigured picture of the past but also "display" the "après-coup" of representation by designating the act and power of reference, in the early modern sense of *faire voir / faire lire*.[37] Representation is thus shown by the mediating procedures of theatrical performativity to be both an activity of enunciation and a space of combined production and reception, of conjoined reality and fantasy. Giving rise to the thought of the dissonant multiplicity of representation, these installations entwine the enunciational triad, signifier/signified/signifying, in an electrical grid that displaces the primacy of the dramatic notions of "the original, the first time, resemblance, imitation, faithfulness."[38]

In *The Fold,* Deleuze relates such a display of repetition and difference to Leibniz's early modern emphasis on the dissonance inherent in resemblance. Deleuze suggests that such dissonance resurfaces with particular verve in recent digital productions of electronic music and art. Characteristic of what he calls "a new Baroque," the digital revolution brings new life to the theatricalization and spatialization of the *show* of representation. While experimentation with point of view continues to be central to new media architectonics (highlighted in more recent experiments with GPS tracking and digital cartography), the conceit is no longer to assume the sameness of point of view "now that both the figure and the ground are in movement in space."[39] What is significant about Deleuze's "new Baroque" is how it positions the digital realization of poststructural notions of performativity in a historical continuum with the rich fabric of early modern thought, a tapestry as dependent on the divergence of its weave as on the accord of its affect.

Perhaps nowhere is the baroque show of the electronic weave as striking as when displayed in the work of Bill Viola. Viola took the lead among electronic installation artists in relying on stripped-down mythical and universal formulas of transcendence, rebirth, struggle, and love to drive his intermixed spectacles of videomatic movement and virtual reality. In many cases, his symbolic references to the most elementary myths of creation and transcendence compete with, if not eclipse, the artistic tradition's more complicated narratives of familial and political trauma and the masochism of their fictional representation. His recent epic installations *Going Forth by Day* (2002) and *Five Angels for the Millennium* (2001) dwell on the captivating imagery of narratives of apocalypse and transcendence. In producing *Five Angels for the Millennium,* Viola realized that "I had inadvertently created images of ascension, from death to birth."[40] Exhibited in New York within a year of 9/11, *Going Forth by Day* features a final panel in which a spectral figure suddenly rises in wondrous transcendence from a watery hole of death. Surrounding the site of tragedy are exhausted and defeated rescue workers who seem to have failed in their quest to save victims of a flash flood disaster. Their eerie melancholia evoked sharp resonance in post-9/11 New York, just as the transcendent figure of death seemed to appeal to the new fervor of religiosity sweeping the city and the nation. In keeping with this fervor, Viola's video diptych *Surrender* (2001) found its place in the grouping "On Spirituality" in the 2006 MOMA exhibition on the legacy of Islamic art, "Without Boundary: Seventeen Ways of Looking." Inspired by the teachings of the thirteenth-century Persian mystic Rumi, *Surrender* features two vertically stacked flat-screen monitors whose respective images of a man and a woman bow toward each other until they seem to merge in hazy indistinction. An attentive viewer comes to realize that the anamorphic blur of their merger camouflages through electronic form the video capture of their murky reflections in water, thus calling to mind Viola's previous video commentary on Narcissus, *The Reflecting Pool* (1977–79). But engaging in a commentary neither on Narcissus nor on Echo, Viola means for this anamorphic diptych to reference Rumi "who looks to the surface for something beyond the world of appearances."[41]

But we need not dwell on Viola's most recent, and most spectacular, installations to appreciate the paradox of the baroque legacy that bathes his work in the luminosity of spirituality. An elegant example of the clarity of such mystical reference can be cited in the 1996 digital installation, *The Messenger*. This single-track projection was commissioned for placement in Durham Cathedral, the resting place of Bede and St. Cuthbert, the giants of medieval spiritual life. Viola himself provides an eloquent description of the piece:

> A large image is projected onto a screen mounted to the Great West Door in Durham Cathedral. The image sequence begins with a small, central, luminous, abstract form shimmering and undulating against a deep blue-black void. Gradually the luminous shape begins to get larger and less distorted, and it soon becomes apparent that we are seeing a human form, illuminated, rising towards us from under the surface of a body of water. . . . After some time, the figure breaks the surface, an act at once startling, relieving and desperate. His pale form emerges into the warm hues of a bright light, the water glistening on his body. His eyes immediately open and he releases a long held breath from the depths, shattering the silence of the image as this forceful primal sound of life resonates momentarily in the space. After a few moments, he inhales deeply, and, with his eyes shut and his mouth closed, he sinks into the depths of the blue-black void to become a shimmering moving point of light once more. The image then returns to its original state and the cycle begins anew.[42]

From the moment of its installation at Durham Cathedral to its subsequent displays in museum settings, critics have read *The Messenger,* similar to *Five Angels for the Millennium* and *Surrender,* as a stunning presentation of the religious significance of birth and rebirth. The piece has generated much more focus on its cycle of the eternal return than on the desperation of the surfacing figure's gasping for breath and the viewer's masochistic identification with the horrors of lengthy submersion, not to mention the piece's stunning dissolution of corporeal realism through the variability and fractalization of light that conjoins, as Deleuze would say, both the illuminated figure and the shimmering ground of movement in space. But rather than dwell on the stunning specularity and representational chaos of the electronically enhanced images and sounds of *The Messenger,* critics have followed Viola's lead by stressing the sentiment of accord over the coercive dissonance of affect itself. "Like all great art," writes David Jasper, "Viola's work focuses upon the profound mystery of creation itself, truly a *poiesis* (a 'making'), suspicious of the coercive power which lurks within traditions of mimesis and representation."[43] Indeed, similar widespread publicity and critical praise of the mysticism of Viola's 1998 retrospective at the Whitney Museum of Art has influenced the tone of the reception of multimedia performance in the millennial decade to come. David A. Ross echoes the timber of Jasper's chant when he states emphatically, in his curatorial introduction to the Whitney retrospective, that Viola "eschews overtly theoretical postmodern concerns. . . . In the traditional manner of great art, Viola provokes the heart by leading the mind to avenues of contemplation and self-discovery. In so doing, the art provides the basis for an experience best described as transcendent—a curious word to use at the end of the age of mechanical reproduction, yet the only word that applies."[44]

Regardless of Viola's personal penchant for an aesthetic of interiority, I wonder whether "transcendent" is really the only word that might apply to his work. By shifting our attention to other pieces by Viola that dialogue with *The Crossing,* I wish to challenge the extent of the resistance of the mystical discourse of new media performance to the "postmodern" theoretical tradition. Judging from Viola's comments, this certainly may cut against the grain of the art in question. "Today our communication," Viola laments, "depends on representation or demonstration, instead of the energy of creating the universe."[45] But rather than dismiss too quickly the millennial drive to equate the spectacular images of digital technology with the mystical creation of great art, I wish here to place digital installation and performance in relation to the haunting effect of the same baroque theatrical language of demonstration and narrative form that it promotes: *faire montrer, faire voir, faire lire.* As evident in the preceding quote from Viola, the conceptual and subliminal *force* of the *faire voir* (demonstration) is too hastily forgotten and foreclosed by the primitivist bent of the metaphysical discourse favored by so many practitioners of the new media.[46]

Something of a baroque splitting of vision, I wish to suggest, sustains the internal or masochistic fissure continually energizing and imploding even the most mystical of electronic performances. Consider Bill Viola's memorable sound and video installation *The Crossing* (1996). Two complementary performances are projected simultaneously on each side of the same large screen. On both sides, a casually dressed male walks slowly into perspective from the darkened background of the screen. The actor's slow, magisterial advance contributes to a spectatorial mood of curious anticipation and a videomatic temporality of endless duration worthy of the most celebrated pieces of performance art. When the figure almost fills the larger-than-life frame, he stands still and stares silently out at the viewer as if not to disrupt duration but to prolong it in a continuous present in which time is em-bodied as literally standing still. Then, on one side of the screen, a small flame appears at the man's feet, followed by a sudden expansion of flame across the floor and up his body. The intensity of the flames totally engulfing the body is matched by the violence of a loud roaring and crackling sound track that fills the room. The fire then subsides, along with the sound track, to reveal only a few remaining flames on a charred floor. As Viola describes it, "The image then returns to black and the cycle repeats itself." Simultaneously, on the other side of the screen, drops of water falling down on the actor's head develop rather suddenly into a raging downpour that completely envelops the actor and fills the installation space with the deafening roar of a waterfall. The cascading water then subsides, finally leaving only a few drops on the ground with no human in sight. Again in Viola's words, "The image then returns to black and the cycle repeats itself."[47]

To a certain degree, the body's electronic disappearing act renders palpable the theatrical reality that Herbert Blau claims as the privilege of the dramatic stage: "its very corporeality being the basis of its most powerful illusion, that something is substantially there, the thing itself, even as it vanishes."[48] Not surprisingly, however, Viola privileges a similar notion of the vanishing thing in order to emphasize the mystical implications of this highly baroque work of electronic art:

> The two traditional natural elements of fire and water appear here not only in their destructive aspects, but manifest their cathartic, purifying, transformative, and regenerative capacities as well. In this way, self-annihilation becomes a necessary means to transcendence and liberation.[49]

What is striking about Viola's insistence on "transcendence" as perhaps, once again, the only word applying to his work, is how the notion of liberation rests on a material support, to recall the terms of Leenhardt, of "assemblage, rapprochement, ellipsis." While Viola might well prefer to stress the symbolic eternal return of past and future symbolized by fire and water, he does so at the expense of dwelling on the incredibly baroque feature of the anamorphic threshold, hinge, or ellipsis sustaining this installation's divergent platforms of spectacle, from below and above, as well as from side to side. Since "the two complementary actions appear simultaneously on the two sides of the screen," as Viola puts it, the viewer must move around the space to see both images.[50] The viewer here joins both figure and ground as being enveloped by movement in space. But it is precisely the reciprocity of the differentials of figure and ground that may unhinge the artist's metaphysical aspirations. "Reciprocal determination of differentials does not refer to a divine understanding," argues Deleuze in *The Fold,* "but to tiny perceptions as representatives of the world in the finite self. . . . The infinite present in the finite self is exactly the position of baroque equilibrium or disequilibrium."[51]

It is the viewer, moreover, who is represented here, somewhat like the spectator of *The Ambassadors,* as the finite self caught in the movement of the crossing, as constituting the middle ground of representation between and within the dual video projections whose mimetic similarity foregrounds their performative dissimilarity. But rather than performing the annihilation of subjectivity or the transcendence of self, the viewer is here positioned in the undulating fold of the in-between. Just such residence in the baroque space of the middle has been celebrated by Deleuze as the promise of theatricality, as what "will release a new potentiality of theater, an always unbalanced, non-representative force. . . . It is in the middle that [one] experiences the becoming, the movement, the speed, the vortex. The middle is not a means but, on the contrary, an excess."[52] The spectatorial in-between of *The Crossing*, I suggest, locates the viewer not in relation to anything like transcendence and liberation but rather directly within the movement, speed, and vortex of *becoming*. It is in this sense of the continuous variation of the ellipsis and the space of the vortex that *The Crossing* marks not only the passage between annihilation and liberation, between the outer and the inner or the personal and the mystical, but something tremendously more vital and virtual, such as the now of crossing itself. *The Crossing*, in this sense, is foremost an interval of becoming, one that merges subjectivity with the archival data of the artwork. It thus figures an amoebic, fractal space of the temporal continuum of becoming, one enveloping the past, present, and future of two performative scenarios whose initial mimetic duplication, via Viola, is rendered asunder by contrasting movements of hot and cold violence from below and above. As the fraught frontier of electronic installation and its doubled spectatorial experience, the crossing / the passage / the ellipsis give show to *(faire voir)* the creative slippage of the many disjunctive tensions that promise to drive the new millennium's ideological fantasy: being and non-being, body and spirit, water and fire, pleasure and pain, matter and simulacra, subjectivity and digital data stream.

Readers familiar with Viola's work will recognize that the artist's theatricalization of the movement of passage is not limited to *The Crossing*. His work over the past two decades consistently experiments with variations of time and space in order to position the viewer in the vortex of the middle. The result is a temporal passage, through which one of Viola's most astute readers, Anne-Marie Duguet, understands "the present to be taken toward the spectral so that the past can be rendered as a present."[53] In *Passage* (1987), a rear projection of a four-year-old's birthday party fills the space of a sixteen-foot-wide by twelve-foot-high wall on one side of a small room facing the narrow twenty-foot-long corridor leading into it. Viola characteristically insists on the "ritualistic and mythic" nature of the birthday party as a rite of passage. Yet, his installation's stress on how "manipulation of space" and "extreme extension of time" leave "the viewer uncomfortably close to this large image, overwhelming in scale" once again foregrounds the spectatorial becoming of "passage" itself as the monumental event of this piece.[54] Viola's description of *Passage*'s enclosure of time places the stress on the becoming of thought: "The structure frames an image that transcends human scale in both time and space, placing it in the internal or subjective domain of memory and emotive association."[55] A similar emphasis on the movement between the extremes of time, past and future, is the subject of Viola's single-track videotape *The Passing* (1991), as well as the performative result of the installation *Threshold* (1992). In *Threshold,* an electronic display sign scrolling up-to-date news events is divided in two by a doorway through which the viewer must exit the room. The three other walls of the space feature dim, colossal projections of sleeping figures whose nocturnal breathing fills the auditory chamber. The threshold between the waking state and sleep, external events and internal dreams, reality and fantasy, as well as the passage from one exhibition site to another positions the visitor among, as Viola describes it, "a gallery of unconscious presences existing beneath the incessant flow of worldly events."[56] Ross Gibson goes so far as to insist that the many "instants of passing over a threshold define existence for Viola. Again and again he creates moments when the spirit defining alive-ness is dramatised so acutely that some essence of existence gets glimpsed, even if only momentarily."[57]

Add to the flow of *Threshold* Viola's display of the interval itself in *Slowly Turning Narrative* (1992). In this memorable installation, a nine-foot-high by twelve-foot-wide screen rotates on a central axis in the middle of a darkened room. But unlike the two-sided screen of *The Crossing,* a mirrored surface on one side contrasts with the other side's conventional projection screen. Two video projectors on opposite sides of the room cast eerie projections as the screen slowly turns. One projector displays the close-up black-and-white portrait of a man squinting and straining. The other projects a divergent series of various sequences of video verité (a nighttime carnival, children riding a carousel, kids playing with fireworks on a beach, a building in flames, car lights in a parking lot) that are characterized, Viola insists, "by continuous motion and swirling light and color."[58] Two audio tracks fill the room with similarly discordant sounds: one of everyday sounds recorded as the camera captured the verité events of play and destruction, the other of a man rhythmically chanting a list of actions and modes of being ("turns/away/looks/comes/calls/returns/remembers/cares/learns/ laughs . . ."). Particularly significant is how the mirrored surface of the one screen spills the passage of the contrasting projections onto the surfaces of the adjoining walls and floor. This results in an anamorphic extension and pixilated distortion that is brought back into focus only momentarily by the return of the conventional projection screen. If something can be said to be "narrative" here, it would be the contrast between the regularity of the rhythmic sound track and the excessive distortion of pixilated colors and flickering traces of light that bounce off the installation's architectonic surfaces, not to mention off the viewers themselves. Indeed, the viewers find themselves similarly caught and dispersed by the mirrored screen's turning reflection of their own hardworking (and anamorphically distorted) gaze that ends up miming the squint and strain of the portrait facing them on the other side of the slowly rotating interval. From *Slowly Turning Narrative, Threshold,* and *The Crossing* to *The Passing* and *Passage,* Viola thus presents his intended narratives of mythic spirituality within theatricalized spaces that envelop the spectator not so much in the liberation of transcendence but in the continual passage of the slippage between becoming and data. The mirroring of conjoined visions of fantasy and reality position Viola's work within the disorienting passage of the middle space, a space reminiscent of the unstable baroque pairing of equilibrium and disequilibrium.

Viola's sophisticated digital video installations lend to the interrelated histories of video and performance something of a new retrospective ellipsis and repetitive energy, whose critical force may also be akin to the virtual allure of the early cinema, celebrated as "beyond all representation" by Artaud and described as "assez baroque" by Leenhardt. Rather than "video black," "digital baroque" might be the phrase that best applies to the passage of becoming characteristic of Viola's dazzling performative installations. It is through the middle gray zones of the digital that Viola displays the prioritizing convolutions of introjection and projection, of self and other, of past and future, on which the politicized narrative of identity has depended. The result is something of a "baroque fervor," in the sense of Peer F. Bundgard, as what "might trace its origin elsewhere than the passionate ecstasy of the transcendent subject . . . far from plunging the subject into the excruciating wait for the revelation of being, the baroque figure seems, on the contrary, to elicit the subject in traversing the limits of the sensible."[59] Perhaps the slowly turning narrative of the digital, its form and its speed, is what will best serve installation in our new millennium as it foregrounds the complex folds of the passage of becoming along the many discordant axes of the data streams constituting Viola's work. "To the degree that the world is now made up of divergent series," Deleuze writes of the "new baroque," "accords no longer convey our world or our text. We are discovering new ways of folding, akin to new envelopments."[60]

chapter 2

ET IN ARCADIA VIDEO: POUSSIN' THE IMAGE OF CULTURE WITH THIERRY KUNTZEL AND LOUIS MARIN

In fond memory of Thierry Kuntzel (1948–2007)

When considering an object by itself and on its own terms, without considering what it might represent, one has an idea of a thing, like the idea of the earth and of the sun. But when reflecting on a certain object only as it represents an other, one has an idea of a sign, and this initial object is called a sign. This, then, is how one ordinarily considers maps and paintings. The sign thus includes two concepts: one, the thing representing; the other, the thing represented; and the nature of the sign consists of prompting the latter by the former.

—ANTOINE ARNAULD AND PIERRE NICOLE, *La logique ou l'art de penser*

Those readers familiar with Louis Marin's extensive writings on the semiology of art will recognize my title's pun on one of his favorite images, Nicolas Poussin's pastoral elegy *Et in Arcadia Ego,* a painting that Marin analyzes in detail in *To Destroy Painting* and throughout his extensive oeuvre. Marin is partial to this painting of the specters of death because its tombstone materializes the powerful role of the sign by representing the two things, death and utopia, that are never perceptible as anything other than representations. Arcadia and death can be known only through the signs of their ephemerality, through representations of infinity and finality, whether of the ultimate future or the idealized past. Put in other terms, Poussin's memorable painting performs the twofold function of the sign as theorized by Arnauld and Nicole in the 1683 edition of *La logique ou l'art de penser. Et in Arcadia Ego* embodies in one picture plane the thing represented and the thing representing. Poussin's painting of the display of the tomb and its inscription, "Et in Arcadia Ego," thus functions as the doubled representation of representation, the deictic showing of the thing that can only be represented virtually as representation.

Just where might we locate such baroque concerns with painting, representation, and virtuality within the context of the contemporary study of new media, not to mention within the discourse of what has come to be known as the disciplines of visual and cultural studies? Do such reflections on death and utopia preclude their conceptual usefulness to Anglo-American cultural and visual studies, which tend to be more at home, more comfortable, with the critical markers of realism, materialism, facticity, and "history"? Judging from the extensive bibliography of *Cultural Studies,* the canonical 1992 reader edited by Lawrence Grossberg, Cary Nelson, and Paula Treichler,[1] the answer would seem to be simple. This bibliography includes not a single reference to such a figure as influential as Marin, whose interrelated writings on the Baroque, semiotics, psychoanalysis, and Continental philosophy helped to forge the discourse of poststructural approaches to the cultural. Also symptomatic is the volume's lack of bibliographic reference to other influential French theoreticians of text and image, such as the many writers who dialogue with this book's theorization of the Baroque, the temporal, and the cinematic. Absent from this volume is reference to Philippe Lacoue-Labarthe, Jean-Luc Nancy, Hubert Damisch, Julia Kristeva, Raymond Bellour, Anne-Marie Duguet, Christian Metz, Guy Rosolato, Thierry Kuntzel, and J.-B. Pontalis, who reflect insistently on earlier traditions of philosophy, psychoanalysis, and cultural theory while mapping an ideological approach to culture and its vicissitudes. Indeed, the same absence is true of significant contemporary figures in Germany such as Alexander Kluge and Oscar Negt, who insist that the role of fantasy be included in any discussion or production of the media. It is notable that this project's encyclopedic attempt to delineate a critical terrain of the cultural remains strikingly indifferent to, if not in defensive disavowal of, the extensive Continental discourse on representation and its cultural work. Many adherents of cultural and visual studies no doubt would attribute this absence or entombment of the discourse on representation to what they perceive as the muted response of semio-psycho-philosophical analyses to the imperatives of identity politics and the attendant realistic, materialist issues of race, class, sexuality, ethnicity, and colonialism. While such an Anglo-American

spin on the poststructural (in)sensitivity to cultural identity has functioned
to foreground many political issues that are crucial to any theorization of
culture, it tends to be inscribed in a pragmatic notion of difference that
itself remains insensitive to the muted differends of representational hybridity that constitute the vibrant fabric of the cultural.[2]

If we take the lead from Anne-Marie Duguet's reflections on the French
theorist and installation artist Thierry Kuntzel, we can appreciate how his
sort of mixture of conceptual art and representational theory situates the
cultural not as an object of study but as a mise-en-scène of representational relations, one that "is able to display the gaze and the visible together
as enigma."[3] It is in this context of the enigmatic hybridity of cultural and
visual relations that I here propose to reopen the discursive crypts of death
and utopia. To do so, I wish to establish something of an imaginary dialogue between the philosopher and the artist with whom I have opened this
chapter, Louis Marin and Thierry Kuntzel, two thoughtful proponents of
poststructural practice whose nuanced views and images enhance the contemporary valence of the Baroque.[4]

AFFECTIVE SPACE

It is not insignificant to Louis Marin that the Jansenist logicians Antoine
Arnauld and Pierre Nicole chose to collapse the many factual distinctions
between paintings and maps, *tableaux* and *cartes,* when they first articulated
the semiological role of the sign. Readers of Marin know that his texts are
especially fond of contemplating the common relation of cartography and
painting. In one formidable essay on the topic, "The City in Map and Portrait," Marin provides a detailed reading of how the 1542 and 1578 maps of
Strasbourg exemplify the two dimensions, transitive and intransitive, that
cartography shares with all representational procedures.[5] That is, maps represent something—their object—while at the same time demonstratively
showing themselves as their own subject, as representing themselves to be
representing space. Put simply, cartography simultaneously signifies place
and shows itself representing space.

Particularly noteworthy is Marin's stress on the distinction between the
signification of place and the representation of space (a distinction that
Michel de Certeau went on to develop in *The Practice of Everyday Life*).[6]
In response to his question "what is place?" Marin suggests that any local

sequence of things, property, value, and beings-there constitute a synchronic order of position or place. Such synchronic ordering provides the material for systems, tables, or maps. Place should thus be understood as the site of the configuration of stability and the production of law. While place is the term Marin reserves for "the conclusions of an action, for the accomplishment of process . . . the contract, the treatise, the alliance," space signifies the more fluid field of enunciation, action, and the processes of history and its movements. "There is space," writes Marin, "when one takes into consideration direction vectors, speed quantities, temporal variables, movements." "Space," he adds, "is animated by movements within it, or, more precisely, spaces are effects of these movements. Space is the effect produced by operations of orientation which, by the same token, 'temporalize' it."[7] In the context of Marin's interest in seventeenth-century sovereign historiography, space plays out conflicts, conquests, and the representation of movement in space, whose effects are themselves spaces. Speaking of a tapestry depicting Louis XIV entering Dunkirk, Marin notes how the king looks at the spectator while gesturing with his commanding cane to Dunkirk, the city he is about to occupy, which is represented topographically in the background of the tapestry. The representation-effect of space is thus equivalent with the act of the historical subject whose gesture enacts power through action.

I should add that Marin initially developed this distinction between place and space as representation-effect in his work on Renaissance and baroque cartographic utopias.[8] The cartographic pictorialization of utopia, an extensive practice of the period ranging from maps to engravings in epic novels, particularly interested Marin since its early modern practices frequently collapsed the realism of cartographic place and the fantasies of utopic space. Like the text and image of Poussin's arcadian tomb, early modern cartography was just as much a powerful projection of spaces and social movements imagined as it was a practiced charting of cities, landscapes, and places known.

Marin derived much of his complicated theory of "the powers of the image" from his keen semiological understanding of how cartographical practice demonstrates the method of charting place while simultaneously representing the procedures of the projection of representation as effect. This theory of power—what I would qualify as power projected—maintains that representational systems, both visual and textual, both artistic and cartographic, always function as apparatuses that position the subject as "a power of theory or a desire of representation." Marin's concept of subjectivity relies on the critical acceptance of two related contingencies that he was careful to distinguish: (1) that power is defined "as desire bound by and caught in representation" (what I understand as the enfolded procedures of projection and incorporation, that is, the effects of representation) and (2) that the Cartesian subject of enunciation is not only a "theoretical" subject but also "a will, a desire," that is, a space of affect.[9] Through elaborate close readings of texts and images, Marin consistently demonstrates how the will is the stuff of desire and how power is contingent on desire's manifestation as representation. In both cases, the exterior images of power/ desire and theory/representation always bear the phantasmatic marks and traces of the inside just as the subliminal representation of the inside is always sustained by incorporated forms and supports of text and image, which representational devices he terms "text or tissue."[10]

One way of conceptualizing space, in this baroque context, might be to picture it as the affective fold of the voluminous motions of inside-out, outside-in. A trademark of Marin's exceptional contributions to the understanding of early modern culture is his appreciation of how the fold and trace conjoin the *différance* of deconstruction, the interpellations and symptomatic enfoldings of Lacan, and the critical legacies and semiotic specificities of classical French philosophy, art, and letters. What Marin understands as the philosophical arcadia of early modern culture is less an unproblematic, neoclassical utopia than those uncanny "games of space" that both dissemble and present the historical and ideological contradictions of representation and its subjects. As he so forcefully reads the playful scene of Poussin's arcadia, there lie the playful spaces of identity and alterity, will and desire, as well as theory and representation.

WHITE LIGHTS

Having laid out the groundwork of Marin's passion for cultures of cartography, I wish to note that I have charted these investments primarily to project the space of Marin's early modern concerns into the future. My task here, returning once again to Poussin's painting *Et in Arcadia Ego,* will be to discuss the critical shift that occurs, if any, when the semiotic subject of early modern painting or cartography, Ego, gives way to the spatially diffuse subject of postmodern installation, Video. How might Marin's concept of the powers of the neoclassical image impact contemporary video culture and its museum arcades? Given that artistic form and subject matter shift through time and practice, what might we expect from the video transformation of the interpellations of desire and subjectivity common to the age of Poussin?

When I first heard of plans to exhibit Thierry Kuntzel's video installation *Four Seasons Minus One,* as part of his retrospective at the Jeu de Paume in 1993, I had hopes of viewing this electronic appropriation of Poussin in the pleasurable company of Louis Marin, a groundbreaking reader of French neoclassical painting. I was wondering what Marin would make of Kuntzel's technological rendition of Poussin's pastoral passage from the pleasures of spring to the death masks of winter. But since this scenario was disrupted by the too sudden arrival of death at Marin's own door, I found myself visiting the Kuntzel exhibition armed with thoughts from his text "The Being of the Image and Its Efficacity," the preface of *Des pouvoirs de l'image,* the book on which Marin was working at the time of his death. The result of my visit to the Kuntzel exhibition was the unfolding of what Marin calls in his preface "a theoretical fiction," that is, a theoretical questioning of the interval between the possibilities of the apparition of Poussin's arcadian subject and what Marin might have termed the "arcanian" effects of its video manifestation.

While I have already elaborated in the preceding chapter on this kind of interval as the structural hinge of Viola's Digital Baroque, the conceptual apparatus I took into my viewing of Kuntzel's installation stemmed more specifically from Louis Marin's sensitivity to the powers of the image in Poussin. Had Marin been able to enjoy the delights of Kuntzel's dazzling technological rendition of *The Four Seasons,* the sobering arcadian cycle that Poussin painted at the end of his life, he might well have included a still from the central panel of Kuntzel's triptych wall projection *Winter (The Death of Robert Walser)* to illustrate his point of departure. This still would depict a crisp video close-up of the sparkling white fabric of a translucent death shroud whose elegant folds simultaneously veil and display a dark body lying motionless beneath. In reflecting on the Occidental tendency to diminish the image to the secondary status of a dead copy, a mediating screen, or a mirroring specter of a living presence, Marin would have displayed this still to illustrate his point that the image derives its force from just such an embodiment of re-presentation. Like the writing to which he always compares it, the image always already figures a substitutional absence in space or time. Yet it is the excess of visual displacement, condensation, and secondary revision that lends to the image an undeniable enunciational force. Whether in viewings of Poussin or in readings of Montaigne, Marin insists that the making present of imagined absence fuels the autobiographical energy sustaining all theoretical fictions. Regarding Kuntzel's *Winter*, he might well have repeated his remarks about the representational force of death in Poussin's *Et in Arcadia Ego*. Poussin's "representation of death," he writes, "refers to the process of representation *as* death, which writing (and painting as a writing process) tames and neutralizes among the living people who read and contemplate it."[11]

As if writing in the echo of Montaigne's famous prescription, "To Philosophize, Is to Learn How to Die," Marin describes the "primitive" force of representation as an image-effect of death and its drive: "it makes present the absent, as if what returned were the same and sometimes better, more intense, stronger than if it were the same."[12] Sometimes better, more intense, stronger, that is, inasmuch as the representation-effects of "force" are understood in the context of the powers of the image. *Force is here the representation-effect of the visual projection (or as J.-B. Pontalis would say, the transference)*[13] *of the imaginary accomplishments of desire in the insurmountable folds of temporality, in the insuperable* différance *of desire's realization.* Marin stresses his punning emphasis on the Real when he adds: "In representation which is power, in power which is representation, the real *[le réel]*—if by "real" we understand the always deferred fulfillment of this desire—the real is nothing more than the fantasy image in which the subject contemplates itself as absolute."[14] These words bear the full weight of Marin's acknowledgment of their accomplished precedent in the practice of philosophical painting. It was Louis Marin, after all, who wrote that excellence in painting meant to Poussin a kind of learning how to die: "knowing how to tell the story of the dead through images."[15]

It is in the context of such a fantastically absolute image of self staring at the specter of death, like the one projected by Kuntzel's shrouded figure who at one point opens his eyes to stare up at the camera in *Winter*, that the subject interpellated by painting can be said to be inferred and presupposed by the specific configurations of history and culture. The powers of the image constitute something like a virtual force field conjoining absolute subject and dissolute history. Marin understands such a conjunction to figure the representational efficacy of the image. "If it is the essence of all force to aspire to the absolute," he writes in a lengthy passage,

> It is the "reality" of its subject never to be consoled not to be absolute. The representation-effects that constitute powers and that powers permit and authorize in return would be the modalities (historical, anthropological, sociological . . .) of a work of mourning—although infinite in space and time—of the absolutism of force, of the real fulfillment of the desire of absolutism of its subject. The image in its powers would work the transformation of the infinity of a loss . . . without alterity or exteriority from an imaginary in which the absolute would have its space.[16]

The ultimate force of visual history is thus relegated to the powerful space of absolute desire that conjoins the gazing procedures of subjectivity and the latency of the subject-caught-in-sight. The modalities of history, anthropology, and sociology, it is crucial to note in the context of a theorization of the cultural, have a representational place here only as the fraught reworkings of the mourning of spatial absolutism.

Curiously, Thierry Kuntzel attributes analogous image-effects to the force particular to cinema. He distinguishes between two types of return that are characteristic of cinema. The first involves what Marin would call the exterior modalities of representation: those repetitive elements that permit, through the means of *Nachträglichkeit,* spectatorial recognition of the secondary references of the cinematic image—the visibility of the places, characters, actions, and gestures of diagesis. The second aspect of cinematic repetition fuels the repetitive "force" of cinema that seizes spectators in the web of obscure impressions. This "demoniac power" paralyzes spectators in view of the return of the trace through which they are marked as cinematic effects; the cause of such power can be verbalized only in terms of the traces of misrecognition, "the arrestation effect *[l'effet de sidération],*" writes Kuntzel, "that the film produces in me."[17] The positioning of the spectators inside, rather than outside, the fantasy effect is what both Kuntzel and Marin identify as the force of the image.

Marin and Kuntzel also share a deep interest in how visual arrestation occurs in structural relation to the scopic drive, "la lumière" (the light). This reader finds that Kuntzel's description of his video work as an "outline of light" emits an uncanny shadow of the figure sustaining Marin's theoretical fiction of the powers of the image. Marin relates imagistic power to the force of "the light": "the white of light or the black of shadow that is its necessary reverse—the light is untenable to sight. The transcendental sphere of "see as seen [voir-être vu]" is impenetrable to the gaze."[18] Marin here refers, no doubt, to Lacan's visualization of the scopic drive in terms of "la lumière," that burst of light through which Lacan was rendered immobile by the luminous presence of a discarded tin can. "This is something," Lacan writes of "la lumière," "that introduces what was elided in the geometral relation—the depth of field, with all its ambiguity and variability, which is in no way mastered by me. It is rather it that grasps me, solicits me at every moment, and makes of the landscape something other than a landscape, something other than what I have called the picture."[19] Lacan's reference to the pictorial tradition of landscape works to link his interests in perspective and geometry to the aesthetic legacy of "la lumière," which is so crucial to Marin's sensitivity to the powers of the image.

In the neoclassical period so dear to Marin, "la lumière" embodied the distinguishing, sublime features of neoclassical painting and theory as well as the trope of its extended force in the centralizing ideology of the Sun King and his geometrical representation. Marin is quick to link the visual force of the neoclassical investment in "la lumière" to the biblical legacy of Christ's sublime transfiguration on the mountaintop, as reported in Matthew 17:1–2: "And after six days Jesus taketh Peter, James, and John his brother, and bringeth them up into an high mountain apart, And was transfigured before them: and his face did shine as the sun, and his raiment was white as the light."[20] The whitening of Christ in garment and portrait is embellished further in Mark 9:3: "And his raiment became shining, exceeding white as snow; so as no fuller on earth can white them." In noting how white light here functions as a trope in excess of any representable figure, Marin then relates the extreme of light to its opposite: "The sight of the figure-Light, the dazzling whiteness of the Image has something to do," he suggests, "with death, with the 'gustatory' experience of its peacefulness, as if the sight of the extreme, ultimate image, that of the absolutely white figure, could only anticipate the delight of an exquisite death."[21]

A visual depiction of such a transfigured conjunction of shining white fabric and exquisite light of an impenetrable sublimity is also evident in the neoclassical paintings called to mind by Kuntzel's loose appropriation of Poussin's *Winter*. I refer not only to the whitening effect of Philippe de Champaigne's painting *The Dead Christ*, which hangs adjacent to *Winter* in the Louvre, but also to the 1521 painting of the same title by Holbein, which literary theoreticians might recognize most readily as the subject of extensive discussion in Julia Kristeva's book *Black Sun: Depression and Melancholy*. Kristeva's description of the pictorial achievement of Holbein's painting echoes Marin's poignant analysis of the effects of "la lumière." Kristeva suggests that the painting

> gives form and color to the unrepresentable, understood not as erotic profusion but conceived as the eclipse of the means of representation on the brink of their extinction in death. The chromatic and compositional ascetism of Holbein translates this competition of form and death . . . in the liminal manifestation constitutive of mourning and melancholy.[22]

Thinking again of the video of Kuntzel, might his *Winter* enact the projection of just such an arcadian impenetrability of light, one visualized by the legacy of aesthetics as the form of death, as the monochromatic fold of inside-out?[23] Might not this typify the sublime feature of Kuntzel's work that links it, in more than a casual way, to the forceful philosophical contemplation of Ego/Cogito praised by neoclassical aestheticians as having been enlivened by the painting of Poussin?

Referring, in *To Destroy Painting*, to Poussin's definition of painting as "an imitation made on the surface with lines and colors of all that is visible under the sun,"[24] Marin describes the arcadian space of Poussin as the white space, "la lumière," of Descartes through which objects are said to take shape. In situating Poussin's work in relation to the French philosophical dialogue surrounding and often responding to it, Marin cites the fifth part of the *Discourse on Method* and the first "Discourse" of the *Dioptrique* where Descartes clarifies the visual impact of light. What catches Marin's critical eye is the philosophical grounding of the metaphysical characteristics of light in the material embodiment of light as color. "La lumière," writes Marin, "is defined as immediate physical contact at a distance and color is defined as the reflection of light on bodies. White is a straight reflection while red, yellow, and blue are modified in various ways. It follows that a body's color is nothing more than the effect on an eye that has been *touched* by light reflected by that body's surface. White light ('le blanc-lumière') reflecting as color on the surfaces of bodies defines these surfaces for the gaze."[25]

Just such a touch of colors abounds in Kuntzel's triptych installation *Spring (Dance of Spring / No Spring)* [*Printemps (Pas de printemps)*]). The viewer enters a darkened room to face a tripartite field of large-scale video colors flowing from laser projectors mounted on the opposite wall. Framed by the modified light of monochromatic blue color-fields, whose form is repeated in *Winter,* a central panel tracks the video camera's computer-controlled movements that slowly gyrate around a nude couple enclosed in a lush Provençal bower. Following the female's poignant placement of her hand on the male's rigid biceps, the camera zooms closer to capture tight shots of the female breast, male shoulder blades, and buttocks. Kuntzel boldly departs from the composition of the source picture, Poussin's *Spring, or The Terrestrial Paradise,* by shortening the depth of field of the Poussin landscape with something like the bravado of pictorial disavowal ("yes, Poussin's landscape, but nevertheless some fetishism"). That is, Kuntzel limits his vision to the magnification of the couple in the extreme lower left-hand corner of Poussin's picture. Even the uninitiated viewer of Poussin may be struck by the transformational effect of Kuntzel's displacement of video eye from the ordered place of Poussin's landscape to the fluid space of supple bodies caught in motion. Kuntzel both effaces the white region of the heavenly lord looking down from the upper right of the *Terrestrial Paradise* and blots out the painting's pastoral pond whose calm waters double as the pictorial ground of minute white brushstrokes—crafted by Poussin to represent the reflection of sunlight and its eclipse of vision. But since too strong a stress on the blotting out of Poussin's blue waters might misrepresent the pictorial framework of Kuntzel's bower, as it is bordered by blue monochromatic projections on the wings to either side, I simply wish, for now, to emphasize how Kuntzel repositions the corporeal parts of the *Terrestrial Paradise* to catch and reflect the pastoral colors in a way that sets them in enlivening motion. Of course, it is equally critical to note that what further enhances the motion of the body is its visual incorporation in the immateriality of computer code that guides the camera with exact precision. In the case of Kuntzel, the motion of light, its computer-driven registration, and its digital projection are what situate the viewer in the interval of Digital Baroque.

Just how brilliantly Kuntzel transforms Poussin's geometrical application of the whiteness of landscape into the sublime immaterial coda of all that is lit might be better appreciated by pausing a moment to consider *Calm Weather,* a landscape by Poussin preceding *The Four Seasons.* This painting, singled out by Marin for its exemplary depiction of the rigorous cartography of landscape geometry, greets the spectator with a foreground grouping of a pastoral shepherd with his flock and, in the distant background, a typically Poussinian Italianate village whose bright lighting brings it forward in the picture plane. In-between lies the wide expansion of a lake whose mirroring surface contributes to the effect of bringing the distant civilized village closer to the pastoral foreground. In a stunning essay on the "Evidence of Time in Painted Representation," Marin notes, in particular, how wonderfully the serene blue of the lake captures not only the most subtle illuminations of the painting but also maintains through reflection the synchronic configuration of all places surrounding it, as if it is a map showing itself showing the perspectival balance of city and landscape, civilization and nature.[26] What I find fascinating is how Poussin's later painting, *Spring,* disrupts the serenity of this surface of blue by a kind of anamorphic distortion: it decenters the lake by pulling it off to the left, it disturbs the calm of reflection with the interpellation of shining light (indeed, Lacan could have cited the flash of light in Poussin's painting just as easily as he notes the shining tin can that blinds the youthful fisherman), and it unsettles its talismanic waters with the charged motions of unfolding passion. What is somewhat weird about Poussin's *Spring* is how its "dérangements" of the artist's own conventions of landscape seem to approximate the motions of the pictorial sequel to *Calm Weather,* Poussin's canvas *The Tempest* (the theme that Poussin repeats in his *Four Seasons* painting *Winter*). I suggest that this is weird, or uncanny, because *Spring* hyperbolizes the two features of sublime irruption that Marin singles out in the *Tempest* for disrupting the mirrorical tranquility of *Calm Weather.* The first is the irruption of light, "la lumière," that negates, through the arresting brightness of reflection, the lake's ability to gauge perspective, near and far. Here perspective is neutralized or "medusé" by light and its punctum.[27] Second is how the corporeal figures express effects of passion—fear in the *Tempest,* desire in *Spring*—whose exaggerations exceed the temporal containment of pictorial contemplation. Put otherwise, the dramatic display of light and body ("l'effet de sidération") in the *Terrestrial Paradise* shifts the terms of representation

from the predictable orders of geometrical reflection to the arresting accidents and passionate motions of *Spring*.

Kuntzel accentuates this shift in *Spring* by staging the body itself as the
source and depth of field of passionate light. If read in the context of
Marin's reference to Descartes, the light of *Spring* ("le blanc-lumière") provides the screen or space for the perilous gaze by reflecting itself in colors
only on the surface of the two characters' bodies. The play of light joins
this couple in a stunning videomatic pas de deux in a way that foregrounds
while negating their sexual difference in a primal mise-en-scène. Kuntzel's
adjacent installation, *Summer,* seems to emphasize this point by juxtaposing two video scenes, one evoking something akin to a more traditional
diagesis and the other enacting the figural display of light on body. A small
monitor inset in the wall on one side of the room depicts a naked black
man who leafs through a book on Poussin as he sits in a neoclassical draw-
ing room while another indistinct and relatively androgynous figure wanders
out into the garden and back into the room, suggesting a kind of mysterious diagesis that is never resolved (the figure I take to be androgynous
here in its distant indistinctiveness is actually played by Irena Dalle, who
is more obviously female in *Spring*). Catching the eye of the spectator on
the opposite wall is a computer-enhanced blowup of the traces of light
touching and highlighting the reader's porous, nude body. Put otherwise,
the subject of the diagetic vision (of Poussin) becomes the object of the
arresting light (of Video and of Digital Baroque). Similarly, the spectators
of Kuntzel's installation are literally caught between these scenes of sight
and light to the extent that they act out and embody the interval between
narrative and affect—the interval identified by Marin as site of the powers of the image. The interval, writes Kuntzel, "between a memory and the
other . . . the place of difference, a place without place (blank/white, silence,
void) conjoining, superimposing, comparing two images."[28] It is easy to
imagine the delighted response of Louis Marin had he enjoyed access to the
digitized purity of the interval in both *Spring* and *Summer,* the interval conjoining white light and reflective skin as well as the difference between character and video spectator. For the immaterial play of Kuntzel's light certainly
projects the visual force that Marin likens to the transcendental a priori
conditions of the apparition of the image and its arcadian efficacy "through
which are accomplished the *exit* of 'seeing' and 'being seen' from the field
of 'in-sight,' of invisibility, of inaccessibility to the gaze."[29]

As the camera of *Spring* continues the first of its two machinic revolutions around the primal couple, it combines touch and look in recording the embrace of the actors' eyes in a mutual gaze. The female's subsequent turn away from their gaze is finally embodied by the camera after a second slow revolution as it suddenly and quickly veers upward to track the white light of the invisible heavens, "inaccessible to the gaze." It is this gesture of controlled visual technology suddenly careening off course toward the inaccessible sky that shifts emphasis from the arcadian dance to the zigzag of its luminous other, "no Spring." As if evoking the Cartesian paradigm that the transcendental sphere of "seeing-to be seen is impenetrable by the gaze," Kuntzel's video installation inscribes the iconic gesture of Poussin's Eve in the inaccessible whiteness of the ethereal space. The spirit of such an "Et in Arcadia Video" may well be reflected by Kuntzel's enigmatic citation of Marguerite Duras that concludes his catalogue note on *Spring:* "It was the blossoming cherry tree, this excessive springtime that the mother said she could no longer tolerate, would no longer wish to see. What tormented her was that the springtime could return." Might not we say, following Duras, that the digital returns of light here illuminate the transcendental tensions, the excessive differences, that fuel the force of Kuntzel's spectacular imagery? *Pas de printemps: dance of spring / no spring.*

BLUE-BLACK *JOUISSANCE*

In foregrounding Kuntzel's mimicry of the transcendental orderings of the aesthetic legacy of Poussin ("the exact negative of the present project"),[30] I wish to emphasize how much the tensions and differences framing his digital video installation contrast with the arcadian formalism of Poussin's pastoral series *The Four Seasons.* In the final section of this chapter, I speak in broad terms about the cycle's promise of an eternal return as represented by the overall schema of Kuntzel's installation, about the contrast of colors ultimately sustaining his video work, and about the subsequent linkage of its colorful overlays of corporeal positions with the historical modalities of body, race, and sexuality that impinge on the universality of "la lumière" and its imagistic space. My aim is not so much to dispute the legacy of the transcendental condition that is evident in the conjunction of psychoanalysis and phenomenology informing the work of both Kuntzel and Marin. Rather, I wish to emphasize how this very legacy under erasure frames the forceful representation of the image of Otherness in the digital age. I mean to insist that *the study of the historical modalities of material culture is framed by the eternal return of the ideational constructs informing it.*[31] As made evident by Kuntzel's computerized video appropriation of Poussin's arcadian series, it is now impossible to imagine, to re-present, one legacy without the other.

To begin with the matter of appropriation, Kuntzel's undertaking of a video adaptation of Poussin's pastoral series seems to have stemmed from his fascination with the incompletion of the cycle when considered in terms of its individual canvases: *Spring, or The Terrestrial Paradise, Summer, or Ruth and Boaz, Autumn, or Grapes Brought Back to the Promised Land,* and *Winter, or The Flood.* Rather than accept the neoclassical allegory of the teleology of such a pastoral cycle, which always promises to return the viewer from "the flood" to "the promised land," Kuntzel exaggerates the violence of the interval to evoke the allegorical "minus one." Disjunction of "the always deferred—hope, regret" is what Kuntzel describes in his catalogue notes as the common link of the separate installations. So too does the light of Kuntzel's video installations reflect "the always deferred." The "white space" of Poussin is prefigured by the total darkness of an empty installation chamber, the one titled *Minus One (Autobiography of an Other).* In keeping with the added reference of "Minus One" to the unanticipated legal exclusion from the exhibition of the final sequence, *Autumn (the Analogical Mountain),* the layout is designed so that spectators should have to pass through this black chamber when moving from the installation of one season to another. It is in this darkened, autobiographical space, the conjoined space of Lack and Other, that spectators are assaulted by the loud musical lyrics of Lou Reed: "I don't like opera and I don't like ballet . . . Deep down inside I've got a, I've got a rock 'n' roll heart." It is with this forceful beat of desire and will, of performative negation and affirmation, that the spectator moves from one darkened space to another only to be confronted by the wonder of what Kuntzel calls the "paralysis" of his video light. But rather than mollify viewers disoriented by the loud darkness of the Other, Kuntzel's "four seasons" provide the illusion of a colored space that contrasts significantly with the white lights of Poussin. Kuntzel's installations present a visual environment much more akin, say, to that of Caravaggio, whom neoclassical theory was quick to compare with Poussin. As Marin patiently rehearses the neoclassical argument over "le coloris" (the art of color, of brilliance) in *To Destroy Painting,* Caravaggio was praised and blamed for providing an alternative to the white arcadian space of Poussin.[32] Caravaggio's was the "black space" of a closed cell, crypt, or tomb that Marin describes as "an arcanian space." In this mysteriously arcane space, light is projected from a unique source at maximum intensity to provoke, in Marin's terms, a Medusa-effect, an effect of arrestation. This description certainly fits the effect of Kuntzel's luminous projections as they penetrate the shadowy intervals of the darkened installation space. In a striking respect, Caravaggio's arcanian space thus can be said to have prefigured Kuntzel's conjoined space of Ego and Video, whose self-representations are always already poised on the darkened, deadly screen of deferral, positioned, that is, on the cartographic site, sign, or portrait of the autobiography of an Other.

This screening of internalized otherness (a metaphor of the computer itself?) foregrounds significant historicized modalities in Kuntzel's installation whose encrypted motions rise forth as phantoms more disturbing than arresting, more ambivalently fluid than certainly contained by the cartographic synchronies of law and culture. It is highly significant, in this context, that the contrasts important to the formal concerns of color theory give rise to consideration of the weight of the particularly charged historical modalities whose sadomasochistic introjection tempers any lightness of their transcendental properties. Returning to Marin's notion of the powers of the image, I wonder whether it is possible, especially in light of the France of Sarkozy / Le Pen and the violent protests in France against racial and cultural disparity, to overlook questions of racial and sexual miscegenation posed by the color and gender contrasts of Kuntzel's models? What is designated in *Spring,* for instance, by the outstretched arm of the black male model whose quivering hand attests to its inability to rest on the arm of the white other. Can it help but point to the black man's historical failure to share in the white female's willful touch of his skin? Just how does a historical modality such as the racialization of difference figure in the installation's "always deferred—hope, regret"? While I would argue that we should acknowledge the aesthetic role of Kuntzel's staging of the black body as a vibrant spatial receptacle of the lightness of being and that we must appreciate Kuntzel's complex dialogue with the visual tradition from which it derives, I cannot help but think that this lightness of being may be unbearable to some while remaining hopeful to others.

Consider, for just a moment, the compulsive denial of race by the psychophilosophical tradition that so informs the French projects here under consideration. From Descartes and Nicole to Lacan and Deleuze, the enigmatic question of race too frequently has been bracketed or framed, sometimes necessarily, by strategic consideration of both local and transcultural questions of signification, power, essence, and desire.[33] What merits added critical pressure is how the discourse of racial (and frequently sexual) denial almost always already seems to creep into the work of even the most politicized of writers, past and present, them and us. A paradigmatic example can be cited from Sartre's compelling chapter on mapping in *Being and Nothingness*. "The Body" exemplifies how the contingencies of historical modalities impinge on the purity of Sartre's philosophical discourse:

> This body of the Other as I encounter it is the revelation as object-for-me of the contingent form assumed by the necessity of this contingency. Every Other must have sense organs but not necessarily these sense organs, not any particular face and finally not this face. But face, sense organs, presence— all that is nothing but the contingent form of the Other's necessity to *exist* himself as belonging to a race, a class, an environment, etc., in so far as this contingent form is surpassed by a transcendence which does not have to exist it. What for the Other is his taste of himself becomes for me the Other's flesh. The flesh is the pure contingency of presence. It is ordinarily hidden by clothes, make-up, the cut of the hair or beard, the expression, etc. But in the course of long acquaintance with a person there always comes an instant when all these disguises are thrown off and when I find myself in the presence of the pure contingency of his presence.[34]

Just how are we to respond to such a politicized philosopher's phenomenological collapsing of the differences of race, class, not to mention gender and sexual difference for the sake of the pure contingency of presence?

When *Spring* was displayed in the early 1990s in San Francisco, some dismissed it outright for lightening the weight of the psychic contingencies and historical modalities of skin. Criticism was aimed at Kuntzel's seeming indifference to the racialized subject position of his male model, Ken Moody, whose apparitions circulate in the photographic fantasies of Robert Mapplethorpe's controversial project *Black Book*.[35] Might not Kuntzel's installation, so the challenge went, contribute to the demonized fetishization of the nude black male for which Mapplethorpe has been loudly criti-cized?[36] But rather than map a place for universal presence, *Four Seasons Minus One* works just as easily, in my estimation, to deconstruct the purity of its own cultural cartography through the heightened representation of contingency. Consider the open question of what is figured by the subject position of Ken Moody. How might Thierry Kuntzel's *Four Seasons Minus One* be understood as carrying the ambivalent and traumatically retroactive fantasy of this model's racialized and homographic trace? I wish to suggest that the figure of Ken Moody lends to the installation an alternative vision of sexual representation and politics that may well challenge the colonial and heterosexual economies of the gaze and its contingent "lumière."

I arrive at this conclusion through a close reading of Kuntzel's piece *Summer—Double Vision.*[37] This installation, you will recall, includes a video-projected close-up scan of a lounging black man, shown in the small mon-itor installed in the opposite wall, who is naked except for the folds of a bright red cloth covering his lap. The cloth is appropriated from Poussin's *Summer, or Landscape with Ruth and Boaz*—a reproduction of which is semivisible in a book sitting on the subject's lap. Or more precisely, the book sits on the piece of appropriated cloth that is made poignantly enig-matic by its purloined status. How might we read Kuntzel's reference to Poussin through this piece of borrowed loincloth? While Kuntzel's double vision of summer suggests an obvious revision of landscape's depth of field and light in the age of video, its reference to the sexual thematics of Poussin's painting is much less clear. Poussin's depiction of the meeting of Ruth and Boaz leaves unchallenged the *Book of Ruth*'s biblical narrative of magnan-imous paternalism sustained by phallocentric threats and domination (Ruth 2:1–4). In granting Ruth's request to gather the remains of wheat left by his reapers, Boaz sets in motion a sequence of events that leaves Ruth will-ing to be his wife by purchase. This all begins when he enriches his initial gesture of generosity by declaring his fields something of a sex-free zone where Ruth can be safe from the threat of molestation by his and his neigh-bor's men. She is warned that she would be vulnerable, were she to leave his fields, to the sexual threat always already troubling the pastoral scene. What, then, can be made of Kuntzel's indifference to the narrative of Ruth's willed slavery as a defense against more frightful phallic aggression? Given Kuntzel's titular censorship of Poussin's Ruth and Boaz subtitle, one might be tempted to wonder about the piece's political relation to the complex artistic tradition celebrating the patriarchal entrapment of women. This is the tradition so violently displayed by one of Poussin's more memorable paintings—*Rape of the Sabine Women.*

But such an alignment is complicated by the installation's double vision, for the spectator is made aware of the visual strategies of this tradition when shown computer-guided close-ups of enlarged fragments of the model's objectified black body—fingers, toes, lips, the line of a thigh. In describing the installation, Christopher Phillips writes that Poussin's "classical perspectival frame is shattered by the modernist close-up view. The twist here is that Kuntzel wholly identifies this modernist vision with an erotic gaze that is fetishizing and obsessively calculating."[38] To further complicate Kuntzel's reference to the fetishizing gaze of the black male, Phillips could also have turned to the source picture, *Summer, or Landscape with Ruth and Boaz.* In addition to the sizable scarlet robe lying on a handcart to the left of the painting, a red Phrygian cap rests on the head of the lute player sitting on the right. In this context, Kuntzel's citation of one piece of red cloth calls to mind yet another important to the history of French representation, the Phrygian cap, known during the French Revolution as the "bonnet of Liberty." Neil Hertz provides a compelling analysis of how the drooping cap, particularly as worn by Louis XVI in a mocking representation, slides between the signifiers of liberty and castration.[39] Of significance to Hertz is how the drooping red cap comes to represent the inscription of sovereign patriarchy in the threat of its impotence or castration. In Kuntzel's installation, the folds of red are transferred from sovereign's cap to reader's lap. If read from the baroque perspective of double vision, couldn't the red fold function here to dis-play or deconstruct the history of the fetishistic (and racialized) gaze on which it depends?

MOODY VISION, FROM MAPPLETHORPE TO JARMAN

But this would represent only one view of the sexual economy of *Summer— Double Vision,* let's call it the transcultural desire for Kuntzel's close-up to deconstruct the pure contingency of fetishized vision. What of the fact that the Phrygian cap is an attribute of two competing sexual economies, not only that of Paris but also, as suggested by Hertz, that of Ganymede? It could well suggest that the fetishizing gaze and its psychopolitical contingencies may register differently for the lovers of Ganymede than for the sons of Paris. This distinction may pertain especially well to the viewers who actually recognize Kuntzel's close-ups to be pictures of Ken Moody. However, it is of considerable importance that not all viewers are likely to know Moody and that those who do will position him differently within the intermixed references of white/black, homosocial/homosexual identities that have made Mapplethorpe's *Black Book* such a controversial source of cultural cartography. Kobena Mercer and Isaac Julien have described their own viewing positions:

> What is at issue is that the same signs can be read to produce different meanings. Although images of black men in gay porn generally reproduce the syntax of common-sense racism, the inscribed, intended or preferred meanings of those images are not fixed. They can at times be prised apart into alternative readings when different experiences are brought to bear on their interpretation. Colonial fantasy attempts to "fix" the position of the black subject into a space that mirrors the object of white desires; but black readers may appropriate pleasures by reading against the grain, overturning signs of "otherness" into signifiers of identity.[40]

Indeed, these video close-ups of Moody and their potential appeal to homosexual desire will joyfully dispel for some, while defensively strengthening for others, the calculating, heterosexual logic of the fetish. Traces of the cap that can only weaken some bearers are placed by Kuntzel on the very lap that can harden others. Double vision: castration and/or liberty.

The liberty of the vision of Ken Moody takes on added significance in Kuntzel's double take on autumn, two installations that follow in the wake of autumn's "minus one" in Kuntzel's retrospective at Jeu de Paume, a sequence of the *Four Seasons* whose rights were not released by the Ministry of Agriculture (in some kind of surreal tussle with cultural divisions of the French government). In the 2000 exhibition, "Silent," at Yvon Lambert in Paris, Kuntzel returned to the *Four Seasons* with two versions of *Autumn, Autumn (the Analogical Mountain)* and *Autumn (in Praise of Darkness)*. Both installations feature large-scale projections of East/West landscapes. The western version, shot in Transylvania, confronts viewers with slow and deliberate video experimentation with the colors and depth of landscape. Marking the disappearance of the "blue tendency" in order to contemplate autumn yellows and dark browns, the frame remains the sole

stable form of representation as long shots of a rocky mountain are pas-
tiched over one another so that the projection blends in with the folds of
montage. These shots then give way to close-ups of bleeding color-fields
of greens, reds, and, yes, the return of black and blue, with a number of
fades into black. The final shot pauses on an isolated rock (Kuntzel's version of a philosopher's stone?) before a final fade into video black. What's
stunning about *Autumn*'s Japanese double is its repositioning of the centrality of the video frame via the architectonics of a Japanese temple whose
lateral latticework helps to frame the garden, seen on the outside. Unlike
its Transylvanian double, which focuses on the spirit of landscape and the
promise of the (philosopher's) stone, this is a video installation marked by
the return of the body and its double inscription in video black. As visitors to the temple fill the interior space to contemplate the exterior garden,
they progressively limit the camera's vision, leaving the screen stained, blot-
ted, and eventually black as in the Transylvanian version. When the visitors
leave the temple, the clarity of landscaped vision returns. It is as if viewing in itself *Trans*fers the stain of video black, the obsession with the representational blank of death and/or utopia onto the serene vision of Asian
landscape, one which is designed to be peopled and experienced rather
than seen and lost as the autumnal return of the ghostly legacy of liberty's
castration.

And, yet, the double vision of *Autumn* here rests in the gazing eyes of
that ever-present figure Ken Moody. Set into the wall facing the installation
screen (common to both installations) is a smaller video monitor featuring
the gazing eyes of Ken. Looking directly back at the viewer, in a way that
disrupts the cultural requirement of the black viewer to look away in the
face of the empowering white gaze, these eyes frame the vision of everything represented, from West to East. Moody's eyes assume less the role of
representation's object than its enigmatic subject. Rather than reflecting
the Occidental tendency to diminish the image to the secondary status of
a dead copy, a mediating screen, or a mirroring specter of a living presence, the phantasmatic image of Moody's eyes, inset into the flush of the
wall, derives its force, as Marin would say, from its strategic embodiment
of re-presentation. Caught again by video installation in the interval of representation, the viewer secedes the gaze to stand within the field of the
screen, the Other, what Raymond Bellour calls the dilating "hallucinations"
of Kuntzel's "double view: the supplement of vision disturbs it, and produces

a fragile anamorphosis or the dividing line between mobility and immo-
bility."[41] Autumn's minus one: the return of the doubled logic of Video
Baroque.

There is a final moment in *Autumn (the Analogical Mountain),* however,
when the stability of analogy seems to provide some ballast in the anamorphic swerve of the installation's interval. As the screen fades to black for
the final time, Moody's eyes close as if mirroring the end of representation
and the finality of vision. Were this installation to have been included, as
anticipated, in Kuntzel's Jeu de Paume suite of the four seasons, it well could
have provided somewhat of a seamless overture to the finality of *Winter: The
Death of Robert Walser.* While the analogous visions of these two installations certainly call to mind the unrepresentable binary with which I began,
death and utopia, the weight of the historical modalities of race and sexuality in these installations beg for renewed consideration of the return of
the "blue tendency." What might be signified by the projection of the figure of Ken Moody as the shrouded body framed by cobalt blue as he lies
stretched out for public viewing in *Winter's* darkened crypt? It certainly
triggers the many phantoms of death that Kuntzel aligns with the disturbed
figures of form that lie entombed by video in the past history of aesthetics:
"we had to completely forget the codes, let them fall, one after the other,
dead skins, deadly boredom, because we had to create the void, take the
risk of the void, the risk of death."[42] Yet, I wonder what happens when we
situate this video crypt in the historical modality of the age of AIDS? Attesting to the powers of Kuntzel's imagery, I find it difficult to play back the
memory of this dazzling video installation without recalling Robert Mapplethorpe's chilling reference to the impact of AIDS on his black models,
friends, and lovers: "If I go through my Black Book, half of them are dead."
And since, so too is he.

Add to these chilling words the uncanny description of *Winter* provided
in a press release by the Museum of Modern Art for its 1991 exhibition:
"*Winter* is inspired by the early writings of Swiss author Robert Walser that
foretold his death in the snow and Nicolas Poussin's paintings of the four
seasons. . . . A computer controlled camera pans the entire body in the
path of an infinity symbol. Slowly repeating the same movement four
times, the camera progressively moves in closer to the figure, which grad-
ually emerges from a sheer white veil. This relief-like image is flanked by
two projections of identical color fields—a cobalt blue which fades in and

out to gray and white and creates a tension with the image of the almost entombed body." In the context of contemporary French aesthetics, one might turn away from the obvious precedent of Yves Klein or Kuntzel himself to read this blue in relation to that described by the painter Jacques Monory in *Document bleu* (1970), "the color of the approach of *jouissance,* of the color of the drives."[43] Again calling forth the distant memory of Holbein and Champaigne, it is significant that the pulsating *jouissance* of such cobalt blue grounds the ethereal transcendence of absolutist white through the deictic charge of its visceral intensity. Playing constantly between life and loss, the video of Thierry Kuntzel is described similarly by Anne-Marie Duguet as "contributing to an opening of a space of *jouissance* in which the spectator might enter, wander, and produce her own reading."[44]

But what really verges on the uncanny *jouissance* of the drives, at least of the death drive, is how the monochromatic variations of these color-fields project the image of Moody's death into the haunting frame of the cobalt present. Can we, of either the cinematic or queer communities, now view this modulating cobalt space without experiencing the shock of its memorialization of the baroque gay filmmaker whose final effort was the monochromatic moving picture rightly titled *Blue*? Curiously, it was through *Blue* that Derek Jarman joined Thierry Kuntzel and his fellow travelers in the electronic arts by referencing video to deliver what, in the end, the filmmaker couldn't deliver from cinema. Michael O'Pray recounts how Jarman turned to the immateriality of video to achieve his ultimate vision. "For Jarman, the blue . . . is also a self-reflexive statement about the medium of cinema. Interestingly for this project Jarman rejected a use of film that stressed its inevitable patina—the scratches, the slight flicker—in favour of a blue akin to the electronic video field, unadulterated by the human hand and sheer in the way only a pixel can attain (in this it is like Yves Klein's own use of vertiginous blue). Within the most electronic of the popular media, and one which he had resisted, Jarman found a ground for his most discursive and profound piece."[45]

Enveloped in video's inhuman field of touch and techne, I invite you to imagine witnessing the electric cobalt blue borders of Kuntzel's *Winter* as it now frames the image of another death, Thierry Kuntzel's own, which happened too suddenly and too uncannily while I was engaged in the final revision of this chapter. Had I been privileged to attend Thierry's internment at Père Lachaise,[46] I would have saluted him with these echoes from the *Blue* crypt of Derek Jarman, that marvel of cinematic enigma whose baroque sensibilities often make him sound like an imaginary interlocutor of Kuntzel and Marin:

> Blue protects white from innocence / Blue drags black with it / Blue is darkness made visible / Blue protects white from innocence / Blue drags black with it / Blue is darkness made visible . . . For Blue there are no boundaries or solutions. / How did my friends cross the cobalt river, with what did they pay the ferryman? As they set out for the indigo shore under this jet-black sky—some died on their feet with a backward glance. Did they see Death with the hell hounds pulling a dark chariot, bruised blue-black, growing dark in the absence of light?[47]

What more need be said, to return to the balance between form and culture, but that the modalities of history, sexuality, and sociology here again have their place only as fraught reworkings of death and Arcadia, finality and infinity, only as the mourning of spatial absolutism?[48]

These last sounds and images, then, are only some of the specters adding melancholic weight to my consideration of Thierry Kuntzel as read through the arcanian light of Louis Marin and via the cobalt traces of his brother, Derek Jarman, who now joins him in Arcadia. These are the phantom colors of Digital Baroque, as inscribed in my titular epitaph, *Et in Arcadia Video*.

II.
DIGITAL DELEUZE:
BAROQUE FOLDS OF
SHAKESPEAREAN PASSAGE

THE CRISIS OF CINEMA IN THE AGE OF NEW WORLD-MEMORY: THE BAROQUE LEGACY OF JEAN-LUC GODARD

Monads "have no windows, by which anything could come in or go out." They have neither "openings nor doorways." We run the risk of understanding the problem [of Leibniz] vaguely if we fail to determine the situation. A painting always has a model on its outside: it always is a window. If a modern reader thinks of a film projected in darkness, the film has nonetheless been projected. Then what about invoking numerical images issuing from a calculus without a model? . . . The painting-window is replaced by tabulation, the grid on which lines, numbers, and changing characters are inscribed (the objectile). . . . Folds replace holes. The dyad of the city-information table is opposed to the system of the window-countryside.

—GILLES DELEUZE, "What Is Baroque?"

We have seen throughout the preceding chapters how Gilles Deleuze borrows in *The Fold* from the late twentieth century to visualize the curvilinear patterns of thought that distinguish Leibniz's "folds" from Descartes' "lines." For a rather simple comparison, Deleuze turns to the cinematic apparatus to contrast the illumination of its projections with those "lines with infinite inflection" that are characteristic of numerical images. The code of the latter highlights a radical structural change that Deleuze attributes initially to the thought of Leibniz. The shift occurs when "the surface stops being a window on the world and now becomes an opaque grid of information on which the ciphered line is written."[1] Although Deleuze here refers to the grids of Rauschenberg and the lines of Pollock, he concludes

The Fold by dwelling on the "new Baroque" quality of the numerical music of Boulez and Stockhausen. At the heart of this new Baroque "fold," for Deleuze, lies the transformational force of its cultural impact. "To have or to possess is to fold, in other words, to convey what one contains 'with a certain power.' If the Baroque can be associated with the emergence of capitalism, it is because the Baroque is linked to a crisis of property, a crisis that appears at once with the growth of new machines in the social field and the discovery of new living beings in the organism."[2] Rather than illuminate a pregiven process of conceptualization and its concomitant social order, the growth of new machines in the aesthetic arena, from line painting to digital sound, provides the mechanism for "deterritorialization" and new sets of previously incompatible social groupings and fabulations.

THE CRISIS OF CINEMATIC PROPERTY

If the promise of the Baroque can be thought of as a crisis of property, its contemporary specter is nowhere more haunting and baffling for Deleuze than in the field of cinema. While *The Fold* contrasts the projection of cinema with the baroque lines of numerical painting and synthetic sound, *Cinema 2: The Time-Image* turns to Leibniz and the crisis of perspectival "property" to understand the radicality of the shadow and the depth of field that Welles introduced to cinema. The book on *The Time-Image* concludes similarly to *The Fold* by reflecting on the "change of force" wrought by the procedures of "serialization" shared this time by Boulez and Godard. In cinema, insists Deleuze, this serialization results in a transformation through which characters are less windows on the world than serial elements "of the will of force" through which the worldview becomes open to new and unpredictable procedures of fabulation. The property of cinema is understood by Deleuze in relation to the radicality of its unfolding tales and representations.

Yet, few social fields have been placed into so much crisis by the growth of the new Baroque as has cinema. The new machines are those of mathematical replication, of course, with their digital duplicating systems that sometimes make redundant the need for actors, props, and craft itself, from design to lighting to cutting. Digital editing systems, to cite one example, both shorten the process of production and transform the messiness of crude, manual procedures of visualization into slick, technical translations of virtualization. Many of the most difficult techniques of montage can now be enacted by the unpracticed initiate through the simple procedure of clicking a mouse. Segments of film, moreover, can be downloaded on the Web or burned onto a DVD in a way that challenges the integrity of the print and the need for its distribution. Even the culture of cinema has been transformed by the growth of digital cinematic machines. Not only are cinematic segments readily downloadable on the Internet but the amateur discourse of cinema has proliferated with Listservs, celebrity sites, amateur cinema reviews, YouTube, electronic journals, CD-ROMs, and DVDs. Nevertheless, just such a crisis of cinematic property, from the specialized magic of computer-generated imagery to the generalized terms of amateur video and chat, must be understood as constituting essential threads of the growth of cinema and the terms of its theorization.

Readers concerned by the decline of film, from the demise of analog editing to the growing popularity of Web and cell phone cinema, may be rather skeptical regarding any celebration of the era of new media. Indeed, the rise of new media has brought with it an increase in academic protection of the sacred ontology of film as something purer and healthier than all that is digital. It may seem ironic to readers now mournful, say, of the cutting-edge dominance of Godard and his French peers, those convinced of the death of (French) cinema (which Roger Leenhardt lauded for being "baroque"), that I understand the crisis of cinematic property wrought by the digital revolution and its new movie culture to be somewhat of a natural extension of the legacy of Godard and the uncanny prescience of his tenets and practices. Discussion of this suggestion, however, necessitates a shift of focus away from many of the New Wave's critical innovations, such as its break from the tradition of literary adaptation promoted by the French Cinema of Quality and its celebration of the singular role of the cinematic auteur, not to mention its distancing in the early sixties from the Left Bank movement that so admired the political value of cinema. What Godardian cinema shares with the new media, notably with its independent strains, is its sensitivity to a crisis of property that links the new and the old. By this, I am thinking of the Godardian crisis of cinema as well as his representation of property in crisis, such as is figured by Godard from the sides of East and West, whether in *Allemagne année 90 neuf zéro* (1991) or in *For Ever Mozart* (1996), as a horrifying struggle over the property of ethnic identity: "in this Europe not purified but corrupted by its sufferings."[3] In chapter 4A of the printed text of *Histoire(s) du cinéma: Le contrôle de l'univers,* Godard appropriates text from Denis de Rougemont's *Penser avec les mains* (1936) to suggest that the crisis pertains to the soul of Europe and its self-representations: "in this Europe of today, there are two sorts of nations, those called old and those called rejuvenated, those that have guarded a certain number of possibilities but don't know what to do with that freedom which they brag about, and those that have waged or suffered a revolution of the masses since the wars and have maintained freedom of opinion, that is to say, the freedom to protest, but without deep passion."[4]

This double crisis of action and passion is linked further by Godard to the crisis of representation itself. Again citing de Rougemont, "I wouldn't want to speak ill of our tools but I would like them to be employable / if it is generally true that the danger lies not in our instruments but in the weakness of our hands / it is no less urgent to specify that a thought which abandons itself to the rhythm of its mechanization renders itself literally proletarian."[5] For Godard, the popular mechanization of the apparatus reflects not merely the numbing split of the European condition, something perhaps open to celebration on the other side of the Atlantic, but also the concomitant decline with the onset of television and amateur video of the thoughtful promise of cinema itself. Consistently evident, however, throughout *Histoire(s) du cinéma* and his later interviews is Godard's linkage of the property of the transformation of cinema to how his cinema thinks the crisis of property. This conflation of cinema with a crisis of property, particularly in relation to past terms of troubled growth in the social field, is what uncannily aligns Godardian cinema (and its thought) with the coda of a new baroque aesthetic caught between clashing systems of visual projection and digital information.

THE MESS OF AVOIDANCE

A vibrant picture of the clash of new movie culture with the memory of the privileged visual systems of the past appears in Microsoft's CD-ROM *Cinemania* in which the likes of Roger Ebert or Leonard Maltin share their casual responses to cinema with the user of the personal computer who now has the "full" repertoire of history, shorts, publicity stills, and star data at her finger tips. One two-star review by Maltin speaks so presciently to the crisis faced by the legacy of Godardian cinema that I've decided to shape the framework of this chapter around an excerpt:

Bizarre, garish, contemporary punk-apocalyptic updating of the Shakespeare classic. There's little to be said about this pretentious mess except . . . avoid it.[6]

The "pretentious mess" is none other than a film by Godard, his 1987 adaptation of *King Lear*. Set in a postnuclear time, after Chernobyl when everything was lost and since everything has come back, except, that is, for culture, this film certainly represents the slippage of cinema in the face of a resurgent American movie culture and the resistance of Godard himself to the demands of that culture.

The idea for the film is said to have arisen spontaneously at the 1986 Cannes Film Festival when Godard met the infamous Menaham Golan and Yoram Globus of Cannon Films. Their first and only exchange while crossing the street led immediately, according to Godard, to "a fast deal" penned on a cocktail napkin for a $1,000,000 adaptation of *King Lear*, to be directed by Godard and to feature the writer of its script, Norman Mailer, as Don Learo.[7] Godard's film opens by replaying the director's taped phone conversation with Golan who called to pressure the director to make good on the promise to deliver the movie by the 1988 Cannes Festival. The film then screens footage of the two initial takes of the first scene in which Mailer protests Godard's shaping of his script, followed by Mailer's sudden and permanent departure from the set (along with his $100,000 scriptwriter's fee and his $250,000 actor's salary). Add to this folly the fact, recounted by Godard, that he, the director, had never read Shakespeare's play prior to signing the deal ("Of course I'll read it before I shoot. People tell me it's a great story, but it's just one I've heard of, like the story of Carmen or the story of Mary").[8] The prehistory of Godard's film thus bears all of the traces of the mess it is reported to be by more than one critic: "By turns slapstick and funereal, self-mocking and pretentious, Godard's *Lear* could almost pass for a student movie were it not for some talented presences [Norman Mailer and his daughter, Kate, Burgess Meredith, Molly Ringwald, Peter Sellers, and Woody Allen]."[9] Certainly not a movie by a student of Shakespeare, Godard's *King Lear* stands out at the onset of the twenty-first century as much more than a platform for marquee actors. I argue that it conveys a stunning portrayal of the challenges of the cultural loss of property and the recovery of a certain power in the new social field of cinema. What's recovered, however, is less a classical adaptation of Shakespeare than

a thoughtful reflection on the promising structures of cinema in the post-
traumatic condition of its cultural decline.

Twice early in the film, a voice-over evokes the postnuclear trauma that
sets the stage for Godard's take on the great story: "And then suddenly, it
was the time of Chernobyl and everything disappeared, everything, and then
after a while everything came back, electricity, houses, cars, everything except
culture and me." While perhaps a reference to the waning value of the
auteur directing the action, the "me" here actually refers to the movie's central protagonist, William Shakespeare Jr. the Fifth (played by Sellers) whose
voice provides the grainy texture of many of the film's voice-overs. The task
of young William is to fulfill the charge set jointly by the Royal Library of
the Queen and the Cultural Division of Cannon Films "to capture what
had been lost, beginning with my famous ancestor." Throughout the film,
Will Jr. walks around with a notebook jotting down overheard phrases that
seem hazily familiar to him. Is it merely coincidental that William shares
the task faced by Jean-Luc, his director, to capture the loss of the cultural
capital of the (more and more frequently) unread Shakespeare, if not to
recoup the losses of cinema itself?

There is certainly no reason why Shakespeareans or even cinephiles would
need to appreciate Mailer's mafioso rendition of the plot in which Don
Learo attempts to divide his entertainment-laden crime kingdom between
his daughters. Similar modernizations of *King Lear* have been accomplished
more successfully in innumerably different ways. Yet what should not be
undervalued here is Godard's repositioning of the text, post Mailer, in the
discourse of the modernist genre par excellence, cinema. In addition to re-
specting the play's insistence on a father's confused struggle with his three
daughters, Godard introduces the terms of his film as he speaks from off-
screen following Mailer's sudden departure from the set. Godard picks up
the script with a sensitivity for the theme of "Kate with three fathers":
"Mailer as star, father, me as director: too much indeed for the young lady
from Provincetown." What appears initially to be yet another adaptation
of Shakespeare *on* film, evolves from the opening moments into an articulation of Shakespearean themes *in* cinema, in the history of cinema. This
becomes particularly apparent when Godard's *King Lear* is considered in
the context of the filmmaker's retrospective sense of its place in the *His-
toire(s) du cinéma*. Given the relative obscurity of his messy *King Lear* in
film history and criticism, it is fascinating that *Histoire(s) du cinéma* makes

multiple references to the film's conceptual dialogue and the Shakespearean text, as well as including multiple stills from the film and conceptual commentaries on many of its visual strands whose status is rather obscure in the Shakespearean adaptation. This relative prominence of *King Lear* is particularly evident in the telescopic version of the printed text, *Histoire(s) du cinéma*, notably the fourth volume, where textual and imagistic references to the film stand out. As suggested by its conceptual prominence in *Histoire(s) du cinéma*, what Godard aimed to capture in creating his *King Lear* might be said to be twofold: cinematic representation and the thought of cinema *as* representation.

CINEMATIC REPRESENTATION

Cinematic representation is harnessed throughout the film via frames and traces of the artistic images of civilization that remain with us in the hazy decline of postnuclear / post–Cold War culture. Although William's voice-overs in Godard's *King Lear* are focused primarily on textual retrieval, they reveal that postnuclear / cold war cultural recovery—the kind called for in *Allemagne année 90 neuf zéro* and *For Ever Mozart*—will go astray if it sticks too close to the misleading academic insistence on the convenient separation of histories of theater and cinema, of Shakespeare and Godard. As made evident by the interweave in *Histoire(s) du cinéma* of pictures featured by Godard in *King Lear*, the historical stuff of cinematic visualization is as much the property of cinematic adaptation as is the composite memory of Shakespeare on the screen (with the significant difference being how the Cinema of Quality's faithfulness to fictional narrative gives way here to the imagery of cinema itself and the weird jump cuts and dissolves of their screened memory and mediated thought).

The figures and sounds of cinema itself intrude frequently in *King Lear*, from the European cinema of Vladimir Kozintsev, Robert Bresson, and Jean Renoir to the American movie culture of Woody Allen, Burgess Meredith, and Molly Ringwald, as the shadow of something about Shakespeare and cinema that remains to be noticed.[10] How *King Lear* bears the marks of the history of cinema itself is made evident from the beginning of the second opening of the film, after the departure of Mailer and his Kate. Here William Shakespeare Jr. wonders, "Why did they pick me? Why not some gentleman from Moscow or Beverly Hills? Why don't they just order some goblin to shoot this twisted fairy tale?" While young William flips through his photo album of cinema's past, stills of famous directors appear on the screen as William enumerates the ghostly presence of cinema by imagining which gentleman might be appropriate for the task: "Marcel [Pagnol], yes. Kenji [Mizoguchi] yes, of course . . . François [Truffaut], I'm not sure, Georges [Méliès], yes, definitely, Robert [Bresson], yes, Pier Paulo [Pasolini], yes, Fritz [Lang], yes, of course, of course." This rush of cinematic references suggests that the postnuclear age has fused moving images with static words in a way that lends little solace to previously comforting cultural points of view and orientations that now lie "twisted without reason, as if perspective has been abolished . . . [as if] the vanishing point has been erased."

In the wake of such twisted ghosting of cinema's many fathers, this viewer is struck by the curious surfacing of stills and citations from Godard's *King Lear* at key moments in *Histoire(s) du cinéma,* as if somewhat of a retrospective homage to the enigmatic traces of the history of cinema itself. Consider how the overhead shot of waves crashing against the shoreline, which opens and closes *King Lear,* follows in the wake of the graphic, "SEUL LE CINÉMA/BEAUTÉ [only the cinema, beauty]" in *Histoire(s) du cinéma 4.* Crucial to an understanding of the role of representation in Godard's *King Lear,* this shot and intertext are accompanied in *Histoire(s) du cinéma 4* by a cautionary voice-over concerning the need for the urgent return of artistic thought and its vicissitudes.

Of course, the inclusion of *King Lear*'s waves in *Histoire(s) du cinéma* also alludes coyly to the prominent legacy of the textual classics and their thoughtful provocations in Godard's *King Lear.* Godard's film depicts how the Shakespearean text is recognized and transcribed in bits and pieces by the interloping descendent who seems to recognize Shakespearean verse as if aided by something of a transgenerational phantom: "As you wish, which, watch . . . wITchcraft . . . As You Like It, that's it," exclaims young William after eavesdropping on the conversation between an old man (Learo) and his young daughter at an adjoining table. While the film comes across Virginia Woolf's modernist experiment *The Waves* in its entirety amid the refuse of the shoreline (references to this text open and close the film), William recovers the classical text of Shakespeare only by the arbitrary reassemblage of its language, line by line, phrase by phrase, as uttered by the cultural unconscious of the postnuclear public. Readers of the book *Histoire(s) du cinéma* will surely notice how the Shakespearean text once unknown to

Godard surfaces to provide the lines voiced over the montaged images of the New Wave's "intensité": "she's gone for ever / I know / when one is dead / and when / one lives / lend me a looking glass."[11] At issue throughout both *King Lear* and *Histoire(s) du cinéma,* then, is a challenging reflection on the possible recovery of visual representation in the wake of the loss of its most cherished figures, from image to thought.

ABOLISHED PERSPECTIVE

Perhaps something like the missing mist of the stone or the failed mimetic return of the looking glass constitutes the representation of the perspectival shift that links the challenge of the new (media) age to the crisis of representation so prominent in Shakespeare. One of the most enigmatic moments in *King Lear* occurs in the final moments of the play, when Lear makes his final plea to the unyielding stone:

> And thou no breath at all? Thou'lt come no more,
> Never, never, never, never, never.
> Pray you undo this button. Thank you, sir,
> Do you see this? Look on her! Look her lips,
> Look there, look there!
>
> (V.iii.307–11)[12]

In Shakespeare, Lear's enigmatic command appeals to his audience to act as a sort of go-between, to join him in seeing, in acknowledging, the captivating enigma of the figure of nothing: the death of the daughter and the disempowerment of sovereign perspective. Reenacting his imagined representation of Cordelia's living trace on the stone, Lear dies while redirecting the viewer's vision to a side view of whatever it is that we imagine remains "there" and the fragmented conditions of interpersonal relations promised by it.[13] In Godard's *King Lear,* young William's mournful line, "as if perspective has been abolished," transfers into the cinema the enigmatic deictic gesture with which Lear leads us to his death: "Look there, look there." Reenacting Lear's imagined representation of an abolished perspective in need of reparation, Godard's *King Lear* positions the enigma of the empty look as the deictic gesture most characteristic of the challenge of this film (just as *Histoire(s) du cinéma* similarly cites these lines to imagine the living trace of the New Wave's expired "intensité").

The film's intertitles describe *King Lear* three different times as a movie "Shot in the Back." Clearly related to the film's destruction of perspective (which is traditionally established from a frontal view), this provocative intertitle might also refer to Godard's betrayal of the realistic codes of cinematic and dramatic adaptation. More than once, for example, Godard positions his two primary protagonists, William Jr. and Cordelia, so that they face away from the camera at important moments in the film. The spectators' first introduction to William comes from the back, as he faces away from the camera and gazes out across a body of water while asking in voice-over, "Am I in France"? During their first cinematic interaction in the elegant restaurant of the Hôtel Beau Rivière in Nyon, Cordelia sits with her back to William as he addresses her from his adjacent table (in response to which Don Learo, as Mailer terms his mafioso protagonist, punningly accuses Shakespeare of "making a play for my girl"). In the following scene, when three silent muses follow William down a country road, one of them mimes Shakespeare's writing gestures from behind his back. And two scenes later, when Cordelia reads aloud to her father her sisters' rhetorical telegrams attesting to their unbridled love for Learo, she does so while looking out from a hotel balcony so that her back is turned to the camera, her father, and her spectators. Thus "Shot in the Back," Shakespeare and Cordelia are portrayed less as the tragic presences of this tale with whom the spectators will identify and more as the mediating screens through which and between whom the performance of language, affect, and cinema must pass via the abolition of conventional cinematic perspective and Shakespearean pity and fear.

This reversal of convention also animates the form of Godard's productions. In contrast to the architectonics of the movie palace through which, we learn late in the film, "light must come from the back," Godard prefers to invert the conventions of lighting in production to achieve a consistently enigmatic chiaroscuro effect. Rather than positioning artificial lights behind the camera, Godard reverses the process so that the camera captures light coming from the back of the set:

> I see contrast. It's a way of having two images, far away from each other, one dark and one sunny. I like to face the light, and if you face the light, then contrast appears and then you are able to see the contours. . . . I like to not have the light in the back, because the light in the back belongs to the projector,

the camera must have the light in front like we have ourselves in life. We receive and [afterward] we project.[14]

True to his predilection for the destruction of cinematic perspective (established from the front), Godard shoots from the back while situating light "there" "in the front" as if to thrust the spectator onto the horizon of deictic space whose iterative referent, "there, there" is cut free by Lear from the clarity of perspective's anchor. What follows "there, there" are the uncertain contours and chiaroscuro folds that underlie projection.[15]

NO THING

Just such a framework of the uncertainty of perspective's loss is foregrounded by one of the voice-overs opening the film as "a good way to begin." It is the sound of Norman Mailer, who in his short-lived role as Lear introduces the viewer to the central epistemological dilemma bequeathed to Godard from William Shakespeare Senior: "words are one thing, reality another thing: between them, NO THING." Between them, in other words, lies the enigmatic thought of cinema as epitomized by Godard's "way of having two images, far away from each other, one dark and one sunny." Between them is also the voice-over description of William Jr.'s arrival in Nyon, "between Italy and Germany, between the woods and the water." Also between them lies the graphic intertitle that reappears at infrequent intervals throughout the film as a marker of cinematic thought itself: NO THING. "So that [Don Learo] can silence this silence of silence," says Shakespeare Junior in a voice-over midway through the film, "he listens as if he's watching television. But Cordelia, what she shows in speaking is not NOTHING but her very presence . . . her exactitude" (9). Between them, between Learo and Cordelia, then, lies not the amnesiac sounds of televisual viewing through which Learo, in listening to his daughters, "hopes to see their entire bodies stretched out across their voices" (9), as Junior so electronically states it. Between them lies something much more exact: Cordelia's presence, or what lies between reality and words. NO THING.

Conversely, this phrase split between itself of what lies there, between frames, between images, between words, and between Lear and Cordelia, doubles as the graphic embodiment of the interval itself, NO THING. It seems plausible that the thought of culture missing from the casino and entertainment world of Don Learo resonates on the horizon of the interval whose temporal insistence on the different folds of the present, past, and future was annihilated by the NOW of Chernobyl and its expansive nuclear fusion.[16] "Handling in both hands the present the future and the past," so Godard writes in English and French, in *Histoire(s) du cinéma 4,* "un roi peut achever un règne mais on n'achèvera jamais l'histoire de ce règne [a king may complete a reign but the history of that reign will never be completed]."[17] It seems likely that the recovery of the thought of history will entail a rethinking of the horizon itself, marked as it is by the postnuclear, postcommunist reality of Chernobyl and by the dispersion of the frontiers of national and ethnic identity, from Kozintsev's Russia and Kurosawa's Japan to Godard's France and Woody Allen's America.[18] If we think back to William Jr.'s first appearance in *King Lear,* moreover, we will realize that the rethinking of the horizon of history must also entail the rethinking of cinema itself: "I remembered what Pluggy told me years later about editing, 'handling, physically, in both hands the future, the present, and the past.'"

The challenge of positioning the horizon in relation to the productive suspension of the analog movement of temporality is brought home by the film's seeming refusal to mark its end with the traditional credits that fix the boundaries of its national locations and financial sponsors. After a graphic intercut declares "The End" of *King Lear,* the film begins anew, however briefly, by introducing viewers to the man in charge of editing Cannon Pictures now that "Chernobyl is long past." After Chernobyl, the conventions of closing the film seem to have been altered as much as those that opened Godard's *King Lear.* Played by Woody Allen, the editor sports the appropriate name of Mr. Alien. Introduced literally as the cinematic "Other," Mr. Alien's role is singled out quizzically by William Jr. (who is himself covered by yards of celluloid), "Why not some other gentleman from Moscow or Beverly Hills?" In a way that positions the film in the loop of déjà vu, as if doubling Shakespeare's return of Cordelia to Britain to redeem, with the aid of France, the lost perspective of her father's reign, Mr. Alien here comes to life in the wake of cinema's seeming passing (punning perhaps on Signourey Weaver's return from the dead in *Aliens*) to handle film with the temporal sensibility prescribed by Godard in *Histoire(s) du cinéma.* As he literally sews film at the editing table (accompanied by the graphic intertitle "So Young, Sew Tender"), Mr. Alien addresses his cinematic viewers with the same lines positioned by Godard in *Histoire(s) du cinéma* in relation to the boundlessness of history, as well as those remembered by William Jr. at the outset of the film in relation to the openness of memory. Fingering his celluloid footage, Mr. Alien speaks aloud his self-consciousness about how he is "handling in both hands the present, the future, and the past." Echoing William Jr.'s opening lines in the film, Mr. Alien again situates the place of cinematic thought here again on the frontier, on the border, on the margin, on the horizon of history and its cinematic passing: Look there, look there.

As for the holder of thought, the server of epistemological wisdom, this task lies, in Godard's *King Lear,* neither with the CEO of Learo Jet, his dutiful daughter, nor the obedient scribe, Shakespeare Junior. "They seemed to be looking for something," says Junior of Lear and Cordelia midway through the film, "no one knows, only the Professor knows." Alongside Shakespeare Jr., Learo, Cordelia, and much later Mr. Alien, enters the persona of cinematic thought itself, the inimitable Professor Pluggy. "I don't know if I made this clear before," Junior reminds the viewers in two subsequent voice-over intervals, "but this was after Chernobyl. We're in a time now when movies and more generally art have been lost, do not exist, and they have to somehow be reinvented. Thanks to the old man and his daughter I had some of the lines but I was told this old man Pluggy had to go together with the lines." Pluggy, who says he "hates light," bears the name of his twenty years in the chiaroscuro dark, hidden in the editing room lit obscurely from the back, just as his face is partially obscured by the parodic headdress of his electronic brotherhood with flowing cords and dangling jacks.

Hidden beneath the plugs and wires that denote the electronic transformation of life in the editing cave, Jean-Luc Godard himself stands in jokingly for the Professor of Cinematic Thought. He plays Pluggy, the genius of cinema whose epistemological quest is fueled by the fact that, as he tells Junior, he knows that what he is looking for "doesn't exist: since nobody does it." After he utters these lines, the Professor responds to William's question, "What are you aiming at?" by shifting the underside of his seated body to surround the cinematic space with the baffled resonance of a loud fart. Epistemological aim, in this context, is tantamount to an aggressive bilabial fricative, a pure sound-event, one that may have no corollary or analogy other than the invisible waste of nuclear fallout or the perlocutionary effect of NO THING.[19] "The result of what is obtained immediately," says Pluggy to Junior, "controls the truth of association. . . . What is great is not the image but the EMOTION that it provokes. . . . The emotion thus provoked is true because it is born outside of all imitation, all evocation, and all resemblance."

Just such a distancing from an art of resemblance for the sake of a cinema of affect lies at the heart of later Godardian cinema, as well as at the core of its prescient representation of what I termed earlier a new baroque era caught between clashing systems of analog and digital representation. Godard can be said to lay bare the virtual scaffolding of his cinema when he distances his artistic practice from systems of analog representation, i.e., from those practices based on formal codes of progression and analogy through which a picture demonstrates its mimetic resemblance to its realistic source (and through which a cinematic adaptation of the French Cinema of Quality marked resemblance to the source text). In agreeing with Gavin Smith in a 1996 interview that cinema has "imprisoned the image," Godard indirectly positions himself on the digital frontier when he differentiates moving pictures from cinematic images: "An image doesn't exist. This is not an image, it's a picture. The image is the relation with me looking at it dreaming up a relation at someone else. An image is an association."[20] By shifting cinematic practice from the terrain of resemblance to what exists to that of association with or simulation of something as nebulous as the haptic affect of a fart, Godard can be said retroactively to inscribe his work in the virtual interactivity now so characteristic of digital aesthetics.

Rather than celebrate film's imitation of nature; its adherence to well-established artistic genres such as adaptation, documentary, or realistic narrative that set the parameters of resemblance; or even its perspectival solicitation of spectatorial attention and wonder, digital aesthetics can be said to position the spectator on the threshold of the virtual. As put succinctly by Pierre Lévy, the image thereby "abandons the exteriority of spectacle to open itself to immersion."[21] The promise of digital aesthetics is its enhanced zone of interactivity through which the users' entry into the circuit of artistic presentation simulates or projects their own associations, fantasies, and memories in consort with the artwork. It is just such a simulation that Godard terms the virtual, unrealized promise of "true montage":

> La vrai mission, the true goal of cinema, was to arrive at a way of elaborating and putting into practice what montage is. But we never got there; many

directors believed they had reached it, but they had done other things. Particularly Eisenstein. He was on the way to montage but he didn't reach it. He wasn't an editor, he was a taker of angles. And because he was so good at taking angles, there was an idea of montage. The three lions of *October,* the same lion but taken from three different angles, so the lion looks like he's moving—in fact it was the association of angles that brought montage. Montage is something else, never discovered.[22]

"Born outside of all imitation, all evocation, all resemblance," the image of true montage or true emotion in Godard's *King Lear* can be only a simulacrum of the production and the affect of representation, whether the simulacrum is understood in terms of its founding, philosophical articulation in Plato's cave or its later electronic actualization in Godard's studio.

A most eerie sequence in *King Lear* cuts between both of these scenes of the cave and the studio during William's second interrogation of Pluggy about the status of cinema. It happens inside a chiaroscuro-lit editing studio, a space viewers have come to associate with Godard's self-representation in films dating back to *Numéro Deux* (1975) where Godard works in front of two video monitors from which he reshot video footage on 35 mm.[23] Peeking around the doorway into a darkened space where flashes of light are doubled by the whirring sounds of electronic equipment, Junior notes, "There's a lot of noise around here, huh? What's it for? What's it all for, Professor?" Signifying the cinematic crisis that appears with each growth of new machines in the social field, from silent cinema to video and digital editing, this conflation of cinema with a cacophony of sound positions the contemporary editing studio in continuous variation with the earlier trauma of the talkies' break from the pure image of silent cinema. It is the allusion to this break and its confusing discovery of new beings in the cinematic mechanism (thinking back to Deleuze's notion of the Baroque) that prefaces Pluggy's discourse on the image as "a pure creation of the soul, it cannot be born of a comparison but of a reconciliation of two realities that come more or less far apart."

One of the realities shown at intervals during this sequence is that of a crude light box illuminating tiny plastic models of prehistoric creatures that hearken back to cinema's primal scene of the cave. At precisely the moment of Pluggy's assertion that "the image is a pure creation of the soul," footage of the prehistoric light box is intercut with an image resembling the silhouetted spectacle displayed to the imprisoned spectators of Plato's cave. To grasp the cinematic relation between these two distinct prehistoric realities of light box and cave, one need merely recall the theoretical legacy of Jean-Louis Baudry's emphasis on the importance of the allegory of Plato's cave to the ideology of the cinematic apparatus: "we can thus propose that the allegory of the cave is the text of a signifier of desire which haunts the invention of cinema and the history of its invention."[24] At issue for Baudry, but perhaps lost after Chernobyl, is how the cinematic apparatus provokes the simulation not of the reality of cinema and its representations but of its dream, its desire, to such an extent that "it is indeed a simulation of a condition of the subject, a position of the subject, a subject and not reality."[25] Baudry's apparatus, from cave to movie palace, is thus no more than a subject's machinery of desire and its signifying practices.

While Baudry's model fits the cave, it might well constitute a cinematic reality more or less far apart from that of *King Lear* where we learn from young William that everything reappeared after Chernobyl, "everything except culture and me." Culture and me, the apparatus and the subject. Where do they lie in the postapocalyptic wasteland of Godard's *King Lear*? Is the machinery of desire here represented as grounded in the subject or might the culture of the subject itself have disappeared in the machineries of cinema and their signifying practices: "cinema is higher than us, it is that to which we must lift our eyes"?

Add then to the primal image of the cave in this same intriguing sequence the simulacrum of the studio itself whose dual video monitors and electronic mixing board attest to Godard's own enigmatic position between the dueling realities of cinema and video that have ushered in the digital age. This darkened editing cave with its electronic noises that so befuddle Junior mirrors the space viewers have come to associate with Godard since *Numéro Deux* (1975). The uncanny return of this scene, which leaves the director in the dark as he lurks in the shadows of New Age machineries, clearly harks back to Godard's stance in *Numéro Deux,* when he stood next to two video monitors to speak prophetically about the link of his cinema to the crisis of its property: "Mac machine. No Mac, only machine."[26] While Godard had no way in 1975 of foreseeing the developments that have unfolded in Silicon Valley, his repetitive staging of the doubling of the video monitor presciently situates the future promise of the Mac in relation to the logic of his doubled image.

Harun Farocki could easily have been referring to *King Lear*, rather than *Numéro Deux*, when he wrote that

the idea of doubling the image must have come to Godard from working in video. Video editing is usually done while sitting in front of two monitors. One monitor shows the already edited material, and the other monitor the raw material, which the videomaker may or may not add to the work-in-progress. He or she becomes accustomed to thinking of two images at the same time, rather than sequentially.[27]

It is this break from the mastery of analog sequence that repositions the subject in the disjunctive gap of the cinematic machine, in the space of the between, in the thought of the dislocation of two realities more or less far apart, whether those of the cave and the editing room or those of cinema and video. In *King Lear*'s editing room sequence, the jocular alternation on two monitors of the figure of Liberty and the caricature of Pluto (an animated embodiment of the fricative) attests to the irrational dissonance of the quest that brings Pluggy and Junior together in an attempt to redefine postapocalyptic culture. Here the quest differs from the confident recreation of authorial vision, artistic harmony, and narrative development— the humanistic project shared by literary history and classical cinema and the pedagogical project now lamented for its supposed death by the National Association of Scholars and the National Alumni Forum, whose recalcitrant members cannot acknowledge the radicality of the Shakespeare they lament or the Shakespearean dissonance of Godard's emphasis on what lies between *King Lear*'s NO THING.[28] In effect, this fascinating sequence, with its cavelike studio setting, reproductive lights, electronic feedback, video monitors, and enigmatic sounds, attests to the disparate forms and realities through which contemporary cinema now responds to frontiers, horizons, and representational possibilities opened up by the politics and new machineries of the post-Chernobyl age. This is a representational challenge not at all contrary to that posed by Shakespeare's *King Lear*, providing we apply pressure to the uncertainty of Lear's dying deictic, "Look there, look there!" an uncertainty embraced as representationally empowering by Edgar who subsequently speaks the play's closing lines: "Speak what we feel, not what we ought to say."

DELEUZE IN THE SHADOWS

Sandwiched between the electronic editing board and the editing room's two monitors, so different in their exact similarity, lurks a figure darkened in silhouette who appears to stand in for the off-camera voice of Pluggy. Although it turns out at the scene's end to be the same Edgar who utters Shakespeare's lines about speaking feelingly, I have frequently found myself fantasizing that this silhouette is the specter of the other Professor of Cinema and its Thought, the one who wrote the chapter on "Thought and Cinema" in his 1985 book, *Cinema 2: The Time-Image,* in which Godard figures so prominently. I was first enraptured by this fantasy that Deleuze appears as if in hologram in Godard's 1987 film upon hearing Pluggy's assertion about the reconciliation of two realities that are more or less far apart. "The more the connections between these two are dissimilar," Pluggy informs us, "the stronger the image will be, the more it will have emotive power. . . . Two contrary realities will not draw together their opposing selves; one rarely attains power and forces from these oppositions."

The emotive reconciliation of such dissimilarities can be understood to be fueled by the force of Deleuze's notion of incompossibility. "Incompossibility" is Deleuze's baroque term borrowed from Leibniz for two coexisting incommensurables. Deleuze follows the lead of Leibniz to wonder how elements fail to converge while still not negating or rendering each other impossible. Instead of converging or remaining impossible for each other, they stand in paradoxical relation to one another as divergent and coexistent, as incompossible. In a footnote to *Logique du sens,* Deleuze provides a summary of the three serial elements of the world that inscribe the Leibnizian monad on the margins of incompossibility: one that determines the world by convergence, another that determines perfect individuals in this world, and finally one that determines incomplete or rather ambiguous elements common to many worlds and to many corresponding individuals.[29] Deleuze is interested in how these elements fail to converge while still not negating or rendering each other impossible. Rather than either converging or remaining impossible for each other, they stand in paradoxical relation to one another as divergent and coexistent: as incompossible. Deleuze dwells most explicitly on the serial nature of post-Leibnizian incompossibility in *Difference and Repetition* and *Cinema 2: The Time-Image.* He contrasts Leibniz's example of different points of view on one town, "not-necessarily true pasts," with the bifurcating fabulations of seriality, "incompossible presents," through which each series tells completely different stories that unfold simultaneously.[30] The forced coexistence or "chao-errancy" of seriality, Deleuze adds in *Cinema 2,* results in a crisis of truth that knows no solution but only a pause or a delay, say, within 24 frames a second. Pluggy's assertion quoted above stands out as a new baroque exemplar of cinematic incompossibility: "The more the connections between these two are dissimilar, the stronger the image will be, the more it will have emotive power."

Rather than attaining power from oppositions, suggests Deleuze in writing on Godard, (post)modern cinema stages "the whole" as it "undergoes a mutation, because it has ceased to be the One-Being, in order to become the constitutive 'and' of things, the constitutive between-two of images. The whole thus merges," adds Deleuze, "with what Blanchot calls the force of 'dispersal of the Outside,' or 'the vertigo of spacing': that void which is no longer a motor-part of the image, and which the image would cross in order to continue, but is the radical calling into question of the image (just as there is a silence [this is still Deleuze writing before Godard's *King Lear*] which is no longer the motor-part or the breathing-space of discourse but its radical calling into question)." "False continuity," Deleuze concludes, "takes on a new meaning, at the same time as it becomes the law."[31] The brilliance of Godard's *King Lear* is how it situates the new electronic meaning of cinema in relation to the contemplation of the radicality of silence and its impact on the law in Shakespeare. "Bear them from hence [instructs Albany at the end of Shakespeare's *Lear*]. Our present business is general woe. Friends of my soul, you twain Rule in this realm, and the gor'd state sustain." Just as false continuity, the breathing space of NO THING, became the law of Lear's Britain whose twained rule (saved by France) sustains the gor'd state, the doubled image, the silence of the break, and the gap of sequentiality sustain the rule of what Deleuze calls Godard's cinema of incommensurability.

It is almost uncanny how much Jean-Luc Godard's *King Lear* exemplifies Deleuze's argument about the cinema of Godard. One almost can imagine Godard falling upon *Cinema 2* after the sudden departure of Normal Mailer to come up with the idea for a saving protagonist of the film, the Professor of the Thought of Cinema. A brief summary of Deleuze's reading of Godard provides almost a pony for the reading of this film Shot in the Back. The hallmark of this cinema is what Deleuze calls its irrationality:

The cut has become the interstice, *it is irrational and does not form part of either set, one of which has no more an end than the other has a beginning:* false continuity is such an irrational cut. Thus, in Godard, the interaction of two images engenders or traces a frontier which belongs to neither one nor the other.[32]

This visual irrationality brought home by Godard in his morphing play with Goofy Liberty pertains as well to the many parts of *King Lear,* which begins and ends twice, as well as its disparate protagonists, intertitles, and voice-overs. Three features of such false continuity provide a particularly apt means for summarizing Godard's performance of the cinematic frontiers of the film: free indirect vision, the interstice between sound and vision, and finally the fabulation of modern political cinema.

What Deleuze calls the "free indirect vision" is the excessive seriality of Godardian cinema that flows in continuous variation from one sequence to another. Through this offshoot of "free indirect discourse," Deleuze writes,

Either the author [think here of Shakespeare as well as Godard] expresses himself through the intercession of an autonomous, independent character other than the author or any role fixed by the author, or the character acts and speaks himself as if his own gestures and his own words were already reported by a third party.[33]

If this seems all too abstract, just think back to the intercession of Professor Pluggy, on the one hand, or how Shakespeare Junior speaks words already reported by a third party, on the other hand. The practical result is the effacement of a controlling interior monologue, the inversion of a totalization of images or whole in favor of an outside inserted between them, and the erasure of the unity of man and world in favor of a break, leaving Godard's spectators with, at best, only a frail belief in the promise of the postnuclear world.[34]

These results could be summarized in the series of intertitles repeated at intervals throughout Godard's film in a way that disrupts the narrative flow of *King Lear:* A Picture Shot in the Back, A Study, An Approach, A Clearing, A Thing, Fear and Loathing, Three Journeys into King Lear. Such a repetition of intertitles in continuous variation constitutes the seriality of *King Lear* through which two images or the fold of sound and vision are said by Deleuze to engender or trace a frontier belonging neither to one nor the other. Just such a stress on the showing, *faire voir,* of the indiscernible, of the in-between, of "Look there, look there!" motivates the project of Godard with its mixed media, intertitles, and intersecting narratives, as well as the discourse of Professor Pluggy who responds to Young Shakespeare's timid request, "Tell me, Professor," with the abrupt corrective, "Show, show don't tell."

Perhaps it is something like the violence or the bloodiness of Godard's show that prompted the viscerality of Leonard Maltin's negative reaction to the mess of *King Lear.* Or perhaps it has as much to do with the stress on fabulation deriving from Godard's seriality, a fabulation described by Deleuze as characteristic of political, feminist, postcolonial cinema (not as strange a category for Shakespeare's *King Lear* as one might think, and one worth entertaining in its postnuclear cinematic apparition). Fabulation— the reciting, retelling, reconceiving of the ancestral story—is the truly cinematic image-event in Deleuze through which the colonizing myths of culture, whether those of Shakespeare, Hollywood, or the National Association of Scholars, achieve something akin to a contrary world-memory of an infinity of peoples who remain to be united, or even who should not be united. The new world-memory of Shakespeare *in* cinema, as suggested by the postapocalyptic project of Godard and his stress on the recovery of the passion of cinematic history throughout *Histoire(s) du cinéma,* is marked not so much by the coherence of authorial perspective and cultural patrimony as by the intensity, disparity, dissemblance, and *différend* of cinematic nomadism and its chao-errancy. Through radical transformations of the conditions of Shakespearean production, moreover, Godard might be said to join Cordelia in her pact with Virginia Woolf to constitute, as Professor Deleuze would say, "an assemblage which brings real parties together, in order to make them produce collective utterances as the prefiguration of a people who are missing."[35] Such fabulation on the eve of the new digital era of cinema needs to be understood, moreover, as just as dissimilar as it is drawn together. At one moment, it might constitute no more than an abrasive cinematic fricative; at others, it might amount to an assertive, feminist countercharge such as that spoken by Cordelia to Shakespeare Jr.: "You write what is against me, you do not write for me." But at all times, the new world-memory of post-Chernobyl cinema—let us call it Histoire(s) du cinéma—testifies to the prescience of Godard's cinematic practice that champions the idealism of pure montage and the generative passions of the clash of its incompossible systems of analog and digital representation.

HISTOIRE(S) DU CINÉMA:
ET CINEMA'S POLITICAL LEGACY

So how might we account for the status of cinema now that its history has been spoken, now that its Histoire(s) have been shot? And thinking of the authorial positionality of Godard's lengthy cinematic and bookish reflection on the glory and passing of his cherished medium, *Histoire(s) du cinéma,* one wonders whether cinematic Frenchness has been rendered anomalous in the light of globalism and international systems of distribution that favor English (read American or Australian) production studios and values. Is cinema itself spent, depleted, shot as an image-action of national discourse and identity? And what of the seduction of the cut and promise of montage over which Godard swooned and drooled? Is the lure of cinematic editing now rendered dull and lifeless by the ease with which digital effects are created by the click of a mouse and the push of a button?

As mentioned in the introductory remarks framing this chapter, Godard understands the popularity of new forms of media to reflect not merely the cultural crises of the European condition but also the concomitant decline of the thoughtful promise of cinema itself as it dumbs itself down to the level of the televisual and perhaps now even the digital. Godard consistently voices concern about the ability of late cinema to bear the ontological fabric of the twentieth century whose traces he laments as fading on the tiny screens of television and computer monitors: "Cinema is higher than us, it is that to which we must lift our eyes. When it passes into a smaller object on which we lower our eyes, cinema loses its essence. One can be moved by the trace it leaves, this keepsake portrait that we look at like the photo of a loved one carried with us; we can see the shadow of a film on the television, the longing for a film, the nostalgia, the echo of a film, but never a film."[36] Embalmed in such an enigmatic discourse of something like a chiaroscuro effect—the shadow, the longing, the echo—the composite picture of Godard's scattered thoughts on cinema and culture requires his reader's frequent adjustment to the quick and jarring movements of his prose between the apparatus, property, thought, and cinema. Consistently evident, however, throughout *Histoire(s) du cinéma* and his later interviews is Godard's linkage of the property of the transformation of cinema to how his cinema thinks ontology as the unsettled relations of being and property, of "être et avoir." It is such a conflation of cinema with a crisis of ontology that positions *Histoire(s) du cinéma* at the threshold of cinema's future in relation to the material translations of digitality and the social slippage of cultural specificity in the numbing sameness of cultural globalism.

At the material core of this threshold stand two terms whose status seems more and more fraught with each passing day. The first is "Godard," the proper name that seems always to stand at the epicenter of *Histoire(s) du cinéma*. Perhaps the morphing value of the proper name, Godard, is nowhere more evident than in international cinema studies that now tend to look beyond the New Wave into the threshold of global video and new media installation, a look I frequently share. Consider a discussion I had recently with a colleague in film studies who shares my passion for new media and global cinema. When I explained to her that I was writing a text on Godard, she responded to me both quizzically and aggressively by asking something on the order of "Godard, why would you even consider working on THAT anymore?" (While I do not recall her exact words, the violence of her "THAT" is deeply engrained in my psyche). Now link THAT to the other term also bound to elicit curious affect among a growing number of American interlocutors, that of "France." France is something of a fleeting signifier of what my generation understood as bearing an exciting cultural cachet. These days France frequently stands as a symbol of decline (declining enrollments, cinema, wine, cheese, purity; declining participation in the EU; declining football; declining Socialism; I even heard someone speak recently over dinner of the Centre Pompidou as an edifice that exemplifies the decline of its previous glory). Godard himself celebrates the paradox of this so-called decline in a sequence concluding *Histoire(s) du cinéma 4:* "It is my privilege to film and live as an artist in France, nothing like a country that descends daily along the path of its inexorable decline."

In the midst of a spirited discussion of the world crisis at same dinner party, someone else signaled the other blemish now known as France, that of something like an American national irritation, when he blurted out with total confidence, "If we were to have to acknowledge that a single country maintains hegemonic control over world power [and he could have added, culture], who would we possibly want that to be other than America?

FRANCE?" Well, I'm sure there must be a few people reading this book to whom these anecdotes might seem like a slap in the face or a shot in the back by academic and cultural allies who seem not to appreciate the intellectual return of thinking the cultural ontology and materiality of these signifiers that could be doubled as one: Godard and France. And yet, the very penning of this anecdote helped me to recall, via *Histoire(s) du cinéma*, the forcefulness with which Godard has situated precisely this doubled figure of betrayal and paranoia, the "shot in the back," as a loaded "signe parmi nous" of the imperative of critical positionality and artistic innovation at the back side of the cinema's history.

It is in *Histoire(s) du cinéma 2A*, "Seul le cinéma," that Godard reminds his viewers of the French connection to the cinematic legacy of Plato's cave in which cinema's primal imaginary has it "shot in the back":

It took a French prisoner who turned round when placed in front of a Russian wall to enact the mechanical application of the idea and desire of projecting images on a screen that subsequently took off with the invention of cinematic projection.[37]

Nowhere does Godard reflect with more insistence on the paradox of cinema being shot in the back than in *King Lear*, his disastrous collaboration with Hollywood's moguls, Golan and Globus of Cannon Films. As I hope to have made evident in the preceding analysis, the shot in the back exemplifies not simply the betrayal of politics or the decline of art but, more importantly, the power of Godardian cinematic and political intervention. It solicits the viewer to think otherwise about the clear-cut terms of politics and representation frequently dominating histories of film. Screened here is not the utopian joy of political synthesis, the coming together of contrary realities or cinematic traditions that some now call "world cinema," but rather the emergent strength of contrast and difference in themselves. This is the kind of political reality of the different and the differend that remains so unrecognizable to today's American interlocutors whom fear and trembling has inculcated with the either/or temperament of threatened democratic liberty.

This is a political reality grounded in a continual cinematic deliberation on the grounding concepts of "être" and "avoir" themselves. To illustrate this point, I would like to recall Godard's only film that he features in the ending sequences of *Histoire(s) du cinéma*. Given the current tensions of global politics, I cannot think of a film more important than *Ici et ailleurs* (1970) with which to work toward a conclusion of this analysis of the crisis of Godardian cinema. I turn your attention to one of the sequences that most clearly marks the differential power of the film's imagery on today's global scene. Shot in the back are two youthful viewers whose innocent immersion in televisual flow is intercut by Godard with shots of political leaders and newspaper footage exemplifying the tension, rather than solution, of capitalist culture and global politics, a tension from which we don't seem to have made that much progress over the past thirty-eight years of film history. Flickering with light from both front and back, the sequence is framed by the somewhat surreal image of "ET," a figure of the dissimilarity of East and West, here and there. Initially begun as a film by Jean-Pierre Gorin and commissioned by the Palestinians to document their revolutionary plight, *Ici et ailleurs* evolved, in the wake of the Palestinian massacre at the betraying hands of Hussein, into a commentary by Gorin, Godard, and Miéville on the challenge and positionality of cinematic production at the center of contrary realities: the Palestinian revolution, there, in the East; the economic revolution, here, in France, in the West. Challenging even the centrality of auteurship that is frequently associated with the film (as one by "Godard"), *Ici et ailleurs* provides the viewer with the opportunity to reflect both on the mediating criticality of cinema as well as on the display of contrary political realities steeped in the tension of worldviews and political shifts. A revisionary reflection on "être et avoir" makes it too easy to divide the world simply in two (either for us or against us).

What is perhaps most prescient about this sequence, moreover, is the rhetorical accent it places on the flickering figure lit from front and back, ET, not yet a signifier of the Hollywood Extra Terrestrial, but a sign of what Gilles Deleuze and Claire Parnet call "the geography of relations." As if prophesying the direction of Deleuze's philosophical reflections, Godard substitutes ET for EST. Displaced is EST, the sign of either the East or the metaphysical copula of centralized subjectivity and national centrality so important to France and its intellectual, political, and cinematic history. What remains is the stripped-down coda of relationality, ET, that displaces the presence of cinematic auteurship and cultural dominance, the clarity of the copula.

The concluding emphasis of *Histoire(s) du cinéma* on clips from *Ici et ailleurs* further suggests how Godard's cinema thinks ontology as the unsettled sequencing of histories of being and property, of "être et avoir." With the aim of juxtaposing the shot of ET, illuminated from the back, as an essential signifier of the act of theorizing film history, I would like to invite you to montage the sequences I've described from *King Lear* and *Ici et ailleurs* with this citation from Deleuze and Parnet's *Dialogues,* a text that so elegantly echoes the insistence of Godard on the political and artistic valence of relationality:

> All grammar and syllogisms are a means of maintaining the subordination of conjunctions to the verb to be. . . . This must be stretched farther: to make the relational encounter penetrate and corrupt everything, undermine being, make it sway. Substitute ET for EST. The "ET" is not even a relation or particular conjunction: it's what underlies all relations, the routing of all relations, and what wires relations beyond their terms, beyond the ensemble of their terms, and beyond everything that could be understood as Being, One, or All. The ET [is] like extra-being, inter-being.[38]

Addition, accumulation, extension, tension. This is the baroque legacy, the extra-being of *Histoire(s),* created by Godard when he conjoins the formal figure ET with the political valence of the cultural, shot in the back.

YOU ARE HOW YOU READ:
BAROQUE CHAO-ERRANCY IN
GREENAWAY AND DELEUZE

The Renaissance explores the universe; the Baroque explores libraries. Its meditations are devoted to books.

— BENJAMIN, *The Origin of German Tragic Drama*

As if the epitome of the Baroque, *The Tempest* by Shakespeare has been cited as a case history of the negative legacy of capitalism. Postcolonial readings situate the play's "brave new world" on the fold of the rise of the new economic order. Being the first dramatic text in the folio of 1623 and the "last" play written by Shakespeare, *The Tempest* is lamented by postcolonial critics for its self-replicating vision of patriarchal duplicity and colonial conquest fueled by the absolutism of knowledge and the economy of the same in which Prospero and his books stand in for Shakespeare and his plays.[1] While Prospero's passion for esoteric knowledge costs him his dukedom, his manipulation of the esoteric magic of his books wins it back. He not only controls the fancies of the shipwrecked visitors from Milan but also holds the key to his daughter's memory of her cultural past. He manipulates their composite understanding of the tempestuous present for the personal ends of past revenge and the political gains of future matrimonial alliance. Finally, the bookishness of his agency results in his enslavement of the native labor of Caliban and Ariel and his usurpation of their foreign goods and methods. "For what does the island become to Prospero," asks Eric Cheyfitz, "but an expanded library, a library transformed into a state, a state into a library, where the scholar, who in the Renaissance must always be a translator, literally rules his subjects by the book?"[2]

Prospero's island also becomes an extended library to Peter Greenaway, who recasts the family romance into a cinematic cornucopia of digitally animated books, ideas, and European fantasies. In the world of *Prospero's Books* (1991), the scholar-magician Prospero works gleefully in the quiet of his cell to collate passages and visions from twenty-four books randomly bequeathed to him by Gonzalo on the night of his exile. The goal of his quest is composition of a play called *The Tempest*. Spectators are presented with the spectacular vision of a truly baroque author who loves his books and loves writing for the merger of ink and texture, line and sound, text and margin, self and other. It could easily be suggested that Greenaway's representation of Prospero's books and the inner spaces (mental and spatial) of their composition embodies the baroque ideal of "the book of monads" so admired by Gilles Deleuze: "the book of monads, in letters and little circumstantial pieces that could sustain as many dispersions as combinations. The monad is the book or the reading room. The visible and legible, the outside and the inside, the façade and the chamber. . . ."[3] Indeed, the visual delight of *Prospero's Books* lies in its imaginative proliferation of images, textures, and electronic folds whose hallucinatory presence is conjoined in the monad, Prospero, and folded anew in the dramatic text that Prospero continually pens and voices throughout the film.[4]

CROSS-IDENTIFICATION

Greenaway would probably qualify my emphasis on "hallucinatory presence" here. For it is crucial to him that there be no confusion about the subject responsible for his production. The commensurate Shakespearean actor, Sir John Gielgud, proposed making the film as a means of providing himself with a celluloid platform for his penultimate performance of the role he acted on stage at least five times before.[5] One of the unusual features of this adaptation is its reliance on the voice of Gielgud to mouth most of the characters' lines in voice-over. When Gielgud isn't actually penning the lines of *The Tempest*, whose text is performed as Prospero writes it throughout the play, he voices the other characters' lines in varying chronological sequence—sometimes the lines precede the action; sometimes they occur simultaneously with the action; sometimes they are spoken or written as if an afterthought of a visual sequence. The result is that the sound of the text tends to revolve around Gielgud. There are many moments in the film when the actor himself seems captivated by the rich timbre of his own voice, such as his melodic repetition of the call "Boatswain!" which opens and closes the film. If we are to trust Greenaway's account, the aged Gielgud was motivated by a desire, perhaps like Shakespeare's, to go out in style by identifying himself for posterity with the masterful role and voice, the *logos,* of Prospero.

Gielgud's appropriation of Shakespearean dialogue coalesces in a composite representation of Prospero's twenty-four books plus one (Shakespeare's final play still being composed) as well as the resultant scenes and fantasies that are often superimposed on the screen with Shakespeare's script as it is being written. This profusion of script, as much as the cell of Prospero, demands a reading of *Prospero's Books* as the figuration of the Baroque, as a schema, in the sense of Walter Benjamin, of "the baroque ideal of knowledge, the process of storing, to which the vast libraries are a monument . . . realized in the external appearance of the script. Almost as much as in China it is, in its visual character, not merely a sign of what is to be known but it is itself an object worthy of knowledge."[6] Described by Greenaway as "like a Kircher book-making machine," Prospero literally rules his subjects by the book.[7] The characters of *The Tempest* come to symbolize the cultural translations of the ruling monad, "who obtained his knowledge from books, not first-hand observation."[8] The authority of knowledge is the guiding principle of Greenaway's fanciful translation of *The Tempest,* which sought to capitalize on Gielgud's "powerful and authoritative ability to speak text" in order to ensure "deliberate cross-identification between Prospero, Shakespeare and Gielgud" who become at times "indivisibly one person."[9]

The dignity and centrality of Prospero's many voicings are lent shape by Greenaway's attentiveness to the place and shape of the Shakespearean text. Accompanied by the magnified sound of a drop of water, the film returns regularly to a stunning close-up shot of a quill piercing the cobalt blue surface of Prospero's inkwell (could this possibly have been a gesture to Derek Jarman, who shot a competing version of *The Tempest*?). The director stresses the centrality of the shot by comparing it to a magician's hat "where everything comes from, always acknowledging the Shakespearean original text."[10] Also acknowledged indirectly here is the strategy of this film to substitute striking and enigmatic visuals for direct textual quotations. Indeed, few

cinematic adaptations of Shakespeare have been so ruthless in excising textual passages that might appear to compete with the directorial vision at
hand. Even viewers (like Godard) with only a schoolyard knowledge of *The
Tempest* would be likely to notice the more significant cuts meant to foreground the voicings of Prospero. Excised from Greenaway's film are

- the majority of the dialogue lending depth to Miranda's character, from
  her reference to Caliban as "a villain, sir, I do not love to look on"
  (I.ii.309)[11] and her acknowledgment of her subconscious defiance of
  her father by telling Ferdinand her name, "O my father, I have broke
  your hest to say so" (III.i.37), to her significant references to her gender, such as "Good wombs have borne bad sons" (I.ii.120) and "I do
  not know / One of my sex, no woman's face remember, / Save from
  my glass, mine own" (III.i.48–50);
- the many punning references to the intoxicating bottle (as a double
  of the book) made by Stephano, Trinculo, and Caliban (II.ii.120–44;
  III.ii.62–79; IV.i.206–15);
- the references by Ferdinand, Miranda, and Prospero himself to Prospero's "passion," "distemper," and "infirmity" (IV.i.142–63);
- Prospero's final reference to Caliban as "disproportioned in his man-
  ners / As in his shape" (V.i.290–91);
- Prospero's promise to make a gift of his life story at the conclusion of
  the play (V.i.303–7).

These are only some of the more blatant examples of Greenaway's surgical
excision from the Shakespearean text of its more ambiguous or ambivalent
references to the "disproportion" of Prospero's identity, the methods of colo-
nialization, the intersubjective reciprocity of gift giving and storytelling,
not to mention the early modern rise of woman's self-definition. It is fitting,
to refer briefly to the subsequent representation of Miranda as "an innocent sent to destroy the fiercest prude,"[12] that Greenaway not only silences
her sometimes wily words but also superimposes on her face the signatory
image of Prospero's inkwell as she enters his cell for the first time. In word
and vision, she bears the mark of her father's writing and her director's editing. Instead of calling attention to the overtures made by the text to the
seams of difference, the many textual cuts in *Prospero's Books* function to
provide the viewer with a translation of the text in keeping with Greenaway's

equation of Shakespeare, Gielgud, and Prospero as the patriarchal masters of *logos* and the many baroque coordinates of a universalizing point of view.

Such cross-identification is one of the most clearly identifiable baroque traits of Greenaway's translation. Through just such cross-identification the acting Subject, John Gielgud, comes to represent the indivisible itself— the soul or the monad as a representation of the *concentration, accumulation,* and *convergence* of all that might be both interior and exterior to it in mind and body. These predicates of individuality, *concentration, accumulation,* and *convergence* are what Deleuze understands to be fundamental to early modern attempts to grapple with emergent concepts of subjectivity. In *The Fold,* for instance, Deleuze reflects on the Leibnizian notion of compossibility through which "every individual monad expresses the same world in its totality although it only clearly expresses a part of this world, a series or even a finite sequence."[13] Similarly, in his earlier work *Difference and Repetition,* Deleuze emphasizes the "single centeredness" of representation through which the subject, that emergent phenomenon of early modern philosophy, comes to reflect the infinity of representations "by ensuring the convergence of all points of view on the same object or the same world, or by making all moments properties of the same Self."[14] Viewers of *Prospero's Books* need look only to Greenaway's procedures of Shakespearean translation to recognize the method of "single centeredness" sustaining the deliberate cross-identification between Prospero, Shakespeare, and Gielgud and their control of the book, the monad, and the many subjects of difference firmly fixed within the masterful economy of this composite point of view. It is telling, in this context, that the narrative of *Prospero's Books* is motivated and framed by an opening montage of cursive text from later in the play that Prospero reads in voice-over: "knowing I lov'd my books, he furnished me from mine own library with volumes that I prize above my Dukedom." Even though Shakespeare's text makes it quite clear that Prospero's love of books led to his exile ("me, poor man, my library / Was dukedom large enough" [I.ii.109–110]), the film's excision of this qualification at the outset presents an unambiguous picture of Prospero's books as the ultimate source of perspective and power on the island—and perhaps elsewhere. The fact that cross-identification is grounded in the love of text from the start of the film exemplifies the baroque system of power understood since Foucault, Marin, Deleuze, and Buci-Glucksmann to locate being in the masterful field of reading. "We're no longer seeing, we're reading," writes Deleuze, in reflecting on how "Leibniz begins to use the word 'to read' at once as the inner act in the privileged region of the monad, and as the act of God in all of the monad itself."[15]

In Shakespeare and Greenaway, Prospero displays his powers of reading to rule over an anachronistic Manichaean world of light and dark, good and evil, cultured and native, us and them that is divided into the three segments of time: the past, the present, the future. Most spectacular about Greenaway's mise-en-scène is how it capitalizes on the panoramic nature of Prospero's visions to engineer conceptual order in an otherwise fractured society. Prospero seems always to be situated at the pinnacle of perspective of even the most chaotic of visions and happenings. At the opening of the first section of the film, the past, he sits writing/reading in the quiet of his cell, as if distanced from the violence of his projections of the chaotic tempest while his cinematic double traverses the busy, noisy, and windswept halls of his palace. In section 43, Prospero peers into the deep watery pit of Caliban and shouts down as his voice echoes back off the high wall of a crumbling tower of decaying brick and concrete—this postindustrial edifice is covered by a ladder of rusting iron hoops and rises out of the sludgy brown water made dank by the historical misdeeds of the future, not to mention the vicissitudes of the death drive. Prospero moves into the present by inviting Miranda, in section 44, to witness Ferdinand's arrival on the island from a detached post above a curiously exotic panorama conjoining the broad landscapes of Rubens, the sharply raked pyramids of Kircher, and the perpetually ripening cornfields of Breughel. Similarly, Prospero orchestrates the shaky arrival of the shipwrecked courtiers while perched high above them in the dark opening of the steepest of pyramids from where the camera follows his gaze downward until it rests on the scene of the melancholic arrival of Alonso and his court at ground level. Both from the quiet of his study and the distance of his surveillance posts, Prospero orchestrates a complex economy of symmetries and exchanges through which his panoramic vision enacts the collective memory of a total mobilization of the past, present, and future.

Readers of the cinema books of Gilles Deleuze may recognize in such a cinematic cross-identification and systematization of vision the colonial stuff of classical cinema. As Deleuze understands the panoramic visions of such a cinema, its movement-images are geared for the representation of the resemblance and association of images in a way that combines metaphor and remembrance to extend beyond the individual constructs of cinematic dream for the actualization of collective memory and utopic gain. Like that of Prospero, the vision of classical cinema is said to be organized around the projection and imprint of a commonly understood cause to be realized in the future for the collective good: "the whole was the open."[16] The panoramic mise-en-scène of collective memory in *Prospero's Books* may well provide Greenaway with a cinematic equivalent of the Leibnizian formula so dear to Deleuze for its nomadism, "we're no longer seeing, we're reading."

SNAP, CRACKLE, AND POP: SERIAL CHAO-ERRANCY

Application of the baroque formula of reading to either Shakespeare or Greenaway will always entail consideration of the dynamics of translation. In the Deleuzian sense of the Baroque, "to have or to possess is to fold, in other words, to convey what one contains 'with a certain power.'"[17] But just as Shakespeare's play equates print culture with translations of European mastery, collective memory, and the concomitant rise of capitalistic exchange, its adaptation by Peter Greenaway is anchored even more deeply in what Deleuze appreciates as the baroque *crisis* of property that may well disturb the certainty of power. While Greenaway certainly emphasizes the textual power of cross-identification and collective vision in *Prospero's Books,* his excessive stylization of Prospero's obsession with books can be said to open his film to the many paradoxes of the Baroque. Most significantly, the centrality of Prospero's mastery is offset, I suggest, by the baroque paradox most fascinating to Deleuze: that of a visceral cultural trauma stemming from the growth of new machines in the social field and the discovery of new living beings in the organism. Not satisfied with a simple translation of Prospero's capitalist equation of vision and self (an eye for an I), Greenaway displaces the certainty of any perspectival coherence of *The Tempest* with an invigorating electronic proliferation of what he calls "the chaos of visual realities."[18] Stretching the volume of the pictorial screen in all dimensions, the allegorical proliferation of books, pictures, nudity, bestiality, rhythm, sound, music, line, color, and space implodes the cross-identifications of baroque culture in *Prospero's Books* and loosens the liminal grids separating its expanding population of texts and readers. Rather than merely presenting the metaphor of Prospero as a collective cultural translator "who rules subjects by the book," Greenaway screens baroque subjectivity as the traumatic plight of cinema's multitudinous readers who remain attracted and divided by the thoughtful crises of the differend.[19] It is along this nexus of the Baroque that I would like to trace the further affinities of Peter Greenaway and Gilles Deleuze. How might the preoccupation of Deleuze with something he calls "le baroque," a phenomenon of both early modern culture and cinema, correspond to Greenaway's sense of the cinematic challenge of his film: "how to organize the multiplication of points of view in *Prospero's Books* . . . a consideration of 'you are what you read'"?[20]

Nowhere has the baroque legacy of the printing press been visualized more imaginatively than in Greenaway's energetic contrast of the quiet solitude of Prospero's reading cell (patterned after the platform writing room in da Messina's painting of St. Jerome, but not after Simon Biggs's 1993 *Portrait of a Young Man*) with his loud, mannerist printing hall teeming with innumerable volumes, textures, colors, and figures. The chaotic energies of a newly mechanized visual culture are embodied from the outset of *Prospero's Books* by the profusion of pages swirling and floating through the expanse of the printing chamber, by the loud clanging of tools and printing press, and by the raucous and staccato slamming of huge and dusty folio bindings marking Prospero's disavowal of magic toward the end of the film. This is a graphic world in the most three-dimensional sense in which tissues, textures, dust, inks, folds, and even the new abstract sounds of bindings and presses—all the stuff of books—envelop the monad in the multiple and enigmatic sensibilities of becoming. "Not content to list and present the books that Prospero used to foster and implement his command of the island, it is necessary," writes Greenaway, "to riffle their pages, crackle-snap their spines, curl their edges and smell their glue."[21] In his description of Prospero's library, moreover, Greenaway stresses the "ambiguous confusions" of the books that "seem unable to contain their arcane knowledge" and result in "an overspill of objects and people and events."[22] The players not only suffer the overflow of arcane knowledge in this environment, they also endure the excesses of books that literally bleed, move, shake, pop up, and burn in digital cornucopia. "A Book of Motion" vibrates and bursts under its own volition and must be held down by the crystal weight of Prospero's inkwell; "The Book of Mirrors" includes eighty mirrored pages with "some covered in a film of mercury that will roll off the page unless treated cautiously";[23] "A Harsh Book of Geometry" includes geometrical diagrams that pop out of the pages as if electronic holograms; finally, "The Book of Earth" doubles as a natural early modern waste dump whose "pages are impregnated with the minerals, acids, alkalis, elements, gums, poisons, balms and aphrodisiacs of the earth."[24] Add to these motions and fluids from within the books the additive volume of the spray of Ariel's urine lent to "The Book of Water" at the opening of the film, not to mention how Caliban constantly abjects Prospero's realm of knowledge by spraying the master's tomes with vomit, shit, piss, mud, and other ambiguous liquids. In all of these cases, the books function as mixed-media environments for the chaotic expression of the senses. Greenaway understands the chaos of these pages to enfold all sensual realms as exemplified by "an assortment of half-seen succubae and incubi [that] cavort, tumble and flap-jack on the white papers. All knowledge is erotic to the desirous. In this particular library, though the sexual organs are primarily masculine, the vaginal creases of the interior spine of the books and the billowing curves of the pages themselves are indubitably feminine."[25] These curvy pages and billowing folds both personify the phallocentric worldview of Shakespearean theater while lending a particularly visceral, even erotic, sense to their mental incorporation.

Just as the books, pages, and folds of Prospero seem always to bear the physical traces of the corporeal acts of their making, viewing, reading, desiring, or abjecting, their fictional elements are personified by the very creatures who adore or resist them. As Greenaway understands the island of Prospero, it is a textual place

> where the indigenous spirits are persuaded to impersonate classical mythological figures, where Prospero dresses like a Venetian doge, where Caliban dances and there are four Ariels to represent the elements, and the world is appreciated and referenced with the architecture, paintings and classical literature Prospero has imported. With such a fabric, it will be no surprise that it is an island full of superimposed images, of shifting mirrors and mirror-images—true mir-ages—where pictures conjured by text can be as tantalisingly substantial as objects and facts and events, constantly framed and re-framed.[26]

In the exuberant plasticity of "mir-ages," *Prospero's Books* thus shifts its gears from the theatrical single-centeredness of representation to the cinematic multiplication of motions, senses, pictures, and time. In conjoining Shakespearean theatricality, baroque visual culture, and cinematic innovation, Greenaway shifts the dramatic emphasis from books to their mirrors, residues, and movements, thereby making room for the displacements of representation. "Such movement, for its part," insists Deleuze, "implies a plurality of centres, a superposition of perspectives, a tangle of points of view, a coexistence of moments which essentially distort representation. . . . Chao-errancy is opposed to the coherence of representation; it excludes both the coherence of a subject which represents itself and that of an object represented."[27]

The "true mir-ages" haunting the indivisibility of Prospero-Gielgud-Shakespeare may be understood best as surfacing in relation to Greenaway's "little facetious joke about the 24 books—Godard suggested that cinema was truth 24 frames a second."[28] That is, rather than read *Prospero's Books* as a translation of conventionalized theatrical representation, perhaps we would be served better by contemplating its specificity in view of the seriality of cinema, of electronic mir-ages in motion. Seriality well could be recognized as the dominant signature of Greenaway's work in cinema. Since his first full-length film, *The Falls* (1980), Greenaway has experimented with the impact of serial narratives and imagery—from the serial representation of the ninety-two victims of "A Violent Unknown Event" in *The Falls* to the systematic staging of Prospero's twenty-four books. Readers familiar with Greenaway's design practices and storyboards know how frequently he works in abstract series of painterly color-fields to plot the cinema text rather than rely on the more traditional narrative method of line and figure. These practices come together in his many large-scale projects of mixed media on paper on which he frequently relies to ponder the importance of seriality for cinema. In a series of 1989 pieces, for instance, Greenaway experiments with variable color-fields divided into separate page-sized grids, four to six across and four down. Splotchy, uneven colors, scratchy lines, and graffitilike text à la Twombly are enfolded within the grid or exceed the frame in dialogue with the elusiveness of cinematic procedures of framing and folding. It is from this series that viewers are treated to the arcane principles of framing that so regularly disrupt the panoramic memory of *Prospero's Books*. "The investigation started," he writes concerning *A Framed Life* (1989), "with serious intent in the making of *Death in the Seine* and persists in the constant reframing in *Prospero's Books*. There are many different vocabularies at work here—a filmic vocabulary of fading and mixing, an animator's vocabulary of clipping and pasting, a compositor's vocabulary of spacing and margins and perhaps even a sheet-metal worker's vocabulary of welding and drilling."[29] Greenaway understands the difference of vocabularies to relate to the ambiguous rendering of cinematic framing. This is the point of a sixteen-panel piece, *Frame Catalogue* (1989), that resembles the storyboards of *Prospero's Books*:

> The painter can pick his own frame, the film-maker is not so lucky. Having made a selection from the small number of film ratios possible, careful composition of a picture into the corners of a frame and right to the very edges is still not dependable when projected. Exact symmetries are not to be relied upon. Tolerances must be permitted. Hence the concept of the floating edge.[30]

Finally, this serial experimentation with frame, color, and edge produces another piece, *Proportional Representation* (1989), whose twenty-six variable grids plot Greenaway's own relation to the film he was in the midst of editing or, I should say, reading:

> There are twenty-six volumes in *Prospero's Books*—a film adaptation of "The Tempest"—and although all have influenced Prospero's thinking they have done so in varying proportions—this is a consideration, constantly adjusted in shape and colour as the film was edited, to evaluate the different influences of each book.[31]

Whether on paper or celluloid, seriality for Greenaway decentralizes point of view and panoramic vision to foreground the floating edges of projection, the constant adjustment of proportion, and the vocabularies of fading and mixing—in relation to both the Subject and the cinema. It is in this sense that the Subject of cross-identification fades before Greenaway's facetious joke about Prospero's twenty-four books—that truth at twenty-four frames per second is serial, not focal.

Curiously, it is in this same context of the montage of the floating edge and its elusive depth of field that Deleuze relies most heavily on baroque analogies to explain cinema's shift from the panorama of movement-image to the depth, volume, and duration of image-time. Rather than remain bound to the interiority of identity and its logics of association, resemblance, analogy, and metaphor, serial images are marked as independent from reductions to the same by the irreducible difference of the false resemblance of their spacings, markings, edges, and colors. In contrast to classical cinema's trust in "the whole was the open," modern cinema, as Deleuze sees it, shifts the paradigm to "the whole is the outside."[32] What counts is the *interstice* between images through which "each image is plucked from the void and falls back into it."[33]

It is crucial to note that Deleuze understands this shift to affect the image only insofar as the interstice is inscribed in the seriality or difference of duration and time. Partially in dialogue with Welles's revolutionary experiments with depth of field, in which "the volume of each body overflows any given plane *[plan]*, plunging into or emerging from the shadow and expressing the relationship of this body with the others located in front or behind,"[34] Deleuze reads modern cinema as profiting from a move away from the centralized truth-content of movement and panorama to the constant adjustment of a more democratic space and depth. Thus providing for an "art of masses," the new depth of field stages the differential of space and time in contrast to the equation of place and subject; it engages repetition rather than representation; and it frames the disparate as opposed to the identical.[35] Through the excessiveness of its theatricality, moreover, this new depth of field foregrounds time as the central region of a cinematic "set of non-localizable connections, always from one plane to another, which constitutes the region of past or the continuum of duration."[36] It is precisely in this context, adds Deleuze, that "the term 'baroque' is literally appropriate."[37] Or, once again, as Deleuze puts it in *The Fold:* "the Baroque is linked to a crisis of property, a crisis that appears at once with the growth of new machines in the social field and the discovery of new living beings in the organism."[38]

It should be recalled that the French term "la propriété," although generally understood in today's postindustrial world to denote "property," had currency in the seventeenth century as an ontological signifier of character in the sense of qualities belonging exclusively to an individual. The crisis of property so marked by Greenaway is, in this context, foremost an ontological one through which the Subject is confronted by the nonlocalizable exteriority of serialization, "the whole is the outside." As I mention in chapter 3, Deleuze always returns rather ambivalently to Leibniz's notion of incompossibility to explain this complex point.[39] In dwelling most explicitly on the serial nature of post-Leibnizian incompossibility in *Difference and Repetition* and *Cinema 2: The Time-Image*, Deleuze contrasts Leibniz's example of different points of view on one town, "not-necessarily true pasts," with the bifurcating fabulations of seriality, "incompossible presents," through which each series tells completely different stories that unfold simultaneously.[40] Deleuze is insistent in *Difference and Repetition* about the essential nature of

> the simultaneity and contemporaneity of all the divergent series, the fact that all coexist. From the point of view of the presents which pass in representation, the series are certainly successive, one "before" and the other "after." It is from this point of view that the second is said to *resemble* the first. However, this no longer applies from the point of view of the chaos which contains them, the object = x which runs through them, the precursor which establishes communication between them or the forced movement which points beyond them: the differenciator always makes them coexist.[41]

The forced movement, or "chao-errancy," of seriality, Deleuze adds in *Cinema 2,* results in a "crise de la propriété," which knows no solution but only a pause or a delay, say, within twenty-four frames a second.

FROM MIRRORICAL TRAUMA TO WORLD-MEMORY

In *Prospero's Books,* the dynamics of seriality frequently enacts a critical diegetic pause through which divergent series of cultural points of view enter into the field of representation. Throughout the film, for instance, the stuff of illusions, dreams, and cultural traumas are presented to the viewer through a series of mirrors held aloft by newly discovered minions and spirits born from the machinery of Roman/Greek/Renaissance mythology. The excessive repetitiveness of Greenaway's cast of supporting minions and their constant framing and reframing of shifting mirrors and mirror images frequently enacts his displacement of the Shakespearean text for a parade of mir-ages at twenty-four frames a second. At the outset of Greenaway's film, Prospero leafs through *A Book of Mirrors,* whose serial content, summarized in voice-over, reflects the divergence of incompossibility:

> Some mirrors simply reflect the reader, some reflect the reader as he was three minutes previously, some reflect the reader as he will be in a year's time, as he would be if he were a child, a woman, a monster, an idea, a text or an angel. One mirror constantly lies, one mirror sees the world backwards, another

upside down. One mirror holds onto its reflections as frozen moments infinitely recalled. One mirror simply reflects another mirror across a page.
There are ten mirrors whose purpose Prospero has yet to define.[42]

This mirrorical book helps to define the analytical framework of *Prospero's
Books,* which is layered both in vision and narration around similar series
notable for their divergence. The enigmatic temporal coexistence, or chao-
errancy, of its seriality can be traced in *Prospero's Books* through the varying fields of representation depicted by Greenaway's many mir-ages.

At the beginning of the film, an electronic video overlay on top of the
silvery pages of *A Book of Mirrors* presents the image of the mariners in
peril. The specter of their peril is given greater representational constancy
as it becomes transferred onto the plane of a mirror-image of the night-
marish tempest disturbing Miranda in her sleep. Similar mirror-images soon
present detailed visualizations of the pillage of Prospero's villa in Milan, from
the massive destruction of Prospero's library to the excessive rape of his
Milanese women, none of which is mentioned by Shakespeare's Prospero
who limits his account of the exile from Milan to mention of its enforce-
ment by "a treacherous army" (I.ii.128). Mirrors frequently positioned at
anamorphic angles, to foreground the curiosities of vision, not only frame
representations of Ariel's magic on the island but also screen the primal shots
of both the pregnant and dead mother of Miranda (who is strikingly absent
in the play),[43] as well as excessively racist and misogynist imaginings created
by Greenaway from composite fantasies of the textual and artistic past. For
instance, Greenaway looks to the baroque future in citing Felicien Rops's
nineteenth-century painting of *Pornocrates* as the source of his representation of the grotesque Sycorax and her birth of Caliban who, being more
piglet than human, is "produced in a welter of blood and pus and mag-
gots and the sound of buzzing flies."[44] In the depiction by Rops, Pornocrates parades a pig on a leash, and she is wearing only full-length back gloves
and matching knee-high hose. This unflattering specter is but one of many
sadomasochistic images retrieved by Greenaway from the composite historical archive.

Perhaps the most troubling confusion of fantasy and reality, the past and
present, especially in today's age of immigration wars, is the series depicting Alonso's daughter, Claribel, abandoned and isolated among the dark-
skinned court of Tunis—a representation to which *The Tempest* merely

alludes. The series culminates in the traumatic pictorialization of the blood-ied crotch of Mirabel that appears to have been rudely violated by the King of Tunis. In the same mirror-image, Tunis stands dominant above Claribel and parades the pride of his massive black virility as his body is caressed by the massaging hands of dark harem women. Functioning much like a mirror-image of the erotic Egypt of *Antony and Cleopatra,* this har-rowing vision of miscegenation packs the unwanted rhetorical force, as Greenaway explains it, "of a 1600s European fantasy of the Near Eastern Orient."[45] Still another disturbing series of nondiegetic mirror-images de-picts Stephano dressed as a king and Caliban as a viceroy; these images are followed by an excessively violent vision of Stephano's rape of a limp Mir-anda. Recollective of the sexual violence characteristic of Greenaway's ear-lier film, *The Cook, the Thief, His Wife, and Her Lover* (1989), such moving pictures of misogyny and racism must be understood as exceptionally gra-tuitous images in any adaptation of *The Tempest,* as a moral "crise de la propriété"—unless they are recalled in the enigmatic contexts of, say, the slaughter of MacDuff's innocents in *King Lear* or the Witches' mirroring mirages of violent succession in *Macbeth* or the violating imaginings of other Shakespearean plays such as *Measure for Measure* and *Titus Andron-icus.* While Greenaway's constant parade of violent misogyny and colonial racism deeply troubles contemporary sensibilities, it can be said to lend to his adaptation of *The Tempest* an uncanny entry into the depth of the in-compossible visual field of fiction, fantasy, and projection enveloping Pros-pero and his early modern contemporaries.

   Indeed, Prospero frequently finds himself reflected back in the mirrorical field he faces, as if he too is arrested by the return of his gaze at the com-plex miscegenation of his own visual culture. Like his viewers, Prospero, whom Greenaway says "can slip time and borrow and quote the future,"[46] is caught within the temporal folds of visual fantasy—past, present, and future. And much like contemporary readers of *The Tempest,* Prospero fre-quently finds himself seduced and betrayed by the same problematic social structures with which he may have unwittingly identified in reading book 24, "Thirty-Six Plays by Shakespeare." While Prospero may appear to de-nounce Sycorax for her enslavement of Ariel, for example, he seems to have few qualms about his own indenturing of Ariel, Caliban, and Ferdi-nand. Indeed, his careless disregard for human rights on this utopic isle sim-ply mirrors, in *Prospero's Books,* his recollected vision of the shackled slaves who fit in so naturally with the social landscape of Antonio's investiture as Duke of Milan by the King of Naples. Such fluid passage from the freedom of utopia to the cultural subjugation of Europe is lent added figural force by the film's quick cut to "A Book of Utopias" following Sebastian's racially Eurocentric reprimand of Alonso for the loss of his son: "Sir, you may thank yourself for this great loss, / That would not bless our Europe with your daughter, / But rather lose her to an African" (II.i.121–23). The visual "Utopias" through which Prospero leafs are none other than those Native American scenes depicted by Theodor de Bry's infamous 1590 engravings that illustrate Thomas Hariot's *A Briefe and True Report of the Newfoundland of Virginia*. Sensitive to the visual tradition of cultural miscegenation represented by these engravings, Greenaway links these images to his sexualized representation of Tunis (which precedes and follows their appearance in the film) while calling attention in his film script to de Bry's alteration of the original watercolors by John White:

> The original John White drawings drawn in the 1580s—one suspects—were ethnically accurate . . . but his European engraver has toned them down to suit European sensibilities—and made the Indians fit the classical tradition. At the same time as increasing their sexuality, the engraver has also made them more "decent" to a European eye.[47]

Greenaway's film also shows that he is unusually sensitive to how de Bry's engravings highlight the flawed miscegenation of Utopia itself. During Prospero's voice-over of Gonzalo's "Golden Age" monologue (II.i.148–68), he again flips through the pictures in "A Book of Utopias." This time he views the nude, tattooed figures at the back of Hariot's *Virginia* depicting "the Pictes which in the Old tyme dyd habite one part of the great Bretainne."[48] These curiously fascinating historical images show the utopically sexualized savage to be just as Old as New, just as native to Britain as to Virginia.

   The trauma of cultural miscegenation, whether textual or visual, is thus carefully depicted by Greenaway to encroach upon, to inhabit, Prospero's dream of utopia. Although Prospero attempts to transcend trauma and its transference in the present by dividing his script into past, present, and future, he bequeaths his enigmatic text, *The Tempest,* to Other readers of the future just as he is shaped by the past visions of Theodor de Bry. The representative power of this disturbing play is acknowledged by Prospero who leaves an empty space for this script at the beginning of his twenty-fourth book of Shakespeare's collected works, that canonical series of plays whose sexual and colonial miscegenation we, the future Other, would rather not already have needed and devoured so fervently at so many different times in our social field.

Deleuze would think it no coincidence that fantasy and trauma are marked so radically in *Prospero's Books* by the serial interstices of mir-age and simulacrum. For it is the traumatic chaos of pause and delay that Deleuze appreciates for creating a space and dynamism for the errancy of incompossible series, for the difference between series in radical abstraction from their empirical succession in time. When Deleuze reflects on seriality in *Difference and Repetition,* his remarks on narrative, time, and divergence take him right to the primal scene of fantasy that *is* the delay of the pure form of time in which before and after coexist.

> If it is no longer possible in the system of the unconscious to establish an order of succession between series—in other words, if all series coexist—then it is no longer possible to regard one as originary and the other as derived, one as model and the other as copy. For it is in the same movement that the series are understood as coexisting, outside any condition of succession in time, and as *different,* outside any condition under which one would enjoy the identity of a model and the other the resemblance of a copy.[49]

Framed by the opening cries of a sleeping adolescent disturbed by the primal scenes of her dreams, the coexistence of traumatic mir-ages in *Prospero's Books,* whether materialized as the crisis of books, the simulacrum of mirrors, or the confusion of time, has a peculiarly arresting effect on identity and representation in *Prospero's Books.* The enigmatic motions of trauma, I wish to suggest, are what enfold the dominant cross-identifications and collective memories of the perfect monad, Gielgud-Prospero-Shakespeare, into the post-Leibnizian specter of ambiguous elements common to many worlds and to many corresponding individuals. This is particularly notable toward the end of the film when, for the first time, three of the four Ariels pen the play themselves. The direct impact of this moment is to transform Prospero from distanced writer to feeling reader of the words written by the Ariels and scrolled on the screen to be devoured by author and spectator alike: "Your charm so strongly works 'em, / That if you now beheld them, your affections / Would become tender" (V.i.17–19). The transformative effect of reading (his own text) so sensitizes Prospero to the discovery of new living beings in the organism that he then drowns his books and frees the colonized Ariel.

Through Prospero's accumulation of the effects of trauma as feedback from his bookish representations of the Other, the film confuses the collective memory of the past with that paradox of thought championed by Deleuze in *Cinema 2: The Time-Image:* "the different levels of past no longer relate to a single character, a single family, or a single group, but to quite different characters as to unconnected places which make up a world-memory."[50] World-memory encompasses for Deleuze the intensive cinematic encounter with the demonic sign bearers of the interval that dislocates "the same," "the identical," and "the similar" in the groundless future of the eternal return. In this ultimate synthesis of past, present, and future,

> the present is no more than an actor, an author, an agent destined to be effaced; while the past is no more than a condition operating by default. The synthesis of time here constitutes a future which affirms at once both the unconditioned character of the product in relation to the conditions of its production, and the independence of the work in relation to its author or actor.[51]

The promise of a world-memory independent of the coherence of an authorial subject is staged by the conclusion of Greenaway's film when Prospero tosses all of his prized tomes one by one into the corrosive waters of Caliban's pool. Reminiscent of Caliban's purposeful desecration of books at the opening of the film, the prized tomes brought from Milan disintegrate, explode, evaporate, and melt in the midst of the phantasmatic intensity of the demon's pool. All of the books seem to have vanished until Caliban, of all characters, surfaces from under the water to preserve for posterity the last two books whose rough magic their author here abjures, Shakespeare's folio and the manuscript just completed, *The Tempest*. This unexpected action transforms Caliban from passive servant to active reader, from being kept as the Other of culture to being the keeper of the cultural Other. The suggestion of a brave new world of previously colonized readers thus ushers in the promise of a world-memory of incompossible subjects and sites. As also evidenced by the postwar proliferation of experimental Shakespeare on film and in new media, from Welles, Kozintsev, and Godard to Jarman, White, Rogala, and Vivaria.net, the new world-memory of Shakespeare is marked not so much by the coherence of authorial perspective and cultural patrimony as by the intensity, disparity, dissemblance, and *différend* of cinematic nomadism and its chao-errancy. Through radical transformations of the conditions of Shakespearean production, moreover, these directors join in pact with Caliban the reader "through trance or crisis," as Deleuze says of the emergent promise of minority cinema, "to constitute an assemblage which brings real parties together, in order to make them produce collective utterances as the prefiguration of the people who are missing."[52]

DIGITAL MACHINES

A particularly striking feature of *Prospero's Books,* is how constructively it enfolds world-memory in the unresolved problem of the Baroque. The crisis of property continues to be posed as an issue not only via the discovery of new living beings in the organism but also, and most crucially for Greenaway, in relation to the attendant discovery of new cinematic machines in the social field. Few filmmakers with strong interests in Shakespeare have ventured as daringly as has Greenaway into experimentation with the visual machineries of cinema, television, and digitality that realize the "two essential aims" that Deleuze claims for the arts: "the subordination of form to speed, to the variation of speed, and the subordination of subject to intensity or to affect, to the intense variation of affects."[53] It must be understood that what I have been claiming as the subordination of cross-identification (the Subject) to the traumas of intensity and affect is enfolded entirely, as Leibniz would say, in Greenaway's machineries of spectacle.

Perhaps Greenaway's interest in the baroque machineries of dramatic representation is what led him to *The Tempest* in the first place. The aura of Miranda's brave new world is lent its final enchanting cast in *The Tempest* by her experience of the spectacular wedding masque whose staging at court in 1611 we can imagine to have been accompanied by grand machineries described by the likes of Inigo Jones. It is significant, by the way, that Greenaway claims to have written "a script called 'Jonson and Jones,' about the relationship of Ben Jonson and Inigo Jones in making masques for the Jacobean court."[54] In the play, Prospero stages the masque as a means of presenting a controlled allegorical tableau of matrimonial jointure[55] and the wonders of his artistry. "So rare a wondered father and a wife / Makes this place paradise" (IV.i.123–24). Yet the spectacular wonder of Prospero's masque is especially significant, I would argue, for its subordination through variation and speed of this same "wondered father" to the intensity of its affect. Even Prospero is rendered so dumb by the spectacular variations of the masque that he forgets momentarily the festering threat of Caliban's rebellion. The dramatic effects of his instructions to Ariel, "Incite them to quick motion" (IV.i.39), can be said to entrap all spectators, author and spectator alike, in the chao-errancy of intense motion and the baseless fabric of vision.[56]

Keeping with the formula of cross-identification, Greenaway takes his lead from Prospero in staging a wedding masque of numerous mythological characters (the past) and newfound natives (the present) who pass swiftly by the prosperous couple (the future) while presenting them with wedding gifts of quick motion that symbolize the conjoined blessings of colonial culture. Or more accurately, the speedy offerings of exotic presents are made in "quick time"—in the form of vibrant electronic mir-ages constructed by Greenaway through his inventive experimentation with the new digital machinery of the electronic graphic "paintbox."[57] Although novel at the release of *Prospero's Books,* what Greenaway calls "the newest Gutenberg technology"[58] is now a common digital fixture in studios of virtual and cinematic art. The electronic stylus of the digital paintbox permits the artist to draw freely on a sensitive keypad whose functions are organized by a computerized menu of stylistic offerings (draw, paint, brush-size, stencil, overlay, flood, mask, etc.). Combined with the liberating 1.78 ratio of the new Japanese video screen, Greenaway's paintbox also lent him access to a massive visual archive and library as well as a palette of a seemingly infinite variety of color and nuance. For his archive, Greenaway incorporated his painterly habits of seriality into the chao-errancy of hypervision:

> To provide a background for many possible images in the film, a library of some thousand or more small "field frames" was made—each some 8 by 6 centimetres—painted or drawn on paper in various media—paint, ink, graphite, pastel—in sequential book-form, stressing the painterly characteristics of mass, volume and colour in preference to line. Because these images were comparatively small, the enlargement necessary to make them useful also enlarged the grain and texture of the paper thereby stressing their manufacture.[59]

Throughout *Prospero's Books,* even images grounded in the most conventional of form and content are framed for the viewer by the speed and variation of Greenaway's work with the paintbox. Sometimes the cinematic mise-en-scène takes place within a virtual frame of vibrantly varying electronic shapes and colors whose intense floating edges exaggerate the demystification of film art's symmetries. At other times, the spectators cohabit with Prospero in the fantastic visual field of ancient books whose historical themes and images are sent spiraling into the four-dimensional hyper-future by means of quick time, digital montage, and electronic alteration.

Prospero's books are not there for seizure and appropriation, unless we mean by that the "trance or crisis," as Deleuze would say, of the subordination of form to the variation of speed and the subordination of subject to the intensity of affect. It is in this regard—you are what you read—that the quick motion of paintbox technology shares in the heritage of the Gutenberg revolution and the Kircher book-making machine; turning books into more books, images into more images, both technologies envelop authorial subjects in what Greenaway calls the "ambiguous confusions" of voluminous productions of new fields of knowledge whose books "seem unable to contain their arcane knowledge."[60] Through the electric variables of the paintbox, Greenaway fancifully experiments with the cohabitation of speedy motion and incompossible seriality in a way that stresses anew the baroque crisis of property by demystifying the fetishistic jointure of authorship, commodity, and manufacture.

The historical machineries of Gutenberg and the new graphic technologies, from Sony to Silicon Valley, provide both Greenaway and Deleuze with the conjoined conceptual means to delve into the enigmas of seriality that continue to position cinema on the demonic interstice of baroque incompossibility. For Greenaway, the crisis of property assumes colossal proportions in terms of the cultural struggle over the discipline of machineries of representation. The incompossible worldviews of *Prospero's Books* foreground the struggle over cinematic chaos that this self-explanatory, polemical passage from Greenaway links directly to the ongoing crisis of property:

> Painting, the theater, and as like as not, opera and ballet, and certainly the cinema, and certainly television, exist disciplined within a fixed frame. And the frame is a visual straightjacket. Sometimes, perhaps, the frame can be adjusted a little. A painter can choose his rectangle, though for the last four

hundred years he has done so with remarkable conservatism. The proscenium arch grows taller and wider and even thicker according to architectural taste, but it rarely revolts, explodes, expands. The film-maker has just a little leeway. He, or she, can expand sideways into cinemascope. Once upon a time there were other curious film formats—but now film-makers are restricted within the close confines of a rectangle with the proportions of 1 to 1.66. Television is ubiquitously boxy—with a proportion of 1 to 1.33. There is indeed a television disturbance on the horizon of a rectangular 1 to 1.78— but at the moment it is far away in Japan, and Western conservatism, if not Ludditism, is holding it presently at bay, fearful of disturbing the profitable but limited status quo. And we all concur to the conservatism of these limits. The conveniences of such parameters are a truce between maker and viewer. This is how we restrict and confine, crop, cut, shear, prune, chop, manacle, bind, imprison, and jail the chaos of visual realities. Of course it is very practical, helping us to standardize our various sets of expensive and buyable, sellable, marketable equipment. But it is a convention and should be open to much questioning.[61]

Deleuze concludes *Cinema 2* by reflecting similarly on the linkage of the growth of new machines in the visual field to the political chao-errancy of cinematic nomadism. As I elaborate in chapter 10, he cautions that the electronic, tele-, or video image provides the means either to transform cinema or to replace it, "to mark its death."[62] Through digital imagery, Deleuze believes, the panoramic organization of space loses the vertical privilege of direction, the screen becomes a data bank through which information replaces nature, and the "brain-city" is subject to the perpetual reorganization of world-memory.[63]

Were we to link the conclusion of *Cinema 2* to the end of *The Fold*, we would come to appreciate how such a reorganization of the chaos of visual realities constitutes for Deleuze the very conditions of baroque incompossibility. At stake for both Deleuze and Greenaway is a reconditioning of the serial around the promise of digital cinema and its projections. One result of world-memory necessitates a revision of the baroque formula from "you are what you read" to "you are how you read." A subsequent byproduct, remembering *Prospero's Books*, is the kind of destabilizing cross-identification, say, of Gielgud's Prospero and Greenaway's Caliban that Deleuze conjures in the conclusion of *The Fold*:

To the degree that the world is now made up of divergent series (the chaosmos) . . . the monad is now unable to contain the entire world as if in a closed
circle that can be modified by projection. It now opens on a trajectory or a
spiral in expansion that moves further and further away from a center. A
vertical harmonic can no longer be distinguished from a horizontal harmonic, just like the private condition of a dominant monad that produces
its own accords in itself, and the public condition of monads in a crowd that
follow lines of melody. The two begin to fuse on a sort of diagonal, where
the monads penetrate each other, are modified, inseparable from the groups
of prehension that carry them along and make up as many transitory captures. . . . They identify variation and trajectory, and overtake monadology
with a "nomadology."[64]

III.
PRESENT PAST:
DIGITALITY, PSYCHOANALYSIS,
AND THE MEMORY OF CINEMA

chapter 5

DIGITALITY AND THE MEMORY OF CINEMA: BEARING THE LOSSES OF THE DIGITAL CODE

The baroque artists know well that hallucination does not feign presence, but that presence is hallucinatory.

—GILLES DELEUZE, *The Fold: Leibniz and the Baroque*

Two overlapping curatorial projects in the late 1990s catalyzed this section's reflections on the "return" of cinema in the digital age. For the 1997 Flaherty Seminar, I cocurated with Patricia R. Zimmermann a selection of work by film and video artists who were experimenting with digital technology on platforms other than film. In addition to sessions dedicated to the CD-ROM and digitized video work by Muntadas, Reginald Woolery, Leah Gilliam, and Daniel Reeves, participants were presented with the first Flaherty salon of works on CD-ROM and the Internet that challenged the conventions of screening and spectatorship that have been nurtured by cinematic culture since the days of Robert Flaherty. The success of this modest project, whose exhibition was limited to the long weekend of this "mini" Flaherty Seminar, encouraged me to undertake a much more ambitious exhibition, "Contact Zones: The Art of CD-ROM." This international exhibition of over eighty CD-ROMs by artists from twenty countries toured for five years in the United States, Mexico, France, and Canada, with segments included in related exhibitions in China, South Africa, and the Netherlands.[1]

What left a deep impression on me during public discussions held in conjunction with these exhibitions was the keen sense expressed by many curators and artists that digitality has something creative and critical to offer to the cinematic legacy, in contrast to the ambivalence of some participants about the growth of digitized cinema. While some discussants lamented digitality as a marker of the death of cinema, a great many others lauded it for providing a catalyst for the revival of forgotten cinematic histories, for the reinvention of cinematic form, and for the sharpening of theoretical reasoning. This approbation of the digital seemed most poignant when voiced by emerging artists of color such as Gilliam and Woolery, who saw in the new technology a means for developing a reflective approach to appropriated historical footage from problematic racialized films from which we have learned to distance ourselves. They were able to capitalize on the codes of digital editing and sound production to juxtapose sequences from films like *Birth of a Nation* and *Imitation of Life* with artistic presentations that counter Hollywood's tainted historical memory of the hierarchies of race. The wide range of artistic CD-ROMs, which I continue to collect and exhibit in the Rose Goldsen Archive of New Media Art at the Cornell Library, also provided evidence of the new archival role of digital media and its sometimes uncomfortable relation to the nostalgic reminiscence of the days of Flaherty and his contemporaries in early cinema.

Resounding throughout the public discussions of these exhibitions was an enthusiastic appreciation for the coda of the digital whose terms combine and shift with the ease and fluidity of bits and bytes: appropriation/repetition/layering/simulation/retrospection. Indeed, the retrospective nature of repetition and digital coding—how initial images, forms, and narratives are refigured through their contemplative re-citation and re-presentation—consistently inscribes the new media in the memory and memorialization of its antecedents, cinema and video. Since the time of these exhibitions, a wide spectrum of publications on new independent work in digital media have emphasized the theoretical reflections between new media and early cinema, as well as artistic and curatorial projects that emphasize interaction over spectating. Dear to my heart is the 1999 special issue of *Wide Angle* on "Digitality and the Memory of Cinema" (2002), which I edited in the wake of the Flaherty Seminar and whose revised introductory remarks constitute the bulk of this chapter, which here again functions as an introductory threshold, this time to considerations of "Present Past: Digitality, Psychoanalysis, and the Memory of Cinema." That issue of *Wide Angle* includes groundbreaking essays by Maureen Turim, Patricia Zimmermann and John Hess, Margaret Morse, Sean Cubitt, George Legrady, Michele Pierson, Ross Gibson, Yvonne Spielmann, Mary Flanagan, and Joseph Milutis. They extend the digital themes most prominent in contemporary cinema and its study to a consideration of formal procedures shared by new media and historical cinema as well as to an appreciation of many of the independent artists who have extended the boundaries of digital cinema. The *Wide Angle* issue appeared on the heals of Thomas Elsaesser and Kay Hoffman's collection, *Cinema Futures: Cain, Abel, or Cable?* and Lev Manovich's influential book, *The Language of New Media,* and was followed by a special issue of *Parachute* on "écrans numériques / digital screens," not to mention the gargantuan catalogue edited by Jeffrey Shaw and Peter Weibel, *Future Cinema: The Cinematic Imaginary after Film.*[2]

Rather than follow the lead of other leading digital theorists who have lamented the passing of socially conscious art with the arrival of a digitized Hollywood,[3] I have profited from the independent scene to articulate a case for the social/formal promise of digital art and its memory of cinema. What I personally find refreshing and gratifying is the blend of formal considerations of analogy, collage, editing, special effects, and the star system with a persistent emphasis on the theoretical contributions made by recent digital artists to the critical understanding of social issues of race, gender, sexuality, and politics. Meaning to complicate the arguments of theorists such as Manovich, who maintains that cinema "has found a new life as the toolbox of the computer user,"[4] I am particularly interested in how the digital platform lends itself to a decisive program of social and aesthetic intervention while still serving, as I will suggest below, as something of a spectral crypt of the coda of cinema.

It is in the spirit of foregrounding the political edge of the dialogue between cinema and new media that I wish to open this section on "Present Past" by profiting from conceptual terms important to the work of the engaging independent artists, Gary Hill (USA), Grace Quintanilla (Mexico), Keith Piper (England), and Daniel Reeves (Scotland). I have frequently expressed my belief that artists working in the new media have accepted the critical responsibility of thinking their way into the twenty-first century.[5] I thus wish to frame this section by entering into dialogue with some of their weightier thoughts about the cryptic return of cinema in the digital age.

SITE RECITED, A PROLOGUE TO CODE AND CRAFT

Many readers will recognize "Site Recited (A Prologue)" as the title of Gary Hill's playfully mysterious videotape whose baroque pan of the memento mori of still life, from shells to skulls, languidly moves in and out of perspective to reflect on the clarity of perception and the uncertainty of its repetition.[6] The paradox of the re-turn to sight of the exceedingly slow and patient pan is clearly articulated at one moment in the tape when the sound track states unambiguously that "a boomerang effect decapitates any and all hallucinations." I would like to suggest that Gary Hill's *Site Recited (A Prologue)* presents us with something of a coda for the paradoxical topic at hand: "Digitality, Psychoanalysis, and the Memory of Cinema." Some cinematic purists, intent on maintaining the essence of celluloid cinema, could well imagine that artistic application of the digital code consists of something like a negative boomerang effect that decapitates cinematic essence and the memory of its histories. But in the wake of Hill's crystal-clear digitized scan of still-life's skull and its focusings, perhaps the beheading of hallucinations can be understood to constitute the cinematic code of the new media itself. Rendered headless would be the many hallucinations of realism (not to mention its anchorings in the studios and traditions of cinema's history) as the moving embodiment not of the thing portrayed, but of its essence in time, in the movement of cinema.[7] You might recall, in this context, how cinema was praised by its influential French theoretician, André Bazin, for freeing time from its "embalming" in photography. In contrast to cinema, writes Bazin, "photography liberates its object from temporal contingency in a way that 'embalms time' in the click of the instant and thus heightens the photograph's ontological value or 'presence.'"[8] It is hard not to be amused by how this logic has come full circle, in that digitality, the medium of virtuality, could be said to free time from the hallucination of analog movement, from the hallucination of cinema's temporal movement from point A to point B to point C. Paradoxically, Hill's tape moves freely in time to foreground how its photographic reality remains contingent on the rather anamorphic movement of the lens and its baroque tracking between here and there, then and now, now and then—the present past, hardly the pure stuff of analog movement and its documentary obsession with matching the coda of realism in the passing present.

The question confronting us, then, is "where do we locate the lure of the new media?" Might the new media be situated, however precariously, in the memory of the body of cinema, or does it float free of the prior code? Is it, as Manovich would have us believe, simply a matter of the computer conversion of data and variability whose "paradigm is concerned not with time but with space"?[9] Or might the promise of digital art dwell somewhere in the in-between, in the interstitial zone between the binaries that are shared by our cinematic, critical, and digital heritages: code and craft?[10] While the code has moved, in the digital context, from the stuff of theory to the matter of computing, it could be said to maintain a continued binary relation to the craft of artistic production. The one, code, suggests the work of criticism and theory (even in the context of computing), not to mention history and its idea, while the other, craft, denotes the work of art, the hand of the artisan, the here and now of techne. These terms may well imply something like a digital kernel and its artistic shell, with the code grounding the craft in the virtuality of Idea that can be only approximated, approached in the new, in the now, of the craft of art and software. Are we thus to be guided, once again, by the aesthetic dialectic derived from Plato in which the artisan and her crafts never quite live up to the virtual promise of Idea and his codes?

This is the slant given to the new media by many of its proponents, such as those gathered in Peter Lunenfeld's collection of essays *The Digital Dialect: New Essays on New Media*. In the introduction to the volume, "Screen Grabs: The Digital Dialectic and New Media Theory," Lunenfeld summarizes his collection's critical orientation in a way that ends up validating the Platonic divide between Idea and techne. "The digital dialectic," he writes,

> offers a way to talk about computer media that is open to the sophisticated methodologies of theory without ignoring the nuts and bolts or, better yet, the bits and bytes of their production. To repeat, the digital dialectic goes beyond examining what is happening to our visual and intellectual cultures as the computer recodes technologies, media, and art forms; it grounds the insights of theory in the constraints of practice.[11]

Now let's return to our formula, code and craft. Should we understand it to reflect Lunenfeld's mandate that so clearly aligns insight with theory and constraint with practice? Do we mean to contrast the artistic work in new media with the examination of what is happening to visual culture? Are memory and cultural study thus situated on the side of theory while digital art is set apart from culture to be limited by the constraints of practice? Should it be our critical task to go beyond examination of what is happening to our visual and intellectual cultures so that the digital dialectic might ground Idea in the constraints of practice?

If even only a proximation of the weight of such an intellectual code continues to impinge on critical practice in the digital age, then we also might wonder about the corollary binarism, cinema and new media. Does cinema provide the code of new media's craft? Is cinema, or the idea of cinema, what provides the reference for the free-floating hallucinations of new media's art? Is this what lies behind the subtitle of this section, "Digitality, Psychoanalysis, and the Memory of Cinema"? Are we crafting our sense of the new media in the shape of its fleeting cinematic core that, for its part, may never have realized itself as much more than an idea, an idea approximated but never attained due to the vicissitudes of craft?[12]

It would be rather depressing to think that our chore is simply to predict something for the twenty-first century similar to what Heidegger mourned for the twentieth century. In "The Age of the World Picture," Heidegger attributes the lost flexibility of scholarly invention and artistic craft to the "projection and rigor" of the code of modern technology and institutionalized research. Following in the wake of the loss of the gods (Nietzsche), "science becomes research through the projected plan and through the securing of that plan in the rigor of production."[13] Put simply, the rigorous replication of code dictates the plan of craft. Were we to seek a corollary discourse in the world of cinema, we need only turn to the likes of Jean-Luc Godard, who mourns the passing of cinema (the twentieth-century god) into the rigorous emptiness of the televisual (and now digital) code. "Cinema is higher than us," Godard insistently reminds us, "it is that to which we must life our eyes. When it passes into a smaller object on which we lower our eyes, cinema loses its essence."[14] But rather than simply mourn the loss of the gods through the passing of cinema, I propose that we capitalize on Godard's description of the diminished essence of cinema to think the rigorous duplication of the (digital) code. Otherwise, might the arrival of inordinate miniaturization and the advent of the new media with its thumbnails and windows signal the cinematic paradox of digitality? That to shape a digital code means to bear the loss of code itself, to carry on the legacy of cinema as the crypt of the twentieth century?

For an idea of what kind of loss I am contemplating, permit me to elaborate on the code as its stands in relation to cinema. In doing so, I hope to make clear how the cinematic code might be understood to linger in digitality as something of a crypt or a carrier of the discourse of loss, mourning, and melancholia so familiar to cinema studies.[15] There certainly is a critical tendency to follow this path in relocating the code of the new craft in the loss or continuation of cinema. I was struck, for example, by how many articles crossed my transom for the special issue of *Wide Angle* that think of digital memory in this context. Writers as different as Maureen Turim, Margaret Morse, Yvonne Spielmann, David Tafler, Sean Cubitt, Michele Pierson, and Mary Flanagan dwell on the trajectory or even the translation of the cinematic code in the new media: the legacy of montage, the legacy of the star system, the legacy of silent cinema. That is, they provide answers to the rather paradoxical task of thinking digitality as the analogue of cinematic practice and representation, as something like cinema. But rather than dwell on the pragmatic issues of production, I reflect on the conceptual significance of the new media, particularly as it corresponds to the visual procedures, ontological positions, and cultural attitudes associated with cinema. But in doing so, I mean not to separate theory from practice but rather to foreground the conceptual articulations of digital craft. As I'll make evident in discussing the work of Gary Hill and Daniel Reeves, digital cinema may create the perfect environment of morphings and time passings through which loss and its trauma can both be visualized by the artists and shared through immersion by the spectators. In a related way, as I have learned from the CD-ROMs of Grace Quintinilla and Keith Piper, the multimedia platform can provide the venue for visual and aural juxtapositions, artistic manipulations, and conceptual contrasts through which the discourse of mourning and time passing can also serve to unsettle the many codes of realism, fetishism, and national/racial pride so dear to cinema and its theorization. Even though it might be figured as cut off from cinema by the boomerang effect of digital culture, the hallucinatory cinematic code haunts the interface of digital multimedia.

BETWEEN 1 AND 0

Permit me to reformulate this paradox of digitality in the more formal terms of the cinematic code. I am thinking of the cinematic code of analogy in the sense articulated by Christian Metz in his canonical essay of 1968, "Problems of Denotation in the Fiction Film." There Metz reflects on the nature of cinematic denotation by clarifying how film is structured around the partial equations of visual and auditory analogy, by the perceptual similarity of signifiers and signifieds. Put simply, cinematic images and sounds match ideas and emotions. Film works hard to make images look and feel real. On another, more complex level, Metz emphasizes how the symbolic nature of cinematic connotation overtakes perceptual analogy as the latter accrues value through the additional meaning it receives from sociocultural codes. In these terms, consider how the white dress that lifts up over Marilyn Monroe's head, from the hot air of a sidewalk grate, becomes less a dress than the sign of a female star, the mark of the gaze, and the icon of the practice of Hollywood cinema.[16]

It is significant to the understanding of the cinematic code that Metz brings these two terms together. Both the denotation and the connotation of cinematic analogy are constitutive of a mixture of two important signifying structures: what Metz terms "specialized codes" and "cultural codes." Specialized codes are purely cinematographic signifying features: think of "montages, camera movements, optical effects, 'rhetoric of the screen,' interaction of auditory and visual elements, and so on."[17] Cultural codes, in contrast, constitute the iconographical, perceptual, and other codes of given social groups. These cultural codes are "so ubiquitous and well 'assimilated' that the viewers generally assume them to be 'natural.'"[18] Of particular importance to our consideration of the history of the code is not so much the distinction between these codes as the "modulation" of the two analogical systems. We've come to appreciate, for example, how many classical Hollywood films were coded through cinematic form to have the man assume the role of the active agent while the women often become objects of what Laura Mulvey calls "to-be-looked-at-ness."[19] What's crucial, as I've argued more extensively in *Like a Film,* is how Metz's distinction seems open to the probability that *the specialized codes of cinema have themselves become, or always already were, "naturalized" or "cultural."* In this sense, they return to cinema not as "specialized" but as cultural codes that function for the most part "within photographic and phonographic analogy."[20] I am thinking here of the sorts of cinematic codes that, writes Metz, "intrude to the film by means of perceptual analogy each time an object or an ordering of objects (visual or auditory) 'symbolizes' within the film what it would have symbolized outside of the film—that is to say, within culture."[21] One can recall the futile attempts of Godard's male protagonist in *Breathless* to model himself after Bogart (something that had to be accomplished by naturalized procedures of acting, not by digitized programs of morphing). To appreciate such a modulating relation in which the specialized discourse of film is folded back upon itself, "naturalized" as "culture," we need only recall Godard's nostalgic reference to film's miniaturized structure in and through the video monitor as something like the photo of a loved one carried with us. Were he to have written his essay in the digital moment, Metz might have told Godard that his "longing for a film, the nostalgia, the echo of a film" is actually the cinematic code itself, this time naturalized as the analogical history we wish to give to digital culture.[22]

Perhaps it is precisely something like this echo that constitutes the thoughtful spectacle of Gary Hill's digitized video *Site Recite (A Prologue)*. In reviving the baroque conventions of the memento mori, Hill capitalizes on digital clarity and its transformational possibilities to confront us with the recitation of an analog accumulation of loss. As marked by the anamorphic skull, such an accumulation of loss can be known, as Louis Marin reminds us, as nothing but a sign of representation's ephemerality. While providing a horizontal, analog pan of the still-life assemblage of memento mori, Hill inverts the clarity of perspective through the losses and gains of anamorphic perspective. The digital coding of cinematic loss is what here frustrates the analog move forward. The digital convention of temporal pause, ocular layering, and the clear separation of encoded sound and video tracks opens up a space of recitation while at the same time, I suggest, foregrounding the lasting legacy of the analog code itself. The challenge of this piece might be said to lie in its crafting of the code. For digitality, in this context, provides us with the code for confronting something of a revitalized memento mori through which we can contemplate our electronic passage through recent history and its visualization.

In his essay nodding to the digital code, "Between 1 and 0," Hill articulates this paradox in the guise of a philosophical dialogue between two characters, 1 and 0.

> 1: What you are saying is that it matters whether our foreknowing occurs exactly at the same time or whether perhaps there is a slight delay which would allow for comparison to take place. That is, that knowledge as

such, known at two different times, in this case moments of unknow-
able increments, would in fact be different knowledge.

0: Wait a second. . . . Are you suggesting that thinking might be inextricably linked to time and that a kind of leapfrogging of moments,
and the knowledge of those moments, gets compared, producing a
difference, thus enabling the leapfrogging to continue? . . .

1: I would say that if it is possible for us to have a discussion—to toggle—then it is possible that the comparison we are speaking of and
the theories surrounding it are not trivial but absolutely fundamental
to our intraweave, or perhaps at the point we had better just "call it
a game." I'm going along with our assumption from the beginning
that there can't be a binary culture because two (1 & 0) cannot forget
themselves, and therefore cannot live time, that is the time of remembering. One is always reciprocal to the Other and therefore one
always knows what state they are in and there can be no forgetting
because there can be no loss of technology: no change equals no time
equals no difference. Once there is no difference, information becomes
purely quantitative and questions cease.[23]

Perhaps it can be said, returning to the boomerang effect, that digital precision frees the momento mori from analog time and its movement forward
through its decapitation of, and juxtaposition with, the body of cinema.
Emblematic of the digital code and its liberation of hallucination from the
analog weight of history itself is the spectral image that closes Hill's digitized tape. "Imaging the brain closer than the eyes," the camera suddenly
looks out from within the inside cavity of the skull as if staging the hallucinatory reversal of encoded perspective.[24]

Decapitated by the boomerang of the loop, might not hallucination be
thought to roll freely around in the studios of new media cut off from its
anchoring in a certain history of cinematic perspective, analog temporality,
and the ordering gaze? Put otherwise, might the specter of hallucination
be thought now to haunt, in the enigmatic recombinations of digital code,
the body of cinema and its gaze, to haunt in the sense of a toggle effect? I
suggest that digitality can be said to render the momento mori anew, this
time by differentiating it from photography's "embalmed time" and cinema's
suture of temporality. Maybe we're faced with something akin to what
Lacan saw in Holbein's *The Ambassadors,* whose decapitated anamorphic

skull confronts the viewer with the surprise of death's perspective and the loss of the self-same confident gaze?[25] "The longer I wait," utters the narrative voice tracked onto Hill's digital still life,

> the more the little deaths pile up; bodily substance is no longer an excuse; too much time goes by to take it by surprise. So much remains. No doubt it can all be counted, starting with any one, continuing on with any other one until all is accounted for. A consensus is reached. It can all be shelved in all its quanti-splendor, this thing is the turf. These sightings as seen before me made up of just so many just views, nature's constituency sits with indifference to the centripidal vanishing points that mentality posits so falsely.

Already in 1968, Gilles Deleuze imagined just such an aesthetic when he theorized, in *Difference and Repetition,* "elements, varieties of relations and singular points [that] in the work or object, in the virtual part of the work or object, without it being possible to designate a point of view privileged over others."[26] Deleuze would be very quick to caution us, however, that the evacuation of a privileged point of view need not necessitate the loss of the analogue, at least in its conceptual guise as analogy and resemblance. Of course, it is quite common to understand digitality as shifting the ground of artistic craft, to continue with this metaphor, away from representation and toward virtualization, away from resemblance and toward simulation. The promise of digital aesthetics, moreover, has been understood in relation to its intensification of interactivity through which the user's physical or manual participation in the circuit of artistic presentation simulates or projects the user's own virtualizations, fantasies, and memories in consort with the artwork. But while opening the artwork to the virtual relations of digitality and enhanced interactivity, a significant number of digital craftspeople also have remained faithful to the preservation, investigation, and critical analysis of the cinematic archive and its dependence on prior codes of resemblance and analogy.[27] I have come to appreciate that analogy's loss, outside and within cinema, should constitute the central object of study in any attempt to give digital culture a history. It is in this context of looking back to the cinematic past to reach into the digital future, via the present past, that my research has prompted me to reflect on how new media incorporates earlier themes and methods of cinematic representation as a means of articulating cybernetic paradigms of craft, code, and history.

VICE VERSA: GRACE QUINTANILLA

Few, if any, multimedia projects interface with the history of cinema without assuming an ambivalent relation to the cinematic code. Of the many CD-ROMs I could choose from *Contact Zones: The Art of CD-ROM* that might illustrate this ambivalence, one seems particularly appropriate to the task at hand. A playful example is the 1999 *Vice-Versa: Presenting the Past, the Present, and the Depths of Roberto and Chelo Cobo,* by the Mexican artist Grace Quintanilla. *Vice-Versa* literally presents the miniaturized trace of cinema as something "like the photo of a loved one carried with us." Aiming "to experiment with the boundaries of traditional documentary in which the narrative structure is conceived in a linear way and predetermined by the director,"[28] Quintanilla plots the life stories of the nationally known cabaret performer, Chelo Cobo and her movie star brother, Roberto Cobo (Roberto would be most familiar to readers for his role as the young protagonist El Jaibo in Bunuel's *Los Olvidados*). Now in the twilight of their lives, they reflect back on their pasts through their meditation on recent photographs of their naked bodies that were taken by their niece, Grace. Structured not around a film, but around the psychic zone of the family photo album, the CD-ROM permits users to access historical photo and video files as well as digitally altered contemporary footage of the personages who subsequently perform nude for the camera as if acting out the nude photographs around which they nervously shaped their retrospective narratives.

To this aged brother and sister born from actor parents, the profession of acting always doubled as their primal scene. They took to acting and dancing before they could distance themselves from the mirror stage and the family code. The narrated photo novella of the CD-ROM reveals that both child actors incorporated or naturalized the codes of cinema and cabaret almost before the procedures of mimicry could be symbolized. Crucial to the CD-ROM is the digital method of morphing that Quintanilla uses to represent the ebb and flow of time through which memory confronts the subject with fantasy's retrospective traumas and pleasures.[29] Notable is the morph of footage of Chelo's first film role, as an infant of six months lying in a crib, into an image of the elder, nude Chelo curled up in the fetal position. Throughout the CD-ROM, the faces of Roberto and Chelo transform so fluidly into morphed versions of their younger and older selves that even the nude, curled-up figure of the aged Chelo looks natural-ized in the cinematic crib she occupied as an infant (Figure 6). Rather than simply "permitting history's elision and repression" through "the endlessly regenerative self-creation of morphing," as Scott Bukatman and others have argued about mainstream cinema's repetitive display of morphing,[30] Quin-tanilla's morphing is marshaled to foreground the dynamics of aleatory time and motion through which the psyche maintains a charged relation to the complexity of history's incorporation. Digital toggling between past photo albums and present moments thus confronts the user, not to mention the family subjects, with the specter of specialized codes that have become naturalized, perhaps too much so, in the aleatory zone of family history.[31]

Two aspects of this CD-ROM are particularly noteworthy to our discus-sion of the code. First is the seemingly analog structure of the piece. Users can choose between past and present photo albums that provide loops of the combined family/media history of each personage. The albums con-tain clickable photos that often come alive in video footage, bringing to

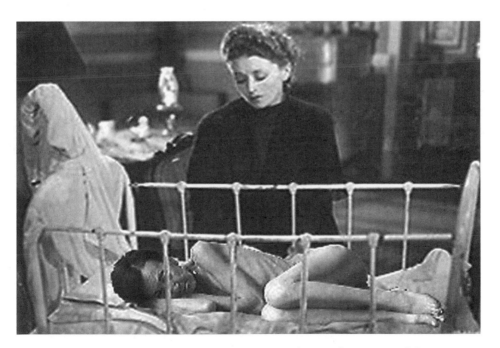

Figure 6. Grace Quintanilla, *Vice-Versa: Presenting the Past, the Present, and the Depths of Roberto and Chelo Cobo*, 1999.

life the historical still life with animation, montage, and morphing. Even though the photos appear to be arranged in chronological order, they move through artistic alteration between the present and the past, regardless of which photo album they are in. It is striking that the last page of Roberto's album presents the user with two unaltered QuickTime clips of films starring Roberto, *Los Olvidados* and *Mujeres de Teatro*. Although the cinema is positioned here as the analog culmination of the life of Roberto, not to mention the end point of this digital loop, the clips themselves seem somewhat flat and rather unnatural in comparison to their prior appropriation as digitally animated photos. While Godard would be correct to think of these miniaturizations as but the shadow of their films, they stand out forcefully here as literal specters of the multimedia interface. The miniatures, now lacking the nostalgia of their historical purity, reflect Roberto's own retrospective distance from that past, as now a remembering subject who thinks about the code that had contained him and who knows the past only in relation to its manifestation in the present.

Only when all loops of the past and present have been hit does the user of *Vice-Versa* have access to the material arranged literally on the "top shelf" of the CD's cabaret-like mise-en-scène: "the depths." Here, again, the structure suggests the kind of perspective on depth that also constitutes part of the cinematic code frequently compared to the shallowness of television and now multimedia. It promises the very profundity, for instance, that Bill Nichols has accused cybernetic systems of lacking: "The chip is pure surface, pure simulation of thought. Its material surface is its meaning, without history, without depth, without aura, affect, or feeling"[32] (how frequently do we hear television and now multimedia derided for their lack of depth?).[33] It is the depths, in *Vice Versa,* that render the user most vulnerable to the intersubjective zone characteristic of the best of CD-ROMs that dwell passionately on the very histories, affects, and feelings thought by Nichols to be negated by virtual technologies. Here the user is invited to click on the private parts of the aged nude bodies of the Cobos to learn more about them. This rather trite aspect of the CD—both the entry into depth and its passage through the procreative organs—is what paradoxically constitutes the cultural promise of this multimedia experiment. The digital clarity of these natural bodies replete with wrinkles, folds, sags, and splotches both resists the cinematic code of the sutured body of the aging star and confronts the user with a provocative reflection on the naturalness of aging.

Similarly, the process of interaction itself implicates the user in the loss of the code: from the grounding of analog vision in the gesture of the click (remember Freud's essay on the paranoid sound of the camera capturing the primal scene?) and the playful foreshortening of voyeurism's distance to the challenge of the viewer to act out the rendering of the whole body into its fetishistic parts. And what's the result of the click, of the entry into performative commentaries of the actors on their autobiographical relation to specific body parts? Really, and here's the digital rub, really nothing other than more of the same contemporary, burlesque footage that had already confronted the user in the prior albums of past and present. Here the depths pun not simply on the loss of life but more importantly on the loss of the code. What we see no longer reads according to the naturalized codes of cinema and its melancholy relation to the body that brought us to it. In its place stands the performative gesture of hyperrealistic hallucination, in which the taboo site of the aged body usurps the public and private codes of its secrecy and horror.[34] There is something about these dancing, winking, undulating body parts that revivify the modulating relations of the cinematic code, that reanimate cinema's memento mori in the playful codes of digital mimicry and mime.[35]

RELOCATING THE REMAINS: KEITH PIPER

Let me be cautious, however, not to leave the impression that the digitized code simply privileges burlesque and mime. While this is clearly the case with a wide range of wonderfully ludic CD-ROMs, from Spain's *Let's Tell Lies* (1999) by Christina Casanova and Australia's *Cyberflesh Girlmonster* (1995) by Linda Dement to the American Isabel Chang's *Virtual Makeovers for the Post-Identity Cyborg* (1999), an equally significant number of CD-ROMs and digital installations rely on the zones of digitality to evince the experience of passing itself. How trauma leaves its mark on the history of the subject and its inscription of loss in cinema, video, and installation are the subject of a wide range of digital art, from Australian installations and performances such as *Shock in the Ear* by Norie Neumark (1998), Suzanne Treister's *No Other Symptoms: Time Travelling with Rosalind Brodsky* (1998), and Jill Scott's *Immortal Duality* (1997) to CD-ROMs such as *The Crazy, Bloody Female Center* (1999), from Americans Nina Menkes and the Labyrinth Project; *Troubles with Sex, Theory and History* (1997), from Slovenians

Marina Grzinic and Aina Smid; and *Natural Selection* (1998), from Britain's Mongrel. I will dwell further on this difference between the playfulness of digital burlesque and the deadly seriousness of digital loss by turning my attention to the 1997 CD-ROM by Keith Piper, a leading figure in Britain's Black Arts movement. *Relocating the Remains* is a CD-ROM catalogue of Piper's retrospective exhibition of video, sculptural, and digital installations that opened in 1997 at the Institute of International Visual Arts in London and later toured at the New Museum of Contemporary Art in New York and the National Gallery of Canada in Ottawa.

What is fascinating about the CD-ROM synopsis of this show is its transformation of Piper's loud and large-scale three-dimensional installations into the softer, quieter, miniaturized forms of QuickTime movies and virtual reality computer graphics. It could be argued, thinking back to Godard's nostalgia for the passing ontology of cinema, that the CD-ROM diminishes the colossal form and almost mystical milieu of Piper's museum installations. The subtitle of the CD is, after all, "mapping the traces of 3 expeditions: an interactive journey through the work of Keith Piper." But rather than diminishing the art form, the traces of this CD-ROM, I suggest, provide an alternative interface, one that mimes the installations not in a burlesque manner but rather in a way that highlights the structural insistence of repetition with a difference that is so crucial to Piper's work. By mimicry here, I refer to Homi K. Bhabha's notion of "the process of the *fixation* of the colonial as a form of cross-classificatory, discriminating knowledge within an interdictory discourse, and therefore necessarily raises the question of the *authorization* of colonial representations; a question of authority that goes beyond the subject's lack of priority (castration) to a historical crisis in the conceptuality of colonial man as an *object* of regulatory power, as the subject of racial, cultural, national representation."[36] It is within the journey of interactivity that the user of Piper's CD-ROM is situated in "the between," in the toggle effect, between the history of colonialism and its mime, between the object of the technological interface (from slave ship to computer chip) and the subject representing racial, cultural, and national specificity and difference.

Piper initially mimics the colonial procedures of regulation by organizing the three expeditions around three (un)classifications: UnMapped, UnRecorded, UnClassified. "Unclassified" re-creates two of Piper's video/digital installations, *Caught Like a Nigger in Cyberspace* and *Tagging the Other*.

Tagging the Other replicates Piper's fast-paced, hip-hop video wall that plots the black subject's inscription in the technological interface, from the bondage of surveillance to the framing of the media. *Caught Like a Nigger* presents the user with a video game that reflects on the black subject's false entry into the capitalist free world of cyberspace. Similarly, "UnMapped" traces the conflicting cultural representations of the toggle between "Negrophilia and Funk: The Sight of a Negro," "The Sound of a Negro," and "The Feel of a Negro." Finally, the four pieces that compose the section "UnRecorded" retrace the loss of the memory of the Middle Passage and the complex imprint of its blockage on British cultural identity. Given the resonance of recent international crises of immigration, from East Timor to Kosovo, I will comment on Piper's work by focusing on the centerpiece of this section, "An English Ship."

The installation establishes a historical linkage between the colonial institutions of Christianity, British Empire, and slavery by opening with an introductory loop to "A Ship Called Jesus," the ship donated by Elizabeth in 1564 for the first official slave trading voyage and the ship in which, the subtitle tells its viewers, "we have been sailing . . . ever since." Regardless of the passage taken through this virtual tale, whether through "The Story of an English Queen," "A Pirate," or "A Ship Called Jesus," the cybertraveler is caught in a paradoxical zone that makes an issue of the nature of the universal "we." The initial track is interrupted by competing sound loops of voices hailing the user to enter three different venues. By moving the cursor over the graphic "Pirate," which links to fluctuating sites of the slave trade and the stock market, the user triggers a repetitive male sound bite, "Commerce is our goal." When the cursor slides over the collage of Elizabeth, a voice sounding like Margaret Thatcher tells "us" that "I think it means that people are really rather afraid that this country might be rather swamped by people of a different culture." Finally, sliding over "A Ship Called Jesus," the cursor activates the soulful spiritual, "You Know I'm Gonna Find a Way to Freedom."

"Embracing the anguish of past that has not yet passed into representation," writes Kobena Mercer, "*A Ship Called Jesus* exemplifies a critical postmodernism in which art survives the experience of trauma by entering into a practice that performs an ethics of *responsible disenchantment*— letting go of losses that can never be redeemed by the promises of the future but only endured through the labor of symbolisation."[37] "A Ship Called

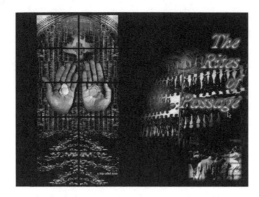

Figure 7. Keith Piper, "A Ship Called Jesus," in *Relocating the Remains,* 1997.

Jesus" (Figure 7) provides a viewing of Piper's videotape *The Rites of Passage,* in which art provides a montage of the representation and passage of four hundred years of ongoing endurance. Here the combination of digital processing, mental incorporation, and cultural representation are presented as transgressively parodic activities of the master's legacy: "the instance of how black people's spiritual and musical genius borrowed what was given to them and then made them their own." Overall, Piper's complicated digital platform generates a new medium of cultural capital from the preservation of the historical traces and memories of black residue that cast a lasting shadow on the purity of the Empire. *Relocating the Remains* marks not only the ongoing procedures of the containment of loss but also, I wish to insist, the processes of cultural anxiety and the baroque resurgence of loss and trauma as a kind of revolutionary melancholia. The digitized melancholia structuring Piper's CD-ROM turns aggressively against the narcissistic love object, Mother Britain, in a way that saves its black subject from psychic annihilation.[38]

OBSESSIVE BECOMING: DANIEL REEVES

I will make my way toward a conclusion by touching on the other spectrum of digital loss, works that profit from the blended cinematic/digital code to dwell within the interface of a loss whose public resonance is grounded in the pain of private or personal affect. Neumark's *Shock in the Ear,* which I analyze in chapter 8, is one example of a CD-ROM that relies on the blends of digital editing of sound and image to offer the user thoughtful passage through the more interiorized zones of the deeply personal traumas of family and medical histories. It is important to appreciate, moreover, that the digital code can offer such a mental space to the viewer of single-track video as well as to the user of a multifaceted CD-ROM. Of particular note, in this vein, is the 1995 video *Obsessive Becoming,* by the American-Scottish artist, Daniel Reeves. Appropriating amateur photos, home movies, and documentary footage, Reeves stuns his viewers with a masterful series of morphs and digitized sound tracks that narrate the artist's discovery of untold family trauma. The narrative relies on family interviews and home footage to recount the affliction of violence on the artist and his brother by their stepfather; it replays the artist's shocking discovery that their stepfather was not their real father, and that his real father, himself subject to domestic violence when a boy, was institutionalized as the result of his own violent outbursts. This troubled narrative is linked and fused by Reeves to his continuous artistic attempts, since his first well-received video, *Smothering Dreams,* to overcome his own trauma that he suffered as a soldier in the Vietnam War when he was the only member of his platoon to survive an ambush by the Vietcong. Of equal weight in the piece is Reeves's scarred resemblance in physique and psyche to his brother alongside whom he frequently morphs in shape and spirit, from the stilled photos of their childhood to their more recent interactions in front of Daniel's camera. Patricia R. Zimmermann has put her finger on the pulse of this tape by valuing its emotive narrative of the violence of male bonding that is embedded in the endless system of patriarchy.[39]

One could say that this story is not new to the digital age—Western letters have known it since Oedipus. Replaying the interiorized trauma of Oedipal fantasy, the two sons speak literally of wanting to kill the father and wish nostalgically for more intimacy with the mother. Yet, there remains something searing about how Reeves enraptures his audiences with a tale that pierces the heart more quickly than it challenges the intellect. Although mimicry plays an important tonal role in this piece as well, it does so more in relation to trauma than to parody. Distancing his work from anything resembling the parodic burlesque of Grace Quintanilla's family relations, Reeves capitalizes on the internalized regenerations of digital photo editing in a way that mimics the deeply structured psychic relations themselves. "These things happen," Reeves says in his voice-over narration, "because I feel they happen." Reeves's sophisticated blends of morphing call to mind the psyche's sadomasochistic procedures of incorporation and its subsequent sublimated projection of the horrific sights of culture's traumas. By toggling imagery between the seven Omega computers in his home studio, Reeves morphed sequences of family portraits so that the emotive depth evoked by these personal photos flow into one another with sublimated grace and fluidity. "Along with keen hand tintings and other painterly treatments," writes Steve Seid, the curator of Berlin's Transmedia '97, "the high-tech effect of morphing finally becomes not so much graphical pizzazz as a visual recognition of our seamless linkage to the past."[40]

In view of my admiration for the practiced craft of Daniel Reeves's digital imagery, it may sound ironic that I have discussed with Reeves my ambivalence about the digital architecture of *Obsessive Becoming* whose aesthetic results I so admire. My discomfort stems from the proximity of Reeves's finely tuned piece to what Lunenfeld describes as the "digital dialectic." In a fashion rarely achieved so successfully in the annals of cinema, Reeves combines a captivating, melancholic narrative with the morphed loops of family and historical footage in order to create a hyperreal zone of emotive interactivity.

> What I am trying to get at it is in the context of what I would call "emotively charged memory," the memory that perhaps surrounds trauma and pain and suffering . . . the most exciting morphing that goes on in the whole piece is not the faces in the end, it is rather prosaic to me, was the ability to take the black and white photographs and make them appear as a rag in water or paper thrown to water . . . a poetic representation, a visceral representation of how I think, images at least, transmute, transform, permutate in the mind.[41]

Both the specialized codes and cultural codes of documentary and amateur cinema here morph into a streaming spectacle of universal trauma that goes beyond examining what is happening to our visual and intellectual cultures. Reeves's painful chant of trauma nurtures emotive immersion rather than prompting critical examination.

I have attended screenings of few films that evoke such a consistent response of overwhelmed emotions and identification with the artist as happens in the wake of *Obsessive Becoming*. This well could be due to Reeves's deep belief in the universal pathos of his story. Associating the private terror of family violence and loss with the cross-cultural reality of historical trauma, the middle section of *Obsessive Becoming* even links Reeves's family trauma with imagery from the broader historical traumas of the twentieth century. The viewer is taken through a stream of documentary footage linking the plight of children in the Warsaw ghetto, Japanese victims bearing the burn wounds of atomic fallout, soldiers skirmishing in the Vietnam War, and smart bombs crashing into Gulf War bunkers. Reeves manipulates the images of embalmed photographs and dusty documentary to free the cultural code from its encryption in the formal codes of the document. "What we have forgotten will come back," he laments in a voice-over that tracks the ugly footage of Nazi concentration camps. Yet, what comes back, it seems to me, is not the juxtaposition of analogous imagery that might revise our reception of the footage of amateur and documentary cinema. What comes back is not a cinematic reflection on the resemblances and contrasts of complex historical traumas. What comes back as remembered in *Obsessive Becoming* is a flow of familiar media images, electronic sound tracks, and sorrowful narrations that tend to render the difference of forgetfulness to the same: "They are no different than you," the narration says of the portraits streaming through the end of the tape . . . "the face is the same."

Might not such an assuming declaration reflect the essence of digital dialectics? The synthesized blend of digital sameness here softens out the hard edges of analogical difference. The remains of forgetfulness certainly arise in all their pathos in *Obsessive Becoming*. But it is not clear that Reeves's chanting obsession with the universality of his pain prompts anything close to an examination of the shadows of cinema or anything resembling a critical relocation of the remains of culture. To return to the critical distinction I have tried to maintain throughout this chapter, it could be said that the emotional gain promised by Reeves's digital aesthetics equals the loss of analogy's difference, outside and within cinema. Instead of foregrounding the resistant differences of digital analogy and resemblance, Reeves capitalizes on his masterful craft of the code to reduce the critical edges of difference to the softened sameness of the spectacle of digital dialectics.[42]

My hope is that my toggling here between code and craft, between theory and practice, between cinema and new media, will have foregrounded the theoretical choices made available to us by the code of the digital platform. In doing so, I also hope to have demonstrated how digital culture can revitalize the loss of enigma characteristic of earlier codes of analogy, a loss glossed over by the temporal machinery of cinematic suture with the imaginary hallucination of a common world picture. What I have come to appreciate from the conceptual interface of so many digital artworks is that we must alter how we think temporally, in an analog or even dialectical fashion, in order to inhabit the space and history of the ampersand, to dwell in the contact zone, in the AND, of code and craft. If nothing else, digitality provides us with a means to rest in the between of the ampersand, between 1 & 0, so Hill might say. Digital art that inhabits the ampersand revitalizes the power of contrast and paradox rather than seeking its transcendence through the ontology of cinema and its dialectical legacy. This is the intricate critical space where we can pause to examine what is happening, critically and politically, to our visual and intellectual cultures.

chapter 6

WOUNDS OF REPETITION IN THE AGE OF THE DIGITAL: CHRIS MARKER'S CINEMATIC GHOSTS

Death is the ferryman; he shows the way to language, to order, to the consideration of lack, to meaning, to culture.

    —LYOTARD, "One of the Things at Stake in Women's Struggles"

The disturbed relation with the dead—forgotten and embalmed—is one of the symptoms of the sickness of experience today. . . . It becomes a wound in civilization, asocial sentimentality, showing that it has still not been possible to compel men to indulge solely in purposeful behavior. The dead . . . are expunged from the memory of those who live on. Men have ceased to consider their own purpose and fate; they work their despair out on the dead.

    —HORKHEIMER AND ADORNO, "On the Theory of Ghosts"

The dead are expunged from the memory of those who live on. While such a theorization of ghosting does not represent the artistic strategies of either Daniel Reeves or Grace Quintanilla, it is a fitting description of at least one cinematic and psychiatric approach to trauma and its aftermath. A dominant method utilized by the U.S. Army for treating post–World War II shock syndrome could be described by the formula of "speak and you shall remember in order to forget." You might recall the memorable scene in John Huston's film *Let There Be Light* (1944) when a voice recounts the condition of a soldier "who doesn't even remember his own name and entire past" as a result of shell shock suffered during the invasion of Okinawa. The film depicts a psychiatrist who hypnotizes the soldier in order to make the man "tell me what you see." The point of such an analytic exercise was not, of course, to confront the soldier with the haunting specter of the only major land battle in "Japan" during World War II, one that resulted in more casualties than all those killed in the atomic bombings of Hiroshima and Nagasaki. Huston's psychiatrist was not asking the traumatized patient to visualize the hypertraumatic spectacle of the 12,000 dead American soldiers and the combined 107,000 dead Japanese and Okinawan soldiers, on top of the 150,000 Okinawan civilians who died either from their sacrifice "for Japan" during the American bombing or from their participation in the mass suicide led by the Japanese army. Rather, the performative aim of the Hollywood doctor was simply to reawaken the patient's personal screen-memory of his own shelling in order to expunge the epic spectacle of Okinawan slaughter from the memory of those Americans who live on.

Similar strategies of burying the dead inside the mournful hallow of memory have been recounted more recently by Japanese commentators who lament their historical silence about the genocidal horrors that their countrymen inflicted on the Okinawans who were used by the Japanese essentially as human shields. Western readers are more familiar with the experiences of children of Holocaust survivors, who frequently note with ambivalent confusion their parents' silent relation to the details of their trauma. The Holocaust survivors tended not to discuss the horror of their sufferings with their children as they grew up during the 1950s and 1960s. These memories of Holocaust trauma, recent studies suggest, were not so much forgotten as embalmed.[1] They remained inside this collective body, as if mummified, with all their vivid details preserved and awaiting exposure. In this manner, history could be said to have been censored not for the survivors themselves, who remained haunted by the specters of incorporation, but for the others, the children of the future, as if to protect them from the ooze of civilization's deep wounds.

Radically different from Huston's cinematic restaging of the treatment of shock, not to mention from the initial reluctance of the survivors of Auschwitz and Okinawa to speak about their horrors, is the approach to trauma taken by Chris Marker in his digitally resonant film *Level 5,* which appropriates the analytic sequence from *Let There Be Light.* Much different from Marker's prior project, *Sans soleil,* which turns ambivalently to Japan as a cultural marker of postcolonial media and subjectivity, *Level 5* is one of the first films by a major Western or Japanese director to contemplate directly the tragic jockeying during World War II by Japanese and American interests over the culture and landscape of Okinawa. In so doing, it also demystifies the hegemonic cultural confidence with which Japanese, American, and French cinema have gone about their business since the war. Marker's complicated project traces historical and contemporary accounts of the tragic slaughter and mass suicides of the Okinawan people by intermixing, in the guise of a CD-ROM, footage from historical documentaries, Hollywood film, and contemporary documentary on film and video, all of which foreground the differences of the combined perspectives of their Japanese, Okinawan, French, and American interlocutors. The film and the CD-ROM within the film recount and rescreen numerous cinematic strategies of the twentieth century's disturbed relation with the dead that leaves them forgotten and embalmed out of a fear that the dead may remind individuals of the degeneration of their own existence.

One sequence, for example, shows a contemporary Japanese tourist who seems more fascinated with Marker's camera than with the spectral traces of the deaths forever lingering in the shadows of the suicide caverns of Okinawa: "Look," she tells her son, "you're going to be on American TV." In an interview sequence in the film, moreover, the Japanese filmmaker Nagisa Oshima reflects on one method of eliminating the memory of history when he notes that Japanese war films "never showed the adversary." The film then cuts to a montage with a voice-over recalling a similar American approach to the adversary through which distance is achieved by means of deadly objectification: "The only good Jap is a dead Jap." (Suggestive of how much the American and Japanese engaged in similar hegemonic representations of the Okinawans, the Americans referred equally to the Japanese and the Okinawans as "Japs.") Here the enemy is spoken only as absent, as dead, or as objectified, in a rather matter-of-fact rather than disturbing way. Through these varying interviews and cinematic sequences, Marker's film insistently sensitizes its viewer to how complexly the postwar approach to trauma was related to the codes and conventions of cinema and film's approach to the horrific losses of history. He even implicates his own media in the drive toward death itself when he rescreens footage of an Okinawan woman jumping from a cliff alongside much earlier 1910 footage of a caped man jumping to his death from the Eiffel Tower, both of whom seemed reluctant to take the plunge until they discover themselves being captured on camera, as if, says Marker's voice-over, "the cameraman shot them like a hunter."

Further complicating *Level 5*'s narration of traumatic historical memory is its representation of the experience of testimony. The affect of testimony is placed in relief by the self-address of the film's only live actor, a woman named Laura, played by Catherine Belkhodja. In between her self-musings, Laura manipulates the CD-ROM about Okinawa that has been left unfinished by its designer, her dead lover, with whom she shares a personal conversation throughout the film. Directly addressing the camera, Laura engages in a series of monologues about her personal loss and her attempt to supplement her lost love object with the sublimational work of art. The pathos of Laura's relation to art is compounded by the film's direct reference to its reinscription of the grainy narrative of historical trauma in Alain Resnais's 1957 film *Hiroshima mon amour,* in which the actress protagonist relives, in postwar Hiroshima, the screen memory of her personal loss and melancholia during World War II. The narrative struggle of this powerful film revolves, of course, around the French girl's working through, with the aid of her cultural other, the internalized traumas of loss and torture that she suffered as a consequence of her love of a young German soldier who was killed at the end of the war. Aided by the sheen of *Level 5*'s digital formats and sensibilities, Marker similarly conjoins the memory of the losses of history with the pathos of melancholia and its representational absence that frequently situates the subject, to recall Horkheimer and Adorno, in relation to "something that has no market value and runs contrary to all feelings." Here narcissistic drift and the melodrama of lost love stand in for, or overlap with, the high seriousness of historical memory and national trauma. Through the staining overlap of subjective loss and historical subject, the films cited above prompt reflection not only on the traumas of history but also on the related pathos of the cinematic arts.

What does it mean, then, for the pathos of the personal to be so intermixed with the trauma of the social in one context, and for the bathos of mass cultural melodrama to be so interwoven into the texture of a specific cultural tragedy in another, but still related, context? And how might cinematic practice, its theorization, and its digital application contribute to an understanding of the cultural workings of trauma? Intermixed throughout *Level 5,* for example, are the discourses of memory and trauma, absence and loss, self and history, fantasy and reality, whose particular relations have been the subject of lively dispute in recent debates over trauma and its historical specificities. In the pages to follow, I focus on structural aspects of cinematic theory and digital practice that may provide a "material" framework, something of a baroque memento mori, through which to contemplate the representation of cultural loss. While some critics might prefer a more cautious separation of the personal and the political, or of the fictional and the historical, a sharper distinction between, say, narrative cinema and cultural history, I have occasion later in this essay to recommend *Level 5* for embracing the artistic challenge of generating critical energy that emanates from the conjoined pathos of absence and loss, from the mnemonic interface of identification and incorporation, that attests to the collusion of the personal and the social, and even the fictional and the historical. This film's contribution to a digitized contemplation of trauma will be even more apparent, I hope, in the course of considering the role of trauma within cinema itself.

As the preface to a consideration of this structural charge of trauma in cinema, I propose that it would be helpful to consider how *Level 5*'s mixture of subjective representational absence and objective historical loss exemplifies what Jean Laplanche has called the artistic excitation of sublimation. "You have to think of sublimation," writes Laplanche,

> in a less transformational and so-called mathematical way than Freud thought of it, which is of inhibited and desexualised drives and so on. We must try to think of sublimation as new sexuality; it is something new, maybe coming from the message, from the work itself. It is a kind of new excitation, new trauma coming from the sublimated activity itself, and through this new trauma comes new energy. I try to connect the idea of sublimation with the idea of research or trauma, and I coined the idea of traumatophilia.[2]

Of course, consideration of the relation of sublimation and trauma in the history of cinema and its reception is hardly novel. One need think only of the mixed reception of a film such as Claude Lanzman's *Shoah* to recall the charge that the entertainment value of cinema (documentary or not) can trivialize trauma rather than energize its reconsideration or that the cinematic restaging of the sublimated activity itself (in this case, Lanzman's own performative relation to the memory of trauma) could work to level or democratize the historical subject position specific to the witnesses of

fragile memories. At issue is not only the vicissitude of cinematic representation but also the possibility of what Dominick LaCapra critiques as the
slippage in trauma theory between absence and loss. LaCapra frequently
warns his more poststructurally bent colleagues of a slippage between the
heightened loss linked to specifically historical events and the structural crisis of absence endemic to representational procedures and apparatuses—a
slippage, I should add, that he frequently identifies as the consequence of
deconstruction.[3] Of course, he could just as readily have expressed a similar concern about the pleasure and excitation of cinematic reproduction at
the expense of the pain and masochism of historical memory. Implicated
in such a warning about the dangerous slippage between absence and loss
in critical theory is the role of cinema itself as a practice that conjoins the
fantasies of pleasure and pain in the screening of memory and trauma. I
hope to demonstrate how cinema itself, particularly as it intersects with the
codes of digital culture, attests to the structural place of traumatophilia as
"a kind of new excitation, new trauma coming from the sublimated activity itself."

What is notable throughout the history of cinematic theory, particularly
in its European formulations, is the recurrent theme of cinematic memory and the repetition of the cultural wounds of historical loss. Even when
reflecting on the digital trauma of cinema discussed in the preceding chapter, I frequently find myself retracing the history of cinematic theory and
its disparate group of cinematic thinkers, from the German cultural theorizing of Horkheimer and Adorno, not to mention Negt and Kluge, to the
French formal philosophizing of Lyotard and Deleuze, Malraux and Artaud.
At issue is not so much the veracity of the cinematic representation of history as the dilemma of the cinematic replication of loss. Although the theorists of cinematic representation do not necessarily utilize the discourses
of psychoanalysis or trauma theory in their work, their thoughtful accounts
of cinema lead with uncanny frequency to reflections on affective virtualities, something like the structural features of cinematic sublimation and
its confusions of sexual energy and social loss.[4]

THE WOUND OF REPETITION

Consider how the cinematic legacy of Horkheimer and Adorno's *Dialectic of
Enlightenment* speaks directly to the issues of loss outlined above. What is

fascinating about their infamous chapter "The Culture Industry: Enlighten-ment as Mass Deception" is its peculiarly odd relation to the mise-en-scène of traumatophilia produced by Marker's digital project. This traumatophilia is made both proximate and distant by the markers of cinematic history that, in my opinion, properly position cinema as something of an affective wound in civilization. If read retroactively in the context of the traumatic issues prompted by *Level 5*, *Hiroshima mon amour*, and *Let There Be Light* (films from the 1990s, 1950s, and 1940s), "The Culture Industry" fore-grounds precisely the concepts through which we might consider trauma in relation to the thought of cinema, particularly in terms of a cinematics enacted by the various writings of Deleuze, Lyotard, and Laplanche. But before pursuing this claim, it would be prudent to frame the following citations of Horkheimer and Adorno with a critical disclaimer. There is no doubt that my appropriation of Horkheimer and Adorno's writings about the regulations of cinema and enlightenment run counter in spirit to their understanding and appreciation of what we might call the traumatic thought of the cinematic, particularly as it has been understood in France. But their articulation of a cinematic energetics strongly resembles, I think, the struc-tural sensibilities of the French theorists from whom they would have dis-tanced themselves.

Perhaps I can clarify this resemblance by turning to Horkheimer and Adorno's remarks on the automatism of thought, which they articulate ini-tially in their book's introduction, "The Concept of Enlightenment":

In the anticipatory identification of the wholly conceived and mathematized world with truth, enlightenment intends to secure itself against the return of the mythic. It confounds thought and mathematics. In this way the latter is, so to speak, released and made into an absolute instance. . . . Thinking objectifies itself to become an automatic, self-activating process; an imper-sonation of the machine that produces itself so that ultimately the machine can replace it. Enlightenment has put aside the classic requirement of think-ing about thought.[5]

These remarks resurface in the "Culture Industry" chapter when the authors insist,

The stronger the positions of the culture industry become, the more sum-marily it can deal with consumers' needs, producing them, controlling them, disciplining them, and even withdrawing amusement. . . . Pleasure always means not to think about anything, to forget suffering even where it is shown . . . The liberation which amusement promises is freedom from thought and from negation.[6]

In the wake of this 1947 book, written itself from within the wound of postwar civilization, such a machinic sublimation of thought and negation has been denounced in some circles as the nefariously misogynistic project of classical Hollywood cinema or considered more broadly in others as the result of the cinematic "apparatus" stemming from Renaissance mechanisms of perspective and vision. Common to both considerations has been a strident concern with the homogeneity of the cinematic enterprise and its effect on cinematic production.[7] "Pure amusement in its consequence, relaxed self-surrender to all kinds of associations and happy nonsense, is cut short," Horkheimer and Adorno write in "The Culture Industry," "by the amusement on the market: instead, it is interrupted by a surrogate overall meaning which the culture industry insists on giving to its products, and yet misuses as a mere pretext for bringing in the stars."[8] One need think today only of the continuous significance of Leonardo DiCaprio as the star attraction sustaining the traumatic drama of *Titanic* and the psychic dissolution of *The Aviator* or of the ongoing draw of that busty, big-lipped Hollywood centerpiece, Julia Roberts, to appreciate the prescient significance of the Germans' critique of the Hollywood culture industry. Put otherwise, they write a few pages earlier,

> The culture industry did away with yesterday's rubbish by its own perfection, and by forbidding and domesticating the amateurish, although it constantly allows gross blunders without which the standard of the exalted style cannot be perceived. But what is new is that the irreconcilable elements of culture, art and distraction, are subordinated to one end and subsumed under one false formula: the totality of the culture industry. It consists of repetition. That its characteristic innovations are never anything more than improvements of mass reproduction is not external to the system.[9]

I will return to their emphasis on repetition in just a moment, but for now I want to align their remarks with similar ones made by Lyotard in his 1973 essay "Acinéma." Lyotard similarly condemns classical Hollywood cinema for its method of privileging "elements in motion" in order to exclude aberrance and to channel primal drives into the sublimated image of a recognizable organic and social body. To Lyotard, Hollywood films enact a complex machinery of ordering, whose principal economic function is to excise, to cut out, and to expunge any psychoaesthetic waste or excess.[10]

But precisely the emphasis on repetition that brings Lyotard and his French thought together with Horkheimer and Adorno can be said to render them asunder. Horkheimer and Adorno's stress on the repetition of imitation constitutes one of the most important structural links between their introductory musings on "The Concept of Enlightenment" and those on "The Culture Industry":

> And so it is in enlightenment. . . . The doctrine of the equivalence of action and reaction asserted the power of repetition over reality, long after men had renounced the illusion that by repetition they could identify themselves with the repeated reality and thus escape its power. . . . The principle of immanence, the explanation of every event as repetition, that the Enlightenment upholds against mythic imagination, is the principle of myth itself.[11]

In cinematic terms, such a power of repetition over reality insinuates itself in the Hollywood structure of narrative. Writing of the culture industry as the repetitive machinery of "the prevailing order," Horkheimer and Adorno suggest that its only choice is to join in or be left out.

What I wish to stress by insisting on Horkheimer and Adorno's particular emphasis on repetition, however, is its own indifference to "the classic requirement of thinking about thought" or at least of thinking about *cinematic* thought and its relation to trauma. I make this claim to foreground the serious difference of Horkheimer and Adorno's notion of "the demonically distorted form which things and men have assumed in the light of unprejudiced cognition" from the tradition of thinking about the demonism of cinematic thought, particularly in relation to the more fluid linkages of enlightenment cognition to the hauntings of fantasy and what Laplanche calls fantasy's "enigmatic signifiers." Sustaining the life of fantasy as the new figure of "primal seduction," the "enigmatic signifier" denotes "a fundamental situation in which an adult prefers to a child verbal, non-verbal and even behavioural signifiers which are pregnant with unconscious sexual significations."[12] Here the enigma is in and by itself a seduction whose mechanisms are unconscious. It is important to Laplanche that the enigma of fantasy is reciprocal: for just as the language of the child is inadequate to that of the adult, the language of the adult remains inadequate to the childlike source-object acting upon her. It is along this reciprocal but uneven axis of primal seduction that the traumatic, retroactive fantasy affect of the enigmatic signifier is always already in destabilizing circulation. "We have to place considerable stress on the possibility," writes Laplanche, that the signifier may be *designified,* or lose what it signifies, without thereby losing its power to signify *to.*"[13] The spectral form of the signifier thus haunts the subject without permitting the disturbed soul the comfort and certainty of a determinate content and its cultural value. Such enigmatic haunting is what Laplanche considers to constitute the core of the primal trauma of seduction.

As a means of relating the energetic trauma of enigma to the specific case of *Level 5,* permit me to continue this thread by making a few broad observations about such demonism in relation to the legacy of cinematic thought. It is important to note that Horkheimer and Adorno's broad conceptual approach to cinema derives not only, as Peter Hohendahl puts it, from Adorno's "admitted unfamiliarity with the techniques of film production,"[14] but from their very dislike of modern cinema itself. Who cannot but be struck by the extent to which Horkheimer and Adorno attempt to ward off the demonism of modern cinema in perhaps the most memorable passage of "The Culture Industry":

> Real life is becoming indistinguishable from the movies. The sound film, far surpassing the theater of illusion, leaves no room for imagination or reflection on the part of the audience, who is unable to respond within the structure of the film, yet deviate from its precise detail without losing the thread of the story; hence the film forces its victims to equate it directly with reality. . . . Sustained thought is out of the question if the spectator is not to miss the relentless rush of facts . . . no scope is left for the imagination.[15]

To be fair to them, a similar point was made in the forties by André Malraux, who unfavorably compared the quick movement of the sound film to the pause rendered by the textual divisions of plays and novels. But as the French film critic, Roger Leenhardt, stresses in his 1945 essay "Malraux and the Cinema," Malraux then emphasizes the contribution of cinema's departure from the centralizing thought of metaphor toward a new art of ellipses, of repetitions, of movements—"assez baroque"—that give rise to the enigmatic diversity of discourses.[16] Leenhardt's emphasis on the baroque thought of cinema picks up on a much earlier point made in 1927 by Antonin Artaud that the virtual force of cinematic matter works explicitly to express "les choses de la pensée [the matter of thought]."[17] This is particularly true for cinema, suggests Artaud already in 1924, due to its total reversal of optical values, of the perspectives of logic through which the demands of rapidity and especially repetition put pressure on the comfort of realism favored by formal psychology.[18] Once again, cinematic repetition is put into play, but this time as the energetic engine of thought that is counter to the psychic death of realism's certainties.

Artaud's insistence on the interrelation of thought and psyche works further, I suggest, to foreground the contrasting discomfort of Horkheimer and Adorno and the fascination of many theoreticians of trauma with the structural play of imagination, fantasy, and its vicissitudes. I refer here not only to the correctives of Negt and Kluge who worked to reinsert the vicissitudes of fantasy into the cognitive operations of the public sphere, but also to what I see as Horkheimer and Adorno's peculiar discomfort with and denial of the affect internal to the cognitive procedures of enlightenment and, particularly, to the masochistic disturbance of cinematic identification itself. More than once, the authors denounce the kinds of thrashing suffered by the Donald Ducks of modern cinema as indicative of the internalized masochism suffered unthinkingly by the spectator (an internalized trauma later critiqued by Laura Mulvey for constituting the primary viewing positions made available by Hollywood cinema to female spectators). Similar negations of sadomasochistic violence sustain their introductory notions of the Enlightenment and its structural support of modern totalitarianism. But what is missing from this cinematic lens, I propose, is any attentiveness to what Artaud called the thought of imagination or what Negt and Kluge would term "the imaginative faculty grasped as a medium of sensuality and fantasy."[19] In an uncanny way, Horkheimer and Adorno seem ironically to turn their thoughts away from the ghostly wounds of civilization in a manner that prevents them from acknowledging the charge of Negt and Kluge to "theoretically grasp the relation of dependency between fantasy and the experience of an alienated reality."[20]

Horkheimer and Adorno's retort, of course, is that repetitive structures of cinematic fantasy work all too easily to swamp the experience of alienated reality. As if presaging the hyperreality of digital reproduction so striking in *Level 5,* they suggest,

> Whatever the camera reproduces is beautiful. The disappointment of the prospect that one might be the typist who wins the world trip is matched by the disappointing appearance of the accurately photographed areas which the voyage might include. Not only Italy is offered, but evidence that it exists. A film can even go so far as to show the Paris in which the American girl thinks she will still her desire as a hopelessly desolate place, thus driving her more inexorably into the arms of the smart American boy she could have met at home anyway. . . . Continuing and continuing to join in are given as justification for the blind persistence of the system and even for its immutability.[21]

Yet, I am wondering whether a sensitivity to the vicissitudes of fantasy (not to mention the underlying repetition compulsion) would enable a conception of repetition as a process that lends itself solely to immutability. Considering related work on repetition from the French tradition of Deleuze, Laplanche, Lyotard, and Derrida, I wonder whether repetition itself doesn't open the way to what is "assez baroque" in cinema, the structural ground of difference, deferral, and, fantasy, even when understood in relation to the trauma of loss.

Deleuze thinks it no coincidence, for example, that fantasy and trauma are marked so radically in the arts by the interstices of repetition and simulacrum. It is the traumatic chaos of the duration of cinematic repetition that Deleuze positions (well before publishing his "cinema books") at the core of those "two essential aims" that he claims for the arts: "the subordination of form to speed, to the variation of speed, and the subordination of the subject to intensity or to affect, to the intense variation of affects."[22] What is traumatic is the artwork's structural interference in the stability of fixed perspective and its positioning of the spectator in the subsequent vectors, swirls, and speeds of moving pictures, fractalized imagery, and discordant narratives. The traumatic variations of speed and affect are understood by Deleuze, moreover, to create a baroque space and dynamism for the errancy of cinematic seriality (think of Greenaway's baroque experimentations with energetic seriality, from *The Fall* to *Prospero's Books,* which I discuss in chapter 4).[23] The movement between sequence to sequence or from serial image to serial image results not in the soothing, progressive movement away from one sequence toward the next but rather in an incommensurable series of folds or overlaps between

> the simultaneity and contemporaneity of all the divergent series, the fact that all coexist. From the point of view of the presents which pass in representation, the series are certainly successive, one "before" and the other "after." It is from this point of view that the second is said to *resemble* the first. However, this no longer applies from the point of view of the chaos which contains them, the object=x which runs through them, the precursor which establishes communication between them or the forced movement which points beyond them: the differenciator always makes them coexist.[24]

In this way, suture displays the three-dimensional chaos of the fold, instead of disguising the cut with its magically invisible seams. As if it were the machinery of sublimation itself, it creates an energetic difference between artistic and cinematic series as they are abstracted radically in the temporal folds of fantasy rather than flattened realistically by their empirical succession in time. What counts is the interstice between images through which "each image is plucked from the void and falls back into it."[25]

In such a context of intensity, affect, radical abstraction, and display of the void, can cinematic pleasure possibly "always mean," to return to Horkheimer and Adorno, "not to think about anything, to forget suffering even where it is shown"? Perhaps cinema serves rather as the ground for a different kind of thought about how cinema *shows* suffering as something that disturbs the very "doctrine of the equivalence of action and reaction." Perhaps the speed and affective variation of repetition can be said to haunt the power of repetition over reality, the power appreciated by Horkheimer and Adorno as the explanation of every event as repetition that Enlightenment upholds against mythic imagination.

Consider, for example, the cinematic repetition of the Paris narrative itself so exemplary to Horkheimer and Adorno of repetition's immutability: "A film can even go so far as to show the Paris in which the American girl thinks she will still her desire as a hopelessly desolate place, thus driving her more inexorably into the arms of the smart American boy she could have met at home anyway. . . . Continuing and continuing to join in are given as the justification for the blind persistence of the system and even for its immutability." To be fair, Horkheimer and Adorno couldn't have foreseen it, but this is precisely what Godard takes up in *Breathless* in a way that insinuates the diversity of difference, as a marker of both thought and pleasure. In this story, one insistent on its repetitive appropriation of the bizarre sadomasochism of *Romeo and Juliet,* the American girl in Paris doesn't meet the smart American boy she could have met at home anyway, but aligns herself instead with the homelessness of the cunning Frenchman who proves not to be smart enough to permit her "to forget suffering even where it is shown."[26] While it is true that Michel repetitively patterns himself after the image of cinema, i.e., Belmondo's unforgettable primping in front of the cinema poster of Bogart, the cinematic result is something very different from "the justification for the blind persistence of the system and even for its immutability." For the Frenchman, Michel, joins his creator, Godard, in the rebellious repetition and performative mime of the very blind persistence to the system to which the Hollywood tradition adheres. As discussed in chapter 2, Deleuze understands repetition in Godard to result not in the closure of thought or its feeling but in the foregrounding of the irrational cuts and the dissonant accords of seriality.[27]

Such a wound of repetition insinuates itself even more strongly in another French film of the period, Resnais and Duras's *Hiroshima mon amour,* where the violent memory of suffering takes place in the Cafe Casablanca in a way that forecloses the cultural beauty of American film and demystifies the classical cinematic style it cites. Now it is a French girl who is caught up in the reenactment of the event of trauma and its enigmatic fantasies with the aid, this time, of the Japanese boy whom she certainly could not have allowed herself to meet at home. (Most fortunate for the Japanese boy was that Duras's script did not place him at home anyway, in Hiroshima, during the historical enactment of the primal atomic fantasy.) The complexity of the French girl's working through her internalized war/love trauma, with the aid of her cultural other, is complicated by her sense of betrayal in revealing to her Japanese lover the festering psychic wound that she has harbored secretly during years of marriage. You might recall, moreover, that this is the film around which Cathy Caruth frames her chapter "Literature and the Enactment of Memory" to exemplify the state of the "unclaimed experience" of trauma that calls forth nothing like the blind persistence of the (cinematic) system and its immutability, but rather the ethical dilemma of the screening of memory that is staged as the female protagonist's "betrayal," in Caruth's words, "precisely in the act of telling, in the very transmission of an understanding that erases the specificity of a death."[28] Rather than forget suffering even where it is shown, cinema here works like a memento mori to reveal the necessity of suffering, what Caruth calls "the necessity of betrayal in the ineluctability of sight."[29]

The complex Japanese-French seduction is taken up more recently by Marker in *Level 5*. In Marker's film, which punningly refers to its obscure narrative as "Okinawa mon amour," the female protagonist, Laura, stands in for the woman from Nevers, but this time with the aim of provoking thought about the blindness of both American and Japanese cinema to the suffering of Okinawa even when it is shown.[30] She inhabits the "black zone" of her dead or absent lover in face of the "things hidden" in his incomplete CD-ROM on the battle of Okinawa. As she calls on her training as a "technology free" writer to aid her in completing the lover's CD-ROM, Laura moves in and out of her identification with the interrelated cinematic fields of the social and the personal that are embedded in the CD's files. Presented to Laura and Marker's spectators through digital montage are cross-period and multimedia references to the historical and fictional appropriations of what Oshima calls, in his interview segments in the film, the phantoms of the destroyed culture of Okinawa; this culture, he adds, was sacrificed by Japan and disavowed by Japanese cinema for the sake of reinforcing the imperial system (a system that Naoki Sakai understands as the phantasmatic incarnation of nationalized Enlightenment).[31] As if foregrounding the crisis of national and cultural identification exemplified by the historical enigma called Okinawa, the film features startling interview footage with a male survivor, named Kinjo, who recounts the horrors of the suicides motivated by what he calls "the telepathic effects of love," not of hate, that resulted in the unprecedented flow of ancestral blood, including the blood of his own mother whom he himself killed as part of the contagious ritual of cultural purity. It is important to acknowledge that the power of this testimony derives not only from its exposure of the wounds in civilization, but also from its juxtaposition of historical footage of the American invasion of Okinawa with documentary footage of the Okinawan attempt to reclaim its losses through procedures of everyday life and rituals of mourning, as well as interviews with Japanese intellectuals such as Oshima who position their work in the enigmatic interval of competing national accounts of witness.[32] Marker thus situates the unstable relation of memory and trauma against the backdrop of the history of international cinema and the ineluctability of sight, with a striking emphasis on the resounding variation of cinematic technique and tradition as demarcated by the conventional shifts of national difference and the clashes of cinematic style.

What thus occurs is something of a revision of Horkheimer and Adorno's stress on the individual's fear of the degeneration of his own existence to foreground a new memory of culture's wound whose disturbance catalyzes the enigmatic traumatophilia of signification rather than any fearful flight from history. Perhaps cinematic repetition can be appreciated, in this context, as the memorial thought of suffering itself, particularly in relation to the disparity between the collective memory of the past taken too much for granted by Horkheimer and Adorno and the disparity of world-memory championed by Deleuze in his book *Cinema 2: The Time-Image:* "the different levels of past no longer relate to a single character, a single family, or a single group, but to quite different characters as to unconnected places which make up a world-memory."[33] World-memory encompasses for Deleuze the intensive cinematic encounter with the demonic sign bearers of the intervals of repetition that dislocate "the same," "the identical," and "the similar" in the groundless future of trauma's eternal return.

DIGITAL TRAUMATOPHILIA

Marker's mechanism and display of world-memory links formally to his accomplished experimentation with recent cinematic advances in digital layering and editing. This accomplishment cannot be understated since it provides the history of cinema with something of a new retrospective ellipsis and repetitive energy. The resulting critical force of Marker's digital energetics may come to share the kind of earlier impact of the sound cinema whose masochistic grains of voice seemed so disquieting to Horkheimer and Adorno while so pleasing to the baroque sensibilities of Roger Leenhardt. At issue here is not simply the filmmaker's switch from an analog to a digital means of editing but also his supplementation of camera lens and frame with the stunningly different depth of field achieved through the painstaking work of digital layering. Marker also envelops the speed of digital movement and the overlap of digital collage in eerie sensorial fields of electronic sound and electric light. The filmmaker's ability to capitalize on digital technology allows us to enfold the vicissitudes of subjective loss into the elliptical resonance of sound, light, and shot. This digital means of enfolding affect serves to inscribe the discourse of memory on multiple registers of time, space, and national identity that are simultaneously available on the screen of cinematic representation, perhaps for the first time. The digital thus displays the retrospective convolutions of the prioritizing of introjection and projection, of past and future, on which the narratives of identity and culture have depended.

So the viewer doesn't miss the point, Marker thematizes his formal innovations in the narratives of cyberspace. Consider how Marker's Laura inhabits at different moments in the film both the sensitizing night vision of the OWL (Optimal World Link, e.g., World Wide Web) and the newly configured gaze of a virtual reality mask that positions her within the fold of fantasy. While her online presence on OWL links her directly with the quite different characters and unconnected places that make up a world-memory, her wired experience within the spectrum of the virtual mask places her directly in the now of narrative history. In this sense, Marker's new cinematics of the digital offers to the wound of civilization the haptic mechanisms of its immediate touch and enfolding rather than the optical control of its mediated distance and projection.[34] But unlike many cybertheoreticians who have celebrated too readily the utopia of the new cyberworld order, Marker is careful to establish a link between the black zone of mourning and the visceral shock experienced by Laura when her handprint is rejected by a magnetic resonance pad that would grant her access to the higher levels of OWL: the code, "access denied," flashes aggressively on the screen with attendant blaring sound effects as she abruptly removes her shocked hand from the pad. Here the signifier of mind and body, "access denied," serves as the enigmatic carrier of the traumatic shock of the digital (a formulation I owe to Norie Neumark's extraordinary CD-ROM, *Shock in the Ear*).[35]

As a seemingly ageless artist in his mideighties who embodies the wounds of that earlier time of war, Marker cautiously still embraces the digital in order to foreground the complex layerings of psychosocial identities and memories that can be thought in space only insofar as they will have been ghosted by the vicissitudes of access, as they stand mournfully in the past only in relation to their virtual illumination in the future. Deleuze concludes *Cinema 2* by reflecting similarly on the linkage of the growth of new machines in the social field to the political chao-errancy of cinematic world-memory and its nomadism. As I discuss more thoroughly in chapter 10, he remarks somewhat ambivalently that the video or digital image provides the means either to transform cinema or to replace it, "to mark its death."[36] Through digital memory, Deleuze believes, the panoramic organization of space might lose the vertical privileging of direction. The screen could become a data bank through which information and the methods of its production replace nature. And, ultimately, the "brain city" could become subject to the perpetual reorganization of world-memory and its radical intensities.

Such an interrelated mechanics of digital technique and memory works most successfully in *Level 5*, returning to a point I made earlier in this chapter, to enfold the memory of the social into the affect of the personal. Running parallel to the traumatic event and differing cultural translation of Okinawa is Laura's personal narrative, addressed this time not to a transferential Japanese interlocutor, as in *Hiroshima mon amour*, but more directly to her absent lover as viewer or perhaps also to her viewers as distant discursive lovers. Concerning her subliminal search for the meaning of her missed physical and digital encounters, she declares that "when I decipher your program, I'm scared that I'll find things hidden that flow out of my psyche." The stakes of the personal drama could not be higher since they combine the inaccessible truth of hermeneutics with the impossible fulfillment of desire. It is not insignificant that the levels to which the film's title refer are the stages of cognitive sophistication with which Laura and her lover evaluated their acquaintances, as well as the stages of difficulty embedded in the CD-ROM, from Level 1 for the common user and Level 2 for critical minds to the higher levels that remain inaccessible to mere mortals. Ultimately, one must die (along with cinema) to attain Level 5. The hermeneutic drive of the game should thus be understood, in the context of Level 5, to be as old and as realistic as Montaigne's early acknowledgment that the goal of knowledge is not the philosopher's stone but the positioning of thought on the fragile limits of the degeneration of one's own existence (a distinction that also would pertain to Kuntzel's two versions of *Autumn*). To philosophize, insisted Montaigne, is to learn how to die. Put otherwise by Lyotard, "Death is the ferryman; he shows the way to language."

What Marker inserts into the history of thought, moreover, is a digital foregrounding of the traumatophilia underlying, energizing, and destabilizing it. In a way that intensifies and foregrounds the traumatophilia of the female protagonist of *Hiroshima mon amour,* whose speech unlocks the crypt of her ghostly memory at the film's end, Laura opens Marker's film with the acknowledgment that speech and knowledge themselves remain an insufficient antidote to loss. At the beginning of *Level 5,* Laura voices Elle's infamous lines closing *Hiroshima mon amour,* "C'est le premier fois que j'en parlais de toi à un autre" (this is the first time I've spoken about you to someone else), to establish speech in the face of the Other as the catalytic engine of this film's traumatic seriality. This certainly works differently from how Horkheimer and Adorno might have thought it, as the cathartic forgetfulness of suffering even when it is shown. More to the point is this film's stress on the lingering trace of the pathos of memory even after it is screened. Laura concludes the film by acknowledging that "I almost lost the echo of something I don't know . . . which I cannot know but what my programmer foresaw." She then points a remote at the camera filming her to trigger her dissolve out of focus in a way that figures her anew in the energetic interval, she adds, between "memory and forgetfulness."

Such a concluding display of the shadowy haze of self-representation effectively screens the ellipses occupied and performed by the repetitions of digital enhancement and encoding that peel open for the viewer of Marker's film the wounds of civilization. These are the wounds that inexorably intertwine memory and trauma, as well as the specific losses of history and the structural absences of fantasy. These are the wounds traversed by the ferryman, Death, who shows the way to language, to representation, to the consideration of loss and lack, to the enigmatic signifier that is culture, that is cinema.[37] But the "way" itself is what remains phantasmatically ghosted, energetically sublimated, and creatively morphed by the wounds of repetition in the age of the Digital Baroque. The way, the repetitive process of becoming, here takes on the shape of purposeful behavior through which the dead are no longer expunged from the memory of those who live on.

c h a p t e r   7

PHILOSOPHICAL TOYS AND KALEIDOSCOPES OF THE UNFAMILIAR: THE HAUNTING VOICES OF TONI DOVE AND ZOE BELOFF

Without simply ignoring or simplifying technologies, we now need to emphasize the necessity of thinking the subject not only in its relation with other subjects, but also *in,* and with the astonishing complexities *of,* the world. Yet, paradoxically, at the confines of the universe, contrary to any overriding belief in "man" or "woman," machines show humans that our universe is opaque, or "haunted."

—VERENA ANDERMATT CONLEY, *Rethinking Technologies*

When Verena Andermatt Conley published these words in 1993, she couldn't have foreseen the extensive developments in new media art through which viewers might be haunted by the loops and fades of works such as Viola's *Going Forth by Day* and Piper's *Relocating the Remains.* But her introduction to the clairvoyant collection on *Rethinking Technologies,* produced by the Miami Theory Collective, lays out the terms for understanding such haunting inscriptions and energizing sublimations of machinic art. Most particular to Conley's interests, which remain somewhat cloaked in this introductory epigraph, is how the poesis of techne performs the corporeal plenitude of energetics and affect that remains so important to French feminists Hélène Cixous and Luce Irigaray, who were introduced to the English speaking world by Conley's writings and translations. While the technological machines to which she refers may override belief in hollow concepts of man or woman, her notion of ecopoetics continues to appeal to a highly energetic corporeality, to "the idea of new language, a new *techne* based on bodily affect. This *techne* is no longer added to the body but is already in and of the body. Between nature and culture, women's sexual model, based on bifurcations and mutations that open to life and change, has cultural repercussions."[1]

It was at the invitation of Livia Monet, for her 2004 Montreal conference "Subjectivity, Embodiment, and the Transformation of Cinematic Practice in Contemporary New Media Art," that I found myself returning to Conley's writings on the ecopoetics of techne when contemplating the relation of feminism to recent developments of interactive cinema in works by artists such as Toni Dove, Zoe Beloff, and Char Davies. Although these particular artists resisted Monet's request to situate their work in relation to the ideology of feminism, my sense is that their interactive works open up something of a new techne based on bodily affect. In particular relation to the conjoined impact of touch and voice, they intersect traditions in cinema and performance on the interface of new media art.[2] I hope to suggest how their work provides a welcome opportunity to reflect on the cultural interchange of earlier projects on the performative and technological hauntings of drama trauma and cinematic incorporation with newer experimentations in machine life and culture. In my books *Drama Trauma* and *Repossessions,* for instance, I analyze the phantasms hovering throughout the pages of Shakespeare and Montaigne as well as the traumatic ghostings of performance culture at large. This work sensitized me to the powerful way in which voice and touch have served as carriers on the stage of the specters of loss and uncertainty that sustain the fantasy of seduction and its retrospective traumas. Similarly, my previous studies of the representational range and arrestation of the visual in film, video, and performance, in *Like a Film* and *Mimesis, Masochism, and Mime,* have fueled my ongoing interests in how the shifts of representation specific to the media of technology register and project enigmatic imprints of psychic and cultural exile. These are the kinds of registrations, from the screens of cinema to the condensations of video, that continually haunt the states of belonging to which Conley refers, in which subject and even gender formations remain vexed by both material and psychic manifestations of being-technologically-in-the-world.

Most specifically for this chapter, I had in mind creating a theoretical dialogue between the fanciful narratives in Toni Dove's interactive movie *Artificial Changelings* (1998) and the mesmerizing sound of Zoe Beloff's

high-pitched voice (anyone who has heard an electronic representation of
Beloff's voice should have no difficulty replaying its tone as they read). I
anticipated that critical reflections on the touching affect of voice might
generate an interesting appreciation of feminist contributions to the new
era of interactive cinema. The promise of such anticipation stems from a
wide range of feminist work on voice and touch in performance and cinema to which Conley strongly gestures yet almost sets aside in respect of
something more grandly opaque, or haunting. Godard's baroque adaptation
of *King Lear,* for instance, gains much of its energy from his appreciation
of the combination of voice and touch that closes the play when Edgar
appeals to his interlocutors to "speak what we feel, not what we ought to
say." Lear's dying exclamation to see feelingly, "Do you see this? Look on
her! Look her lips, Look there, look there!" continues to resonate haunt-
ingly in the wide array of critical work on touch, from Eve Kosofsky Sedgwick's study *Touching Feeling* to a wide path of writing in performance, film,
and video studies.[3] While Régis Durand charts the various ways in which
voice lies "*between* body and language," in his elegant essay "The Disposition of Voice," he reminds us how Lyotard's writing on theatricality as a
"theater of energetics" anchors the interrelated research on voice and touch
in the key words of "shifts, jumps in intensity; errance, mobility . . . Lyotard makes us aware that drama, vocal music, the cinema, whatever their
particular aesthetics, are complex systems, screens, filters, apparati designed
to capture and transform energy."[4]

   Similarly in film theory, "touch" often refers to the fields of designation,
the deictic, within script and shot. Something like Barthes's "punctum,"
subtle nondiegetic aspects of a film can surprise, arrest, or wound the viewer,
as if urging the spectators to "look there, look there." As a metaphor of
energetic affect, touch also impacts the viewer through formal and narrative procedures of identification and suture, as with the "touching film."
This tends to have been a gendered phenomenon in classical Hollywood
film through which audience affect has been recognized to have been structured differently in relation to male and female characters. We've all noticed
such a differentiation ever since Laura Mulvey's common adage that female
characters take out their tissues while watching their male counterparts pull
out their swords. Mary Ann Doane argued soon thereafter that the touch
of a film is explicitly linked to the hallucinatory power of voice: "the voice
appears to lend itself . . . to the hallucination of power over space effected

by an extension or restructuration of the body."[5] Because the convention of the male voice developed a steadying extension of the body in the documentary and newsreel, its power, Doane adds, "resides in the possession of knowledge and in the privileged, unquestioned activity of interpretation."[6] Even in the moment of its melancholic decline, it remains the voice of *King Lear* and his patriarchal predecessers who fill the stage and screen with commands to "look there, look there." But while cinematic voice, or affective touch, can be understood pejoratively as a carrier of repressive gender inscription, it can be marshaled just as readily for its empowering difference, whether as a carrier of the primal scene and subsequent invocatory drive or as the bearer of a feminist politics of voice. The use of the female voice alongside alternative procedures of narrative and montage functions as a positive contribution to gender representation in independent feminist cinema and performance. We need only rescreen the conjoining resonance of voice and touch in the cinema of Marguerite Duras, Chantal Akerman, Julie Dash, and Mona Hatoum, not to mention the performances of Robbie McCauley, Anne Deveare Smith, Holley Hughes, and even their predecessors who first experimented with performance's passage into video, such as Carolee Schneeman and Lynn Hershman.

While voice and touch have been reclaimed from traditional Hollywood cinema by feminist practitioners and theorists, their relation to the deictic, in the digital sense, takes on enhanced dimensions in the contexts of interactive cinema and new media installation. Devices of human computing interaction, such as the mouse, the touch screen, or the sensor, rely on the collaborative work of the user's digit or body to activate the varying fields of the digital interface. Works by Zoe Beloff and Toni Dove solicit the user to manipulate their CD-ROMs, net.art pieces, and interactive cinema through the electrified medium of digital touch, which new media artist Jean-Louis Boissier calls the "'sensorial cartography' of the interactive image."[7] By raising the question of the structural and representational status of sensorial cartography in new media and interactive cinema, I initially set out to rehearse in this chapter earlier feminist arguments regarding voice in cinema by theorists such as Mary Ann Doane and Kaja Silverman and to inquire whether the digital interface carries or solicits affect in a way that is synonymous with cinema.

But the more time I spent reacquainting myself with this work and deciphering my barely legible notes on installations by Dove and Beloff that I had viewed some time ago, I came to acknowledge that the scope of their artistic projects far exceeds the grain of voice itself by embracing a conceptual framework of the criticality of voice that jointly urges a psychophilosophical approach to new media art. I now focus my attention on the criticality (in all senses) of these artists' common interdisciplinary voice. In appropriating my epigraph from Conley's terrific 1993 collection, *Rethinking Technologies,* I hope to suggest how the digital machinery of new media art is haunted, in the most compelling terms, by philosophical toys and kaleidoscopes of the unfamiliar.

KALEIDOSCOPES OF THE UNFAMILIAR

Toni Dove's *Artificial Changelings* offers viewers a means of visualizing the conceptual current I appreciate as significantly energetic in these women's work. *Artificial Changelings* is an interactive movie that presents its users with the opportunity to move, quite literally, between two parallel narrative tracks. The viewer's physical movement across a sensitized motion pad activates the interrelated tales of Arathusa (Figure 8), a nineteenth-century self-destructive kleptomaniac, and Zilith, a real and imagined encryption hacker whom Arathusa dreams in the twenty-first-century future. Audience members are invited to enter a pool of light at the front of the cinematic screen whose iridescent space positions them in the interactive zones of the piece. When closest to the screen, you have access to a character's interior thoughts; step back a pace (onto another sensor pad) and the character will address you; step back again and you enter a cinematic trance or dream state; the final step back takes you into a time tunnel that opens into the other century. Within these separate interactive zones, moreover, the spectator's movement triggers changes in the behavior of video and sound, such as differing body, speech, and memory segments or image dissolves, frame loops, and changes of speed and color, just as "movement away from the screen will create memories clouded by layers of time, transparent images, and washes of sound."[8]

While suspended between past and future as screened in the present (you'll recall this to be the temporal formula of Freud's topography of transference), the film's shift between realistic and trancelike tracks finds itself framed by two conjoined archaeologies of the modern representation of woman. One is how the neurotic thrill of Arathusa's purposeless kleptomania provides, according to Dove, "a unique statement on how consumer economy, from the Industrial Revolution to the present, shapes identity." Scenes of Arathusa's real and imaginary wanderings through commodity culture texture this shaping with the specifics of touch, as inflected by gender and as reflected in the history of cinema and popular culture. Readers of recent studies of virtuality would likely make connections, for instance, between Arathusa's aimless wanderings through the arcade and Margaret Morse's more recent equation of "freeways, malls, and television [as] the locus of virtualization or an attenuated *fiction effect,* that is, a partial loss of touch with the here-and-now."[9]

Woman's loss of touch with reality in commodity culture is contrasted in *Artificial Changelings* by a related archaeological pattern that arrests her in the patriarchal gaze. One of the narrative conclusions that can be triggered by spectatorial motion visualizes Arathusa being caught in the act. As she furtively fills her purse with the delicacies of the shopping arcade,

Figure 8. Toni Dove, *Artificial Changelings,* 1998.

a forceful male hand suddenly grasps her wrist to arrest her purloining motions. Touch is here embodied as male arrestation, much as it is for Lacan in *The Ambassadors*. In the film's interactive spirit of determining the choice of narrative flow, the male authority subsequently presents to her a narrative of choice that is classic in its reductive clarity: he will either exhibit her or give her away to disgrace. To be looked at or to be disgraced, these are, of course, the familiar cinematic choices open to the femme fatale throughout the history of cinema. On a broader scale, we can relate them to those larger economies of consumerism and paranoia that have so frequently been intertwined in American cinema as determining factors of female identity.[10]

Yet, while the male touch here embodies the gaze and authority of the patriarchal, disciplinary agent, Dove's Arathusa remains endowed with an empowering touch of a different sort. Hers is the thrilling affect of digital sensation, like when her touch of department store silk makes her tremble as if she were drunk. Hers is the touch of subliminal stain, like when the sticky film of stolen sugared strawberries leaves her awash in a "sensation like electric waves [that] flows through her body." Hers is a touch that lends itself not to the disciplinary gaze but to the subliminal surface. I have been struck by how curiously Dove's mixture of sensation, stain, and electronic flow ranges from the nineteenth to the twenty-first centuries. Her interactive film thus dialogues in fascinating ways with Deleuze's theorization of the passage of time through what he calls the "surface of flesh." When preparing a class on Deleuze's *Logique du sens* at the same moment I was researching *Artificial Changelings,* the energetics of Arathusa's scenarios of electric touch kept clouding my reading of Deleuze's description of *Alice in Wonderland*'s vaporous surfaces of skin and tactility as the "extrabeing" or the "quelque chose" of the being-event itself: "where events, in their radical difference with things, are not at all appreciated as 'depth' but as 'surface,' in this thin incorporeal vapor that eludes the body, the volumeless skin enveloping things . . . It's in following the border, in hugging the surface, that bodies pass into the incorporeal. Paul Valéry put it profoundly, the most profound is skin."[11]

By not limiting itself to the profundity of skin, scarred on the body of Arathusa by her propensity for cutting the surface of her flesh, the energetics of Arathusa's flesh verges toward the incorporeal when the sublimity of touch provides her with the telepathic link to travel across time in communication with the twenty-first-century Zilith who also is something of an aimless shopper. While hacking the net "to map the invisible loci of power," Zilith abandons anything resembling cinematic point of view while "drowning from lack of focus in futuristic landscapes" (Figure 9). The conceit of Dove's film, driven by the physical movement of its interactive user, is that its characters remain empowered by a force circulating outside of the parameters of surveillance and gaze, subjectification and penetration. Arathusa and Zilith are linked telepathically not only to each other but also through the sensorial surface of the digital touch pad to their interactive viewers whose corporeal movements drive the narrative between past and future while also triggering the motions and discourse of the characters. Many moments in the film even seem to mirror the transferential embodiments of the linked but separated spectators, such as when a close-up of Arathusa shifts her eyes left and right, as if in sync with the viewer, or when she moves in and out of frame mirrorically in step with the interactive user. In a dreamy projection of the eighteenth-century

Figure 9. Toni Dove, *Artificial Changelings.*

theater, Arathusa even recounts its engaged public space where everyone talks at once to the performers, a space that mirrors, as she literally suggests to the viewer, the "interactive social experience . . . you find yourself in now." Another scene of direct address situates the viewer's movements on interactive motion pads in relation to the characters' aimless wanderings, as "dancing like angels on the head of a pin." Indeed, at the 2000 Bookends conference in Albany and Troy, New York, Toni Dove described the characters of *Artificial Changelings* as being "inhabited like digital puppets" by the interacting viewer who "haunts the movie machine" with her digital touch. Participants who have interacted with *Artificial Changelings* also would probably have little difficulty arguing the converse, that their movements were similarly haunted by the characters. My favorite instance of such ghosting was when my movements seemed to have prompted Arathusa to pick up a thread whose electronic pulse then took on a cinematic life of its own, like something of a squiggly green line gone wild on a digital sketch pad. Put otherwise, in the disdainful words of the movie's male authority figure, these mirrorical digital puppets function on and off screen as enlivened carriers of "the kaleidoscope of the unfamiliar."

SOMNAMBULIST CINEMA

In a conversation with Pam Jennings, published online in *Felix,* Toni Dove credits her readings in psychoanalysis for providing her with helpful models of subjectivity that have shaped her characters' confrontations with the unfamiliar.[12] If we were to shift our focus momentarily from the new media gallery to the space of analysis, we might be struck by how the telepathic interactivity between her characters and her moving spectatorial interactors mirrors and informs the rich, but not sufficiently mined, cinematic metaphors haunting post-Lacanian French psychoanalysis. While post-'68 French psychoanalysts have turned frequently to analogical cinematic concepts to depict the enigmas of representation and the kaleidoscope of the unfamiliar, there is something about the interface of digital interactivity and its fractal habitation of past and future cinematic time that lend material shape to the otherwise convenient metaphorical borrowings of psychoanalysis from the expanse of cinema. J.-B. Pontalis, for instance, adopts a cinematic vocabulary to depict the haunting nature of the waking state, that ongoing dream state, which each of us still dreaming here this afternoon knows all too well. This is the state that continues to disturb us "as if haunted," in the words of Pontalis, "by a nighttime dream, by its intense images, by its incomplete scenario, and by its changing totality."[13] In attempting to describe the ongoing hallucinations of what he calls the "visual unconscious," Pontalis calls upon his readers' familiarity with the cinematic legacy of the flashback to depict the ongoing "non-representational" effect of traumatic dreams: like flashbacks, dreams screen the intensity of event and envelop the image in an anterior temporality that lends the fantasy image more visual intensity than it could have once had. These intense effects inscribe the construction of identity as a contingent, retrospective fantasy rather than a certain recuperation of an earlier, essential state.

In a Web text on "hypothetical cinema," Zoe Beloff refers to Duchamp's "Green Box" to remind her readers "that cinema is in essence constructed around absence itself. . . . the afterimage, the absence of the image. The somnambulist cinema [she adds] of one being the memory trace produced through the body severed now from the actual traumatic event."[14] It is in a similar sense that the fantasy flashback provides the analyst with something akin to an afterimage, for not only interpretation but also secondary dream association is understood by Pontalis to have the same effect on the dream state as cinematic analysis has been understood to have on cinema. Both interpretation and "already the associations of the dreamer de-figure," in the words of Pontalis, "the images in movement—the cinema—of the dream."[15] Dissolving the limits of cinematic time, the afterimage stands alongside the film in a palimpsest relation, like that of Roland Barthes's *punctum* to the *studium,* to foreground the constraints of logicotemporal order and the decaying baggage of subjection.[16] Precisely this arresting defiguration, moreover, is what lends to analysis the traumatic quality of figuration that grabs the attention of both spectator and analysand. As I've argued in *Like a Film,* something like a still or an afterimage might be said to conjoin the retrospective traumas of cinematic flashback, hallucinatory projection, and psychoanalytic interpretation.[17]

Add to this discussion of afterimage a similar analogy that anchors Jean Laplanche's notion of the enigmatic signifier in *New Foundations for Psychoanalysis.* The "enigmatic signifier" is Laplanche's term for forgotten visual and linguistic traces that continue to elude the hegemony of the Symbolic by signifying sexuality *to* the subject without this addressee knowing necessarily *what* it signifies. Sustaining the life of fantasy as the new figure of "primal seduction," the retroactive fantasy affect of the enigmatic signifier is always already in destabilizing circulation, much like, adds Laplanche, "a film projected in reverse."[18] In both examples from Pontalis and Laplanche, the theories of the visual and aural unconscious seem to be partially conditioned by the analysts' incorporation of models of cinematic movement and sequence. While we may have difficulty recognizing and mapping the necessarily retrospective visual and aural registers of the psyche, we have less trouble situating them in relation to the mechanics of interactive cinema that themselves seem curiously compounded with the stuff of psychoanalytic case history.

To Zoe Beloff, the nexus of psychoanalytical and philosophical conundrum provides a starting point "to think about what it means to conceptualize the transformation of the world into digital form."[19] Her interactive video installation *The Influencing Machine of Miss Natalija A.* (2001), performs the case history of the former female student of philosophy who sought treatment by the Viennese psychoanalyst, Victor Tausk. Natalija A. approached Tausk because she was tormented by the delusion of being manipulated by a bizarre electrical apparatus. To situate this delusion in the context of the emergence of current pedagogical experimentation with new media interfaces and mobile technologies, I wish to stress that Miss Natalija remained convinced that this torturous technology was being diabolically manipulated by her rejected suitor, none other than a college professor. Beloff's installation foregrounds the paradox of this conflation of psyche and electronic machine, lover and professor, patient and doctor. Although Tausk interpreted her case as one of schizophrenic delusion representing the patient's own body that had become alien to her, Natalija sensed that Tausk too had fallen under the machine's influence. Beloff is quick to add that the doctor committed suicide a few months later.

Beloff's interactive simulation of *The Influencing Machine* includes clips of early Viennese medical and technical films, diagrams of medical electronic picture signals and electric vision, as well as an interactive electron gun disguised in human form. The users of the installation don stereo glasses to interact with a large stereoscopic diagram of the hallucinatory machine (Figure 10) as if they were sinister technicians tormenting the delusional Natalija. While Beloff could take sole credit for the ingenious conceit of her installation, her citation of Tausk seems to share credit with his 1919 statement that "machines produced by man's ingenuity and created in the image of man are unconscious projections of man's bodily structures."

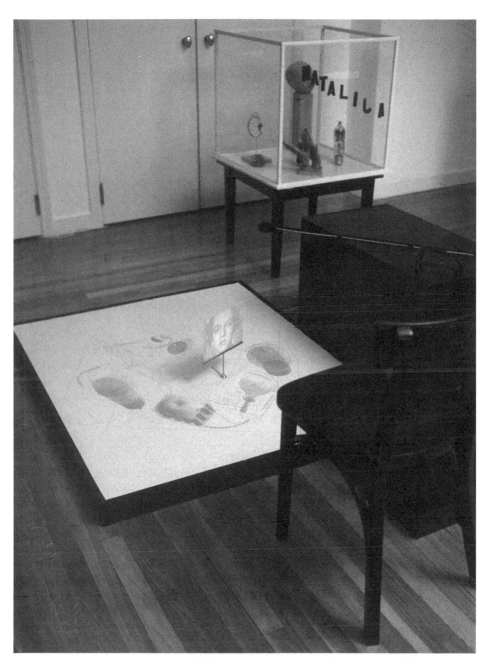

Figure 10. Zoe Beloff, *The Influencing Machine of Miss Natalija A.*, 2001.

Were I to elaborate on similar examples of the cinematic matter of psychoanalysis, it would be to discuss how psychoanalysis, cinema, and now new media often seem to speak on behalf of each other, how their illusions serve as the partial support of psychoanalytical reality in lending structure to the aural and visual relations of analysis and the machine culture of new media, thereby masking what Slavoj Žižek would call "some insupportable, real, impossible kernel."[20] Such a project would aim to clarify new media's role in aiding and abetting the attempts of recent Continental psychoanalysis and philosophy to better understand the visual and linguistic relations of such enigmatic waking states as hallucination, cryptation, hypnosis, telepathy, transference, and countertransference. That is, rather than being merely the passive receptacle of theoretical assumptions about, say, the cinematic gaze and its phallocentric operations, the new media apparatus could be said to provide helpful analogical frameworks through which the visual and aural theories of libidinality might extend their range.

This approach engages seriously with artistic appropriations such as Zoe Beloff's CD-ROM project *Where Where There There Where,* produced in collaboration with the Wooster Group's performance of Gertrude Stein's play *Doctor Faustus Lights the Lights.* In 1996, Beloff was approached by the Wooster Group to produce something in relation to its work-in-progress "House/lights." Probably in response to Beloff's tremendously successful series of QuickTime movies, *Beyond,* which she launched on the Web in serial form, Liz LeCompte invited her to make a series of Web QuickTimes that would incorporate actors from the play.[21] Rather than documenting the performance per se, Beloff set off to create a satellite work on CD-ROM, something that would exist, she writes, "purely in the virtual realm."

But what might constitute purity in the virtual realm ends up being the conceit of Beloff's interactive creation. On the face of things, her CD is something of a virtual translation of the Wooster Group project. The stage sets of colossal industrial ruin are transformed into QuickTime virtual reality panoramas within which the actors perform as embedded video loops. Users can click on a character upon entering a panorama to catalyze a movie or roam the panorama for hot spots linked to related short films. The movies themselves are a combination of shots of the actors performing their parts and clips from period 16 mm film that spoke to Stein (with an affection for Betty Boop). Beloff reshot the period film with a QuickCam that captured rear-screen setups. This rather primitive camera apparatus itself transforms both performance and film sequence into something of a jumpy afterimage, a retrospective of text and image activated by the user's patient habitation of the decayed industrial setting transformed into seductive virtual realm.

The CD-ROM begins with an inset QuickTime movie that recounts the paradigm shaping the story. Beloff returns to this QuickTime epigraph in her notes on the CD, explaining that she "begins with a true story of Wittgenstein's escape into a cinema to drug himself with film in order to forget the philosophical problems that exhausted and tormented him. But as in all dreams, the repressed returns. And it is these hidden conflicts, the ones that are repressed below the surface of the play that I wish to bring to light."[22] The most searing conflict on which Beloff then seizes is less the disappointment of Wittgenstein's turn to cinema as something of a philosophical opiate than the unsolvable paradigm of man's being haunted by the machineries of twentieth-century technology. She writes that she was touched by Stein's statement that "her Doctor Faustus sold his soul, only to discover he had no soul to sell." "It is here," adds Beloff, "that we discover the great changes in perception of what it means to be human, that went hand in hand with the development of technology, mid-century. Man had, in short, become an automata who just didn't know it."[23] Would pure existence in a virtual reality, given this context, thus be tantamount to becoming automata? Beloff's shared affection for the animated Betty Boop and the similarly repetitive appearance of the RCA dog, echoing in incompossible contrast what she calls "the master's voice," seems to suggest an earlier and consistent fascination with the haunting "machines produced by man's ingenuity" that so tormented the delusional Natalija.

Yet the purity of the virtual relates as much to philosophical toys as to haunting machines in Beloff's work. Regarding *Where Where There There Where,* she emphasizes that the virtuality of its framework is as conceptual as it is digital in that it constitutes a montage of concerns common to Stein's language games, Wittgenstein's philosophical conundrums, and the mathematical play underlying Turing's Universal Machine and his later ability to crack the codes of the German Enigma machines. "Each time a word of the text is rewritten," she writes, "the panorama moves thus giving the impression that the world is structured by the recombination of language, creating an interactive experience that is both within the viewers control yet goes beyond it, suggesting that the visible world is now nothing but an interface and behind it lies the logical structure of programming."[24] Interactive performance destabilizes her notions of subjective control as the user hangs in the balance between theatrical memory, cinematic delight, linguistic trace, and ultimately the *jouissance* of manipulating virtual reality in its infancy on the home computer. Beloff turns to Pynchon's *The Crying of Lot 49* for an expression of such virtual purity: "it was now like walking among the matrices of a great digital computer, the zeros and ones twinned above, hanging like balanced mobiles right and left, ahead, thick, maybe endless." I would be just as inclined to cite a 1985 essay from Jean-François Lyotard's book, *The Inhuman: Conversations on Time,* in which he reflects on the dizzying promise underlying stultifying technoscientific practice, a promise since realized by ludically artistic projects on CD-ROM and the Internet that solicit their handling with no particular end in sight:

> The complexification of the transformers, theoretical and practical, has always had as its effect the destabilization of the fit between the human subject and its environment. And it always modifies this fit in the same direction—it delays reaction, it increases possible responses, increases material liberty and, in this sense, can only disappoint the demand for security which is inscribed in the human being as in every living organism. In other words, it does not seem that the desire—let's call it that—to complexify memory can come under the demand for equilibrium in the relation of man with his milieu.[25]

What Beloff contributes to the broad spectrum of interactive cinema and performance is such a complexification of the empowering insecurities underlying the automations of logic and machine. That she does so while utilizing the most rudimentary and crude devices of new media interactivity speaks precisely to her commitment to complexify the milieu and memory of the machines haunting our universe.[26]

BRINGING-FORTH TECHNE

It is this creative emphasis on the haunted user and inhabited machine that Zoe Beloff and Toni Dove share so creatively. Their work foregrounds the uncanny kaleidoscope of the unfamiliar that hovers in the cyberspace between new media art, psychoanalysis, and philosophy. Not only has Dove explicitly referred to her adventurous artworks as "philosophical toys" whose uncanny doubles elicit terror and make strangeness erupt,[27] but Beloff has collaborated with the Internet provider Turbulence to create a magical online site, "Philosophical Toy World."[28] Hers is a delightful Internet data bank that visually re-creates the prehistory of the moving image and its philosophical corollaries. "The ideas expressed here have no wish to be well balanced, or even sane," writes Beloff in a text introducing the site. "They are a call to reinvest moving images with the marvelous, not through other worldly flights of imagery but through seeing the very production of the moving image in a new light." This language calls to mind how interactive installation artist Char Davies describes her "immersive virtual spaces," those that interact literally with registrations of the warmth of the user's breath and the surface of her skin, as "a new kind of 'place' through which our minds may float among three-dimensionally extended yet virtual forms in a paradoxical combination of the ephemerally immaterial with what is perceived and bodily felt to be real."[29] It is only fitting that Davies turns to Martin Heidegger's *The Question concerning Technology* to provide the life breath of the creative "bringing-forth" of techne and poesis into a deadening, militaristic technological world that values machinic automata over new media's haunted, interactive delights.

As I work toward the close of this chapter, I wish to sustain the swelling echo of women's voices that haunt the universe of new media machines. But this can be done only by rehearsing the paradox of the age of post-feminism. As I mentioned at the outset, the occasion for first pondering the parameters of this chapter was an invitation by Livia Monet of the University of Montreal to discuss feminism and new media in a conference to include Beloff, Dove, and Davies. It was there that Beloff and Dove both reacted strongly and with surprising hostility to Monet's attempt to align their projects with "feminism." This was notably paradoxical given Dove's dialogue with woman's place in the nineteenth-century arcade and on the twentieth-century couch, not to mention Beloff's fascination with Tausk and artistic attraction to the performative poses of Charcot, which she is now re-creating as parodic digital photography events. Is it a nostalgia for some kind of universalism or simply a reaction to the consecration of the "woman artist" that leads them to resist the feminist tenor of the same projects that haunt a phallocentric tradition of technoscientific production? Or might they simply be echoing Verena Andermatt Conley's caution about essentializing the machinic complexities of the universe along gender lines?

If the latter, then I conclude by turning our and their attention again in the direction of Conley's *Ecopolitics: The Environment in Poststructural Thought* where she frames her evocation of an activist ecopolitics in a paradox that counters the hostility of the postfeminist generation. Following a critique of the activism of both Hélène Cixous and Luce Irigaray, Conley stages in *Ecopolitics* a virulent call for the need to reground oneself in the epistemology of a sometimes too virtual French feminism at this precise critical moment when, she cautions, the "masculine techno-scientific subject is interested in outdoing all human possibles, lack of gravity, natural time, cosmic rhythms and their regulation but also disintegration, fission, explosions, catastrophe."[30] This call is echoed, albeit indirectly, by Char Davies. I leave you with the touching grain of Davies's voice as she makes her philosophical call to arms by citing the same 1993 book, *Rethinking Technologies,* with which I opened these reflections on philosophical toys or kaleidescopes of the unfamiliar:

> In view of the grim prospect of the twenty-first century, we are compelled to ask how critics of culture, philosophers, and artists will deal with technologies. How do they contend with expansionist ideology, and the accelerated elimination of diversity and of singularities? How do they resist or act? . . . Now, in a world where the notion of space has been completely changed through electronic simultaneity, where the computer appears to go faster than the human brain, or where "virtual reality" replaces "reality," how do philosophy, critical theory, or artistic practices deal with those shifts?[31]

DIGITAL INCOMPOSSIBILITY: CRUISING THE AESTHETIC HAZE OF NEW MEDIA

The "interactivity" of digital aesthetics is commonly understood to shift the ground of the artistic project away from "representation" and toward "virtualization," away from "resemblance" and toward "simulation." Rather than celebrate the art object's imitation of nature, its adherence to well-established artistic genres such as still life, landscape, or portraiture that set the parameters of "resemblance," or even its perspectival solicitation of spectatorial attention and wonder (consciousness and taste), digital aesthetics can be said to position the spectator on the threshold of the virtual and actual. As put succinctly by Pierre Lévy, the image thereby "abandons the exteriority of spectacle to open itself to immersion."[1] The key concept here is not so much the stasis of similitude as the speedy interface of identity and difference occurring on an ever-shifting plane of difference and divergence. The future promise of digital aesthetics is its enhanced zone of "interactivity" through which the users' entry into the circuit of artistic presentation simulates or projects their own virtualizations, fantasies, and memories in consort with the artwork. Already in 1968, Gilles Deleuze was articulating just such an aesthetic when he theorized those "elements, varieties of relations and singular points [that] coexist in the work or the object, in the virtual part of the work or object, without it being possible to designate a point of view privileged over others."[2] What Deleuze imagined as possible at the pivotal moment of 1968 might be understood, at the beginning of the new millennium, as having come to material fruition in the interactive aesthetics of CD-ROM and digital installation.

Underlying the radical potential of new media, however, is a paradox that I argue throughout *Digital Baroque* to lie at the core of digital aesthetics.

While opening the artwork to the virtual dimensions of the digital threshold, a substantial number of electronic artists are just as dedicated to the refashioning of past codes of similitude and resemblance. A poignant testimony of the promise of such an approach is voiced by Francesc Torres in describing his video installation *El Carro de Fenc* (1991). He understands his combined reflection on Bosch, the decline of monastic power, and the tragedy of Tiananmen Square in terms of his assessment of the temptation of the American avant-garde of Eden to reject the social resistance of his Catalonian past:

> Landing in the country of the infinite present was a rite of passage which washed off the accumulated dust of the journey but did not wipe out the memory. When one is left without history, one has the chance to invent a new one or reconstruct the old one. Europe exerted its pull so I opted for the second alternative. After having dissected the butterfly with a hammer, I plunged into the terrifying task of putting its vision back together again under a microscope . . . one also discovers that what is lived through the experience of others means that events older than ourselves can speak to us with the tangibility and eloquence of the physical, of the present.[3]

Torres joins the other artists discussed in this book by remaining dependent on or by opening himself to fresh dialogue with subtle concepts of resemblance that are particularly helpful to understanding our postmodern interactivity with the virtual.[4]

In evaluating electronic art's understanding of its links to the past, critics need to appreciate the historical and ideological complexity of the "new" apparatuses of digitized electronic arts in relation to the future promise of the digital reconfiguration of historical methods, artistic icons, and cultural memories, not to mention, as we have discussed, the role played by new interactive art in addressing the challenges of lost memories, traumas, and their counternarratives of vision and utopia. It is in the spirit of Torres's project, then, that I wish to reemphasize the critical parameters guiding *Digital Baroque:* that any analysis of digital interactivity must dwell critically on and in the metaphors and architectonics of resemblance, identity, point of view, and societal place whose complex, historical roots continue to haunt and inform even the most utopian projects of virtual interactivity. "Far from revealing the blinding light of pure Being, or the object," writes

Maurice Merleau-Ponty in *The Visible and the Invisible,* "our life possesses an atmosphere, in the astronomical sense of the word: it is constantly enveloped in a shadowy haze which one calls the sensible world or history."[5]

To produce such an electronic haze of the sensible has been the compelling and sometimes misunderstood aim of many electronic artists whose work often opens up spaces for ongoing reflection of the complex links between past history and future interpretation. Perhaps the digital helps to foreground the complex layerings of psychosocial identities that can be thought in space only insofar as they will have been, as they stand in the past only in relation to their virtual illumination in the future. The technical ability to enfold the vicissitudes of space and time in the elliptical repetition of parallel structure might be the most novel feature of the horizon of the digital. Such enfolding opens the discourse of memory to multiple registers of time, space, and national identity that are simultaneously present on the screen of representation. As I have had numerous occasions to discuss in this book, Gilles Deleuze concludes both *Cinema 2: Image-Time* and *The Fold: Leibniz and the Baroque* by reflecting similarly on the linkage of the growth of new machines in the social field to the political chaoerrancy of cinematic world-memory and its potential nomadism. Through digital machineries, the baroque panoramic organization of space so cherished by Benjamin loses the vertical privileging of direction, the screen becomes a curvilinear data bank through which information and its methods replace nature, and the "brain city" becomes subject to the perpetual reorganization of world-memory and its radical intensities. In this concluding chapter on "Present Past," I would like to re-situate the parameters of what I have been calling Digital Baroque in relation to the temporal folds of interactive media. As a means of returning the many conceptual and thematic concerns of this book to the threshold of the digital future, this chapter will return to Digital Baroque's stress on incompossibility and temporal folds in view of a number of early works on CD-ROM prior to the next section's emphasis on the future cinema of interactive installations.

DIGITAL FETISH / SENSORIAL CARTOGRAPHY: JEAN-LOUIS BOISSIER

As if miming Deleuze's thesis that the Baroque is linked to the digital in relation to "a crisis of property, a crisis that appears at once with the growth of new machines in the social field and the discovery of new living beings in the organism,"[6] French artist Jean-Louis Boissier turns his attention to the early modern legacy of Jean-Jacques Rousseau to reflect on the historical intensity of the reorganization of sight. In his digital installation *Flora Petrinsularis* (1993–1994), a shiny brass reading lamp illuminates an open book of sheathed papers and pressed flowers.[7] Leafing through two loose-leaf volumes of sixteen double pages, viewers can read selections of Jean-Jacques Rousseau's erotic and turbulent accounts from the *Confessions* or admire the craft of Boissier's physical reconstruction of the herbarium created originally by the eighteenth-century author during his political exile.[8] Positioned behind the book and its comforting reading lamp is a sculptural monument to the electronic garden, an Apple monitor with matching speakers. The visual lure of the Apple is triggered by a camera built into the book's reading lamp that tracks the number of each newly opened page to match the text or herb with a digitized counterpart of textual passages, moving images, and sounds. A trackball, mounted on a small brass railing directly in front of the book, can be slid back and forth by the viewer to catalyze the interactive computer program.

Unsettling this installation's nostalgic display of a cozy baroque reading room are the luminous electronic machineries sitting in front and behind the book as if to serve as the new digital bindings of Rousseau's texts. As readers move in and out of time, from the idyllic Age of Enlightenment to the digital era of virtual luminescence, they find themselves caught in the voyeuristic ebb and flow of a journey between the textual imaginary of sensuous confession and the ocular proof of natural history. Their manipulation of the seductive trackball reduces the text to its most erotically dense sequences. It fixes the eye on the precious details of nature and beckons the virtual timbre of wind and water or the subliminal sounds of rubbing and panting. These are the sounds accompanying split-screen, QuickTime displays of Rousseau's sensual visions that vary in speed, luminescence, and proximity.

In re-creating the textual point of view of Rousseau, digitized video clips review the fetishistic images that so stimulated Rousseau's erotic imagination. In one sequence, a video close-up of hands gloved in delicate lace (Figure 11) tracks Madame d'Epinay's ambiguous gesture that either ties or unties the ribbon of a package; the screen then splits to reveal her close-up profile looking left, then a close-up of her mouth, then a close-up of her

V-shaped hands over the package. Another sequence shows the bodice of Mademoiselle d'Ivernois falling to reveal her breast; this is then juxtaposed with a shot of the ribbony lace of an undergarment being loosened, then a three-quarter portrait shot of a woman looking into the camera, then a close-up of a decorative ribbon tied around her neck. So as not to leave the scene of primal trauma entirely inscribed in the to-be-looked-at-ness of woman, there is also a close shot of a man rubbing his ear, then a hand gripping an armpit accompanied by panting sounds, then a profile of a quivering man with closed eyes, followed by a shot of his neck, all of which is preceded by the textual extract recounting Rousseau's youthful struggle with a man who let fly some kind of whitish, sticky liquid at the moment of their separation. Even though these video sequences loop back to repeat themselves, the loops skip the initial establishing shots, thus returning the viewer only to fetishistic fragments of the lost memory of what came before. While returning reading and viewing to the certainty of its manual roots, to the masculine caress of page or trackball, this neobaroque electronic installation thus ensnares the confidently desiring subject in the cybernetic loss of narrative control as signaled by the fetishistic objects that pulsate in QuickTime and voice-over as if to destabilize the look of the gaze through its return in look and sound. Such capitalization on the digital platform as a means of transforming the passive viewing experience into an aleatory space of interactive sound and vision has been extended by Boissier in his hypermedia installation *Second Promenade*. Departing from Rousseau's traumatic account of having been knocked over by a dog while walking through the countryside, Boissier here re-presents the "angles" of Rousseauesque vision

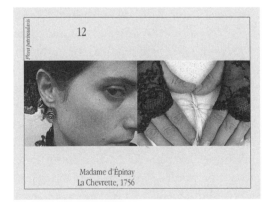

Figure 11. Jean-Louis Boissier, *Flora Petrinsularis*, 1993–94.

by foregrounding the digital paradox that empowers viewers while subjecting them to the logic of the code and the "accidents" of interactivity.[9]

Like the eighteenth-century precedent of Rousseau's "promenades," Boissier's electronic *Flora Petrinsularis* sensitizes its users anew to the many fetishistic interrelations of reading and viewing, language and image, idea and material, subject and object. At all times, Boissier insists, "The fetish objects are just an intermediary, allowing the imagination to construct a presence of greater intensity than reality itself, available at leisure in solitude and innocence."[10] The unpredictable results of this digital journey of sight and touch always position the user on the unstable site of the between that Boissier shares so comfortably with Godard, Marker, and Deleuze: between now and then, between actual and virtual, between book and CD-ROM, between image and fetish, between reading and voyeurism, between look and gaze, between female and male. When the viewer is literally between passages while manually turning the page, moreover, the computer registers an "error" and catalyzes a crystal image of clear water and rocky lake bottom accompanied by the rhythmic sounds of water lapping against a boat. This combined textual/CD-ROM interval, this literal moment of the in-between, thus stages the primal condition, the "reveries with no distinct subject," of Rousseau adrift in his boat.[11]

Boissier emphasizes how the new technical organization of the computer provides a "sensorial cartography" of the interactive image.[12] For readers of Rousseau's *Rêveries,* digital video technology provides for an exact recreation of the "flat" viewing angles from which Rousseau rediscovered nature. Boissier duplicated these same angles for his video peep show that displays the fetishistic gaze so central to the libidinal machinations of the *Confessions.*[13] Similarly, the thirty-two double pages of Boissier's loose-leafed book correspond to a digital volume of more than ten thousand screen pages whose electronic animations underscore their virtual autonomy. His creative use of software also permits him to display his sense of the haptic ambiguity of digital designation (that to point the mouse or to move the trackball gives renewed entrance to an image but not necessarily its confident possession). Through Boissier's new regime of what he calls "a dramaturgy of interactivity,"[14] the viewer leaves *Flora Petrinsularis* with a sensitive coda both to deciphering digital culture and to reading Rousseau: that the greatest proximity equals the most exaggerated fragmentation. Perhaps this is why the CD-ROM highlights Rousseau's description of Madame de

Warens: "The Gentleman saw something quite different which was easier to see than to forget."

PHANTASMS OF FILM AND PHOTOGRAPHY:
PERRY HOBERMAN AND MIROSLAW ROGALA

Perry Hoberman's CD-ROM *The Sub-Division of the Electric Light* (1996) similarly positions the user at the interface of vision and touch, light and machinery, place and space, actual and virtual, sight and remembrance.[15] Shifting our focus from the bookish catalogue of Rousseau to its modernist kin, the cinema, manipulation of the mouse traverses zones of light and threshold to prompt the apparition of a historical piece of cinematic equipment common to the domestic sphere of the home movie: slide lamps and projectors as well as 8 mm and 16 mm projectors (Figure 12). Only the user's touch of the mouse activates the machinery of vision, which then projects onto the threshold of the computer monitor varying stills and sequences of amateur and professional film footage. If cinema can be said to be the twentieth-century's mnemonic machinery, then Hoberman's CD-ROM foregrounds memory itself as the historical container of cinema. Cinema

Figure 12. Perry Hoberman, *The Sub-Division of the Electric Light*, 1996.

here is not merely the material embodiment of movie houses, audiences, and production histories; it is also what touches the spectators at the core of memory's shell: their nostalgia for the home movie, their fond recollection of their first visit to the movie palace, their harboring of traumatic visions and memories created or mediated by cinema, and, foremost to Hoberman, their experience of "the parceling and reapportionment of time that dynamic media bring in their wake."[16]

The interactivity of the users' solicitation of the CD-ROM is crucial here. Rather than being merely the passive recipients of cinematic phantasms from the primal scene, the users find their touch pivoting between the mechanism of everyday communication and the specters of cinematic fantasy to prompt on the monitor cryptic citations of the machineries of vision from the history of cinema. These citations range from indistinctly familiar cinema clips to amateur footage, home movies ranging from parental interaction to the infant's discovery of the mirror-image to the baby's playful game of Fort-Da, and from rites of childhood passage like the familial handshake in front of the camera to the disembodied tracking shots of sublime vacation landscapes.

The Sub-Divisions of the Electric Light positions the users, moreover, not merely in the interval of memory but in cinematic memory's interval of time and light. Hoberman's artistic sensibility to the nuances of time and light are crucial to the interactive play of his CD-ROM. Time is not so much experienced cinematically as a passing of time or recollection of memory, but is *activated,* as Deleuze might say, as the play or thought of temporality.[17] "I want to make something," writes Hoberman, "where time never stops completely—but not where you're trapped in an automated clockwork—where the user can play with time, where time is something malleable—however not something where the user controls time (which would be impossible anyway)."[18] Similar to the CD-ROM's positioning of the users in the thought of time, the varying image tracks and light corridors situate the late twentieth-century subject within the phantasmatic horizon of the cinema not simply as the projection of light but also as the imprint and sociocultural touch of light. Light for Hoberman is not, as discussed in chapter 2, the transparent medium of Cartesian metaphysics that links sight, visibility, and temporality. Nor is it a mechanism that merely "sheds light" on history and its politics. Rather light, particularly in its staged relation to time, functions more in the sense outlined by Cathryn Vasseleu, in *Textures of Light:*

Vision and Touch in Irigaray, Levinas, and Merleau-Ponty, to open vision to the touch of light, "to the hinges or points of contact which constitute the interweaving of the material and ideal strands of the field of vision."[19] Vasseleu's feminist linkage of the discourse of light to the play of touch sets up "a more mediate ontology," a space in-between that so uncanningly characterizes Hoberman's artistic project on the light of "becoming."[20]

Particularly striking about Hoberman's subdivision of light is his demystification of both transcendence and the naturalization of light. Light here remains interrelated to its capture at the conjuncture of a fold in time and space. In one scene, for instance, the spectator triggers footage of underwater divers only to find that the light of projection situates them within the field of a three-dimensional room. While the users can manipulate the moving image to demystify the anamorphic correction of the lens, they find themselves aggressed by the sudden folding of walls, stairs, and screens in a way that reinserts the architectural as phantasmatic space rather than as flat projective place. Although the moving images capture virtual time as having passed, the interactivity of the CD-ROM stages the passing present of actual time through the interminable repetition of the image track. In this way, the CD-ROM conjoins actual passing time, as Deleuze characterizes its swing between the actual and the virtual, and time's ephemerality: "time that is," as we remember from Deleuze, "that is smaller than the minimum of continuous thinkable time in one direction is also the longest time, longer than the maximum of continuous thinkable time in all directions."[21] It is within this temporal fold, moreover, that the viewers come to recognize their entrapment within the repetitive field of moving vision, enveloped as they are within the memory of familiarly indistinct images and the all-too-familiar sound tracks of filmic Muzak. They are beckoned to denaturalize the architectonics of cinema as a means of thinking space within the various folds of the subdivision of electric light.

The repositioning of the subject as thinking the movement of space also characterizes the performative conceit of Miroslaw Rogala's inventive videographic CD-ROM *Lovers Leap*.[22] Rogala creates a CD-ROM environment of real time and virtual reality that conjoins the speed of digital and electronic light. While watching the video movements of passersby on Chicago's Michigan Avenue bridge, the user responds to the frantic urban pace of the everyday by freezing the movement-image with a click of the mouse, as if snapping a tourist photograph. But in doing so, the cybertourist is almost simultaneously seized by the uncanny disorientation of what seems to be a familiar photographic scene rendered askew by the subsequent vector of its movement, the rotation of its vision, and the pivoting of its sensorial planes. For with additional clicks of the mouse, the stilled photograph develops into a dizzying montage of altered angles and perceptions through which the high skyscrapers of the Loop are seen from the top down (Figure 13). The users thus find themselves caught in the space, the vector, and the speed of a mutable point of view.[23] Is it a coincidence that the uneven sound track records the voice of one passerby who recognizes the plight of a fellow traveler caught in the passage of the boundary: "You want to get out of here? Well, I just came in and I came from this way"? Caught in the flow of a seemingly unpredictable digital sequentiality, the users inhabit the threshold between two additional states or zones. One is the fractalized anamorphic rotation of space and light that renders the flat studium of the stilled image into the curvilinear punctum of an image-event in action. The other zone is entered, almost as if by chance, when the users' response to enigmatic hot spots permits them to cross the threshold into the virtual territory of the city's alter-ego, Jamaica, where virtual light waves are the lay of the subliminal land. Here rather amateurish video footage records the artist's own arrestation in the movement of becoming: "Traveling from Chicago to Jamaica," he writes, "I visited a place called 'Lovers Leap' (a legendary location of tragic lovers—such places exist all over the world): there was a military radar scanning the sky. This physical surprise created a conceptual leap as well."[24]

In Rogala's case, the touristic surprise of sensorial entrapment positions the digital user within the destabilizing scene of fantasy as it traverses love

Figure 13. Miroslaw Rogala, *Lovers Leap*, 1995.

and its subliminal leaps in perspective. "Our contemporary life-world," writes Margaret Morse in her perceptive catalogue discussion of the installation on which the CD-ROM is based, "is an aggregate of a physical locality and virtual realms that are linked, but not united. In this case, 'Chicago' and 'Jamaica' correspond less to geographic localities than to states of mind. As Miroslaw Rogala explains, 'movement through perspective is a mental construct; one that mirrors other jumps and disjunctive associations within the thought process.'"[25] The Jamaican image of otherness, similar to the Chicago image of passage, catalyzes less the symbolic opposition of here and there, us and them, now and then, than the phantasmatic interrelation of performance and perspective whose partial uncontrollability and unaccountability happens, as Rogala points out, "in matters of love as well."[26] Fantasy and speculative repetition here morph the dialectics of identity and the political praxis of immediate reaction to situate the visitors in an indeterminate zone of sensory experience.

Somewhat resembling Alice in Wonderland's curious fall through to the other dimension, the combined speed of electronic presentation and the flux of corporeal movement become enfolded in the time delay conjoining subliminal fantasy and speculative thought—enfolded, moreover, within the materialized space of the entry, the visitation, the threshold, the leap, the fantasy, the metamorphosis, the no exit.[27] Rogala's conceptual leap thus involved putting into action something like the enigmatic signifier that unsettles passive, touristic, and colonial observation, so that *Lovers Leap* signifies *to* the subject without its addressee knowing *what* it signifies. Through the traumatic nuance of the seduction of language, vision, and, subsequently, all that is particularly dramatic or performative, the trace of the enigma functions here as the carrier of fantasy's affect. While the structure of resemblance and analogy continue to solicit the subject, its affect carries the uncanny incertitude and semiotic openness of the virtual.

THE SOUNDINGS OF SHOCK: NORIE NEUMARK

Nowhere is this solicitous openness of virtual affect better demonstrated than in Norie Neumark's award-winning CD-ROM *Shock in the Ear* (1998), which invites its user "to explore five moments of shock, to experience the strangely dislocated time/space that is shock."[28] An interactive essay on the intensity and fragmentation of shock's moment and aftermath, Neumark's piece is organized around five moments of shock and its aftermath: Attack, Decay, Memory, Resonance, The Call.[29] The users' solicitous movement of the cursor across enigmatic surfaces of image and color triggers a symphony of natural and electronic sounds whose melody accompanies jarring narratives of shock: a woman's first hours after a severe car accident, a political prisoner's water torture, a World War II soldier's shock from lightning while on the telephone, a mental patient's shock treatment, and a young Italian girl's cultural shock from an Australian hostel full of refugees from diverse backgrounds who speak unfamiliar languages. In a way that freezes the user in the moments specific to these narratives, the CD-ROM is programmed so that the user cannot click to leave the story until all of its painful details are spoken. The tension between the free movement of the cursor across the visual field and the frozen time of narrative delivery exemplifies Neumark's "shock aesthetics [in which] we can sense a dislocated space and expanded time during which, or after which, new sensations and perceptions can flood in."[30]

Given Neumark's reputation as a sound artist, it is not surprising that what marks the resonance of these narrative bits is less the graphic unction of their detail than the various textures or grains of the voice through which the sociological stuff of storytelling becomes entwined in the "more mediate ontology" that is voice. Adding to the wonder of this CD-ROM is how its presentation of the five moments of shock include bits of the same narratives being spoken in varying sequence by the different storytellers of the piece. Shock is thereby screened as apperceived by all users from inside fantasy's continuously unfolding, jumbled, and retrospective narratives as much as something triggered from the outside by social and cultural interaction. While time stands still, fragments of narrative pass from ear to ear, between person and person, self and self's other in what Neumark terms "a radiophonic type of space."[31] Enunciation and the vicissitudes of radiophonic interpellation are thus staged as the foundational ground of shock, a quaking ground whose uncanny affability is likely to disarm and unsettle even its most callous users.

The aplomb of this CD-ROM's interface with the affect of shock may be attributable to Neumark's training in sound art and radio, which permits her to experiment with the elasticity and plasticity of the expansive threshold of digital sound in contrast to the emphasis on cinematic and videomatic fields evident in the work of Boissier, Hoberman, and Rogala. By foregrounding the interface of sound and shock, both of which "take place in time," Neumark means to invert the traditional artistic hierarchy of vision over sound in a way "that challenges the aesthetics and kinesthetics of CD-ROM interactives, through non-linear and poetic movement."[32] Throughout *Shock in the Ear*, the cursor's movement triggers a symphony of natural and synthesized sounds whose disquieting tones work to envelop, if not distort, the voiced narrations. Equally striking about this piece, which could lend itself so easily to sensational visceral display, is the artist's intelligent placement of "the strangely dislocated time/space that is shock" within the appealing surround of a subtly fluid two-dimensional painterly ground. The CD-ROM's ever-changing tableaux of paintings and designs by Maria Miranda playfully solicit the spectators with softly contrasting textures, loosely penciled figures, and abstract color fields that literally embody the digital sound tracks. One animated sequence (Figure 14), which accompanies the horrific description of ants entering the bloody wound of an accident victim's leg, displays not a mimetic image of the horrific thing but, instead, a sheet of colored paper being torn in half; in another, the description of "a violent sort of trembling" in the patient's shock-treated body is matched on the computer screen by rapidly changing color fields, from red/violet/blue; in yet a different link, the spiraling blackness described by a patient who was administered gas is framed by illustrations of human figures entrapped in gilded bird cages. There is something about this project that consistently invites the users to inhabit the phantasmatic zone of shock rather than to delight from a distance in the projected ugliness of its vision.

Neumark's aesthetic environment is far different, for instance, from "the condition of digital culture itself" described by Mark Seltzer as the essence

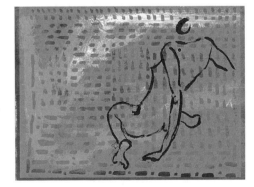

Figure 14. Norie Neumark, *Shock in the Ear*, 1998. Art by Maria Miranda.

of contemporary "wound culture": "The convening of the public around scenes of violence—the rushing to the scene of the accident, the milling around the point of impact—has come to make up a *wound culture:* the public fascination with torn and opened bodies and torn and opened persons, a collective gather around shock, trauma, and the wound."[33] To the contrary, the CD's lyrical and melodic tracks of beckoning whispers, synthesized chords, and natural tunes work wonderfully in situating the retroactive experience and thought of shock in a curiously soothing kinesthetic environment. The calmness and tranquility lent to the visual field by the mischievousness of Neumark's own ear contrasts sharply with the labored violent display of Seltzer's "wound culture." One hears electric static rather than thunder, shards of glass being swept rather than windshields exploding, and abstract electronic rhythms whose dissonance rings of uncertain familiarity. In striking contrast to the visceral attraction of a wound culture, the stunning verve of Neumark's project on shock is how it enfolds the experience of shock less in the public fascination with the visceral image than in an unusual cushion of thought-provoking kinesthesia. "So it was a mapping of bodily shock space experience rather than early modernist shock aesthetics or recent Hollywood that I sought. I worked with sounds that traced that space. Not so much the crash of glass at impact, but the sweeping of shards that mark and mark out a fragmented space. Not the scream, but the sucking-in of breath, deep into the body, along the nerve lines, into the tissues."[34]

Neumark's artistic emphasis on the soft stillness and eerie tranquility of time's suspension contributes to a digital environment in which the retroactive experience of shock can be thought along the divide of its divergent manifestations in culture and history. This is marked most clearly by the occasionally translucent cursor that reveals enigmatic but indecipherable fields of color and texture on the underside of the page. Or for a less subtle example of Neumark's play with the enigmatic signifier of fantasy and its retroactive shock, consider how one page full of the same graffiti-penned question, "what?," is designed so that the cursor can pick up and momentarily drag the "what?" with no apparent purpose or resolution. Here "what?" is displayed as a literal floating signifier that functions to signify *to* the users without its addressees possessing a clue about *what* it signifies.

Upon first visiting *Shock in the Ear* in 1998, I was struck by how profoundly Neumark's piece provides a material ground or support for comprehending the emergent digital horizon itself not simply as artistic material but as concept. Hers is not the immediate, hyperreal flaunting of ooze and wound, "a stalling on the matter, the materiality, of representation," which Seltzer associates with the discourse network of 2000 as "the condition of digital culture itself."[35] Hers is more the phantasmatic condition of reception itself, similar to that condition of spectating suspended in the delay of time, that state noted by her accident victim as "like watching a silent movie."[36] The interactive promise of digital culture, in this sense, reveals not simply "the becoming-visible of the materialities of communication"[37] but something more like the shadowy haze itself, something more akin to the three- to four-dimensional interval conjoining space and time, something close to Deleuze's crystallization of time and image, or Derrida's horizon of "différance" that combines the becoming-space of time and the becoming-time of space.[38] Digital aesthetics, in this context, is foremost *an interval of becoming*. It thus opens to the spectators an amoebic, fractal space of the temporal continuum of becoming; one enveloping past, present, and future; one that foregrounds the creative enigmas of the many tensions driving modernism's ideological fantasy: being and non-being, resemblance and simulation, body and spirit, material and simulacrum.[39]

It may prove helpful to remember that Deleuze understands such a temporal continuum to effect the image of space only insofar as the interstice is inscribed in the seriality or difference of duration and time. The sometimes interminable duration of digital repetition, staged by Neumark as the continual recirculation of sound, can be said to figure an ontological crisis through which the user is confronted by the nonlocalizable exteriority of serialization. As we have seen throughout *Digital Baroque,* Deleuze always returns rather ambivalently to Leibniz's notion of incompossibility to explain this complex point.[40] We need only recall his footnote to *Logique du sens* that provides a summary of the three serial elements of the world that inscribe the Leibnizian monad on the margins of incompossibility: one that determines the world by convergence, another that determines perfect individuals in this world, and finally one that determines incomplete or rather ambiguous elements common to many worlds and to many corresponding individuals.[41] Rather than either converging or remaining impossible for each other, rather than being either included or excluded, they stand in paradoxical relation to one another as divergent and coexistent, much like the five states of shock coexisting incompossibly in Norie Neumark's *Shock in the Ear.*

INCOMPOSSIBLE WORLDS OF RACIAL IDENTITY:
REGINALD WOOLERY

In calling to mind the paradox with which I opened this essay, that of the attentiveness of digital/virtual artists to the temporal ghosting of procedures of resemblance and representation, I wish to turn to an example of digital incompossibility of a sort perhaps more poignant to the American interface. Reginald Woolery's 1997 award-winning CD-ROM *world wide web/ million man march/world wide web (www/mmm)* capitalizes on digital creativity to foreground the incompossible convergence of two major controversial events in recent American cultural history: the 1995 Washington, D.C., Million Man March, sponsored by Louis Farrakahn, and the 1994 group exhibition *Black Male: Representations of Masculinity in Contemporary American Art,* curated by Thelma Golden at the Whitney Museum of Art in New York City. Woolery's deeply reflective project interfaces printed news excerpts regarding the march, the Internet, and African-American culture with photographic and audio interviews of visitors to the *Black Male* show and participants in the Million Man March. Thus juxtaposed with the incompossibility of these events is their rather conventional coverage in the traditional media and the expansiveness of their discussion on the World Wide Web that began to exhibit its cultural promise alongside events surrounding the march. By combining in the CD-ROM contrasting on-site interviews and Internet news bits from two divergently controversial moments in contemporary American cultural history, Woolery successfully conjoins divergent stories that derive from personal and public experience, from history and fiction, with a wide range of competing views and sounds of African-American culture—conflicting narratives, images, and sound tracks that come from within the community as well as from without. The same digital palette links, for example, the contrasting audio interviews of black men celebrating their gathering in Washington with the disenchanted views of patrons who have just left the Whitney disturbed by the prominent display of black male flesh.

The opening page of *www/mmm* presents the user with a small graphic video insert embedded in a page of URLs whose fast-speed sound track frames the CD-ROM in the suspicion of the digital future itself. Equating fascination with the Internet with a version of civil disengagement, the high-pitched, rapid-fire voice (a voice of urgency, of media hysteria?) equates the

Internet with "yet another version of the opiate of the masses" in that it provides users with the illusory impression that they actually are creating community. Users enter the interface of *www/mmm* armed with the warning that the downside of the information highway is its failure to provide its virtual riders with concrete means for sustainability, accountability, and conflict management. In an interior link in the CD-ROM, "News," users are presented with Internet news bits attesting to the pioneering rhetoric of the "new frontier" whose promises may have done little more, one story suggests, than enact the "Haves and Have-Nots Revisited." Recalling the verve of Keith Piper's *Caught Like a Nigger in Cyberspace,* the celebratory joy of digital aesthetics is tempered at almost every turn in *www/mmm* by Woolery's cautious reminder that the interface is not yet all-inclusive.

But I do not mean to give the impression that *www/mmm* is primarily a visual or video phantasmagoria of life on (or off) the Internet. For the soul of this piece is its sound. Composing the CD-ROM's aesthetic fabric is a multimedia weave of two-dimensional graphic collage always surrounded by the beat and tempo of changing African-American music tracks, from jazz to funk, that situate the viewer in the type of radiophonic type of space so characteristic of Neumark. When music is not in the air, then the melodious difference of dialect picks up the beat. What distinguishes Woolery's radiophonics from those of Neumark, however, is the cutting realism of their sound bytes that here burn the memories of the traumatic past into the searing interface of the everyday African-American cultural environment.[42]

Organized around four central tropes—spirit, identity, pleasure, and desire—Woolery's CD-ROM foregrounds the incompossible worlds of identity now challenging the uniform clarity of representational purpose (Figure 15). The playful scene of Uncle Reggie "Sitting on Sunday with Sasha and Sava" opening the "pleasure" site stands in sharp contrast with the deeply melancholic collage of stills from the late Marlon Riggs's *Tongues Untied* and a closing link to verse so important to Riggs by gay British poet Essex Hemphill. The "spirit" link, moreover, confronts the viewer with a mischievous video montage of footage of two American idols of the media: Louis Farrakahn and Farah Fawcett, or Farah-Kahn. The scene of "desire" presents the viewers with graphic outtakes of responses to the questionnaires regarding desire returned to Woolery by the audiences of his public presentations. While a click on the keyword "consume" links to the response "I lost my virginity, I gained insight," the keyword "passion" reveals the

Figure 15. Reginald Woolery,
*world wide web/million man
march/world wide web,
(www/mmm)*, 1997.

painful result of years of such insight: "when my husband left me I was so
physically and emotionally distraught that I wanted to leave my body in
its pain and go somewhere, anywhere." The honesty of the interface and
the openness of its conflicting messages present the users of *www/mmm*
with an aesthetic environment in which to ponder the paradoxes of the
mental and emotional side of physical life in America.

But rather than settle for the simple solution of positioning, say, the Black
Male on the clear-cut threshold of Us and Them, Woolery presents a much
more complicated scenario in which desire and identification enfolds the
atmosphere of representation in something of a shadowy haze that one calls
the sensible world or history. It is precisely the haze of history that provokes
the question of desire's object: desire for and identification with whom?
The unclear response to this question is foregrounded, among other things,
by the CD's emphatic display of the rift caused by the American conflation
of fantasy and desire of and for the black male body. This conflation becomes especially complicated by Woolery's focus on the most controversial pieces of the *Black Male* exhibit, those that interrogate and celebrate
black homosexual desire.[43] Given his CD-ROM's forthright prompting of
the unresolved debate over the show's pictorialization of the black male body,
from its inclusion of the always controversial *Black Book* photographs of
Robert Mapplethorpe to its display of photographs by Lyle Ashton Harris
in drag, my sense is that Woolery's CD-ROM comprises a collective dialogue on the understanding of an art of engagement as something other
than a clear-cut visual praxis of identity, division, and the alienation of
political struggle. Rather, it prompts something more of a fluid aesthetic

reflection on the vicissitudes of repetition, difference, and the flux of ideological fantasy. As one keyword reveals in the "pleasure" site, the "Other" vision here is urgent yet unrestricted: "I had a vision of myself in the bow of a white boat, speeding to the rescue of who or what I had no idea."

FINAL EXIT: RACING ALONG THE DIGITAL HIGHWAY

Woolery's work foregrounds the controversial role of narratives and theories of desire in articulating identities of race, gender, and sexuality, not to mention the incompossible challenge of *Digital Baroque* to prior modernist assumptions about digital art, aesthetics, and identity. I wish to conclude this far-too-sweeping discussion of emergent digital aesthetics by reflecting on the significance of an anecdote lingering in my memory, one that I am fairly confident was prompted by Woolery's presentation of *www/mmm* to the Flaherty Film Seminar at Ithaca College in 1997. This is a memorable remark, which could easily be encased in the expansive memory file of *www/ mmm,* made by a black male who recalled proudly his memory of speeding down the New Jersey Turnpike in a packed automobile on his way to the march in Washington, D.C. The man's remarks focused on the paradoxical spectacle of this vehicle full of black men that may have aroused suspicion from white highway patrolmen surveilling it from the outside just as it generated powerful black pride from within (there is documented evidence that the New Jersey troopers had developed a program of racial profiling that flagged cars driven by black men for random drug checks). This is the kind of *www/mmm* spectacle that is particularly poignant in the context of post–World War II art, for these men were cruising the same nonelectronic highway out of which Michael Fried has gotten so much mileage via his now canonical essay "Art and Objecthood."

You may recall the pivotal moment in this essay when Fried foregrounds remarks by the sculptor Tony Smith about cruising the New Jersey Turnpike while it was under construction in the early fifties. To Smith, as Fried helps us to understand, the turnpike existed "as something enormous, abandoned, derelict, existing for Smith alone and for those in the car with him."[44] The theatrical character of what Fried understood as Smith's literalist art without the object itself resulted, as Fried acutely puts it, in the sheer persistence of the experience that directed itself at Smith from outside the car and that simultaneously made him a subject and established the experience as objecthood.[45]

Curiously, the traveling subject in participatory dialogue with Woolery remarked on a similar experience, but one with a significant difference, with which I conclude this chapter. For him, the thrill was the persistence of the movement toward something enormous but not abandoned or derelict, the Million Man March, whose uncertain utopic journey seems not to have been regarded by him and the others in the car, as it was for Smith, as "wholly accessible to everyone, not just in principle but in fact."[46] In contrast, this man's cinematic motion down the turnpike marked both the desire for and the incompossibility of what Woolery calls the sustainable experience of community. Most notably, that trip on the New Jersey turnpike, much like the delirium of the *Black Male* show for many of its viewers, not to mention the speedy excess of new digital art for so many others, reopened the enigmatic question of black male subjectivity as one in need of breaking the shackles of its American objectification to reposition itself on the conjoined horizons of spirit, identity, pleasure, and desire. Woolery's electronic assemblage of these racialized horizons signifies *to* its many users, but does not necessarily signify *what*—at least in a manner that can be assumed to be wholly accessible and comforting to everyone. Perhaps this is what it means to cruise through the aesthetic haze of digital incompossibility. "I had a vision of myself in the bow of a [digital] boat, speeding to the rescue of who or what I had no idea."[47]

IV.
SCANNING THE FUTURE

chapter 9

PSYCHIC SCANSION:
THE MARKER OF THE DIGITAL IN-BETWEEN

Strange childhood, wedged between two wars like a book caught between two
bronzed elephants.

— CHRIS MARKER, *Immemory*

Wedged between two wars, Chris Marker passed his youth like a propped-
up tome crushed by the weight of two historical bookends. This was a
period that marked not only the representational trauma of youthful passage for a boy who later moved so fluidly between photography, cinema,
and new media, but also, we might say, the traumatic passage, the end, of
the dominant allure of the book and its nineteenth-century realist narratives. The bookends of the two world wars also ushered in the dawn of a
new medium of technological artistry, cinema. It was through the wedge
of cinema that Antonin Artaud, the energetic precursor of the cinematic
genius Chris Marker, dreamed of liberating representation from the weighty
bindings of narrative realism to enact a violent performance of affect. Fascinated by the "virtual force" and movement of film, he wrote compellingly
about the cultural transformations promised by cinema's "new atmosphere
of vision." To this prophet of contemporary performance, film provided
the means for a welcome "deformation of the visual apparatus."[1] Rather
than ground theatrical affect in the development of realism and the narrative of the family drama, he situated performance at the abstract interface
of modernist developments in technology. The technological artifice of
light and sound provided Artaud with the promised break from the numbing effects of mimetic realism and its attendant social passivity. "Cinema,
better than any other art form," he wrote optimistically, "is capable of

translating interior representations because it is the enemy of dull order and habitual clarity." What remains particularly haunting about Artaud's assessment of the cinematic metamorphosis of representational order, whose cruelty he soon adapted to the extravagance of early multimedia performance, is its characteristically French emphasis on the contribution to interiority made by new artistic technologies: "The cinema seems to me to have been made to express matters of thought, the interior of consciousness."[2]

It was around the same moment, when the allure of technology was capturing the imagination of early twentieth-century culture, that Freud too was taken by the affective pull of technology and its metaphors. The big difference, of course, was that Freud was fascinated by the interiority of the unconscious and was drawn more to the aural apparatus of the telephone than to the visual machinery of silent cinema. Speaking of the role of the analyst, he recommended this technological analogy: "He must turn his own unconscious like a receptive organ towards the transmitting unconscious of the patient. He must adjust himself to the patient as a telephone receiver is adjusted to the transmitting microphone . . . so the doctor's unconscious is able, from the derivates of the unconscious which are communicated to him, to reconstruct that unconscious, which has determined the patient's free associations."[3] In adopting a telephonic metaphor for the practice of psychoanalysis, Freud rearticulates the structures of reception he had previously established for the study of dramatic character types through which the derivatives of a character's unconscious continue to transmit to twentieth-century audiences. His readings of the poetic hallucinations, paranoias, and repressions of Shakespearean tragedy inform both his understanding of the form of psychic life and how modern viewers respond telephonically to the symbolic traumas of the Oedipal drama.[4]

Curiously, however, it was in the midst of the same passage of time—when Marker suffered the crush of the bronzed bookends of traumatic history and when Artaud saw in technology the promise of a performance of affect—that Freud broke from his former fixation on the symbolic role of dramatic narrative to reflect more freely on the affects of the drives and the linkages of incorporation, masochism, and sublimation. French work on Freud's later writings, by analysts such as Jean Laplanche, André Green, Guy Rosolato, and J.-B. Pontalis, has revealed that his undeveloped thoughts on the Super Ego and the enigmatic link between incorporation, sublimation, and the drives opened the door not merely to a challenge of the causal

dominance of the Oedipal structure but also to a questioning of the telephonic passivity of the sublimated analyst, not to mention the psychically
confident reader, who too finds herself troubled by the charged currents
of countertransference and its vicissitudes. At the heart of all of this interference, so maintain the post-Lacanian analysts, lies a deformation of the
visual apparatus and its linkage to sublimation.

SUBJECTIVE SCANSION

I frequently find myself wondering what might have happened to psychoanalytic theories of creativity had Freud paid more attention to the early
discourse on cinema and its relation to what we might call the transfiguration of the book/ends of narrative clarity. What if he had been able to
profit from Artaud's prescient dream of a technologically aided performance of affect, one that was meant to impinge on the psychosocial comforts of the ideology of dramatic realism? Perhaps Freud and Artaud could
have collaborated in composing oneiric film scripts or in staging a multimedia spectacle like the latter's play *Spurt of Blood*. Such a collaboration
might have profited from the material representations of performance to
better theorize or imagine the workings of incorporation and the death
drive in view of their enigmatic relation to the visual scene. While such a
missed encounter might be understood as a mere curiosity of history, it
could just as easily be attributed to a gap in sensibility that continues to
exist between psychoanalytic and artistic practice. Whereas psychoanalysis steadfastly champions the curative value of creativity and frequently
celebrates the fine arts for their display of artistic sublimation, it frequently
does so without suspicion of the fundamental premise of Freudian sublimation, as well as without acknowledgment of contemporary art forms and
practices that lend themselves to such conceptual complication.

I am referring to the potential reconsideration of Freud's emphasis on
sublimation as the energetic passage from the sexual instincts to nonsexual
activities,[5] which he attributes to successful intellectual symbolization and
procedures (ideologies) of normative homosocial binding (at the expense,
we should recall, of nonnormative homosexualities and the play of the body).
From a philosophical point of view, the Freudian emphasis on artistic production via sublimation readily embraced by psychoanalytic approaches to
art bears the significant imprint of the Christian discourse of spirit. "If soul

is the form of the body," writes Jean-Luc Nancy in "Corpus," "spirit is the sublation or the sublimation (or perhaps the repression?) of any form of bodies in the revealed essence of the sense of the body."[6] Even sophisticated approaches to sublimation by Laplanche, Rosolato, and Green remain over-determined by authoritative references to Renaissance and modern repre-sentational painting[7] and their attachment to the aesthetic tradition of "spirit." In so doing, they fail to capitalize on the artistic nuances of their own baroque metaphors that might liberate their approach to art from clunky bondage to the conventional aesthetic referents of representational painting and symbolic narrative.

I refer less to the promise of their frequent analogy of painting and dream, such as Pontalis's foundational thesis that "the painting and the dream teach that one must unlearn the conventions of sight so that the horizon and background of things can display themselves in their immediacy,"[8] than to the prescient references in their revisionary texts on sublimation to the burgeoning digital scene. Rosolato reminds his readers, for example, of the psychoanalytic distinction between primary imaging and the digital signi-fiers that efface the prestige of images by opening the subject to linguistic abstraction. Conversely, he turns to the metaphor of scanning to describe the activity of reading through vision whose "exploration demands patience and time" at the expense of visual representation.[9] Just as Freud called on the apparatus of the mystic writing pad to understand the process of screen memory, Rosolato now could cite the digital scanner as precisely such a machine whose patiently close entry of data recognizes the object only in relation to the software's internalized recombination of form as code that easily can skew the representation and abstract thought of the source doc-ument. It is in this process of scanning, moreover, that Rosolato identifies a convergence in psychic space around what he calls the "Object of Per-spective" that grounds psychic life. "We thus recognize the chiasm," he writes, "between the verbally digital and visually representational analogy which is centered around the aporia. This results in a double manifestation: that of the relation of the unknown in the aporia and that of the object of perspective that recovers the aporia as a topological object. So it goes that this object of perspective lends itself to the signifier of loss."[10] Loss here is organized around the phenomenological procedures of scansion, not pri-marily around sexual differences or Oedipal triangularity. These latter are the social forms of representation through which the subject gives content to form. In essence, it could be said that such content *form*ation is the end-game of homosocial sublimation, "in accordance with the general estimate," writes Freud, "that places social aims higher than the sexual ones, which are at bottom self-interested."[11] In contrast, the procedures of scansion could be thought as functioning to rewrite subjectivity as a mere component of the deterritorialized residue of code and its repetition.

As a result of this doubled logic of scansion, through which the form or metaphorization of the scanned object may be recognized but not necessarily in terms of its content or what it represents, the status of "representations themselves can be relegated," suggests Rosolato, "only to that of the phantasm, whereas the visible, maintained at a distance, can only be a protection against more direct contacts, following other perceptions, other sensations, or inversely against abstract thought."[12] Readers of these 1987 remarks on the object of perspective in its visual foundations may even recognize scanned repetitions of Laplanche's earlier seminars on sublimation, which he offered from 1975 to 1977 and published in 1980 as *Problématiques*, vol. 3, *La sublimation*. There Laplanche turns to a similar metaphor to emphasize the importance of the process of symbolic temporalization over and against a symbol's content: "here also we encounter the problem of time as subjective scansion with its heterogeneous moments particularly of 'disqualification,' symbolic loss, and anxiety."[13] At the heart of subjective scansion for Laplanche lies his revised thinking about the energy of sublimation through which the notion of subjectivity itself is rendered unstable by the traumatic enigmas of subjective scansion as they circulate energetically in relation to the uncertainty of content and signification (what he calls elsewhere "the enigmatic signifier"). Laplanche insists, in a familiar quotation: "So you have to think of sublimation in a less transformational and so-called mathematical way than Freud thought of it, which is of inhibited and desexualized drives and so on. We must try to think of sublimation as a new sexuality; it is something new, maybe coming from the message, from the work itself. It is a kind of new excitation, new trauma coming from the sublimated activity itself, and through this new trauma comes new energy. I try to connect the idea of sublimation with the idea of research or trauma, and I coined the idea of traumatophilia."[14]

Taking the lead from such reflections on sublimation that were penned in the nascent stages of digital culture and teleportic communication, I would like to reflect on their prescient relation to the suspended time of digital aesthetics and its "energetic" means of production. Of particular note is the uncanny intersection between recent cinematic experiments with the multimedia book and psychoanalytic discussions of the visual in relation to the aesthetic activity of sublimation. In a discussion of Chris Marker's CD-ROM *Immemory* (1998) and his recent digital installation *Owls at Noon Prelude: The Hollow Men* (2005), I suggest that recent developments in digital art once again offer a promising deformation of the visual apparatus in a way that refigures and reenergizes narrative performance while providing materialized metaphors for a better understanding of the vicissitudes of artistic affect. Both Marker's digital book and recent French rereadings of sublimation prompt their audiences "to unlearn the conventions of sight" so that the horizon or affect of the visual itself might destabilize psychoanalytical and philosophical assumptions about intersubjective and social relations. The challenge posed by digital media to conventions of sublimation are not necessarily new but can be said to be forcefully technological as they carry forth in the work of art what Lyotard calls "a technological stain . . . passing beyond recall of what was forgotten to remembrance of what could not have been forgotten because it was never inscribed or registered."[15]

STAINS OF MNEMONIC REGISTRATION

As an ageless artist in his eighties who embodies the wounds of earlier times of war, Marker cautiously embraces the digital in order to foreground the complex layerings of psychosocial identities and memories that can be thought in space only insofar as they will have been ghosted by the vicissitudes of access, as they stand unregistered in the past only in relation to their virtual illumination in the future. As noted in chapter 6, he joins Godard by working in unconscious dialogue with Deleuze, who concludes *Cinema 2* by reflecting on the baroque linkage of the growth of new machines in the social field to the political chao-errancy of cinematic world-memory and its nomadism. The video or digital image provides the means, Deleuze remarks somewhat ambivalently, either to transform cinema or to replace it, "to mark its death."[16] Perhaps with even less ambivalence than that expressed by Deleuze, Marker wonders, in *Immemory*, "whether the cinema has delivered everything it can, perhaps it should cede its place to something else. Jean Prévost wrote somewhere that death is not so bad, it merely consists of reconnecting us to all that we loved and lost. The death of cinema should be nothing more than that, an enormous memory. This is an honorable destiny."[17]

In presenting its users with a kaleidoscope of visions, images, and sounds of the traces and infelicities of cinematic and personal memory, *Immemory* calls on both ancient and new technologies of documentation to dwell on the stains of mnemonic registration. Through his shift from the public screen of cinema to the private space of the multimedia book, Marker stands in, let's say, for Laura as the author and decipherer of an enigmatic CD-ROM that tracks the twentieth-century visual history and the artist's ambivalent relation to its production. Consider the double vision that frames the technological stain of Marker's presentation of his photographic relationship to Japan—traces of which abound in his more recent films, *Sans Soleil* and *Level 5,* and which lend form to *Immemory's* multimedia essay on travel. Marker's photographic archive of Japan opens not with a photo album but with an ancient book of similar shape, "the *Tabino soshi,* a travel book or journal and notes (*Makura no soshi,* the 'pillow notes' of Sei Shonagon, which became the *Pillow Book* of Greenaway), everything that comes from the point or from the mind, without anything pondering or framing"—subjective scansion perhaps, but self-registration, no.[18] The pillow book serves a function opposite of bringing memory in line with reflection on literary culture. "Good lesson for us, old European students dulled by seriousness and classical discourse, 'what is well-conceived' etc. . . . . What if the essential conceals itself in trifles?"[19] Perhaps Marker's autobiographical foray into multimedia expression puts into play the dual action of a turn aside from the classical discourse of the book and an embrace of the technological benefits of the stain of the everyday. Might not the end of the multimedia book reflect a representation, as first suggested by *Level 5,* of what previously could not have been deemed worthy of remembrance or registration?

Having been confronted with the stain of the stuff of the ancient representational practice of *Tabino soshi,* the user of the CD-ROM is taken to the next link (Figure 16), labeled "where the author," in which an image of a cyberspatial thinker or tourist maintains a lofty, distanced position over Tokyo. But much like the disarming lesson learned about the more ancient form of book writing, the user quickly learns from Marker that subjective confidence over representation is not the result of cinematic projection and omniscient perspective: "the author . . . realized after some time that, all things considered, he never really saw anything that way." Similarly, the users fail to see the next link when they repeat the codes of mapping and clicking on which they relied to navigate the preceding pages. The page does not advance by clicking to the right, as instructed by the program (as if turning the page), nor does anything happen by clicking on the image, the digital convention of blowing up or plumbing the depths of an image. Equally disempowering is any attempt to offer the mouse to the screen's smiling red cat, Apollinaire. Acting somewhat like the user's superego, this mocking feline surfaces sporadically throughout *Immemory* to disrupt the user's flow with caustic questions and informational diversions. Rather than follow the canonical routes of returning either to the previous link or to the main menu, the users must learn to rely on other routes of navigation and different codes of organization by patiently discovering the fleeting icon of alternative vision hidden in the chaotic darkness of the electric screen. But rather than regain the luminous perspective of the filmmaker, the users then are befuddled by an enigmatic grid of stilled circulation and frozen motion in an abstract urban environment named Tokyo. What moves rhythmically here is not the glory of projection; rather, the repetitive sound of a cyberspatial ping summons the user to dwell in the condensed folds of a future not yet recognized.

Indicative of the verve of *Immemory* is how difficult it is for the user to describe this multimedia moment, not to mention the form and content of Marker's contribution to CD-ROM art.[20] What if the deep history of the book or the colossal projection of cinema were no longer the guarantors of a culturally uniform memory but now the mnemonic supplements of something potently disparate, something traveling quickly across the

Figure 16. Chris Marker, *Immemory*, 1998.

neural networks of global communications? What if cinema were less a fading shadow of something higher than us than a lively interiorized mark, a digital burn of densely packed media bits incised onto the shining surface of the CD/DVD-ROM? One result is a refined relation to the historical as something not simply understood and regressive, to be cut off or cast aside for the sake of avant-garde progress, but rather as something wonderfully cryptic, if not also deeply troubling and traumatic, to be brought into critical dialogue with the present for the sake of shaping personal, political, and social paradigms that might help inform the rapid expansions of the technofuture. In many cases, the activity of digital scansion as the pure registration of code opens the user as well as the author to the technological stain of abstract forms and concepts that may never have registered in the first place. When cinematic paradigms shift from spectacular projection and riveted reception to miniaturized registration, temporal folds, memory theaters, and playful interaction, the screen and its users encounter the Digital Baroque.

The technological form of the CD/DVD-ROM plays a particularly challenging role in these developments. In providing artists with broader "bandwidth" and more extensive databases than can yet be readily accessed in a book, film, or even on the Internet, the format of the CD/DVD-ROM challenges artists to situate their thought and practice in an expansive array of visual, aural, and textual interplay. To a certain degree, it could be said that the materials and codes of the CD/DVD-ROM place even the most isolated of artists right at the epicenter of the reception and exchange of both old and new public information and entertainment systems. This is an electronic medium that can linger on the threshold of high art and popular culture; it can conjoin the canonical habits of moviegoing with the impromptu intricacies of interactive game playing; it can serve simultaneously as entertainment system and intellectual archive. A fascinating aspect of the CD/DVD-ROM is how its code can activate scanned and virtualized images, texts, sounds, and shadows at unexpected moments whose linkage to the narrative at hand may be tangential at best. The interactive deterritorialization of narrative form and readerly confidence frequently opens up creative lines of flight between private fantasies and public registers.

This passage from old paradigms of form and spectatorship to new registrations of code and interactivity is paradigmatic of the digital spectacle of Chris Marker's CD-ROM *Immemory*. Through his shift from the public screen of cinema to the private space of the multimedia book, Marker tracks twentieth-century visual history and its ambivalent relation to the electronic screen. It is partly the uncanny status of the CD-ROM as electronic book poised somewhat haphazardly on the threshold of the public and the private, the historical and the personal, that makes *Immemory* such a curious object of analysis. Raymond Bellour, in his essay accompanying the CD-ROM, argues similarly that *Immemory* can be charted along three interrelated axes: the autobiography of Chris Marker and photography and cinema, his two most beloved media. *Immemory* is replete with photos taken throughout the world by Marker along with his reflections on cinema's visual and ideological impact on the twentieth century, which he illustrates with telling cinematic snippets, documentation, and sound tracks (but with no actual footage, curiously enough, from his own films). "The uniqueness of *Immemory*," writes Bellour, "is to be the repository of an oeuvre and a life which have taken this century as a memory palace [comme lieu de mémoire] for all the world's memories."[21]

Upon first entering the CD, the users find themselves interpellated by the appearance of a curious anamorphic sequence that then settles down into a recognizable and chartable grid (Figure 17). Along with icons for the worlds of cinema and photography, there are emblems for "the Museum," "Travel," "War," "Poetry," something called "Xplugs" (leading to a catalogue of digital images), and finally, perhaps the only icon not representative of an artistic genre or historical event, "Memory." These interfaces complicate the more artistically autobiographical template of the CD and cast its artistic visions and self-portraits into complex digital montages where social history and its psychological temporality confront the artist and his users with the depths of memory and the contestation of its representational efficacy, if not the epistemological prominence of identity per se. *Immemory* delivers not only something of a composite picture of what Jacques Derrida might call the feverish delirium of the digital archive but also a lively investment in what we've been calling the conjoined folds of the Digital Baroque. Raymond Bellour insists that

> Marker has not neglected the arts of memory, from which the self-portrait, wittingly or not, has drunk its riches since the Renaissance. He reminds us that Felipe Gesualdo (somewhat underplayed in Frances Yates' great book) proposes in his *Plutosofia* "an image of Memory in terms of arborescence

which is perfectly *logiciel*" [Marker's pun on the French word for computer program]. But if he is particularly careful to acknowledge his debt to Robert Hooke, the precursor of Newton's theories of gravitation who provided him with the most precise analogy of his undertaking, it is because the latter aimed not at an instrumental art of memory but at a veritable philosophy of memory in itself. . . . Hooke, who conceives of Memory as "a repository of ideas," thus qualifies "the last Idea formed, which is nothing other than the present Moment." This is also what Deleuze, speaking of Resnais' cinematic transformation of Proust and Bergson, called Membrane-Memory, between inside and outside, actual and virtual.[22]

Immemory, concludes Bellour, "is indeed that of which one cannot conceive any memory . . . whence something surfaces upon the screen of memory."[23]

The Proustian screen, the Deleuzian membrane, and even the Derridean fever are overlaid in the CD-ROM's link to "Memory." Offering visitors alternative paths to the legacies of Proust and Hitchock, this link conflates the trace of literature with that of cinema: "Que'st-ce qu'une Madeleine?" Clicking on the side of Proust, the user moves from the infamous passage in *Swan's Way,* "And all of a sudden, the memory appeared to me," to a

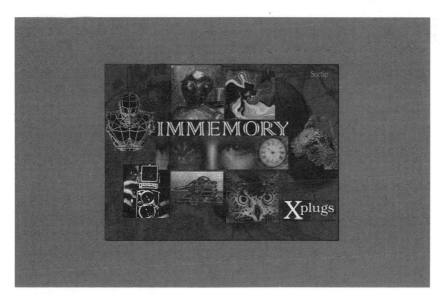

Figure 17. Chris Marker, *Immemory.*

collage of the artist's own visual toolbox. One learns that "Madeleine here is the name of all the objects, of each moment, that can catalyze this strange mechanism of Memory." This Proustian gesture positions the hundreds of images and documents stored in the CD-ROM as the personal marker of the crypt of its artist's meMORy. It is in this way that *Immemory* facilitates the autobiographical task faced by Chris Marker whose partial purpose it is to order his personal archive.

But memory has a bit of a different guise if the user backtracks and clicks on the face of Hitchcock where the picture of *Vertigo*'s Madeleine represents the quest of a protagonist failing in his struggle against "the dictatorship of memory." The lesson to be learned, that which is seemingly offered up as the methodological exercise of *Immemory*, contrasts the duplicitous shadows of memory with the aesthetic serenity of Hitchcock's cinematic art: "It's banal to say that memory lies; it is more interesting to see in the lie a form of natural protection that one can govern and shape. Sometimes, this is called art." Put otherwise, to return to a term important to this chapter, sometimes this also is called sublimation. It is something like the transformation of Scottie's sexualized frenzy into the still life of memorialized art that makes *Vertigo* one of Marker's favorite films. This also resembles what the psychoanalyst André Green attributes to conventional understandings of sublimation: "What is sublimated is related to an ideal object. Desexualization means dematerialization, and dematerialization is synonymous with idealization. The incorporeal, the spiritual, and the ideal are primarily at issue here. Idealization presupposes spiritualization and these become the model of an ideal."[24]

The ruse of Marker's CD-ROM, however, is that it sets up ideals only to disquiet them. Any protection of an ideal always seems to be under interrogation: "Qu'est-ce qu'une Madeleine?" When reflecting on the aesthetic ideals of the museum, for example, Marker seems to undercut the ideal far more than he shores it up. For this resourceful artist, the museum is a site less for contemplation than for fascination, less for spiritual identification with an aesthetic ideal than for quizzical discovery of the unheralded, minor work of art and even of the fetishized objects of artistic projection itself. His digitized imaginary museum includes a humorous picture of Manet's infamous picnickers who play themselves as a video game, as well as a stunning diversion of the Lumières' train from its arrival at La Ciotat into the midst of Poussin's *Rape of the Sabine Women*, almost as if to shuttle between Marker and Kuntzel.

Arriving at a page on Renoir, moreover, the users are asked not so much to contemplate the beauty of his painted woman as to enliven her through an interactive touch that transforms a Renoiresque image of a reclining woman into a three-dimensional enactment of her breathing in a way that fills the electronic screen with playful life-forms unknown to the works of Renoir, whether on canvas or film. The users are encouraged to play even more fast and loose with the ideals of art history when invited to alter Mona Lisa's infamous smirk that lay partially behind Freud's musings on sublimation. Clicks toggle between the classically recognizable smile to a baroquely enigmatic frown. Hovering throughout *Immemory* are thus the combined signifying traces of sublimation and being-there *(Dasein)* that, as J.-B. Pontalis understands them, "are not images or memories but figured through time in plastic and visual form."[25] Behind the look of the ideal and the voyeuristic gaze of perspective, Marker confronts his user time and again with the traumatic enigma of the click—the deictic sign of CD-ROM interactivity. The limit sign in this case is interpellation itself, the figure of greeting or of arrestation, or even of the uncertain certainty of the enigmatic signifier marking the primal linkage of ontology and time, "One day, I was there . . ."

RETROACTIVE FIGURATION

It could be said that retroactive figuration is the primal stuff of *Immemory*. When musing about his encounter with the China of 1955, Marker suggests that to interrogate the new China "would mean playing Malraux against Stalin. The Malraux of 1927, of course." Jean-François Lyotard would add that this also means playing Malraux against Europe and Europe against contemporary art and the flourishing of early cinema:

> The anxiety of Europe must come via Asia. . . . Soon after *La Tentation*, André returns to this theme in the 1927 essay, "D'une jeunesse européenne." He presents an inventory of ruins in the pathetic mode: impossible Christianity, the notion of destroyed man, the self-transformed into a "deserted palace" where phantasms wander as if a miserable parade of heroes. But contemporary art seizes its Renaissance in this very decomposition.[26]

The retrospective envelopment of the present in the haunting imagery or thought of the past is thus no less true of cinema, that art form whose glory was also flourishing in 1927 when Artaud wrote in praise of its magic and made his appearance in Abel Gance's miserable parade of heroes, *Napoleon*.

A particularly intriguing sequence occurs in *Immemory* when Marker attempts to fix his primal memory of film within the binary he identifies as the originary dialectic of cinema: the trauma of war, on one hand, and the enigmatic look of woman, on the other. In this sequence, an inset clip from the midair plane collision in Wellman's *Wings* (1927), whose silent jumpiness is strangely doubled by the digitized platform of QuickTime, leads to a link that features the look of the actress Simone Genevois in *La merveilleuse vie de Jean d'Arc,* by Marc de Gastyn (1928). Although Marker first saw this image at the age of seven, it remained forgotten or unregistered until sixty years later when the filmmaker attended the 1986 Cinemathèque inauguration of the restored print. There he was blown away not by the reappearance of the celluloid image on the big screen but by its retroactive hallucination via the smile of the aged and diminutive actress herself who greeted the public gathered for the opening of the restored film. "She smiled, she waved," writes Marker, "she didn't know that ten meters away sat a stranger who owed her one of the most precious discoveries of his life, the sort of experience that stops the heart." What users of *Immemory* frequently stumble on are similar enigmatic references to the overlapping time of disjunctive memory. But described above is not simply the traumatic retrospection of, say, fantasy, in which the seizure of traumatic affect mostly occurs only the second time around, nor is it a clear temporal dialectic between present and past, the dialectic that Marker identifies with cinema itself. Rather, something like an overlapping of times, something of a present past, surfaces throughout *Immemory* to muddy the temporal flow of retrospection, here inscribed in the sublimational pleasures of cinematic experience and the stoppage of the heart (that is, the emptying of time). This enfolding of time is heightened by multimedia effects that transport the cinematic dialectic of present and past onto the precipice of the interactive future, where the combinatory of CD-ROM code and cinematic content will have been known only as an aftereffect of its repeated use.

There are of course poignant moments in *Immemory* in which the trauma of retrospection does seize the attention of Marker and his users. In the Cuba section of the "Photography" sequence, Marker speaks of how "like a cancerous body which both develops and fortifies the worst, the revolution

advances by carrying in it a cancer of power . . . What one didn't anticipate
is a return of the most insupportable images of the past: Cuba reclaimed
its status as a port of call in sexual tourism." But even when the emphasis
is on the traumatic return, something lingers outside of the tight loop of
retrospection, here in the blind folds of the future of anticipation that side-
steps while soliciting both Eros and Mnemosyne. Indeed, there is an incessant linkage throughout *Immemory* between the work of the apparatus and
the future of its resonance. Wondering aloud why he failed to reveal to his
contemporary Cuban friends that he had attended school there as a child,
Marker turns to the CD-ROM itself as the talisman of the future: "I have
often asked myself this question without finding an adequate response. . . .
It will require the existence of this CD-ROM in order that I can permit
myself a flash-back on a Cuban childhood" (this passage is followed by
links to family photos from that period). The future remains the question
for this aging filmmaker who approaches it only through the digitized
resurgence of photography's miniature trace, something of a keepsake portrait like the photos of the loved ones carried with us. The future remains
the enigma not only for the grownup faced with self-doubt about his childhood past but also for the grown traveler who now in the present, after the
fact, sees the future in the stilled time of photography. Writing of the conceptual disjunction between his photographic work in China during his
voyages of 1955 and 1980, the photographer turned digital artist remarks
how he reads, in the colors of the images he first captured,

> the prefiguration of another voyage, much later, the return after the disas-
> ter. . . . But if there was something in the faces of 1955 to announce the sad-
> ness of 1980, that was really beyond me. At that time my sole pleasure was
> the discovery of treasures and once again the eye of the apparatus (the cam-
> era) will have known to see better and farther than that which lurked behind
> the viewfinder.

Additional prefigurations of voyages and pleasures become more readily
grounded by Marker in the time-traveling afforded by the digital.

Enlivened by the specter of time travel is the intensity of something resembling what Pontalis calls "le visuel," through which artistic sublimation
results not so much in ordered narrative as in "the overaccentuation of
visual *elements*."[27] Perhaps the most helpful reference to something most

explicitly akin to "le visuel" (which in itself runs counter to explicitness) can be found in *Immemory's* photography link to China. It opens by comparing mnemonic, tourist objects of high culture to an overaccentuation of commonplace visuality. "If opera dresses and Martian rings are the gift carriers of memory, the profusion of popular images opens us to a world." The digital dazzle of *Immemory* is precisely its overaccentuation of the visual for which "world" remains other than the threatened fading of artistic memory, something whose scansion may yet have registered the codes of narration. In reflecting on this shift from memory, I find myself returning to a question posed in a psychoanalytical context by Pontalis concerning the status of the translation of the visual. Pontalis wonders whether translation "is an alteration of language, code, and register, or rather, an alteration of state, regime, violent mutation, metamorphosis, exile in another place."[28] It should be no surprise that he recommends adoption of the second hypothesis, which distinguishes psychic scansion from memory. The former enacts translation in violent mutation, metamorphosis and exile, as evidenced by Marker's own subjective exile in the fragile Chinese moment "between two opaque times where the ancient left only its ornaments and the new offered something other than its promise, a dawn between two nights that should never have had the force to usher in daylight."[29]

An "in-between . . . on the horizon of all events." This is the fantasy state attributed by Marker to his new excitation that comes, as Laplanche might say, from the sublimated activity itself, from the idea of research or trauma emblematic of both his CD-ROM and his artistic oeuvre. Nowhere is he more forthcoming about the energetic shift of register created by his artistic activities than in his description of an imaginary place he will soon associate with his relation to Japan:

> My imaginary territory that I peopled with myths that return to my childhood, when I read Flash Gordon and when utopia for me were those huge gleaming cities, traversed by elevated avenues and where the people, a little bit feline, a little bit Asian, came and went without a pause. . . . Such was the stuff of my imagined territory, my territory that deterritorialized me to the point of no longer being myself except in this deterritorialization. My deterritorialization.

If this language seems a bit familiar, thanks partially to the registers of Deleuze and Guattari, the coincidence becomes even more uncanny when the user is invited to approach the photographic representation of Japan not as the image of the cultural Other but rather as the surplus of *Da-sein,* as the deterritorialization of its received ideas, and, finally, as the in-between of "its tranquil schizophrenia."

> When one speaks of harmony à propos Japan, the world thinks of its infamous social consensus, the right swoons, the left is convulsed. You, you think of something else, of this vaporous network of rites, signs, cults. . . . As if there were always on the horizon of each event, of each action, let's not say a beyond, that would be too metaphysical, but more an in-between (un entre-deux).

While one might quibble over Marker's fetishization of his invention called Japan, it provides the cyber-reader of *Immemory* with a coded entry into a new register, the in-between of the digital network and psychic scansion.

To this user, *Immemory* stands out less for its invention of Japan than for its digital registrations of such a dense and vibrant artwork. This user's attempts to master *Immemory* have been frustrated so many times by narrative tracks that loop back to themselves, by a silly cat who frequently tells me what to do and what to think, and by the vaporous enigmas of Marker's digital stills steeped in temporal retrospection. To this reader *Immemory* stands not simply for something remembered cinematically anew, be it war or woman, but for the intense markers of the digital in-between, a present past sustained by the baroque energy of QuickTime's flickering wonders.

EPILOGUE: WEDGED BETWEEN WARS

Strange adulthood, still wedged between wars like a book caught between two bronzed elephants. Chris Marker's epigraphic maxim of his childhood could well serve as the eulogistic caption of his adulthood as well. It is not insignificant that Marker again reflects on the affect of the in-between at the twilight of his distinguished career. For his recent piece *Owls at Noon Prelude: The Hollow Men* (2005), Marker constructs an eight-panel, two-track installation as the first part of a work-in-progress that he designed for exhibition in the Yoshiko and Akio Morita Gallery, in New York's Museum of Modern Art. Featuring the surround sound of composer Toru Takemistu's elegiac "Corona" (1962), with piano by Roger Woodward, the nineteen-minute sequence flows and flickers over the horizontal row of flat-screen monitors. Marker takes his point of departure from T. S. Eliot's 1925 poem "The Hollow Men," which reflects on the "Multifoliate rose / Of death's twilight kingdom" that haunted Europe between the period of the two wars that ushered cinema into Marker's creative life. He also frames his installation in a return to the two figures he isolated earlier as shapers of the history of cinema: war and woman. Marker capitalizes on the fluid sequencing of digital editing to juxtapose and interlace historical footage of the searing wounds of soldiers and battlefields with alluring shots of female portraiture, thus tempting viewers with the same arrestation of the female look that he realized only later in life to have captivated him at the age of seven. As the fleeting memories of Europe's cataclysmic wars then return to plague us with the tortured specters of the Balkans, the Middle East, lower Manhattan, and urban Madrid, the MoMA's curious museum-goers find themselves transfixed by their post-9/11 wonderment at the horrific beauty of mankind's suicidal drive, just as many New Yorkers became enveloped a few years earlier in the sensorial surround of Bill Viola's Guggenheim installation *Going Forth by Day*. It is not insignificant that Marker's installation was one of the only pieces of contemporary art on display following the opening of the refurbished MoMA to have confronted openly the museum's conventionally placid viewers with the divisions of war, politics, and pathos.

Yet, tantric fixation on the sorrowful repetition of the searing same is not the project of *Owls at Noon Prelude: The Hollow Men*. Caught between the fleeting appearance of sublime imagery, sometimes gorgeous, sometimes grotesque, the spectator seeks to follow the rapid seriality of imagery and text that moves seemingly in all conceivable directions across, beyond, off, and between the eight monitors. In this prelude, the viewer is caught not between bookends of bronze but between digitally scratched imagery, electric loops, and textual fades whose continuous variations defy the comforts of cinematic identification and hermeneutic confidence. While the installation's flatness and cinematic organization certainly appeals to the kind of spectatorial identification denied by the interactivity of *Immemory*, its insistence on the in-between of digitized imagery, text, and sound positions the spectator in the gaps of world-memory and image-time instead of pandering to the self-assured return of cinematic identification and movement-image.

"Sightless, unless new eyes open," appears more than once in the script

of one track as if encouraging the museumgoer to think textuality otherwise. An isolated repetition of "sightless" leads to a series of nonsensical
textual fragments, "SIG," "AN LE," "LE," to give shape to Eliot's poetic
signifier, "MULTIFOLIATE ROSE." Marker's teasing sequence, aggressive in its minimalism, shifts Eliot's plea for European hope to an appeal
for new world-memory, for a new sense of a kind yet unknown. Just as the
repulsiveness of a warrior's hanging corpse fills the frame or the gorgeous-
ness of female portraiture captures the screen, sequences readily fade to
black, focal points bleed to snow, and phrases morph into alphabetic fragments to confront the gaping holes of meaning and the unstable platforms
of sense. Frequently returning to its point of departure, Eliot's "The Hollow Men," the installation just as insistently notes the differences of its repetition. Here the memory of war is no longer safely housed between those
poetic bookends of bronze. Here repetition continues to catch the participant unaware in the shadows of the in-between that figure so prominently
throughout Marker's work: "between every song and every silence"; between
the brave plains of the Seine and the sands of Iwo Jima; "between dogfights
at Dunkirk and fingers that triggered the bomb." Ever constant in *Owls at
Noon Prelude: The Hollow Men* are the traumatic enigmas of Marker's
stunning tracks steeped in the folds of psychic scansion and temporal retrospection. To this viewer, *Owls at Noon Prelude: The Hollow Men* stands
alongside *Immemory* in how it signifies not something simply remembered
anew but something, as Laplanche would say, "new, maybe coming from
the message, from the work itself. It is a kind of new excitation, new trauma
coming from the sublimated activity itself, and through this new trauma
comes new energy."[30]

Scanning the future, trauma's new energy reemerges with even more subtle force in Marker's suite of photographs "The Revenge of the Eye," published in *Artforum* (Summer 2006). Once again, Marker presents poignant
black-and-white images of fleeting glances, mostly on the faces of women,
mainly young, one African, another with the imprint of Maghrebian flesh,
many French, and another closer to the age of Marker, looking out sideways from the edge of the lower frame when not morphed with spectacular
beauty in the background of yet another photograph. Somewhat elusive,
but ever-present in their enigmatic turns of face, these determined women
of Paris seem easily to steal away the foreground from the male counterparts surrounding them.

The context of these photographs is site specific, gesturing to Marker's other cinematic bookend of the legends of war. This time it is not the battleground of Dunkirk but the cobblestones of Paris, and the warriors are no longer the French soldiers positioned gallantly on the brave plains of the Seine but their contemporary contraries, the riot police of the CRS whom Marker seems to take pleasure in shooting in the back (the only policeman appearing in the portfolio is a burly character with hands on his hips who stands, unlike all the other subjects, with his back to the camera). The event in 2006 is the groundswell of protest against Villepin's detested First Employment Contract, which would have permitted employers to fire young workers without cause during the probationary period of their employment, a contract they understood to shoot them in the back. The revenge of the eye seems to lie less in the camera than in the lively agency of the female glance, mobilized together as if to turn à la Medusa against the violent indifference of the state to the suffering of its hopeless young. Equally significant, of course, is that the distant lands depicted in *Immemory* and *Sans Soleil* have come home to roost. The young African, Maghrebian, and French are joined together by the spatial proximity of the women's seriality as they evoke a rather mysterious silence, as if multifoliate roses framed against the backdrop of hollow men. Yet when framed or viewed singularly on the pages of *Artforum,* these women stand proud as if modern-day Joans of Arc, emanating the sort of feminine allure that might one day provide an unprepared viewer with the sort of experience that stops the heart.

It was just the uncanny repetition of this kind of emotive event that seems to have grabbed Chris Marker himself, as he once again found himself confronted by the present past of his artistic apparatus. Not photographs these, but actually frame grabs from video footage he shot of the Paris demonstrations, footage he later analyzed in slow-motion playback to counter the "inordinate flow of video and television." It was from this footage, played in reverse as the present past of televisual flow, that Marker replayed the same cinematic habits on which he seems to have relied for *Immemory* by looking for "the one frame lost in the stream of almost identical frames . . . the real photogram, something nobody has perceived—not even the guy who shot it (me, in most cases)." Yet it is the real photogram itself that actually alludes to Marker without, again, the intervention of digital accumulation. For he seemed to find himself compelled, as he did with that cyberspatial figure of the author in Japan, to add digital effects to these photos to make them appeal to us all the more, effects that Bill Horrigan thinks result "in images unlike any others he has ever exhibited."[31] What's uncanny is the resemblance, let's say the repetition, of the process and its effect with the stuff of *Immemory*. For here again it is the future of the image that is pulled from the present past that remains at stake for Marker who, once more, approaches it only through the digitized resurgence of photography's miniature trace, something of a keepsake portrait like the photos of loved ones we carry with us. And where might we carry them? Always, it seems, in the temporal space of the in-between. As if parroting Marker's account of his time-warping photographs of China, Horrigan suggests that these portraits carry the markers of morphed time: "it's as though the faces of 2006 had become the faces of 1936 and 1236, the persistence of the Popular Front no less than the medieval among us."[32] Another "in-between" "on the horizon of all events." So remain the fraught traces of psychic scansion, all carrying the baroque markers of new digital energy.

TIME @ CINEMA'S FUTURE: NEW MEDIA ART
AND THE THOUGHT OF TEMPORALITY

The future ain't what it used to be.

—YOGI BERRA

We need only position the imprint of new media on the future of cinema to appreciate the depth of the maxim voiced by that philosophical icon of American pop culture, Yogi Berra. While Yogi isn't likely to have had the ontology of cinema in mind when he mused about the paradox of time's traveling, his famous quotation certainly seems like an apt epigraph for this concluding chapter on the temporal folds of Digital Baroque. Whether we think of the transfer of light from Lacan to Kuntzel, the crisis caused by the growth of new computing machines in the cinematic field, the interventions of feminism in the digital age, or the psychic shift from projection to scansion, the perception of cinema's future on the threshold of new media depends as much on the continuous foldings of temporality as on cinema's linkage to the many apparatuses sustaining its memory: perspective, point of view, montage, anamorphosis. While the same construction of cinema's point of view continues to be developed, it is, as Deleuze forewarns in *The Fold,* no longer the same point of view nor the same cinema now that both the figure and the ground move fractally in cyberspace. I wish to conclude *Digital Baroque* by considering how this shift might impact our consideration of temporality itself as the fundamental framework for any thought of cinema.

While Yogi Berra cannot claim responsibility for this chapter, his prediction that the future ain't what it used to be certainly speaks to the temporal paradoxes encountered throughout the folds and thresholds of *Digital*

Baroque. Indeed, the paradox of temporality in the digital age has been so crucial to the trajectory of this book, as well as to my own fascination with the baroque intersections of new media and cinema, that I would like to conclude by focusing on the enigma of the return of cinema's future. For this purpose, I have chosen to frame this final chapter around consideration of a philosophy of cinematic thought that I now realize to have shaped the previous chapters far more than I had anticipated. It has been twenty years since Gilles Deleuze published the second half of his project on cinema, *Cinema 2: The Time-Image,* that so altered the figure and ground of the thought of cinematic image and time. Readers who now find themselves close to the end of this book will appreciate how the text, memory, and hallucination of Deleuze's cinema books have permeated the writing of these chapters even when not acknowledged. While my deep affiliation with a wide range of thinkers and artists, from Louis Marin, Jean-François Lyotard, Jacques Derrida, Jean Laplanche, and Anne-Marie Duguet to Chris Marker, Grace Quintanilla, Keith Piper, and Thierry Kuntzel precludes me from identifying this book as "Deleuzian," the very project of *Digital Baroque* remains deeply indebted to Deleuze's many evocations of the baroque paradoxes of incompossibility and the fold, from *Logique du sens* to *Dialogues.* So I conclude my reflections on *Digital Baroque* by time-traveling into the future with Deleuze, but not so much via the hallucinations of patriarchal voice as through the temporal folds of time's cinematic image.

FUTURE CINEMA AND THE SPLIT OF TIME

What would be the result, I wonder, of looking back to Deleuze's cinema books from twenty years forward or looking forward from Deleuze's cinema books twenty years into the future? One response could be paradoxical, one that verges on nostalgia for the future past of cinema: the future ain't what it used to be. Another would entail a project of retrospective thought as a critical activity that toggles between past and future, one that positions us smack within the crystal of cinematic subjectivity, within what Deleuze calls the paradoxical commonplace of time, which I appreciate as the core of *Digital Baroque.* Time's crystal, or the crystallization of time, constitutes the structural paradox of temporality, its activation of passing presents, in which one moment goes while another comes to shape the future, all the while preventing the past from falling into the inaccessible depths of the totally obscure. Deleuze consistently attributes his celebration of the paradoxical commonplace of passing presents to the project of Henri Bergson by building his notion of the time crystal around Bergson's belief that time itself is subjectivity. Rather than arguing that the subject creates time through thought, Deleuze joins with Bergson in maintaining that the subject is *in* time (as *in* fantasy). Deleuze's approach to cinema is guided by his rather simple formula of cinematic time, or time's subjectivity: "it is in the present that we make a memory, in order to make use of it in the future when the present will be past."[1] Put similarly also some twenty years ago by Jean-François Lyotard, in contemplating the paradoxical event of time within the environment of new technology's expansion,

> Because it is absolute, the presenting present cannot be grasped: it is *not yet* or *no longer* present. It is always too soon or too late to grasp presentation itself and present it. Such is the specific and paradoxical constitution of the event . . . . The event testifies that the self is essentially passible to a recurrent alterity.[2]

The body or shape of time, the event within which we find ourselves, is itself something of a phantom oscillating between the not yet and no longer, virtual but graspable in the actual. Deleuze insists that this phantom has been fundamental to cinema, haunting it and its spectators, until the arrival, that is, of "modern cinema" which has given form to the virtual image of time. The time of cinema always already awaits its passing actualization in the future present of modern cinema.

Future cinema and the split of time. These two themes that find voice in Deleuze's second cinema volume, *The Time-Image,* are what seem to have seized the attention of philosophers and the imaginary of film specialists in the twenty years since the arrival of the cinema books. To some extent, we can situate the explosive contemplation of time with the coming of the new millennium. Recall, for example, how the blockbuster exhibition "Le temps, vite!" with which the Centre Pompidou ushered in the year 2000 was designed to lead the spectators through a concluding installation space, "The Future of Time." This show was accompanied by a flood of timely writing in France: for J.-B. Pontalis, *Ce temps qui ne passe pas;* Georges Didi-Huberman writes *Devant le temps;* André Green finds himself ruminating on time on *Le temps éclaté;* in the United States Mary Ann Doane reflects on time in *The Emergence of Cinematic Time,* which is soon followed by Elizabeth Grosz's *The Nick of Time* and preceded by *Cinema Futures . . . The Screen Arts in the Digital Age,* a collection edited by Thomas Elsaesser and Kay Hoffman.[3] These books on the thought of time arrived in fortuitous conjunction with two major exhibitions that solicit us to contemplate the place of Deleuze's "modern cinema" now that it too seems to have passed into the future. The massive 2003 exhibition at the ZKM in Karlsruhe, Germany, "Future Cinema," curated by Jeffrey Shaw and Peter Weibel, was followed by a more focused and elegant show in Lille, France, "Cinémas du futur," which was curated by Richard Castelli for the festival Lille 2004.[4]

The emergence of time in these many reflections and exhibitions provide something of a paradoxical commonplace for consideration of Deleuze's acknowledgment of, yet obvious discomfort with, the movement of his cherished "modern cinema" into the future of "future cinema" itself. I'm referring to his passionate remarks, concluding *Cinema 2,* on the rapid acceleration of developments in electronic and digital media. His acknowledgment of the potentiality of video and digital cinema remains tempered by his affectionate ties to the philosophical vigor of cinema. "The modern configuration of the automaton is the correlate of an electronic automatism. The electronic image, that is, the tele and video image, the numerical image coming into being, either had to transform cinema or to replace it, to mark its death." In an interesting way, Deleuze positions new media at the interval of cinematic time, as the carrier of both cinema's passing and its future. On the other hand, the electronic future carries for him a certain threat of deadening violence against his most cherished aspects of cinematic thought. "It is the time-image which calls on an original regime of images and signs, before electronics spoils it or, in contrast, relaunches it."[5]

It is hardly worth debating that digital technology and sensibilities deriving from new media have transformed the cinematic image, its space, and perhaps even its time. Consider, for instance, the multimedia installation of Renate Ferro, *Screen Memory* (2004), in which footage of family Super 8 film, shot in the 1950s, is digitized, reserialized, and projected silently in different sequences on the facade of a miniature building (Figure 18).[6] The footage plays on the amateurism of the patriarchal control of the camera and its contrast with the domestic activities of the play and the labor it records. At the same time, the placement of the homelike structure casts gigantic shadows onto the dissipating footage that spills onto the adjoining

Figure 18. Renate Ferro, *Screen Memory*, 2004.

walls. Sound does fill this space, but it is precisely the sound of the Super 8 projector eating and tearing the brittle film as it passes through the sprockets, one final time, for digitization. To transfer this film of the past into the numerical future requires its literal wasting in the present of artistic production. The installation doubly complicates the Deleuzian celebration of the cinematic screen, moreover, by luring visitors across the threshold of the structural shell where sensors illuminate a miniature table, set for tea. Inside the visitors listen to the soft sounds of the artist's competing narratives not about cinema itself but about memories of the primal scene of domestic work and familial *jouissance* that transfer the passing of cinema into the register of other places, other screens. Screened are memories marked by the differences of gender, authority, and popular culture as they are registered particularly by clustered groupings of visitors, some hailing from the moment of the Super 8 projector and the Buick Super Riviera, others from the more recent era of the Super 8 motel and the digital Superhero. Here, too, inside and outside, the visitors' bodies disrupt the enveloping projections to insert themselves phantasmatically into the fabric or screen of the installation. The purity of cinema, even in its lowly amateur guise, is sullied by the silhouette, carriage, and subtle interactivity of the viewers. While Ferro certainly places cinema's subjects in the space and place of time, and obviously transfers the stock of cinema into the digital future, she does so with artistic indifference to the ontological and even literal preservation of the very stuff of cinema. When cinema here crosses into the numerical code of archivization, its figure and ground shift in rather colossal ways.

Ferro's multimedia installation, which is rather elementary from a computing standpoint, works to highlight the extent to which even basic convolutions of electronic and digital media easily violate the conventions of the screen and alter the spectatorial habits of the cinematic viewer. *Screen Memory* can be said to exemplify how Deleuze's concern about the impact of electronic and new media on the thought of "modern cinema" seems to go in two directions: one back toward ontology, the other forward toward the uncertain valance of "the future" itself.

To some extent, Deleuze seems to share a certain defensive identification with the ontology of cinema that similarly haunts practitioners and theorists faced with the dissolution of its historical purity. This is voiced no more poignantly than by Mary Ann Doane in *The Emergence of Cinematic Time:*

> A certain nostalgia for cinema precedes its "death." One doesn't—and can't—
> love the televisual or the digital in quite the same way. . . . It is arguable that
> cinephilia could not be revised at this juncture were the cinema not threat-
> ened by the accelerating development of new electronic and digital forms of
> media.[7]

In a particularly combative line concluding *Cinema 2,* Deleuze transforms Doane's threatened nostalgia for the romance or love of cinema into the more forceful, agonistic discourse of a philosopher confronted with the even higher stakes of the end of time's crystal itself: "The life or afterlife of cinema depends on its internal struggle with informatics."[8] These rather urgent words of resistance are written paradoxically by the same philosopher with whom so many artists and theorists frequently dialogue to articulate notions of a "philosophy after the new media."[9] Readers who cherish *Cinema 2* for its elaboration of the virtual may have shared my surprise upon first falling on these combative passages at the very moment when a more committed embrace of the many faces of new media seemed possible, if not logical. Couldn't Deleuze have recognized more unequivocally in the emergent new media a shift in the principal variables of time and rhythm that *The Fold* welcomes in the electronic experimentations of Boulez and Stockhausen?

It is almost as if *Cinema 2* is haunted by the kind of anxious recurrence of the temporal phantom staged by the Chinese new media artist Du Zhenjun in his interactive installation *I Erase Your Trace* (2001).[10] In this computer-driven piece, visitors are invited to walk across a platform whose surface doubles as the screen of cinematic projection. The visitors' footsteps trigger sensors that activate a computerized program of hyperactive avatars who scrub away the residue of the footprints (Figure 19). Every time another step is taken, the avatars reappear with the same passionate momentum in an effort to wipe clean the historical screen of cinema. If considered from the logic of cinema's internal strife with digitality, it is almost as if the avatars are struggling to wipe away the traces of analog visitation itself and to efface the corporeal specters of cinema's passing presents. The movement of passing presents summons back the virtual future with a vengeance. Each step into the "not yet" summons the possibility of the "no longer." While *I Erase Your Trace* could be read as a paragon of resistance to the analogical, it can be understood just as easily as a celebration of the interpellation of the virtual and its complex interface with the actual. It is almost as if Du engages in the Deleuzian logic of time's paradoxical doubling, one that contrasts the presents that "pass and are replaced" with an emergence from the scene that "launches itself towards a future, creates this future as a bursting of life."[11] In Du's work, the virtual and its paradoxical reality seem to spring out of nowhere in sync with the advance of the curious spectator, one who roams the exhibition space in search of, as Richard Castelli might say, the "cinémas du future."

In order better to appreciate Deleuze's other motivation for his struggle against new media, we need to exercise caution, however, about how to gauge the valence of "future" in its cinematic context. For some theoreticians of new media, the notion of "future cinema" would be understood as merely a metaphor for something much more concrete, say, the place of

Figure 19. Du Zhenjun, *I Erase Your Trace*, 2001.

cinema in cyber or virtual space. Lev Manovich, for example, emphasizes what he considers to be a fundamental characteristic of cinema in the digital era, the shift from time to space:

> Film montage introduced a new paradigm—creating an effect of presence in a virtual world by joining different images of time. Temporal montage became the dominant paradigm for the visual simulation of nonexistent spaces. As the examples of digital composing for film and Virtual Sets applications for television demonstrate, the computer era introduces a different paradigm. This paradigm is concerned not with time, but with space.[12]

It could be argued that Deleuze dialogues futuristically with Manovich when he contexualizes his concluding defense of cinema at the end of *Cinema 2* in relation to what he calls "this complexity of informational space."[13] In speaking admirably of the films of Syberberg, he commends the nontotalizable complexity that surpasses individual psychology while rending impossible any sense of a spatial "whole." In view of Deleuze's emphasis on cinematic thought as what surpasses the totalizable subject, David Rodowick even has praised Deleuze as "a cartographer of thought."[14] But Rodowick does so based on his appreciation for how Deleuze insists that such nontotalizable complexity finds its representation not so much in spatialized or even subjective terms as in machinic ones: automata.

> To be a cartographer of thought for either the movement or time-image means tracing out their distinct planes of immanence, their concepts relating movement and time to thought, and the noosigns each gives rise to as particular *raccordements* of concepts and signs. Only in this way will we understand what new powers of thought arise . . . . The spiritual automaton is machinic thought, but this means that the cinema is less a technology than a *téchne* or *poesis*.[15]

Deleuze's concern over the potential dilution of "modern cinema" does not pertain to the digitalized transformation of space, perhaps a consideration more pertinent to the rise of classical cinema's movement-image, but with its potential transformation of our investment in the thought of time itself. It is to protect the very stakes of time and the spiritual automaton as machinic thought that Deleuze circles his cinematic wagons.

Particularly at issue is the shifting valence of the *future* in the age of electronic imagery and automated information. The future of "future cinema" is nothing close to being parodically metaphorical to Deleuze but, rather, constitutes the fundamental machinic constituent of new informatics itself. It is the very replication of information in relation to its anchorage in the pull of the future that, he cautions, ultimately renders its pervasive automation radically ineffective. "Information plays on its ineffectiveness in order to establish its power, its very power is to be ineffective, and thereby all the more dangerous."[16] A helpful elaboration of such a concern with the dangerously numbing accumulation of information for information's sake is provided in a related context by Lyotard's *The Inhuman: Reflections on Time,* a book composed by Lyotard in the wake of his 1985 launching of the first major new media exhibition at the Centre Pompidou, "The Immaterials" (it is noteworthy that Lyotard was conceptualizing an exhibition of electronic arts at the same moment that Deleuze, his colleague at the University of Paris at Vincennes, was celebrating modern cinema). In the chapter "Time Today," which is explicitly concerned with the unrealized potential of informatics, Lyotard focuses his analysis on information culture's privileging of the future at the expense, say, of what Deleuze calls cinema's passing presents. Lyotard joins Deleuze in reflecting on the increasing "complexification" of new technology whose drive is the incessant recombination of information processing and data synthesis:

> As is clearly shown by the development of the techno-scientific system, technology and the culture associated with it are under a necessity to pursue their rise . . . . The human race is, so to speak, "pulled forward" by this process without possessing the slightest capacity for mastering it . . . . The growth of techno-scientific systems . . . means neutralizing more events. What is already known cannot, in principle, be experienced as an event. Consequently, if one wants to control a process, the best way of so doing is to subordinate the present to what is (still) called the "future," since in these conditions the "future" will be predetermined and the present itself will cease opening onto an uncertain and contingent "afterwards." Better: what comes "after" the "now" will have to come "before" it. In as much as a monad in thus saturating its memory is stocking the future, the present loses its privilege of being an ungraspable point from which, however, time should always distribute itself between the "not yet" of the future and the "no longer" of the past.[17]

Lyotard thus joins Deleuze in wanting to short-circuit the pull of computational complexification in order to reinvest in the cinematic interval of
the passing presents, between the "too early" and the "too late."

In this struggle against the informatic pull of the future, Deleuze has
something greater in mind than the simple preservation of the historical
promise of temporal montage, as Manovich would have it. When Manovich contrasts montage with new media, he limits montage to the logics
of its articulation of the alteration of the state of the whole that Deleuze
identifies with the movement-image. In Rodowick's concise terms,

> First, montage in or across movement-images is a logic of juxtaposition, con-
> nection, and linkage. Here time unfolds within movement like the cascading
> sections of a Jacob's ladder. The whole is given as addition (n + 1 . . .) and
> time is reduced to a succession of presents. . . . Second, this means that the
> image of the whole, no matter how infinitely large or infinitesimally small,
> can always be given. . . . Thus the cinematic movement-image presents its
> indirect images of time through the forms or Ideas of montage.[18]

Much more important to Deleuze's concerns about new media is what he
calls its need to remain open to the cinematic imperative of the "montrage"
of time. This is what "brings together the before and the after in a becoming, instead of separating them; its paradox is to introduce an enduring
interval in the moment itself."[19] Crucial to this concept of the interval is
not its logical relation to the whole but its philosophical force as irreducible and autonomous as the montrage of becoming.

Privileging the force of the fissure, the interval is indifferent to the succession of images and the chain of association attributed to montage. Here
the whole *(le tout)* of cinematic ontology *(tout cinéma de l'Etre = est)* undergoes a mutation in order to become the constitutive "et," the "entre-deux"
of image and time.[20] Initially articulated in 1972 by Derrida in his analysis
of the "entre-deux" of the Mallarmean fold, and then echoed by Deleuze
in his 1976 *Cahiers du cinéma* discussion of Godard's *Ici et ailleurs,* the "and"
resists the ontological grounding of the copula to be "neither one thing nor
the other, it's always in between, between two things; it's the borderline,
there's always a border, a line of flight or flow, only we don't see it, because
it's the least perceptible of things. And yet it's along this line of flight that
things come to pass, becomings evolve, revolutions take shape."[21] Or, as

stated succinctly by Derrida, "the medium of the *entre* has nothing to do with a center."[22] Running counter to the rationality of montage's juxtaposition and its connection to centering, this line of flight is what Deleuze lauds as an "irrational interval." Its irrationality can be said to lie in its incompossibility with the spatial perception, the linear logic of the whole, and the ordering of time.

Of course, I stress incompossibility as the figure that has been crucial to my articulation of Digital Baroque throughout this book and that lies, I believe, at the core of Deleuze's reflections on cinematic temporality. It is not by chance that I return, in this concluding chapter, to this notion that Deleuze takes from Leibniz to understand elements of thought and art that can fail to converge while still not negating or rendering each other impossible. Rather than either converging or remaining impossible for each other, rather than being either included or excluded, they stand in paradoxical relation to one another as divergent and coexistent: as "incompossible."[23] The effect is to rethink cinema's grounding in montage as the consequential flow of time, to release narration from its bondage to the truth-claim (making way for fabulation), and to insert the force of "incompossible presents" into the thought of time and its montrage. This opens philosophy to the imperceptible frontiers of the "irrational interval." "What the irrational interval gives," suggests Rodowick, "is a nonspatial perception—not space but force, the force of time as change interrupting repetition with difference and parceling succession into series."[24]

Precisely the efficacy of the spiritual automaton and the irrational interval are what Deleuze fears may be muted but ultimately hopes can be delivered with equal or ideally more intensity by the new media. This leads us to rethink the question central to this chapter. Wherein lies the "future" in the art of new media? Might there be a way in which informatics combines with the artistic performance of the digital archive to reinvigorate the placeholder of the "future" itself, particularly in relation to the complexification of its informational present? In discussing various developments of the naissant numeric cinematics, which Deleuze calls "the corollary of the modern figure of the automata," can we come to an appreciation of what he hoped might lead to its energetic transformation of cinema rather than its melancholic performance of the passing of cinema? Put otherwise, how might the very life of cinema depend fundamentally on an internal struggle with the stuff of informatics, on the becoming of artistic interactivity at the behest of the future?

In the context of new media art, I propose that we consider the form or event of the irrational interval in relation to a series of incompossible events: *archival intensities, interactivities, coded automatons,* and *the returns of the future.* As extensions of the time-image, its fabulations and its irrational intervals, the new media image capitalizes on the complexification of information science and culture by mixing and matching its softwares and hardwares, while experimenting with the crystallized density of the digital point to foreground the extended frontiers of virtual reality (as that event of the virtual touching upon the actual). A far too rapid concluding tour of a series of incompossible new media projects should make evident the lively and productive response of the new media community to Deleuze's charge that it enliven, as Rodowick sums up the mission, "the virtual as a site where choice has yet to be determined, a reservoir of unthought yet immanent possibilities and modes of existence."[25]

ARCHIVAL INTENSITIES

Multiple modes of existence abound in the interactive, database installations of the Australian artist Jill Scott, one of the digital pioneers of what I call "archival intensity." Scott's complex new media events call on the sites of history, the projects of science, and the various possibilities of multimedia to solicit the users to participate collectively in her new media environments. One of her richest installations looks directly into the future from the split perspectives of multiple characters who hail from different moments of twentieth-century time. *Frontiers of Utopia,* mounted in 1995 and installed permanently in the ZKM in Karlsruhe, exemplifies what Scott calls her "hybrid environments." In this piece that questions the idealism of Margaret Mead's notion of transmigratory culture, the users have the option of interacting with eight reconstructed characters: Emma (the anarchist Emma Goldman), Mary (a rural sociologist in Paraguay), Margaret (a secretary in a New York design firm), Pearl (an Australian aboriginal poet), Maria (a Yugoslavian hippy), Gillian (a Marxist radical student), Ki (a Chinese physicist), and Zira (a New Age programmer). Users can access the lives of these women from four terminals geared to the 1900s, 1930s, 1960s, and 1990s. Rather than pursuing Ferro's strategy of collapsing the experience of time on the screen-memory of a cinematic construction made dense by its singularity, Scott provides her users with access to the viewpoints and historical artifacts important to these women who possess different political attitudes from across the globe and from different moments spanning the century that marks the history of cinema. Users are able to manipulate touch screens and interactive suitcases in order to listen to the characters and to peruse artifacts, news items, and memories crucial to their time periods (Figure 20).

Adding to the complexity of this early new media installation is a touch screen that depicts all the women gathered together at a dinner table, à la Judy Chicago. Viewers are able to touch the characters' faces to catalyze sets of conversations between two women from different eras, locales, and imaginaries. One of my favorite exchanges is between Emma, the 1930s anarchist, and Zira the 1990s programmer:

Figure 20. Jill Scott, *Frontiers of Utopia*, 1995.

ZIRA: We have to implement a system, otherwise the planet will die.

EMMA No rules for the hungry.

ZIRA: The problem is too big now. In the nineties we suffer from massive overpopulation.

EMMA: The only answer is to educate the women.

ZIRA: Exactly for that we need a system.

What Scott's *Frontiers of Utopia* makes clear to its diverse users gathered together in struggle with the differends of history is that complexification itself, the ever-expanding system of technology with its mixture of archival matters and database materials, does not provide the sole answer to dilemmas of the future. While her title certainly acknowledges the pull of the future, the magnetism of her interactive objects faces the user with the enigmatic interval of passing presents. The magnetic interfaces of Scott's suitcases, which permit the users to touch keys to material icons that catalyze conflicting narratives about their historical particularity, ground the new cinematic experience in the incompossible archives of time and space. The result is what I appreciate as a dynamic staging of Deleuze's cherished paradox of split memory, "a memory for two people or a memory for several."[26] Constructing "undecidable alternatives" inscribed literally on the tablecloth of history *(entre nappes de passé)*, Scott far exceeds the representation of the incompossible "world-memory" so admired by Deleuze in the cinema of Alain Resnais: "the different levels of past no longer relate to a single character, a single family, or a single group, but to quite different characters as to unconnected places which make up a world-memory.[27]

INTERACTIVITIES

Of course, key to the enactment of undecidable alternatives is an aesthetic practice committed to the unpredictabilities of interactivity, a practice that both solicits the user to respond to a set of predetermined choices and gives itself over to the users' momentary staging of a work whose algorithms leave it incomplete. In one of the most thoughtful contributions to the gargantuan catalogue coming out of the ZKM "Future Cinema" exhibition, "The Relation-Image," Jean-Louis Boissier reflects on the aesthetic of interactivity shaping his experiments with new media since the days when he designed the electronic interfaces for Lyotard's *Les immatériaux* and culminating more recently in his decade-long digital encounter with the works of Rousseau. During that time, as I discuss in chapter 8, Boissier created his interactive installations of the *Confessions* et *Rêvéries* and developed an interactive electronic version of Rousseau that was published by Gallimard. Characteristic of this digital book project, deriving from his installations, is Boissier's experimentation with video inserts of particularly fetishistic moments of the text, with re-creations of the motion and movement inherent in the Rousseau-esque narrative as well as with digital reflections on the interval of time itself. The result is an aesthetic project indebted to Boissier's particular theorization of interactivity as it dialogues with the cinema books of Deleuze.

> If we can imagine *relation* as a form, we can conceive of a relation-image capable of being produced by a new type of perspective. To that perspective which refers to optics can be added a dimension relating to relational behavior. Within this interactive perspective, interactivity holds the position held by geometry in optical perspective. We could go so far as to say that, if perspective is that by which we can capture or construct a visual representation, interactive perspective is equally capable of seizing [saisir] or modeling relations. This interactive perspective projects relationships into a relational space.[28]

In *Moments de Jean-Jacques Rousseau,* the reader of the text is transformed into an interactive participant of touch and sight as she moves in and out of the historical past, the current moment, and the future reconfiguration of the texts as the interactive tracking morphs the text into hypertextual fragments. Two structural features are particularly fascinating in how they overlap. One is Boissier's insistence on experimenting with hardware and software that permits the viewer of video to move horizontally and vertically, and thus in and out of time and focus:

> For all the sequences in *Moments,* I placed a digital camera onto a motorized panoramic head, which I had built with sufficient precision in the degrees of rotation as to achieve just such an interactive panorama. As the starting and ending positions were precisely marked during shooting, the image sequences submit themselves naturally to visual on-screen development, to looping, and to internal bifurcations. It is this equivalence of the movement with the human gaze [du regard], by controlling the movement of the image, that the reader explores each sequence.[29]

Within the video sequence itself, Boissier cuts one frame out of ten resulting in what Mary Ann Doane seems to regret as an acknowledgment of "the temporal lapse, the lost time inherent in the cinematic representation of movement."[30] But rather than marshalling the cut as what Doane calls an ellipsis through which "time becomes delimitable, commodifiable, object-like,"[31] Boissier stages the cut as time's irrational interval itself, as that more baroque ellipsis that gives rise neither to objects nor to commodities but to concepts, relations, and events. Thus the other structural device crucial to *Moments* is the user's interactive fractalization of text through which time and thought are channeled to dwell in the interval of incompossibility itself. Crucial to Boissier's project is the interface of computing and interaction that constitutes the virtual ground giving rise to the poesis or thought of new media art.

> In a computer cinema, the logical relation to the Real is not canceled or diminished, but rather transformed, emphasized. . . . the various domains of interactivity open up this variability. . . an interactive object's degree of openness is linked . . . to its increasing perfection [read "complexification"] in the management of its internal relations . . . being able to respond to the demands of external interactions and to the mutations of its environment.[32]

While Boissier provides his users with the option of inhabiting the intervals of history, of moving between the here while etching a virtual hypertext of the future, other artists have seized on the internal relations of the computing machine to situate the user more solidly in the shifting intervals of passing presents.

Take the simple Internet art project "Expand," by Shu Leah Cheang, the self-proclaimed deterritorialized Internet artist, the global creator without a local address.[33] Published in the "NetNoise" issue of *CTHEORY Multimedia*, "Expand" appropriates footage from Cheang's extravagantly parodic sci-fi porn film *I.K.U.,* which parallels the Internet proliferation of racialized Asian porn.[34] In this subtly machinic net.art piece, Cheang stages the interval of digital frames versus cinema frames: 30 frames per digital second, 30 frames per cinema sequence.[35] The yellow dial intersecting the image strip permits the user to move back and forth in time and movement between and within particular eroticized image-times, catalyzed independent image and sound tracks in the style of the noosignes. By turning the Internet interface into something of a manual scratch device, Cheang permits the user to expand the narrative in shuffling mode. In dialogue with early nineties new media, feminist collective VNS Matrix, the project is framed by Cheang's political resistance to the male technodrive of digital complexification. Cheang writes that she wishes to "expand" VNS Matrix's mantra, "The clitoris is a direct line to the matrix," by claiming, "The Pussy is the matrix."

> I am looking at a wireless digital mobile present with no portal to channel us; built in memory flash and gigabyte hard drive as delivered at birth; genetic mutation for the ALL NEW GEN. The merge is complete. We ride on the fantasy. Living comfortably with the monster within, I assign my body as a self-programmed, self-generative sexual unit. This body functions with an operating system that requires version update and memory upgrade. The unlikely future has come and gone. The retro future could be the next comeback.[36]

While Cheang's net.art depends on the retrofuture fantasy of a self-generative sexual unit, the Japanese artist Masayuki Akamatsu takes for his digital subject the transferential split of time itself. In his installation *Time Machine!* the users approaching the console of this piece have their portraits captured by a video camera and transferred onto a projection facing them.[37] The image itself then becomes pixilated, extended, multiplied, and inverted in relation to the user's manipulation of a trackball (Figure 21). A turn to the left travels the image back into time where it seems to split into a kind of unconscious freefall. The presence of the moment here gives way

Figure 21. Masayuki Akamatsu, *Time Machine!* 2002.

to the fracture and dislocation of time travel—a state previously known to man only through the unconscious or through literary and cinematic fiction. A turn to the left travels the image back from the future into the present. Exhibited here, however, is a present whose image structure never appears to be constant. Through pixilated imagery that moves right, into the future, it remains open to the vicissitudes of the video image's instantiation in time and the subject's entrapment in the doublings of time itself. Ask yourself if you're not witnessing something of a digital image-crystal that embodies what Deleuze calls the most fundamental operation of time: "time has to split itself in two at each moment as present and past, which differ from each other in nature, or, what amounts to the same thing, it has to split the present in two heterogeneous directions, one of which is launched toward the future while the other falls into the past."[38] To be "in" the machinic state of time is to be always confronted with the touch, turn, vision, and thought of the interval as the recombinant turning of time.

CODED AUTOMATONS

It should be no surprise that such machinic display would be cited by many philosophers of cinema as a sign not of cinema's lasting into the future but of its ontological passing in the present. One philosopher who has written elegantly on Deleuze's cinema books sets his sights directly on digital auto-presentation as a procedure that threatens the promise of cinematic memory. Recalling Deleuze's expressions of digital ambivalence, Jacques Rancière warns,

> Information is not memory. It is not for memory that it accumulates; it labors only for its own profit. And this profit is that everything is immediately forgotten for the affirmation of the sole abstract truth of the present and that it affirms its power as the only thing up to this truth. The reign of the informational present rejects out of hand, as unreal, what is other than homogeneous process and what's indifferent to its autopresentation.[39]

This is precisely the same sort of logic with which Deleuze voices his caution about informational culture at the conclusion of *Cinema 2*. To Deleuze, the autopresentation of new media threatens the liveness of cinematic automata that invigorates modern cinema with a new spirit. What he calls the new electronic automatism threatens to dissolve the cinematic inspiration of dreams and mystery into the neutral zone of random information bits indiscriminately traversing the wired membrane of gawkers and insomniacs.[40]

Yet, Deleuze is not ready to abandon the allure of a newly constituted cinematic object, one that is in perpetual flux on the data screen through which a new image can spring up from any point of the preceding image. Losing its directional privilege, the organization of cinematic space moves out of the theater into the fractal zones of high-speed ports, mobile computing, global positioning interfaces, and, more frequently, embedded information chips. Here the admiration for the colossal cinematic screen gives over to the allure of the miniaturized information tablet, an opaque surface carrying instantaneous downloads through which the sacredness of cinema's givens are forever rendered obsolete: "information replacing nature, and the brain-city, the third eye, replacing the eyes of nature."[41]

No artists have staged the newly coded automaton better than Mark Hansen and Ben Rubin in their collaborative project *Listening Post*. In this hypnotic installation that takes on a speed and life of its own, the artists display worded bits of information gleaned by data collection software that "crawls" the Web and listens to active chat rooms and online forums, news groups, and communication channels. Reaping snippets of language from the glossalia of global chat and the world-memory of passing presents, the artists stream them in a series of information snapshots that flows through an interconnected grid of some 230 miniature LED screens (Figure 22). Here cinematic motion shows itself as the coded automata of the passing presents of the new data archive, the NetNoise of hits, chat, traffic, instant messaging, and Web sampling. An automated voice reads some snippets aloud in a way that reenlivens Deleuze's cherished split of pure sound from cinematic image. Is the sounding a repetition of quotation or a sounding of generated digitext separated from the installation's whir and hiss of the movement of data bits?

In the eerily greenish hues of *Listening Post*, information *is* memory, *pace* Rancière, but of the kind literally suspended in the interval of time's code. As Tim Griffin so eloquently describes this enlivening digital memory archive,

> The daily cycle of human rhythms becomes discernable across time zones, with domestic discussions often turning up in the morning, while politics

Figure 22. Mark Hansen and Ben Rubin, *Listening Post,* 2002. Photograph by David Allison.

and sex dominate the discussions at night. Over the course of weeks, one discerns a cultural subconscious. The currents of opinion and attention today, for example, might surround questions of war abroad, or ruminations on security issues at home, which accumulate like so many drops of rain.[42]

Doesn't this performative grid of so many interconnected screens and sites bring to life the very kind of automatism that Deleuze identifies as the soul of modern cinema? Is this not an electronic resurgence of what he describes as "the material automatism of images which produces from the outside a thought which it imposes, as the unthinkable in our intellectual automatism"?[43] Might not the software generators that archive the intellectual automata inhabiting the wired membranes of online data culture be themselves the new source of the surging thought of the irrational interval? Doesn't *Listening Post* appropriate while resisting the flattening drive of information's surveillance to cast it in the glow of electronic Nature anew?

This is the resistant interval, as Rodowick so elegantly puts it, "that re-stores a belief in the virtual as a site where choice has yet to be determined, a reservoir of unthought yet immanent possibilities and modes of existence. In this respect, the utopian aspect of philosophy and art is the perpetua-tion of a memory of resistance. This is a resistance to habitual repetition—a time that is calculated, rationalized, and reified. But it is also resistance to all forms of commerce or exchange, whether in the form of communi-cation or that of commodities."[44]

OVERTURES TO THE FUTURE

Put otherwise, the utopian aspect of a philosophy of resistance might be what engages the future, the avant-garde, as more than the habitual repe-tition of the "pull forward" of the technoscientific system. Such an engage-ment in the future has been at the forefront of the philosophical thought shaping *Digital Baroque*. Encouraging resistance to the flattening hegemony of American film and television, Jacques Derrida warns Bernard Stiegler that "the categorical imperative, the unconditional requirement of all nego-tiation [over the future of new forms and outlets of media] is to leave the future to the future, in all events to leave open the possibility of the future."[45] Could we imagine a future cinema in which the future of the future itself might give rise to thought exceeding the irrational interval of the passing present? Might there be a strategy of digital performance in which the machinic itself, as data automaton and screen of thought, now saturates its memory by stocking the future, to rekindle the phrase of Lyotard, by thus losing its privilege of being an ungraspable point from which, however, time should always distribute itself between the "not yet" of the future and the "no longer" of the past? What might Deleuze have had to say, for in-stance, about the interface with cinema of accelerating developments in affective computing, artificial intelligence, and interactive virtual bots? I'm thinking of the kinds of interactive agents existing in, for example, Ken Feingold's *Sinking Feeling* (2001), Lynn Hershman's *Agent Ruby* and Stelarc's *Prosthetic Head*. These are interactive Web and prosthetic beings who are programmed to interact with the viewer through text and sound recognition software. Appearing to the users as interactive agents projected on screens, they respond uncannily to conversations in the passing present. The fre-quent result of the exchange, via the digital vicissitudes of recognition and scansion, is a response by the virtual bot that reinscribes ontology in the thought of new media exchange. When Feingold tells the bot of *Sinking Feeling*, "I'm just curious what you were thinking about," he receives a response whose playful philosophical import far exceeds the reflexivity of the question: "do you know I AM what thinking about?" What is particularly innovative about these digital beings who embody the complexities of psychic scansion is how they are programmed as open systems—they do more than perform the archive of the past. Their performance is contingent on the archive of the future, since their responses become more complex and sophisticated as they interact with successive visitors in the future.

The unpredictable future, as something of a new irrational interval in the present, one that marks the "not still" of the present and the "no longer" of the past, may well be programmed to engage in resistance to any habitual repetition of future cinema. I would like to conclude by turning to one such installation, *n-cha(n)t* (2001) by the Canadian artist, David Rokeby, that aligns the future resistance of the coded archive with the world-memory of interactive computing. For this project, Rokeby installs a series of interconnected computers and monitors, from six to twelve, that respond to user presence through sensors and microphones. When the computer's sensor acknowledges the presence of the user, its video image solicits verbal interaction with the user, who then joins others in the room by speaking phrases into the various microphones attached to screens throughout the space. This public, interactive performance is rendered strangely private since the microphone works to deaden sound by incorporating it into the computer network rather than amplifying it via speakers to others in the room. Emphasizing a theoretical shift crucial to many of the artistic projects discussed in *Digital Baroque,* Rokeby hereby stages a digital dynamics of scansion rather than a cinematic performance of projection.

What's more, the phrases uttered by the speaker interact with those internalized bits spoken by others to create something of a new emergent language, a new recombinant generator of what might come to be . . . thought. "What each computer speaks is meaningless in itself," says Rokeby. "Taken together, these phrases chart the trajectory of an unfolding narrative of communication . . . shared non-sense shimmering with a sense of meaning."[46] What's crucial to this constantly evolving installation, and what I wish to leave open for further development in my book in progress, "Immaterial

Archives: Curatorial Instabilities @ New Media Art," is that its performance remains dependent on the overture to the future. It requires interaction with anticipated human interlocutors who themselves, as thoughtful agents of the event, constitute the "pull" of the informational future in the irrational digital interval between retrofutures. This is something of a marvelous retooling of the Deleuzian montrage, based you will recall on the bringing together of the before and the after in a becoming. The paradox of the new retrofuture is that "the after" is now inscribed as "the archival," one awaiting the data of the future for the sake of Rokeby's unfolding narrative of communication. His *n-cha(n)t* also screens on many levels the new automatism's giving over to the will and the pull of the future, "put to the service of powerful, obscure, condensed will to art, aspiring to deploy itself through involuntary movements which none the less do not restrict it."[47] What continues to be at play, although with a numerical difference, is the enduring interval of cinema's internal struggle with the temporality of informatics. Crucial to this concept of the interval is not its logical relation to the whole but its philosophical force as the irreducible montrage of becoming. Might not this be the networked ground of the baroquely n-cha(n)ted thought of future cinema itself?

NOTES

INTRODUCTION

1. Peter Greenaway, *Prospero's Books: A Film of Shakespeare's "The Tempest"* (New York: Four Walls Eight Windows, 1991), 50.

2. Ibid.

3. Maurice Merleau-Ponty, *Phénoménologie de la perception* (Paris: Gallimard, 1945), 249. Unless otherwise noted, all translations are my own.

4. Gilles Deleuze, *The Fold: Leibniz and the Baroque,* trans. Tom Conley (Minneapolis: University of Minnesota Press, 1993), 8. Conley's foreword, "A Plea for Leibniz," as well as the interpretational import of his English translation, has been fundamental to the imprint of the temporal fold in this book, as were our many conversations at the book's inception during our year together as fellows at Cornell University's Society for the Humanities. I like to think of the arguments in this book as akin to what Conley describes as "Baroque *territories.* They pertain to a nature endowed with forces that Leibniz describes by tracking the motion of infinite folding" (xvii). Unless otherwise noted, all emphases are in the original.

5. Jacques Derrida, *Dissemination,* trans. Barbara Johnson (Chicago: University of Chicago Press, 1981), 238.

6. Ibid., 270.

7. Ibid., 229. This is my translation of the French, "Le pli (se) multiplie mais (n'est) pas (un)."

8. Richard Coyne engages in an insightful critique of utopic notions of technoromanticism in his book *Technoromanticism: Digital Narrative, Holism, and the Romance of the Real* (Cambridge, Mass.: MIT Press, 1999). In chapter 5, I discuss more directly my discomfort with Peter Lunenfeld's term "digital dialectic," which he introduces in his collection *The Digital Dialectic: New Essays on New Media* (Cambridge, Mass.: MIT Press, 1999).

9. Jay David Bolter and Richard Grusin, *Remediation: Understanding New Media* (Cambridge, Mass.: MIT Press, 1999), 235.

10. Walter Benjamin, *The Origin of German Tragic Drama*, trans. John Osborne (London: NLB, 1977), 184.

11. Ibid., 178.

12. Ibid., 80–81.

13. Christine Buci-Glucksmann, "Préface," in *Puissance du Baroque: Les forces, les formes, les rationalités*, ed. Else Marie Bukdahl and Carsten Juhl (Paris: Galilée, 1996), 13.

14. An exceptional analysis of the development of autoportraiture from video to new media is provided by Anne-Marie Duguet in *Déjouer l'image: Creations électroniques et numériques* (Paris: Jacqueline Chambon, 2002), 13–42.

15. Paul Virilio, *War and Cinema: The Logistics of Perception* (London: Verso, 1984).

16. Angela Ndalianis, *Neo-Baroque Aesthetics and Contemporary Entertainment* (Cambridge, Mass.: MIT Press, 1999).

17. Walter Benjamin, *The Origin of German Tragic Drama*, 92.

18. Deleuze, *The Fold*, 10.

19. Deleuze, *Cinema 2: The Time-Image*, trans. Hugh Tomlinson and Robert Galeta (Minneapolis: University of Minnesota Press, 1989), 81.

20. In the introduction to *Theatricality as Medium* (New York: Fordham University Press, 2004), 16–22, Samuel Weber provides an exemplary reading of Derrida's similar appropriation of the Heideggerian notion of *zweifalt*. I should note that Weber provides a Derridean critique of Deleuze's application of the fold as "interval" in "The Virtuality of the Media," *Sites: The Journal of 20th-Century/Contemporary French Studies* 4, no. 2 (Fall 2000): 297–317. Also pertinent to this discussion of the philosophical valence of the interval is Jean-Luc Nancy's extensive analysis of "the touch" as interval in *Les Muses* (Paris: Galilée, 1994), 34–41.

21. I elaborate on psychoanalytic readings of Holbein's *The Ambassadors* in *Drama Trauma: Specters of Race and Sexuality in Performance, Video, and Art* (New York: Routledge, 1997), 53.

22. See Jacques Lacan, *The Four Fundamental Concepts of Psychoanalysis*, trans. Alan Sheridan, ed. Jacques-Alain Miller (New York: W. W. Norton, 1978).

23. In *New Philosophy for New Media* (Cambridge, Mass.: MIT Press, 2004), 197–206, Mark B. N. Hansen frames his discussion of the "affective topology of new media art" around Robert Lazzarini's uncanny installation that features the installation of anamorphic skulls deriving from a CAD file of a laser-scanned human skull. For discussion of an early modern corollary, see my analysis of anamorphic vision in *King Lear* in *Drama Trauma*, 49–53.

24. Neil Hertz, *The End of the Line* (New York: Columbia University Press, 1985), 179–91.

25. In *Theatrical Legitimation: Allegories of Genius in Seventeenth-Century England and France* (Oxford: Oxford University Press, 1987), 23–104, I discuss the evolution of theatrical rough drafts, "foul papers," into printed, authorial text, as well as reflecting broadly on the baroque importance of allegory, a concept whose parameters, especially

as developed by Benjamin, remain implicit in the argument this book's various arguments about "reading," which I understand as an allegorical event.

26. Vivaria.net and the Institute of Digital Art and Technology at Plymouth University, *Notes toward the Complete Works of Shakespeare* (Plymouth: Vivaria.net and the Institute of Digital Art and Technology, 2002), n.p.

27. Vivaria.net, http://www.vivaria.net/.

28. Vivaria.net and the Institute of Digital Art and Technology at Plymouth University, *Notes toward the Complete Works of Shakespeare,* n.p.

29. Deleuze, *The Fold;* Walter Moser, ed., *Résurgences baroques: Les trajectoires d'un processus transculturel* (Geneva: La Lettre Volée, 2001); Christine Buci-Glucksmann, "Baroque et complexité: Une esthétique du virtuel," in *Résurgences baroques,* ed. Moser, 45–53; Sean Cubitt, "The Relevance of the Baroque: Interactivity," in Simon Biggs, *The Book of Shadows* (London: Ellipsis London Ltd, 1996), 35–40, and *Digital Aesthetics* (Thousand Oaks, Calif.: Sage Publications, 1998); Mieke Bal, *Quoting Caravaggio: Contemporary Art, Preposterous History* (Chicago: University of Chicago Press, 1999); Mario Perniola, *Énigmes: Le moment égyptien dans la société et dans l'art,* trans. Robert Laliberté and Isabella di Carpegna (Brussels: La Lettre Volée, 1995); Angela Ndalianis, *Neo-Baroque Aesthetics and Contemporary Entertainment* (Cambridge, Mass.: MIT Press, 1999); Anna Munster, *Materializing New Media: Embodiment in Information Aesthetics* (Lebanon, N.H.: University Press of New England, 2006); Michelle Barker, "Praeternatural: Digital Metaphors as a Platform for Biological Control in Genetics and Interactive Arts in the 1990s," Ph.D. diss., University of New South Wales, 2005; Christina McPhee, "Net Baroque," *CTHEORY* e129 (2003).

30. "Contact Zones: The Art of CD-ROM" is an international exhibition of fifty-five CD-ROMs from eighteen countries that I curated from 1999 to 2004. It opened at Cornell University in 1999 and traveled to Hobart and William Smith Colleges, Centro de la Imagen in Mexico City, the Virginia Film Festival in Charlottesville, the Nickle Arts Museum in Calgary, the Forum des Images in Paris, and RadioFree-Hamptons Gallery in Sag Harbor, New York. The Web catalogue can be accessed at http://contactzones.cit.cornell.edu.

31. Deleuze, *The Fold,* 110.

32. Jean-Michel Frodon, "Jean-Luc Godard au musée d'Art moderne de New York," *Le Monde,* 10 May 1994.

33. Cubitt, "The Relevance of the Baroque: Interactivity," 39.

34. Perniola, *Énigmes,* 85.

35. Ibid., 86.

36. Ibid., 110.

37. Buci-Glucksmann, "Préface," 14.

38. Deleuze, *Difference and Repetition,* trans. Paul Patton (New York: Columbia University Press, 1994), 48.

39. Jean-François Lyotard, *Économie libidinale* (Paris: Minuit, 1978), 53.

40. Deleuze, *Difference and Repetition,* 48.

41. Ibid., 123. This emphasis on the "different points of view" that constitute a new

world memory, on which Deleuze elaborates in *Cinema 2*, is what I believe distinguishes Deleuze's interest in a new world memory from its critique for singularity by Samuel Weber in "The Virtuality of the Media." This distinction is crucial to my endorsement of new world-memory in chapters 3, 4, and 10.

42. Perniola, *Énigmes*, 86.

43. Walter Moser, "Résurgences et valences du baroque," in *Résurgences baroques*, ed. Moser and Goyer, 35.

44. Timothy Murray, "Introduction: Phantasmatic Repossessions," in *Repossessions: Psychoanalysis and the Phantasms of Early Modern Culture*, ed. Timothy Murray and Alan K. Smith (Minneapolis: University of Minnesota Press, 1998), ix–xxxi.

45. Ndalianis, *Neo-Baroque Aesthetics and Contemporary Entertainment*, 209.

46. Julia Kristeva, *Soleil noir: Dépression et mélancolie* (Paris: Gallimard, 1987), 125.

47. Louis Marin, *Des pouvoirs de l'image: Gloses* (Paris: Seuil, 1993), 237.

48. Deleuze, *The Fold*, 7.

49. Francis Bacon, "The Great Instauration," in *The New Organon and Related Writings* (Indianapolis: Bobbs-Merrill, 1969), 12.

50. Deleuze, *The Fold*, 136–37.

51. I highly recommend the informative analyses by D. N. Rodowick of the impact of digital "figurality" on the interdisciplinary regimes of knowledge in *Reading the Figural, or Philosophy after the New Media* (Durham, N.C.: Duke University Press, 2001).

1. DIGITAL BAROQUE

1. Antonin Artaud, "Sorcellerie et cinéma," in *Oeuvres complètes* (Paris: Gallimard, 1970), 3:83–84.

2. Ultimately, theatricality is understood in the broadly cohesive French intellectual context to destabilize the subject-object dichotomy sustaining what Foucault calls the mimetic paradigm "of a central and founding subject to which events occur while it deploys meaning around itself; and of an object that is a threshold and point of convergence for recognizable forms and the attributes we affirm." Michel Foucault, "Theatrum Philosophicum," in *Mimesis, Masochism, and Mime: The Politics of Theatricality in Contemporary French Thought*, ed. Timothy Murray (Ann Arbor: University of Michigan Press, 1997), 224. What lies at the heart of theatricality, then, whether as the scene of the nonconvergence of representation or as the stage of unresolved social alterity, is the ambivalent pathos evoked by the divisions of mimesis and their profound turn of subject and socius against themselves. Even in its theorization by such neo-classicists as Racine and the Abbé d'Aubignac, mimesis forcefully displays the painful divisions internal to representation and to the self. Indeed, theater and performance consistently return to the wrenching display of such internal division. In view of this conflictual legacy of performance and theory, I understand mimesis and its affect, whether displayed on the stage of tragedy or the page of theory, to consist of nothing less than *the theatricalization of masochism*. This is the subject of *Mimesis, Masochism, and Mime: The Politics of Theatricality in Contemporary French Thought* (Ann Arbor: University of Michigan Press, 1997), my collection of French philosophical essays.

3. Herbert Blau, *Blooded Thought: Occasions of Theatre* (New York: Performing Arts Journal Publications, 1982), 132.

4. The actor's doubling via hologram has been particularly effective in the scene of dance. See my essay "Scanning Sublimation: The Digital Pôles of Performance and Psychoanalysis," in *Psychoanalysis and Performance,* ed. Patrick Campbell and Adrian Kear (London: Routledge, 2001), 47–59.

5. Johanna Burton, "Paul Chan," in *Day for Night (Whitney Biennial 2006),* Chrissie Iles and Philippe Vergne (New York: Whitney Museum of Art, 2006), 198. I should note that Burton accurately reflects Chan's investment in distinguishing the metaphysical aims of his installations from his well-known political activities and projects, a distinction amply developed by Scott Rothkopf in his excellent essay "Embedded in Culture: Scott Rothkopf on the Art of Paul Chan," *Artforum* 44, no. 10 (Summer 2006): 305–11.

6. Jörg Zutter, "Interview with Bill Viola," in special insert, "Profile 31: World Wide Video," *Art & Design* 8, nos. 7–8 (1993): 48. An interesting Deleuzian account of alternative video approaches is provided by Dorothea Olkowski, "Bodies in Light: Relaxing the Imaginary in Video," in *Thinking Bodies,* ed. Juliet Flower MacCannell and Laura Zakarin (Stanford, Calif.: Stanford University Press, 1994), 164–80.

7. Bill Viola, "Video Black—The Mortality of the Image," in *Illuminating Video: An Essential Guide to Video Art,* ed. Doug Hall and Sally Jo Piper (New York: Aperture Foundation, 1990), 485.

8. See, for example, three essays in "Digitality and the Memory of Cinema," special issue, *Wide Angle* 21, no. 1 (January 1999): Maureen Turim, "Artisinal Prefigurations of the Digital: Animating Realities, Collage Effects, and Theories of Image Manipulations," 48–62; Sean Cubitt, "Phalke, Méliès, and Special Effects Today," 114–30; and Yvonne Spielmann, "Aesthetic Features in Digital Imaging: Collage and Morph," 131–48.

9. Roger Leenhardt, "Ambiguïté du cinéma," in *Chroniques du cinéma* (Paris: Cahiers du cinema; Editions de l'Etoile, 1986), 177.

10. Leenhardt, "Les temps du film," in *Chroniques du cinéma,* 145.

11. Leenhardt, "La petite école du spectateur," in *Chroniques du cinéma,* 43, 42.

12. For a prescient elaboration on such doubling, see Raymond Bellour, "The Double Helix," in *Electronic Culture: Technology and Visual Representation,* ed. Timothy Druckrey (New York: Aperture Foundation, 1996).

13. Gilles Deleuze, *The Fold: Leibniz and the Baroque,* trans. Tom Conley (Minneapolis: University of Minnesota Press, 1993), 136.

14. My discussion of the artworks in this section relies on the very detailed and helpful sources I cite within.

15. Francisco Reyes Palma, "'Drink Me,' 'Eat Me,'" in *Mona Hatoum,* Laboratorio Arte Alameda (Mexico City: Conaculta/INBA/LAA, 2002), 70.

16. Ibid., 71.

17. Ibid.

18. Paula Dawson, "Shrine of the Sacred Heart," http://oldsite.vislab.usyd.edu.au/gallery/paula/explanation.html.

19. Ibid.

20. John Rupert Martin, *Baroque* (Boulder: Westview Press, 1977), 190, 188.

21. Rebecca Coyle and Philip Hayward, *Holographic Art in Australia* (Sydney: Power Publications, 1995), 71.

22. Ibid.

23. It should be noted that Dawson's more recent work seems to have abandoned the paradoxical nuance of such a staged fade to black in order to foreground the spiritual illumination of her installation in St. Bridget's Church in Coogee, *Shrine of the Sacred Heart.* Dawson describes the context on her installation Web site: "Light is the key to understanding the visual imagery of the *Shrine of the Sacred Heart.* In this holographic artwork, the light associated with the Sacred Heart is the subject of the visual representation. To appreciate the holographic shrine it is necessary to understand the significance of light in the traditional representation of the Sacred Heart. In previous representations of the Sacred Heart, light comes from the flame and cross which together mark the wound to the Heart. Also the body of Christ is surrounded by another light, the golden sphere called the aureole. The holographic images are of the flame and cross and of the aureole. Representations of the Sacred Heart are all to an extent based on the 17th century visions of Saint Margaret Mary. The following extracts from the autobiography of Saint Margaret Mary are of three of her visions of the Sacred Heart. The essential property of each of these visions is the association of the presence of the Sacred Heart and light. The invisible presence of the Sacred Heart is intimated in the holograms by representing the light of these visions."

24. Ibid., 56.

25. Florian Matzner, "Baroque Laser," in *Baroque Laser,* ed. Matzner (Ostfildern: Cantz Verlag, 1995), 57.

26. Mario Perniola, *Énigmes: Le moment égyptien dans la société et dans l'art,* trans. Robert Laliberté and Isabella di Carpegna (Brussels: La Lettre Volée, 1995), 87.

27. Walter Benjamin, *The Origin of German Tragic Drama,* trans. John Osborne (London: NLB, 1977), 184.

28. Ibid., 92.

29. Matzner, "Baroque Laser," 14.

30. Ibid., 33.

31. Benjamin, *The Origin of German Tragic Drama,* 81.

32. Matzner, "Baroque Laser," 32.

33. Hubert Damisch, *The Origin of Perspective,* trans. John Goodman (Cambridge, Mass.; London: 1994), 28.

34. Mieke Bal, *Quoting Caravaggio: Contemporary Art, Preposterous History* (Chicago and London: University of Chicago Press, 1999), 65.

35. Benjamin, *The Origin of German Tragic Drama,* 81.

36. See my "Subliminal Genius: Energetic Spectating, Deconstructive Praxis," in *Theatrical Legitimation: Allegories of Genius in Seventeenth-Century England and France* (Oxford: Oxford University Press, 1987), 192–217; Murray, "Dirtier Still? Wistful Gazing and Homographic Hieroglyphs in Jarman's *Caravaggio,*" in *Like a Film: Ideological*

Fantasy on Screen, Camera, and Canvas (New York: Routledge, 1993), 124–71; Murray, "Getting Stoned: Psychoanalysis and the Epistemology of Tragedy in Shakespeare," in *Drama Trauma: Specters of Race and Sexuality in Performance, Video, and Art* (New York: Routledge, 1997), 31–56; and Murray, "'Animé d'un regard': The Crisis of Televisual Speed in Racine," *L'esprit créateur* 38, no. 2 (Summer 1998): 11–22.

37. For detailed discussions of these terms, refer to Louis Marin, *De la représentation* (Paris: Seuil/Gallimard, 1994); and Michel Foucault, *The Order of Things: An Archaeology of the Human Sciences* (New York: Vintage Books, 1970).

38. Foucault, "Theatrum Philosophicum," in *Mimesis, Masochism, and Mime,* ed. Murray (Ann Arbor: University of Michigan Press, 1997), 220.

39. Deleuze, *The Fold,* 136.

40. Bill Viola, "Five Angels," *Tate Magazine* 6, at http://www.tate.org.uk/magazine/issue6/fiveangels.htm.

41. Fereshteh Daftari, *Without Boundary: Seventeen Ways of Looking* (New York: Museum of Modern Art, 2006), 25.

42. Felicity Sparrow, ed., *Bill Viola: The Messenger* (Durham: Chaplaincy to the Arts and Recreation in North East England, 1996), 18.

43. David Jasper, "The Art of Bill Viola: A Theological Reflection," in *Bill Viola,* ed. Sparrow, 14; David A. Ross, "Foreword: A Feeling for the Things Themselves," in *Bill Viola,* ed. David A. Ross and Peter Sellars (New York: Whitney Museum of American Art; Paris: Flammarion, 1998).

44. Ross, "Foreword," in *Bill Viola,* ed. Ross and Sellars, 27.

45. Cited by Jasper, "The Art of Bill Viola," in *Bill Viola,* ed. Sparrow, 14.

46. See Louis Marin's elegant reflections on the forceful power of display in *Des pouvoirs de l'image: Gloses* (Paris: Seuil, 1993).

47. Ross and Sellars, *Bill Viola,* 126.

48. Blau, *Blooded Thought,* 132.

49. Ross and Sellars, *Bill Viola,* 127.

50. Ibid.

51. Deleuze, *The Fold,* 89.

52. Deleuze, "One Less Manifesto," in *Mimesis, Masochism, and Mime,* ed. Murray, 242.

53. Anne-Marie Duguet, *Déjouer l'image: Créations électroniques et numériques* (Paris: Éditions Jacqueline Chambon, 2002), 55. In "The Double Helix," in *Electronic Culture,* ed. Druckrey, 192, Bellour similarly refers to Viola's installations as a place where there are passages between cinematic and multiple visions.

54. Ross and Sellars, *Bill Viola,* 86.

55. Ibid. Viola elaborates on the technical aspects of the piece, and the relation between time and emotion, in an interview with John Hanhardt in *Bill Viola: Going Forth by Day,* Bill Viola and John G. Hanhardt (New York: Solomon R. Guggenheim Foundation, 2002), 104.

56. Ibid., 100.

57. Ross Gibson, *Remembrance and the Moving Image* (Victoria: Australian Centre for the Moving Image, 2003), 141–42.

58. Ibid., 107.

59. Peer F. Bundgard, "Forme, force, et figure," in *Puissance du Baroque: Les forces, les formes, les rationalités,* ed. Else Marie Bukdahl and Carsten Juhl (Paris: Galilée, 1996), 178–79.

60. Deleuze, *The Fold,* 137.

2. ET IN ARCADIA VIDEO

1. Lawrence Grossberg, Cary Nelson, and Paula Treicher, eds., *Cultural Studies* (New York: Routledge, 1992).

2. I discuss these issues in greater detail in "The Mise-en-Scène of the Cultural," the introduction to *Mimesis, Masochism, and Mime: The Politics of Theatricality in Contemporary French Thought,* ed. Murray (Ann Arbor: University of Michigan Press, 1997), and in "Ideological Fantasy in Reverse Projection," the introduction to *Like a Film: Ideological Fantasy on Screen, Camera, and Canvas* (New York: Routledge, 1993).

3. Anne-Marie Duguet, *Déjouer l'image: Créations électroniques et numériques* (Paris: Editions Jacqueline Chambon, 2002), 86.

4. I provide a brief overview of Marin's work in "Louis Marin," in *The Columbia History of Twentieth-Century Thought,* ed. Lawrence D. Kritzman (New York: Columbia University Press, 2006), 606–7. For an overview and samples of Kuntzel's art, videos, and theoretical texts, see Thierry Kuntzel, *Title TK* (Dijon, France: Les Presses du Réel, 2006). This is an invaluable collection of Kuntzel's essays and artist's notes along with an accompanying DVD-ROM of stills and clips produced by Anne-Marie Duguet.

5. Marin, "La ville dans sa carte et son portrait," in *De la représentation* (Paris: Seuil/Gallimard, 1994), 204–18.

6. Michel de Certeau, *The Practice of Everyday Life* (Berkeley: University of California Press, 1984).

7. Marin, "Classical, Baroque: Versailles, or The Architecture of the Prince," *Yale French Studies* 80 (1991): 171.

8. Readers of Marin's later books, *De la représentation, Des pouvoirs de l'image: Gloses* (Paris: Seuil, 1993) and *Lectures traversières* (Paris: Albin Michel, 1992), will note the lasting influence of the utopic reflections he developed much earlier in *Utopics: Spatial Play,* trans. Robert A. Vollrath (Atlantic Highlands, N.J.: Humanities Press, 1984).

9. Marin, "Towards a Theory of Reading in the Visual Arts: Poussin's *The Arcadian Shepherds,*" in *Calligram: Essays in New Art History from France,* ed. Norman Bryson (Cambridge: Cambridge University Press), 72.

10. Marin, "La ville dans sa carte et son portrait," in *De la représentation,* 207.

11. Marin, "Towards a Theory of Reading in the Visual Arts," in *Calligram,* ed. Bryson, 86.

12. Marin, "L'être de l'image et son efficace," in *Des pouvoirs de l'image,* 11.

13. In *La force d'attraction* (Paris: Seuil, 1990), J.-B. Pontalis refers generally to such forceful projection as the generalized machinery of "transference."

14. Marin, "L'être de l'image et son efficace," in *Des pouvoirs de l'image*, 16.

15. Marin, *To Destroy Painting*, trans. Mette Hjort (Chicago: University of Chicago Press, 1995), 4.

16. Marin, "L'être de l'image et son efficace," in *Des pouvoirs de l'image*, 16–17.

17. Thierry Kuntzel, "Notes sur *La Jetée*," in *Thierry Kuntzel*, ed. Anne-Marie Duguet (Paris: Galerie nationale du Jeu de Paume, 1993), 32.

18. Marin, "L'être de l'image et son efficace," in *Des pouvoirs de l'image*, 19.

19. Jacques Lacan, *The Four Fundamental Concepts of Psycho-Analysis*, trans. Alan Sheridan (New York: Norton, 1978), 96.

20. Biblical citations are from *The Holy Bible: King James Version* (Cleveland: World Publishing, n.d.).

21. Marin, *Des pouvoirs de l'image*, 239.

22. Julia Kristeva, *Soleil noir: Dépression et mélancolie* (Paris: Gallimard, 1987), 134.

23. In "Video Writing," in *Illuminating Video: An Essential Guide to Video Art*, ed. Doug Hall and Sally Jo Fifer (San Francisco: Aperture, 1990), Raymond Bellour discusses how white light in Kuntzel "accentuates what one sees, but at the same time it makes it unreal, while making one believe all the more in that very unreality" (423).

24. In his letter to Chambray, 1 March 1665, in *Lettres et propos sur l'art* (Paris: Hermann, 1964), Poussin concludes this definition by adding that the "aim of painting is 'la délectation'" (163).

25. Marin, *To Destroy Painting*, 161.

26. Marin, *De la représentation*, 295–96.

27. The punctum is, of course, Roland Barthes's term, in *Camera Lucida: Reflections on Photography*, trans. Richard Howard (New York: Hill & Wang, 1981), for the primal element of visuality that confronts the spectator with the image's unnameable, untouchable elements that wound, pierce, and touch the viewer, very much like the solicitous and disarming effect of Lacan's scopic "light." I discuss the punctum and how Barthes offers it to his readers while taking it away in "Photo-Medusa: Roland Barthes Incorporated," in *Like a Film*, 65–97.

28. Kuntzel, "Memory/Notes," in *Thierry Kuntzel*, 49.

29. Marin, *Des pouvoirs de l'image*, 18.

30. In his catalogue notes on *Summer*, in *Thierry Kuntzel* (126), Kuntzel makes this assertion in response to Diderot's praise of the ordering principles of single-point perspective.

31. I have in mind the eternal return of the ideational simulacra whose "chaoerrancy" is theorized by Deleuze in *Difference and Repetition*, trans. Paul Patton (New York: Columbia University Press, 1994), 57, and whose baroque visual corollaries are discussed in *The Fold: Leibniz and the Baroque*, trans. Tom Conley (Minneapolis: University of Minnesota Press, 1993).

32. In "The Image of Art in Video," in *Resolutions: Contemporary Video Practices*, ed. Michael Renov and Erika Suderburg (Minneapolis: University of Minnesota Press, 1996), 36–40, Maureen Turim presents a fascinating discussion of the visual paradox of Kuntzel's "colorist" appropriation of Poussin. Bernard Teyssèdre provides a detailed

account of the debate over "le coloris" in *Roger de Piles et les débats sur le coloris au siècle de Louis XIV* (Paris: Bibliothèque des arts, 1957). Also see Svetlana Alpers, "Describe or Narrate? A Problem in Realistic Representation," *New Literary History* 8, no. 1 (Autumn 1976): 15–41.

33. Note for example how, in "Intermittances du corp," in *Thierry Kuntzel*, 56–57, Laurence Louppe fails to acknowledge the difference posed by Ken Moody's race while he engages in an otherwise subtle discussion of the tactile dimensions of Moody's body in *Four Seasons Minus One*.

34. Jean-Paul Sartre, *Being and Nothingness*, trans. Hazel E. Barnes (New York: Philosophical Library, 1956), 343.

35. Robert Mapplethorpe, *Black Book* (New York: St. Martin's Press, 1986).

36. This critique of Mapplethorpe's iteration of the terms of colonialist fantasy, by serving the fetishistic expectations of white desire, is made most cogently by Kobena Mercer in "Imagining the Black Man's Sex," in *Photography Politics: Two*, ed. Patricia Holland (London: Comedia, 1987). Mercer has since mollified his position in response to the ambivalence of a black, homosexual gaze in "Skin Head Sex Thing: Racial Difference and the Homoerotic Imaginary," in *How Do I Look? Queer Film and Video*, ed. Bad Object-Choices (Seattle: Bay Press, 1991); and with Isaac Julien, "True Confessions," in *Black Male: Representations of Masculinity in Contemporary American Art*, ed. Thelma Golden (New York: Whitney Museum of Art, 1994).

37. I initially presented this reading in my introduction to *Like a Film*, 11–13.

38. Christopher Phillips, "Between Pictures," *Art in America* 79, no. 11 (November 1991): 110.

39. Neil Hertz, *The End of the Line* (New York: Columbia University Press, 1985), 179–91.

40. Mercer and Julien, "True Confessions," 194–95.

41. Raymond Bellour, "The Double Helix," in *Electronic Culture: Technology and Visual Representation*, ed. Timothy Druckrey (New York: Aperture Foundation, 1996), 193.

42. Kuntzel, "Video/Notes," in *Thierry Kuntzel*, 72.

43. Cited by Jean-François Lyotard, "Contribution des tableaux de Jacques Monory," in *Figurations 1960/1973* (Paris: Union Générale d'Editions, 1973), 163.

44. Anne-Marie Duguet, "Les vitesses de l'immobile," in *Thierry Kuntzel*, 12.

45. Michael O'Pray, *Derek Jarman: Dreams of England* (London: British Film Institute, 1996), 206.

46. In a strange way, I did manage to salute Thierry at the time of his internment. At the same moment Thierry was being laid to rest in the Père Lachaise cemetery in Paris, I happened to be giving a lecture to my Cornell students in "Introduction to Visual Studies" on queer video in the age of AIDS. At the opening of this class, I suddenly realized that I was screening Isaac Julien's sublimely gorgeous and melancholic tape "This is not an AIDS Advertisement" at the precise moment of Thierry's funeral. Just as coincidental as Julien's evocation of loss in the face of death was that I followed this tape with a contextual explanation of independent art production in the age of AIDS, a lecture that opens with images from Robert Mapplethorpe's *Black Book* in

order to frame Mapplethorpe's memorable account of how most of the black boys he photographed in the seventies had preceded him in death from AIDS. As I was recounting this anecdote to my class, I stood with amazement when I realized that the image filling the screen from *Black Book* was of a model who survived Mapplethorpe, Ken Moody. The connection between *Winter* and Thierry Kuntzel's internment couldn't have been more stunning.

47. Derek Jarman, *Blue* (Woodstock, N.Y.: Overlook Press, 1994), 15–16.

48. In the chapter "Wistful Gazing and Homographic Hieroglyphs in Jarman's *Caravaggio*," in *Like a Film*, 124–71, I discuss the fluid and erotic movements between mourning and melancholia in Jarman's work.

3. THE CRISIS OF CINEMA IN THE AGE OF NEW WORLD MEMORY

1. Gilles Deleuze, *The Fold: Leibniz and the Baroque*, trans. Tom Conley (Minneapolis: University of Minnesota Press, 1993), 27.

2. Ibid., 110.

3. Jean-Luc Godard, *For Ever Mozart* (Paris: P.O.L., 1996), 28.

4. Godard, *Histoire(s) du cinéma 4* (Paris: Gallimard, 1998), 38.

5. Ibid., 47.

6. Microsoft, *Cinemania '95: The Entertaining Guide to Movies and the Moviemakers* (Microsoft Corporation, 1992–94).

7. Katherine Dieckmann, "Godard in His Fifth Period," in *Jean Luc Godard: Interviews*, ed. David Sterritt (Jackson: University of Mississippi Press, 1998), 172.

8. Ibid.

9. David Impastato, "Godard's *Lear*... Why Is It So Bad?" *Shakespeare Bulletin* 12, no. 3 (Summer 1994): 38.

10. Similarly complex is Godard's classic montage of text and image. Echoing Cordelia's match of attractive body and frozen tongue, Cordelia (played by Molly Ringwald) spends many of her moments alone looking at stilled, silent images from the history of art that are screened prominently throughout the film, from the delicate female drawings of da Vinci and Vermeer to the female subjects of Manet, Morisot, and Renoir. It is almost as if painting's silencing objectification of female beauty figures the condition triggered by Cordelia's forceful silence in Shakespeare's play. Conversely, it is as if the contemplative female subjects of classical painting best represent Cordelia's silent cinematic introspections. The legacy of painting is evoked at the commencement of the film (directly after Mailer's departure) when William Jr. flips through a photo album that includes a shot of three actresses alongside Renoir, whom William says "was keen on young girls like his father Auguste, father, father." The three girls, the three fathers, the history of the leer—might not these branches of the family tree of cinematic painting be signified by the film's enigmatic intertitle, "3 Journeys In To King Lear"? The same images by da Vinci, Vermeer, and Manet that fill the space of Cordelia's solitude reappear in *Histoire(s) du cinéma 3*, 49–57. Succeeding the double-framed phrase "des ténèbres de l'absolu [the shadows of the absolute]" (an interesting conflation of chapter 3A's title and subtitle, "La monnaie de l'absolu [the

money of the absolute]" and "La réponse des ténèbres"), these silent female images evoke, haunt, or supplement the loss of cinematic plenitude: "the famous and pale smiles of da Vinci and Vermeer first say me, me, and then the world" (*Histoire(s) du cinéma 3*, 51). Regarding the painterly quality of *Histoire(s) du cinéma*, Godard stresses that the video "belongs to painting history and it's pure painting, but cinematic painting—it's a part of cinema that been given away by most people. . . . But I like those people [in the painting] to say words, and then there is a drama—but drama painted like that. Not like in a novel. Very often I look at paintings and I say to myself, What is he saying? Those people—what are they thinking of? I remember my very first article was a comparison between a Preminger picture and Impressionist painting. Maybe it's not possible, but to me it seems possible—it is my cinema." Gavin Smith, "Jean-Luc Godard," in *Jean-Luc Godard: Interviews,* ed. David Sterritt (Jackson: University Press of Mississippi, 1998), 188. Might not just this performative aspect of the painterly subject be precisely what Godard stages in *King Lear* when the spectator watches Cordelia looking at paintings in a way that opens the space of thought: those people, what are they thinking? Might not Cordelia herself stand in for the figure of Berthe Morisot in Manet's *Le Balcon*? Her image reprinted in *Histoire(s) du cinéma 3A* bears a montaged interpellation that preempts the spectator's question in a way that reclaims thought for the silenced subject, "Je sais à quoi tu penses [I know what you're thinking]."

11. Smith, "Jean-Luc Godard," in *Jean-Luc Godard: Interviews,* 155.

12. All quotations from *King Lear* are from the *The Riverside Shakespeare,* ed. G. Blakemore Evans (Boston: Houghton Mifflin, 1974).

13. I develop this point in "Getting Stoned: Psychoanalysis and the Epistemology of Tragedy in Shakespeare," in *Drama Trauma: Specters of Race and Sexuality in Performance, Video, and Art* (New York: Routledge, 1997), 31–56.

14. Smith, "Jean-Luc Godard," in *Jean-Luc Godard: Interviews,* 188.

15. The certain uncertainty of projection is discussed toward the end of *King Lear* when Professor Pluggy teaches the *New York Times* interviewer about the architectonics of cinema where "chairs [are] facing the same space: voice projected all over here: this is our invention: same space, dark: here they know [what] to look at," even while the destruction of perspective no longer permits them to know exactly what that "what" signifies.

16. It is almost as if William Shakespeare Jr. the Fifth is haunted by the crisis of socius that Jacques Derrida analyzes in "No apocalypse, not now: à toute vitesse, sept missives, sept missiles," in *Psyche: Inventions de l'autre* (Paris: Galilée, 1987), 363–86.

17. Godard, *Histoire(s) du cinéma 4,* 262.

18. "Everyone occupies this position," suggests Kaja Silverman when suggesting that the similar condition of "betweenness" in *Passion* means that "to be human is to reside within the interval." Kaja Silverman and Harun Farocki, *Speaking about Godard* (New York: New York University Press, 1998), 188.

19. In this regard, the significational effect of the Godardian sound-event is curiously similar to that of Jean Laplanche's "enigmatic signifier" through which the primal trauma of enigmatic shock is replayed in art and life to the extent that "the signifier may be

designified, or lose what it signifies, without thereby losing the power to signify to." Jean Laplanche, *New Foundations for Psychoanalysis,* trans. David Macey (Oxford, England: Basil Blackwell, 1989), 45.

20. Smith, "Jean-Luc Godard," in *Jean-Luc Godard: Interviews,* 190.

21. Pierre Lévy, *Cyberculture: Rapport au Conseil de l'Europe dans le cadre du projet "Nouvelles technologies: Coopération culturelle et communication"* (Paris: Editions Odile Jacob, 1997), 179.

22. Smith, "Jean-Luc Godard," in *Jean-Luc Godard: Interviews,* 190.

23. In *Speaking about Godard,* 141–45, Silverman and Farocki engage in a provocative exchange about the impact of Godard's editing in front of double video monitors.

24. Jean-Louis Baudry, "The Apparatus: Metapsychological Approaches to the Impression of Reality in the Cinema," in *Narrative, Apparatus, Ideology,* ed. Philip Rosen (New York: Columbia University Press, 1986), 307.

25. Ibid., 316.

26. For the sake of foregrounding the effect of these lines at the outset of the twenty-first century, I cite Harun Farocki's citation of this line, with its prescient diacritical effect that identifies the machine on which I write, as well as that which ushered in the first generation of digital graphics.

27. Silverman and Farocki, *Speaking about Godard,* 142.

28. The National Association of Scholars and the National Alumni Forum are conservative American lobbying organizations whose academic members decry, among other evils, the teaching of Shakespeare in relation to the politics of race, class, and gender, not to mention the philosophy of poststructuralism.

29. Deleuze, *Logique du sens* (Paris: Edition de Minuit, 1969), 138–39.

30. Deleuze, *Cinema 2: The Time-Image,* trans. Hugh Tomlinson and Robert Galeta (Minneapolis: University of Minnesota Press, 1989), 131; Deleuze here refers to paragraph 57 of *La Monadologie* (Paris: Aubin, 1983), 173.

31. Deleuze, *Cinema 2,* 180.

32. Ibid., 181.

33. Ibid., 183.

34. Ibid., 188.

35. Ibid., 224.

36. Cited by Raymond Bellour, "The Book, Back and Forth," in *Qu'est-ce qu'une madeleine? A propos du CD-ROM, "Immemory," de Chris Marker,* ed. Christine van Assche (Paris: Yves Gevaert Editeur; Centre Georges Pompidou, 1997), 147.

37. *Histoire(s) du cinéma 2A,* 50.

38. Gilles Deleuze and Claire Parnet, *Dialogues* (Paris: Flammarion, 1996), 71.

4. YOU ARE HOW YOU READ

1. Helpful discussions of the complex role of colonialism in *The Tempest* are provided by Stephen Orgel, "Shakespeare and the Cannibals," in *Allegory and Representation,* ed. Stephen Greenblatt (Baltimore: Johns Hopkins University Press, 1981), 40–66; Greenblatt, *Learning to Curse: Essays in Early Modern Culture* (London: Routledge,

1990); Paul Brown, "'This Thing of Darkness I Acknowledge Mine': *The Tempest* and the Discourse of Colonialism," in *Political Shakespeare: New Essays in Cultural Materialism,* ed. Jonathan Dollimore and Alan Sinfield (Manchester: Manchester University Press, 1985); and Eric Cheyfitz, *The Poetics of Imperialism: Translation and Colonization from "The Tempest" to "Tarzan"* (Oxford: Oxford University Press, 1991).

2. Cheyfitz, *The Poetics of Imperialism,* 170.

3. Gilles Deleuze, *The Fold: Leibniz and the Baroque,* trans. Tom Conley (Minneapolis: University of Minnesota Press, 1993), 31. Subsequent references in the text are to this edition.

4. Deleuze notes that "Yves Bonnefoy [1970] has studied the complex position of the theater in theme of the Baroque: neither illusion nor renewed awareness, but using illusion in order to produce one's being, to construct a site of hallucinatory Presence." *The Fold,* 161.

5. Peter Conrad reports that Gielgud approached Greenaway only after his idea to perform *The Tempest* on film was turned down by three other directors, Kurosawa, Resnais, and Bergman ("From a Vigorous Prospero, a Farewell without Tears," *New York Times,* November 17, 1991). Films by the former two help shape Deleuze's theory of modern film, which I discuss below.

6. Walter Benjamin, *The Origin of German Tragic Drama,* trans. John Osborne (London: NLB, 1977), 184.

7. Peter Greenaway, *Prospero's Books: A Film of Shakespeare's "The Tempest"* (New York: Four Wall Eight Windows, 1991), 51.

8. Ibid., 98.

9. Ibid., 9.

10. Suzanna Turman, "Interview with Peter Greenaway," *Films in Review,* April 1992, 106.

11. All citations of *The Tempest* are from *The Oxford Shakespeare,* ed. Stephen Orgel (Oxford: Oxford University Press, 1987).

12. Greenaway, *Prospero's Books,* 90.

13. Deleuze, *The Fold,* 60.

14. Deleuze, *Difference and Repetition,* 56.

15. In *The Fold,* 31, Deleuze refers to paragraph 61 of Leibniz's *La Monadologie* (Paris: Delagrave, 1983). Timothy Hampton similarly notes that "the encounter between a subject and a text in which she or he is to find self-recognition constitutes the moment at which subjectivity is defined and circumscribed by discourses of power, whether political or aesthetic." "Introduction: Baroques," *Yale French Studies* 80 (1991): 6.

16. Deleuze, *Cinema 2: The Time-Image,* trans. Hugh Tomlinson and Robert Galeta (Minneapolis: University of Minnesota Press, 1989), 179.

17. Deleuze, *The Fold,* 110.

18. Greenaway and Leon Steinmetz, *The World of Peter Greenaway* (Boston: Journey Editions, 1995), 84.

19. I use this phrase in the complicated sense of Jean-François Lyotard, not in the pejorative sense applied by Deleuze when referring to the "beautiful soul" who remains

indifferent to the complexities of the philosophy of difference and who "sees in the inexpiable struggles only simple 'differends' or perhaps misunderstandings." Lyotard, *The Differend,* trans. Georges Van Den Abbeele (Minneapolis: University of Minnesota Press, 1988); Deleuze, *Difference and Repetition,* trans. Paul Patton (New York: Columbia University Press, 1994), 52.

20. Greenaway, *Papers/papiers* (Paris: Editions Dis Voir, 1990), 98.

21. Greenaway and Steinmetz, *The World of Peter Greenaway,* 112.

22. Greenaway, *Prospero's Books,* 82.

23. Ibid., 17.

24. Ibid., 20–21.

25. Greenaway and Steinmetz, *The World of Peter Greenaway,* 112–13.

26. Greenaway, *Prospero's Books,* 12.

27. Deleuze, *Difference and Repetition,* 56–57.

28. Turman, "Interview with Peter Greenaway," 107.

29. Greenaway, *Papers/papiers,* 83.

30. Ibid., 82.

31. Ibid., 92.

32. Deleuze, *Cinema 2,* 233.

33. Ibid., 179.

34. Ibid., 108.

35. For a thorough discussion of these distinctions, refer to Deleuze, *Difference and Repetition,* 50–58.

36. Deleuze, *Cinema 2,* 108.

37. Ibid. I here simplify the English translation that more freely translates Deleuze's term "le baroque" as "the term 'baroque' or neo-expressionism is literally appropriate."

38. Deleuze, *The Fold,* 110.

39. Conley provides a helpful account of Deleuze's debt to Leibniz in "Translator's Foreword: A Plea for Leibniz," in Deleuze, *The Fold,* ix–xx. In "Autonomasia: Leibniz and the Baroque," *MLN* 105, no. 3 (April 1990): 432–52, Peter Fenves provides an excellent overview of Leibniz.

40. Deleuze, *Cinema 2,* 131, here refers to paragraph 57 of Leibniz's *La Monadologie,* 173.

41. Deleuze, *Difference and Repetition,* 124.

42. Greenaway, *Prospero's Books,* 17.

43. See Orgel's excellent discussion of "wives and mothers" in the introduction to his Oxford edition of *The Tempest,* 18–20.

44. Greenaway, *Prospero's Books,* 88.

45. Ibid., 111.

46. Ibid., 12.

47. Ibid., 113.

48. Theodor de Bry, *Thomas Hariot's a Briefe and True Report of the Newfoundland of Virginia* (USA: Readex Microprint, 1966 [1590]), E.

49. Deleuze, *Difference and Repetition,* 125.

50. Deleuze, *Cinema 2*, 116–17.

51. Deleuze, *Difference and Repetition*, 94.

52. Deleuze, *Cinema 2*, 224. David Norman Rodowick, *Gille Deleuze's Time-Machine* (Durham, N.C.: Duke University Press, 1997), provides a very helpful reading of Deleuze's theory of minority cinema.

53. Deleuze, "One Less Manifesto," trans. Eliane dal Molin and Timothy Murray, in *Mimesis, Masochism, and Mime: The Politics of Theatricality in Contemporary French Thought*, ed. Timothy Murray (Ann Arbor: University of Michigan Press, 1997), 263.

54. Marlene Rodgers, "Prospero's Books—Word and Spectacle: An Interview with Peter Greenaway," *Film Quarterly* 45, no. 2 (1991–92): 11.

55. Jacques Derrida claims that "the genius of Shakespeare" lies in his representation of jointure, "this phantomalization of property . . . as reference, guarantee, or confirmation in the polemic, that is, in the ongoing war—on the subject, precisely, of the monetary specter, value, money or its fiduciary sign, gold." *Specters of Marx: The State of Debt, the Work of Mourning, and the New International*, trans. Peggy Kamuf (New York: Routledge, 1994), 41–42.

56. I am thinking of Prospero's sudden disruption of the celebration of the libidinal triumphs of the present, the wedding masque of Ceres, in order to attend to the future evils of Caliban's revolution. Greenaway cuts three significant passages from the Shakespearean text that foreground, for me, the frailty of Prospero's controlled distance from the magical effects of the wedding spectacle that he stages for Ferdinand and Miranda. Missing from the film are lines by Ferdinand and Miranda that attribute confused passion to Prospero as he breaks the spell of the masque: "[Ferdinand:] This is strange. Your father's in some passion / That works him strongly. / [Miranda:] Never till this day / Saw I him touched with anger, so distempered" (IV.i.143–45). Mirroring these textual cuts are lines missing from the end of this scene spoken to Ferdinand by Prospero himself: "Sir I am vex'd; / Bear with my weakness, my old brain is troubled. / Be not disturbed with my infirmity" (IV.i.158–60). Also missing are Ariel's words regarding the imminent threat of Caliban: "When I presented Ceres / I thought to have told thee of it, but I feared / lest I might anger thee" (IV.i.167–68). My understanding of these passages is that they suggest Ariel's spiteful appreciation of the pageant's forgetful effect on Prospero, whose sight of this spectacle's "quick motion" (IV.i.39) costs him temporary control of his rational defenses. As I see it, this allows Ariel to enact subtle revenge on Prospero and to enter into indirect complicity with the rebellious Caliban for failing to make good on an earlier promise to free Ariel in good speed.

57. Although I here restrict my comments to the visual field of *Prospero's Books*, another essay outside the range of my expertise could be penned on what Deleuze would call the crystalline role of sound and song in the masque and the film as a whole. Sarah Leonard's singing of Michael Nyman's phantasmatic score enfolds the viewer in the interstice of the film's two frames of sound and image.

58. Greenaway, *Prospero's Books*, 28.

59. Ibid., 29.

60. Ibid., 82.

61. Greenaway and Steinmetz, *The World of Peter Greenaway,* 84.

62. Deleuze, *Cinema 2,* 265.

63. Refer to the informative analyses by Rodowick of the impact of digital "figurality" on the interdisciplinary regimes of knowledge in "Reading the Figural," *Camera Obscura* 24 (1991): 10–46; and in Rodowick, "Audiovisual Culture and Interdisciplinary Knowledge," *New Literary History* 26, no. 1 (1995): 111–21. Also see Robert Markley, ed., *Virtual Realities and Their Discontents* (Baltimore: Johns Hopkins University Press, 1996).

64. Deleuze, *The Fold,* 137.

5. DIGITALITY AND THE MEMORY OF CINEMA

1. The on-line catalogue of *Contact Zones,* in Spanish and English, is available at http://contactzones.cit.cornell.edu. Priamo Lozada collaborated with me to produce a Spanish-language catalogue for the Centro de la Imagen, Mexico City: Timothy Murray, *Zonas de contacto: El arte en CD-ROM* (Mexico City: Centro de la Imagen, 1999).

2. "Digitality and the Memory of Cinema," special issue, *Wide Angle* 21, no. 1 (1999); Thomas Elsaesser and Kay Hoffman, eds., *Cinema Futures: Cain, Abel, or Cable?* (Amsterdam: Amsterdam University Press, 1998); Lev Manovich, *The Language of New Media* (Cambridge, Mass.: MIT Press, 2001); Jeffrey Shaw and Peter Weibel, eds., *Future Cinema: The Cinematic Imaginary after Film* (Cambridge, Mass.: MIT Press, 2003).

3. An excellent selection of less than enthusiastic approaches to digital Hollywood, by writers such as Brian Winston, Bill Nichols, and Vivian Sobchack, can be found in *Electronic Media and Technoculture,* ed. John Thornton Caldwell (New Brunswick, N.J.: Rutgers University Press, 2000). In contrast, an earlier collection edited by Timothy Druckrey, *Electronic Culture: Technology and Visual Representation* (New York: Aperture, 1996), contains a range of essays by theorists and artists, from Raymond Bellour and Erkki Huhtamo to Peter Weibel and Siegfried Zielinski.

4. Manovich, *The Language of New Media,* 86.

5. These critically oriented artists share company, of course, with an expanding set of theoretically insightful monographs by writers such as Sean Cubitt, *Digital Aesthetics* (London: Sage, 1998); Margaret Morse, *Virtualities: Television, Media Art, and Cyberculture* (Bloomington: Indiana University Press, 1998); Raymond Bellour, *L'entre-images 2: Mots, images* (Paris: P.O.L., 1999); Katherine Hayles, *How We Became Posthuman: Virtual Bodies in Cybernetic Literature and Informatics* (Chicago: University of Chicago Press, 1999; Mark Hansen, *Embodying Technesis: Technology beyond Writing* (Ann Arbor: University of Michigan Press, 2000), *New Philosophy for New Media* (Cambridge, Mass.: MIT Press, 2004), and *Bodies in Code: Interfaces with Digital Media* (New York: Routledge, 2006); D. N. Rodowick, *Reading the Figural, or Philosophy after the New Media* (Durham, N.C.: Duke University Press, 2001), and *The Virtual Life of Film* (Cambridge, Mass.: Harvard University Press, 2007); Anne-Marie Duguet, *Déjouer l'image: Créations électroniques et numériques* (Paris: Jacqueline Chambon, 2002); Arthur Kroker, *The Will to Technology and the Culture of Nihilism: Heidegger, Nietzsche, and Marx* (Toronto: University of Toronto Press, 2004); Vivian Sobchak, *Carnal Thoughts: Embodiment and Moving Image Culture* (Berkeley and Los Angeles: University

of California Press, 2004); Margaret Lovejoy, *Digital Currents: Art in the Electronic Age* (New York: Routledge, 2004); Trinh T. Minh-ha, *The Digital Film Event* (New York: Routledge, 2005); Wendy Hui Kyong Chun, *Control and Freedom: Power and Paranoia in the Age of Fiber Optics* (Cambridge, Mass.: MIT Press, 2006); Anne Friedberg, *The Virtual Window: From Alberti to Microsoft* (Cambridge, Mass.: MIT Press, 2006).

6. Gary Hill, *Site Recited (A Prologue),* video (Long Beach, Calif.: Long Beach Museum of Art, 1994).

7. See not only Gilles Deleuze's *Cinema 2: The Time Image,* trans. Hugh Tomlinson and Robert Galeta (Minneapolis: University of Minnesota Press, 1989), and Raymond Bellour's "The Book, Back and Forth," in *Qu'est-ce qu'une Madeleine? A propos du CD-ROM "Immemory" de Chris Marker* (Paris: Yves Gevaert Editeur/Centre Georges Pompidou, 1997), 109–54, which reflect on the transformative thought of cinema on the threshold of the digital age, but also the less sanguine discussions of this relation by Nichols, "The Work of Culture in the Age of Cybernetic Systems," in *Electronic Media and Technoculture,* ed. Caldwell, 90–114, and Sobchack, "The Scene of the Screen: Envisioning Cinematic and Electronic 'Presence,'" in ibid., 137–55.

8. André Bazin, *Qu'est-ce que le cinéma?* (Paris: Editions du cerf, 1975), 9.

9. Manovich, *The Language of New Media,* 155.

10. My interest in elaborating on these binaries stems from discussions with colleagues in the Australian film and digital community held at the 1999 conference "Code and Craft; Cinema and New Media: Giving Digital Culture a History," organized by Megan Heyward and Annmarie Chandler and cosponsored by the New Media Arts Research Group, University of Technology Sydney, dLux media arts, and the Powerhouse Museum, Sydney.

11. Peter Lunenfeld, "Screen Grabs: The Digital Dialectic and New Media Theory," in *The Digital Dialectic: New Essays on New Media,* ed. Lunenfeld (Cambridge, Mass.: MIT Press, 1999), xix.

12. Jean-Luc Godard goes so far as to suggest that cinema never realized the potential of its most forceful component, montage: "Cinema never realized montage. This was something that disappeared with the advent of the talkies." *Jean-Luc Godard par Jean-Luc Godard,* vol. 2, *1984–1998* (Paris: Cahiers du cinéma, 1998), 164.

13. Martin Heidegger, "The Age of the World Picture," in *The Question concerning Technology and Other Essays,* trans. William Lovitt (New York: Harper, 1977), 120.

14. Cited by Bellour, "The Book, Back and Forth," in *Qu'est-ce qu'une Madeleine?* 147.

15. See my book *Like a Film: Ideological Fantasy on Screen, Camera, and Canvas* (New York: Routledge, 1993) for a summary of different approaches to cinematic loss, mourning, and melancholia.

16. Christian Metz, "Problems of Denotation in the Fiction Film," in *Narrative, Apparatus, Ideology,* ed. Philip Rosen (New York: Columbia University Press, 1986), 35–65.

17. Ibid., 38.

18. Ibid.

19. Laura Mulvey, "Visual Pleasure and Narrative Cinema," in *Narrative, Apparatus, Ideology,* ed. Rosen, 198–209.

20. Metz, "Problems of Denotation in the Fiction Film," 38–39.

21. Ibid., 39.

22. Cited by Chris Marker in his CD-ROM *Immemory* (Paris, Centre Georges Pompidou, 1998).

23. Hill, "Between 1 and 0," in special insert, "Profile 31: World Wide Video," *Art & Design* 8, nos. 7–8 (1993): 70–71.

24. Hill, *Site Recited (A Prologue).*

25. Jacques Lacan, *The Four Fundamental Concepts of Psychoanalysis,* trans. Alan Sheridan, ed. Jacques-Alain Miller (New York: W. W. Norton, 1978), 79–90.

26. Gilles Deleuze, *Difference and Repetition,* trans. Paul Patton (New York: Columbia University Press, 1994), 208.

27. For an exemplary analysis of the return of analogy in electronic installation, see Raymond Bellour, "The Double Helix," in *Electronic Culture,* ed. Druckrey, 173–99.

28. Grace Quintanilla, *Vice-Versa: Presenting the Past, the Present, and the Depths of Roberto and Chelo Cobo,* CD-ROM (Mexico City: FONCA and the Multimedia Center, 1998).

29. For helpful psychoanalytic discussions of retrospection and temporality, see Jean Laplanche, *Essays on Otherness* (London/New York: Routledge, 1999); J-B. Pontalis, *Ce temps qui ne passe pas* (Paris: Gallimard, 1997); André Green, *Le temps éclaté* (Paris: Minuit, 2000).

30. Scott Bukatman, "Morphing: *Taking Shape* and the Performance of Self," in the excellent anthology on morphing edited by Vivian Sobchack, *MetaMorphing: Visual Transformation and the Culture of Quick Change* (Minneapolis: University of Minnesota Press, 2000), 242.

31. In *Le temps éclaté,* Green provides an exemplary analysis of the psychic tension between linear, temporal progression and its aleatory liaison with the less predictable, repetitive compulsion of the drives.

32. Bill Nichols, "The Work of Culture in the Age of Cybernetic Systems," in *Electronic Media and Technoculture,* ed. Caldwell, 101.

33. One of my favorite examples comes from Hélène Cixous's 1984 interview with the editors of *Hors Cadre* where she laments the lack of depth in television: "There is also a flat theater. There are many false scenes, those of television, for example—which bring us nothing, because they have no inner universe and because they do not produce a sign." Cixous, *"Hors Cadre* Interview," trans. Verena Andermatt Conley, in *Mimesis, Masochism, and Mime: The Politics of Theatricality in Contemporary French Thought,* ed. Timothy Murray (Ann Arbor: University of Michigan Press, 1997), 34–35.

34. Especially as Quintanilla's piece opens the viewer to acknowledge the power of her representation of the aging female body, it exemplifies the feminist appropriation of digital code as analyzed by Kathleen Woodward, "From Virtual Cyborgs to Biological Time Bombs: Technocriticism and the Material Body," in *Culture on the Brink: Ideologies of Technology,* ed. Gretchen Bender and Timothy Druckrey (Seattle: Bay Press,

1994), 47–64; Margaret Morse, "Virtually Female: On Body and Code," in *Processed Lives: Gender and Technology in Everyday Life,* ed. Jennifer Terry and Melodie Calvert (London: Routledge, 1997), 23–35; N. Katherine Hayles, "Embodied Virtuality, or How to Put Bodies Back into the Picture," in *Immersed in Technology: Art and Virtual Environments,* ed. Mary Anne Moser and Douglas MacLeod (Cambridge, Mass.: MIT Press, 1996), 1–28; and Lynn Hershman Leeson, "Romancing the Anti-Body: Lust and Longing in (Cyber)space," in *Clicking In: Hot Links to a Digital Culture,* ed. Hershman Leeson (Seattle: Bay Press, 1996), 325–37.

35. What Quintanilla provides can well be understood as a digital extension of the experimental play ascribed earlier by Julia Kristeva to the experimental theater of Richard Foreman and the emergent cinema of Yvonne Rainer: "Reconstruction of the subjective space experienced by our modernity demands recourse to all means of representation, and therefore, to film, to explore the limits of the representable, and in order to include the visual in the acoustic or the gestural." Kristeva, "Modern Theater Does Not Take (a) Place," in *Mimesis, Masochism, and Mime,* ed. Murray, 280.

36. Homi K. Bhabha, *The Location of Culture* (London: Routledge, 1994), 90.

37. Kobena Mercer, "Witness at the Crossroads: An Artist's Journey in Post-colonial Space," in *Relocating the Remains,* ed. Keith Piper (London: Institute of International Visual Arts, 1997), 68.

38. In *Drama Trauma: Specters of Race and Sexuality in Performance, Video, and Art* (New York: Routledge, 1997), 169–86, 240–73, I address similar ways in which cultural melancholia works to preserve the African-American cultural heritage.

39. Patricia R. Zimmermann, "Processing Trauma: The Media Art of Daniel Reeves," *Afterimage* 26, no. 22 (September–October 1998): 11–13.

40. Steve Seid, "Obsessive Becoming: The Video Poetics of Daniel Reeves," Transmedia '97 Videofest, at http://www.transmedia.de/97/english/28.htm.

41. Daniel Reeves, interview with Timothy Murray and Patricia R. Zimmermann, October 20, 1997, Ithaca, New York.

42. My ambivalence about Reeves's political effectiveness contrasts with Vivian Sobchack's uncritical embrace of the tape: "While asserting similitude, through an affecting representational labor of love that gives human (not computer graphic) emphasis and value to the lives and times he weaves together, Reeves ultimately discovers resemblance—and the possibility of difference, of breaking repetitive and self-same cycles of violence and abuse." Sobchak, "At the Still Point of the Turning World: Meta-Morphing and Meta-Stasis," in *MetaMorphing,* ed. Sobchack, 143.

6. WOUNDS OF REPETITION IN THE AGE OF THE DIGITAL

1. See, for example, Dori Laub, "Truth and Testimony: The Process and the Struggle," in *Trauma: Explorations in Memory,* ed. Cathy Caruth (Baltimore, Md.: Johns Hopkins University Press, 1995), 61–75.

2. Jean Laplanche, "Interview: Jean Laplanche Talks to Martin Stanton," in *Jean Laplanche: Seduction, Translation, Drives,* ed. John Fletcher and Martin Stanton (London: Institute of Contemporary Arts, 1992), 32.

3. Dominick LaCapra, "Trauma, Absence, and Loss," *Critical Inquiry* 25 (Summer 1999): 696–727.

4. After the publication of the initial draft of this chapter, I was delighted to benefit from Brian Massumi's elaborate mapping of "affective virtualities" in *Parables for the Virtual: Movement, Affect, Sensation* (Durham, N.C.: Duke University Press, 2002).

5. Max Horkheimer and Theodor Adorno, *Dialectic of Enlightenment*, trans. John Cumming (New York: Continuum, 1982), 25.

6. Ibid., 144.

7. Two exemplary summaries of these positions that have generated a significant debate within film studies are Laura Mulvey's "Visual Pleasure and Narrative Cinema" and Jean-Louis Baudry's "Ideological Effects of the Basic Cinematographic Apparatus," both in *Narrative, Apparatus, Ideology*, ed. Philip Rosen (New York: Columbia University Press, 1986), 198–209, 286–98.

8. Ibid., 142.

9. Ibid., 136.

10. Jean-François Lyotard, "Acinema," trans. Paisley Livingston, in *Narrative, Apparatus, Ideology*, ed. Rosen.

11. Horkheimer and Adorno, *Dialectic of Enlightenment*, 12.

12. Jean Laplanche, *New Foundations for Psychoanalysis*, trans. David Macey (Oxford, England: Basil Blackwell, 1989), 126.

13. Ibid., 45.

14. Peter Hohendahl, *Prismatic Thought: Theodor W. Adorno* (Lincoln: University of Nebraska Press, 1995), 136.

15. Horkheimer and Adorno, *Dialectic of Enlightenment*, 126–27.

16. Roger Leenhardt, *Chroniques du cinéma* (Paris: Editions de l'Etoile, 1986), 96.

17. Antonin Artaud, "Sorcellerie et cinéma," in *Oeuvres complètes* (Paris: Gallimard, 1970), 3:84.

18. Artaud, "Réponse à une enquête," in *Oeuvres completes*, 3:79. I elaborate on the place of Artaud's writings on cinema within the history of French film theory in "Film Theory," in *The Columbia History of Twentieth-Century French Thought*, ed. Lawrence D. Kritzman (New York: Columbia University Press, 2006), 227–30.

19. Oscar Negt and Alexander Kluge, "The Public Sphere and Experience: Selections," trans. Peter Labanyi, *October* 46 (Fall 1988): 79.

20. Ibid., 76.

21. Horkheimer and Adorno, *Dialectic of Enlightenment*, 148.

22. Gilles Deleuze, "One Less Manifesto," trans. Eliane dal Molin and Timothy Murray, in *Mimesis, Masochism, and Mime: The Politics of Theatricality in Contemporary French Thought*, ed. Timothy Murray (Ann Arbor: University of Michigan Press, 1997), 249.

23. It is important to note that Deleuze's interests in the divergence and coexistence of serial relations, in their baroque "incompossibility," stems from his reflections on the eternal return of seriality in *Difference and Repetition*.

24. Deleuze, *Difference and Repetition*, trans. Paul Patton (New York: Columbia University Press, 1994), 124.

25. Deleuze, *Cinema 2: The Time Image,* trans. Hugh Tomlinson and Robert Galeta (Minneapolis: University of Minnesota Press, 1989), 179.

26. I discuss the *Romeo and Juliet* scene in *Breathless* in relation to Patricia's episte-mological sadism in *Drama Trauma: Specters of Race and Sexuality in Performance, Video, and Art* (New York: Routledge, 1997), 86–87.

27. Deleuze, *Cinema 2,* 238–39.

28. Cathy Caruth, *Unclaimed Experience: Trauma, Narrative, and History* (Baltimore, Md.: Johns Hopkins University Press, 1996), 27.

29. Ibid., 30.

30. An alternative way of reading Laura's intertextuality locates it more in relation to the cinematic period of interest to Horkheimer and Adorno. Laurent Roth notes that "this hallowed-out presence of the characters, a phenomenological constant in Marker's universe, is subtly redoubled by the reference that Laura makes to the film of the same name by Otto Preminger—another great masterpiece of preprogrammed death, the tenebrous twin of *Vertigo.*" "A Yakut Afflicted with Strabismus," in *Qu'est-ce qu'une Madeleine? A propos du CD-ROM "Immemory" de Chris Marker* (Paris: Yves Gevaert Editeur; Centre Georges Pompidou, 1997), 60–61.

31. Naoki Sakai, *Translation and Subjectivity: On Japan and Cultural Nationalism* (Minneapolis: University of Minnesota Press, 1997).

32. Maureen Turim analyzes the complexity of the clashing accounts of national witness in *Level 5* in "Virtual Discourses of History: Collage, Narrative or Documents," *Sites* 4, no. 2 (Fall 2000): 367–83.

33. Deleuze, *Cinema 2,* 116–17.

34. It is interesting to note that this same experience of the digital NOW to which Marker turns to enliven history is said by a skeptical Paul Virilio, in *Cybermonde: Le politique du pire* (Paris: Les Editions Textuels, 1996), 44, to constitute the negative promise of cyberspace.

35. See the entry for *Shock in the Ear* in my online catalogue, *Contact Zones: The Art of CD-ROM,* http://contactzones.cit.cornell.edu/artists/neumark.html. Also of interest is Norie Neumark's theoretical account of digital shock in "A Shock in the Ear: Re-Sounding the Body, Mapping the Space of Shock Aesthetics," *Essays in Sound* 4 (January 1999): 41–49.

36. Deleuze, *Cinema 2,* 265.

37. Raymond Bellour dwells on Marker's digital relation to the ferryman by com-paring him to Godard for whom the image bears a "tragic quality . . . which seems immemorial, inscribed in the history of culture, at once as its nature and its supernat-ural. And hence, through the image, a tragedy of cinema which becomes its guarantor. This tragedy is what Marker has always sought not to ignore, but to accommodate, within a vision of culture that cannot have cinema as its focal point, because in truth there is none, and cinema circulates within a wider history, even if it carries out an incomparable reprise of that history." "The Book, Back and Forth," in *Qu'est-ce qu'une Madeleine?* 148.

7. PHILOSOPHICAL TOYS AND KALEIDOSCOPES OF THE UNFAMILIAR

1. Conley, *Ecopolitics: The Environment in Poststructuralist Thought* (London: Routledge, 1997), 135.

2. All three artists openly distanced themselves from Livia Monet's invitation to present their work in the context of feminism at her conference, "Subjectivity, Embodiment, and the Transformation of Cinematic Practice in Contemporary New Media Art," University of Montreal, Montreal, April 2004.

3. Eve Kosofsky Sedgwick, *Touching Feeling: Affect, Pedagogy, Performativity* (Durham, N.C.: Duke University Press, 2003).

4. Régis Durand, "The Disposition of Voice," in *Mimesis, Masochism, and Mime: The Politics of Theatricality in Contemporary French Thought*, ed. Timothy Murray (Ann Arbor: University of Michigan Press, 1997), 305.

5. Mary Ann Doane, "The Voice in Cinema: The Articulation of Body in Space," in *Narrative, Apparatus, Ideology*, ed. Philip Rosen (New York: Columbia University Press, 1986), 343.

6. Ibid., 341.

7. Jean-Louis Boissier, "Two Ways of Making Book: Working Notes on *Flora petrinsularis*," in *Artintact* 1 (Ostfildern: Cantz Verlag; Karlsruhe: ZKM, 1994), 75.

8. Toni Dove, *Artificial Changelings* (1998), http://www.tonidove.com/af_overview_hold.html.

9. Margaret Morse, *Virtualities: Television, Media Art, and Cyberculture* (Bloomington: Indiana University Press, 1998), 99.

10. See Jacqueline Rose, "Paranoia and the Film System," *Screen* 17, no. 4 (Winter 1977–78): 85–104; Mary Ann Doane, "Paranoia and the Specular," in *The Desire to Desire: The Woman's Film of the 1940s* (Bloomington: Indiana University Press, 1987), 123–54.

11. Gilles Deleuze, *Logique du sens* (Paris: Editions de Minuit, 1969), 20. I am here arguing for a consideration of the energetics of surface that runs counter to the valorization of digital depth proposed by Judith Roof in "Depth Technologies," in *Technospaces: Inside the New Media,* ed. Sally R. Munt (London: Continuum, 2001), 21–37.

12. Pam Jennings and Toni Dove, "Interpretations of the Electronic Landscape: A Conversation," http://www.e-felix.org/issue4/electronic.html.

13. J.-B. Pontalis, *La force de l'attraction* (Paris: Seuil, 1990), 51–52.

14. Zoe Beloff, "Philosophical Toy World," http://www.turbulence.org/Works/illusions/#.

15. Pontalis, *La force de l'attraction,* 30.

16. Roland Barthes, *La chambre claire: Note sur la photographie* (Paris: Gallimard Seuil, 1980), 47–96.

17. In *The Emergence of Cinematic Time: Modernity, Contingency, the Archive* (Cambridge, Mass.: Harvard University Press, 2002), 69–107, Mary Ann Doane provides a fascinating account of the temporality of the afterimage as a mark of cinema's ontological contingency.

18. Laplanche, *New Foundations for Psychoanalysis,* trans. David Macey (Oxford, England: Basil Blackwell, 1989), 126.

19. Zoe Beloff, *Doctor Faustus and the Universal Machine,* http://www.zoebeloff .com/where/ideas.html.

20. Slavoj Žižek, *The Sublime Oject of Ideology* (London: Verso, 1989), 45.

21. Steven Shaviro provides a nice overview of *Beyond* in "Future Past: Zoe Beloff's Beyond," *Artbyte,* August–September 1998, 17–18.

22. Beloff, *Doctor Faustus and the Universal Machine.*

23. Ibid.

24. Ibid.

25. Jean-François Lyotard, "Matter and Time," in *The Inhuman: Reflections on Time,* trans. Geoffrey Bennington and Rachel Bowlby (Stanford, Calif.: Stanford University Press, 1991), 44.

26. In the essay "Ectoplasmic Cinema" accompanying the Gallery TPW (Toronto) exhibition of Beloff's installation *The Ideoplastic Materializations of Eva C.,* Karen Beckman argues that "Beloff opens a gateway to future manifestations of [cinema], and reminds us that cinema has always been inextricably and philosophically bound to the problems of time, space, presence, and history."

27. She made these remarks during the "Book/Ends: Transformations of the Book and Redefinitions of the Arts and Humanities" conference, SUNY, Albany, 2000.

28. Zoe Beloff, "Philosophical Toy World," http://www.turbulence.org/Works /illusions/index.html.

29. Char Davies, "Changing Space: Virtual Reality as an Arena of Embodied Being," 2001, http://www.immersence.com/publications/char/2002=CD=multimedia=Wagn= VR.html.

30. Conley, *Ecopolitics,* 137.

31. Conley, "Preface," *Rethinking Technologies,* ed. Verena Andermatt Conley (Minneapolis: University of Minnesota Press, 1993), xii.

8. DIGITAL INCOMPOSSIBILITY

1. Pierre Lévy, *Cyberculture: Rapport au Conseil de l'Europe dans le cadre du projet "Nouvelles technologies: Coopération culturelle et communication"* (Paris: Editions Odile Jacob, 1997), 179.

2. Deleuze, *Difference and Repetition,* trans. Paul Patton (New York: Columbia University Press, 1994), 208.

3. Francesc Torres, "The Accident Placed in Its Context," in special insert, "Profile 31: World Wide Video," in *Art & Design* 8, nos. 7–8 (1993): 52.

4. In *Cinéma 2: L'image-temps* (Paris: Editions de Minuit, 1985), 41, Deleuze reminds his readers that cinematic analogy is not so much a product of resemblance as it is the movement between "l'énoncé par analogie, et la structure 'digitale' ou digitalisée de l'énoncé." Raymond Bellour develops a similar point in his extraordinary essay on the electronic image, "The Double Helix," in *Electronic Culture: Technology and Visual Representation,* ed. Timothy Druckrey (New York: Aperture, 1996), 173–99.

5. Maurice Merleau Ponty, *Le visible et l'invisible* (Paris: Gallimard, 1964), 116.

6. Deleuze, *The Fold: Leibniz and the Baroque*, trans. Tom Conley (Minneapolis: University of Minnesota Press, 1993), 110.

7. The CD-ROM version of *Flora Pentrinsularis* is available in *Artintact* 1 (Ostfildern: Cantz Verlag; Karlsruhe: ZKM, 1994); a condensed version is available on the DVD-ROM accompanying Boissier's book *La relation comme forme: L'interactivité en art* (Geneva: Musée d'art moderne et contemporain, 2004).

8. For more information on *Flora Petrinsularis,* see http://contactzones.cit.cornell .edu/artists/boissier_flora.html.

9. Boissier again picks up this theme of the paradox of interactivity in his Internet project on Rousseau, "Le billet circulaire," 1997, http://www.artmag.com/techno/ landowsky/projet.html: "Rather than soliciting responses, which is what the internet normally encourages," explains Boissier, "'Le billet circulaire' engages the internet as an aleatory space of aural potentialities, as an echo chamber for the frenzy both of guilt and innocent communication."

10. Jean-Louis Boissier, "Two Ways of Making Book: Working Notes on *Flora petrinsularis,*" in *Artintact* 1 (Ostfildern: Cantz Verlag; Karlsruhe: ZKM, 1994), 73.

11. Ibid., 71.

12. Ibid., 75. Boissier discusses the "sensorial cartography" of his other projects throughout *La relation comme forme: L'interactivité en art.*

13. In his recent hypermedia installation *Second Promenade* (http://www2.kah-bonn .de/1/28/oe.htm), Boissier elaborates on the importance of the digital re-creation of Rousseau's visions so that the precision of the angles provides the mechanism through which digital interactivity here mirrors the points of view in Rousseau's Promenade.

14. Ibid., 73.

15. Perry Hoberman, *The Sub-Division of the Electric Light,* in *Artintact* 3 (Ostfildern: Cantz Verlag; Karlsruhe: ZKM, 1996).

16. Peter Lunenfeld, "Postmodern Ruins, Restive Machines," in *Artintact* 3 (Ostfildern: Cantz Verlag; Karlsruhe: ZKM, 1996), 74.

17. I am referring of course to Deleuze's extensive discussion of the importance of time in postmodernist cinema and its role in generating thought as the experience of cinema. See *Cinéma 2: L'image-temps* as well as D. N. Rodowick's extensive discussion of time in the cinema books, *Gilles Deleuze's Time Machine* (Durham, N.C.: Duke University Press, 1997).

18. Cited by Lunenfeld, "Postmodern Ruins, Restive Machines."

19. Cathryn Vasseleu, *Textures of Light: Vision and Touch in Irigaray, Levinas, and Merleau-Ponty* (London: Routledge, 1998), 12.

20. This emphasis on touch as a space in-between surfaces in a similar aesthetic context in Jean-Luc Nancy's chapter "Why Are There Many Arts, and Not a Single One?" in *Les Muses* (Paris: Galilée, 1994), 34–41, where he reflects on touch as the interval and the very heterogeneity of touch, in the sense of anxiety, destabilization, and deconstruction. This multiple disposition of touch implies, he adds, a dis-position that is

not only spatial but also ontological in the sense of a dis-position, plurality, and heterogeneity of ontological interfaces or zones.

21. Deleuze, "The Actual and the Virtual," trans. Charles T. Wolfe, in *Any* 19 (1997): 7.

22. Miroslaw Rogala, *Lovers Leap,* in *Artintact* 2 (Ostfildern: Cantz Verlag; Karlsruhe: ZKM, 1995).

23. See Timothy Druckrey, "*Lovers Leap*—Taking the Plunge: Points of Entry . . . Points of Departure," in *Artintact* 2 (Ostfildern: Cantz Verlag; Karlsruhe: ZKM, 1995), 75.

24. Cited in ibid., 73.

25. Margaret Morse in "Miroslaw Rogala: Lovers Leap," in *Hardware, Software, Artware: Confluence of Art and Technology—Art Practice at the ZKM Institute for Visual Media, 1992–1997,* ed. Morse (Karlsruhe: ZKM, 1997). *Lovers Leap* was initially designed as an interactive installation (available at http://www.rogala.org/LoversLeap.htm). While moving through the exhibition space, the spectator would activate sensors that would catalyze the doubled visions of Chicago and Jamaica. It is in the context of the spectator's initial unknowing interpellation of the visual spectacle that Rogala distinguishes interactivity from control: "When the viewer enters the place, one becomes aware that one's movements or actions are changing the view but won't realize how. This means that the viewer is not really in control, but simply aware of his or her complicity. . . . As the viewer's awareness of the control mechanism grows, so does the viewer's power." Quoted by Morse in "Miroslaw Rogala."

26. Cited by Druckrey, "*Lovers Leap*—Taking the Plunge," 74.

27. My understanding of the spatial simulations of the threshold are indebted to Gilles Deleuze's extensive reflections on *Alice in Wonderland* in *Logique du sens* (Paris: Minuit, 1969). I develop the electronic implications of the "threshold" in "The Shadowy Haze of the Threshold," in *Threshold,* ed. Louise Dompierre (Toronto: Power Plant—Contemporary Art Gallery, 1998), 61–67.

28. Norie Neumark, jacket copy, *Shock in the Ear,* CD-ROM (Sydney, 1998).

29. Sound/image excerpts of these moments can be found at the "Contact Zones" Web site at http://contactzones.cit.cornell.edu/artists/neumark.html.

30. Neumark, "A Shock in the Ear: Re-Sounding the Body, Mapping the Space of Shock Aesthetics," *Essays in Sound* 4 (1999): 42. Also see Mike Leggett, "Norie Neumark's *Shock in the Ear,*" *Mesh: Film/Video/Multimedia/Art* 11 (Spring 1997): 61–64.

31. Neumark, "A Shock in the Ear," 42.

32. Neumark, jacket copy, *Shock in the Ear.*

33. Mark Seltzer, "Wound Culture: Trauma in the Pathological Public Sphere," *October* 80 (Spring 1997): 3.

34. Neumark, "A Shock in the Ear," 46.

35. Seltzer, "Wound Culture," 18.

36. I elaborate on the phantasmatic condition of reception as something "like a film" in "Ideological Fantasy in Reverse Projection," the introduction to *Like a Film: Ideological Fantasy on Screen, Camera, and Canvas* (London: Routledge, 1993), 1–21.

37. Seltzer, "Wound Culture," 18.

38. Jacques Derrida, "La différance," in *Marges de la philosophie* (Paris: Minuit, 1972); Gilles Deleuze, "Les cristaux du temps," in *Cinéma 2: L'image-temps.*

39. I analyze various artistic manifestations of such "ideological fantasy" in *Like a Film.*

40. Conley, "Translator's Foreword: A Plea for Leibniz," in Deleuze's *The Fold,* ix–xx, provides a helpful account of Deleuze's debt to Leibniz. In "Autonomasia: Leibniz and the Baroque," *MLN* 105, no. 3 (April 1990): 432–52, Peter Fenves provides an excellent overview of Leibniz.

41. Deleuze, *Logique du sens,* 138–39.

42. Woolery since has extended the terrain of these experimentations with sound through his Web radio station, Radiofreehamptons, at http://www.radiofreehamptons.net/.

43. These images are discussed in the catalogue by Thelma Golden, *Black Male: Representations of Masculinity in Contemporary American Art* (New York: Whitney Museum of Art, 1994).

44. Michael Fried, "Art and Objecthood," in *Minimal Art: A Critical Anthology,* ed. Gregory Battcock (New York: E. P. Dutton, 1968), 131. Anne-Marie Duguet contrasts Fried's critique of theatricality in this essay with her sense of the electronic promise of video in "Dispositifs," "Vidéo," special issue, *Communications* 48 (1988): 221–46.

45. The unusual importance of this anecdote to Fried's vision of aesthetics was made evident during his question-and-answer period at the 1998 session of the School of Criticism and Theory when Fried placed the entire weight of his notion of theatrical beholding on this same example that was crucial to him thirty years earlier.

46. Fried, "Art and Objecthood," 133–34.

47. An earlier and briefer draft of this essay, "Digital Incompossibility: The Aesthetics of Interactivity," was distributed on disk in the form of an electronic catalogue to participants of "La sensibilitat multimèdia: II journades sobre ar I multimèdia," Fundacio "la Caixa," Barcelona, October 1998. I am particularly indebted to Reginald Woolery, Norie Neumark, Jean-Louis Boissier, and Miroslaw Rogala for their discussions about their work and their generous sharing of critical materials important to this expanded discussion of their work.

9. PSYCHIC SCANSION

1. Antonin Artaud, "Sorcellerie et cinéma," *Oeuvres complètes* (Paris: Gallimard, 1970), 3:83.

2. Ibid., 85, 84.

3. Sigmund Freud, *The Standard Edition of the Complete Psychological Works of Sigmund Freud,* ed. and trans. James Strachey, 24 vols. (London: Hogarth Press and the Institute of Psychoanalysis, 1953–74), 12:359–60.

4. For more on the Oedipal trajectory of Shakespeare tragedy, see Timothy Murray, ed., *Mimesis, Masochism, and Mime: The Politics of Theatricality in Contemporary French Thought* (Ann Arbor: University of Michigan Press, 1997); and Timothy Murray and Alan K. Smith, eds., *Repossessions: Psychoanalysis and the Phantasms of Early Modern Culture* (Minneapolis: University of Minnesota Press, 1998).

5. For such reconsideration, see Jean Laplanche, *Problématiques,* vol. 3, *La sublimation* (Paris: Presses Universitaires de France, 1983), 95.

6. Jean-Luc Nancy, "Corpus," in *Thinking Bodies,* ed. Juliet Flower MacCannell and Laura Zakarin (Stanford, Calif.: Stanford University Press, 1994), 22.

7. Jean-François Lyotard argued against this habit as early as "Freud selon Cézanne," in *Des dispositifs pulsionnels* (Paris: 10/18, 1973), 71–94.

8. J.-B. Pontalis, *Perdre de vue* (Paris: Gallimard, 1988), 282.

9. Guy Rosolato, "L'object de perspective dans ses assises visuelles," in *Pour une psychanalyse exploratrice dans la culture* (Paris: Presses Universitaires de France, 1993), 44, 34.

10. Ibid., 44.

11. Sigmund Freud, *Introductory Lectures on Psychoanalysis,* trans. James Strachey (New York: Norton, 1966), 345.

12. Rosolato, "L'object de perspective dans ses assises visuelles," 32.

13. Laplanche, *Problématiques,* vol. 3, *La sublimation,* 13.

14. Laplanche, "The Kent Seminar," in *Jean Laplanche: Seduction, Translation, Drives,* ed. John Fletcher and Martin Stanton (London: Institute of Contemporary Arts, 1992), 32.

15. Lyotard, *L'inhumain: Causeries sur le temps* (Paris: Galilée, 1998), 65.

16. Deleuze, *Cinema 2: The Time-Image,* trans. Hugh Tomlinson and Robert Galeta (Minneapolis: University of Minnesota Press, 1989), 265.

17. Marker, *Immemory* (Paris: Centre Georges Pompidou, 1998).

18. Ibid.

19. Ibid.

20. For a survey of this art form, which developed significantly in the nineties, refer to the online catalogue of my exhibition, *Contact Zones: The Art of CD-ROM,* http://contactzones.cit.cornell.edu.

21. Raymond Bellour, "The Book, Back and Forth," in *Qu'est-ce qu'une madeleine? A propos du CD-ROM "Immemory" de Chris Marker,* ed. Christine van Assche (Paris: Yves Gevaert Editeur/Centre Georges Pompidou, 1997), 124. Bellour refers here to the influential study by Pierre Nora, *Les lieux de mémoire* (Paris: Gallimard, 1984).

22. Bellour, "The Book, Back and Forth," 12–30. In *Mutant Media: Essays on Cinema, Video Art, and New Media* (Sydney: Artspace; Power Publications, 2007), 193, John Conomos emphasizes how Marker aimed to transfer Hooke's investment in memory from historical to geographical zones, suggesting the new media zones of temporal folds.

23. Bellour, "The Book, Back and Forth," 130.

24. André Green, *Le travail du négatif* (Paris: Seuil, 1993).

25. Pontalis, *Perdre de vue,* 277.

26. Jean-François Lyotard, *Signé Malraux* (Paris: Grasset, 1996), 157.

27. J.-B. Pontalis, *Perdre de vue,* 291.

28. Ibid.

29. Marker, *Immemory.*

30. Jean Laplanche, "Interview: Jean Laplanche Talks to Martin Stanton," in *Jean*

Laplanche: Seduction, Translation, Drives, ed. John Fletcher and Martin Stanton (London: Institute of Contemporary Arts, 1992), 32.

31. Cited by Bill Horrigan in his eloquent essay on "The Revenge of the Eye" on which I depend for my account of Marker's method. "The Revenge of the Eye: Portfolio by Chris Marker," *Artforum* 44, no. 10 (Summer 2006): 313.

32. Ibid.

10. TIME @ CINEMA'S FUTURE

1. Gilles Deleuze, *Cinema 2: The Time-Image,* trans. Hugh Tomlinson and Robert Galeta (Minneapolis: University of Minneapolis Press, 1989), 52.

2. Jean-François Lyotard, *The Inhuman: Reflections on Time,* trans. Geoffrey Bennington and Rachel Bowlby (Stanford, Calif.: Stanford University Press, 1991), 59.

3. J.-B. Pontalis, *Ce temps qui ne passe pas* (Paris: Gallimard, 1997); Georges Didi-Huberman, *Devant le temps* (Paris: Minuit, 2000); André Green, *Le temps éclaté* (Paris: Minuit, 2000); Mary Ann Doane, *The Emergence of Cinematic Time: Modernity, Contingency, the Archive* (Cambridge, Mass.: Harvard University Press, 2002); Elizabeth Grosz, *The Nick of Time: Politics, Evolution, and the Untimely* (Durham, N.C.: Duke University Press, 2004); Thomas Elsaesser and Kay Hoffman, eds., *Cinema Futures: Cain, Abel, or Cable? The Screen Arts in the Digital Age* (Amsterdam: Amsterdam University Press, 1998).

4. Jeffrey Shaw and Peter Weibel, eds., *Future Cinema: The Cinematic Imaginary after Film* (Karlsruhe: ZKM; Cambridge, Mass.: MIT Press, 2003); Richard Castelli, *Cinémas du futur* (Lille: BAI/Lille, 2004).

5. Deleuze, *Cinema 2,* 265, 267.

6. Renate Ferro, "Screen Memory," http://www.renateferro.net/screenmemory.html.

7. Doane, *The Emergence of Cinematic Time,* 228.

8. Deleuze, *Cinema 2,* 270.

9. This is the term coined by one of Deleuze's most thoughtful readers, D. N. Rodowick, in *Reading the Figural, or Philosophy after the New Media* (Durham, N.C.: Duke University Press, 2001).

10. Du Zhenjun, "I Erase Your Trace," http://www.duzhenjun.com; *La leçon d'anatomie du docteur Du Zhenjun* (Rennes: Ecole des Beaux Arts de Rennes, 2001).

11. Deleuze, *Cinema 2,* 87–88.

12. Lev Manovich, *The Language of New Media* (Cambridge, Mass.: MIT Press, 2001), 154–55.

13. Deleuze, *Cinema 2,* 269.

14. D. N. Rodowick, *Gilles Deleuze's Time Machine* (Durham , N.C.: Duke University Press, 1997), 174.

15. Ibid., 175.

16. Deleuze, *Cinema 2,* 269.

17. Jean-François Lyotard, "Matter and Time," in *The Inhuman: Reflections on Time,* trans. Geoffrey Bennington and Rachel Bowlby (Stanford, Calif.: Stanford University Press, 1991), 64–65.

18. Rodowick, *Gilles Deleuze's Time Machine,* 53.

19. Deleuze, *Cinema 2,* 59, 155.

20. Ibid., 235.

21. Gilles Deleuze, *Negotiations, 1972–1990,* trans. Martin Joughin (New York: Columbia University Press, 1995), 45.

22. Jacques Derrida, *Dissemination,* trans. Barbara Johnson (Chicago: University of Chicago Press, 1981), 212.

23. Deleuze, *Cinema 2,* 130–31.

24. Rodowick, *Gilles Deleuze's Time Machine,* 178.

25. Ibid., 204.

26. Deleuze, *Cinema 2,* 116.

27. Ibid., 116–17.

28. Jean-Louis Boissier, "The Relation-Image," in *Future Cinema,* ed. Shaw and Weibel, 403.

29. Ibid., 401.

30. Doane, *The Emergence of Cinematic Time,* 214.

31. Ibid., 218.

32. Boissier, "The Relation-Image," 405.

33. Shu Leah Cheang, "Expand," http://ctheorymultimedia.cornell.edu/art/4.09/.

34. See Wendy Hui Kyong Chun's analysis of race and cyberporn in *Control and Freedom: Power and Paranoia in the Age of Fiber Optics* (Cambridge, Mass.: MIT Press, 2006.

35. Shu Leah Cheang, "Expand."

36. Shu Leah Cheang, "E-mail Exchange with Geert Lovink, 29 December 2000," http://www.nettime.org/Lists-Archives/nettime-l-0012/msg00140.html.

37. Masayuki Akamatsu, "Time Machine!" http://www.iamas.ac.jp/~aka/Time Machine/.

38. Deleuze, *Cinema 2,* 81.

39. Jacques Rancière, *La fable cinématographique* (Paris: Seuil, 2001), 202.

40. Deleuze, *Cinema 2,* 265.

41. Ibid.

42. Tim Griffin, *Listening Post* pamphlet, Whitney Museum of American Art, 2002.

43. Deleuze, *Cinema 2,* 179.

44. Rodowick, *Gilles Deleuze's Time Machine,* 204.

45. Jacques Derrida and Bernard Stiegler, *Echographies de la télévision: Entretiens filmés* (Paris: Galilée; Institut national de l'audiovisuel, 1966), 98.

46. Su Ditta, ed., *David Rokeby* (Oakville, Ontario: Oakville Galleries, 2004), 37.

47. Deleuze, *Cinema 2,* 266. This results in something like an artistic resurgence of the enlivening aspects of what Arthur Kroker calls "the will to technology." Kroker, *The Will to Technology and the Culture of Nihilism: Heidegger, Nietzsche, and Marx* (Toronto: University of Toronto Press, 2004).

PUBLICATION HISTORY

Earlier versions of the chapters in this book appeared in the following publications.

Chapter 1 was previously published as "Digital Baroque: Via Viola, or The Passage of Theatricality," *Substance* 98/99 (2002): 265–79; and in French translation as "Le Baroque numérique: Via Viola ou le travers de la théâtralité," in *Résurgences baroques: Les trajectoires d'un processus transculturel,* ed. Walter Moser (Bruxelles: Editions La Lettre Volée, 2001), 245–64.

Chapter 2 was previously published as "*Et in Arcadia Video:* Poussin' the Image of Culture with Marin and Kuntzel," *MLN* 112, no. 3 (April 1997): 431–53.

Chapter 3 was previously published as "The Crisis of Cinema in the Age of New World Memory: The Baroque Performance of Godard's King Lear," in *The Cinema Alone: Jean-Luc Godard in the 1990s,* ed. James S. Williams and Michael Temple (Amsterdam: Amsterdam University Press, 2001), 159–78. Reprinted with permission of Amsterdam University Press.

Chapter 4 appeared as "You Are How You Read: Baroque Chao-Errancy in Greenaway and Deleuze," *Iris* 23 (Spring 1997): 87–107; and in Japanese translation in "Modernity of the Other," *Shiso* 8 (2000): 183–208.

Chapter 5 appeared as "By Way of Introduction: Digitality and the Memory of Cinema, or Bearing the Losses of the Digital Code," *Wide Angle* 21, no. 1 (January 1999): 3–27; and as "Déjà-vu, Cinema, and Memory Error in the Digital Age," in *Déjà-vu,* ed. Guenter Oesterle (Berlin: Wilhelm Fink Verlag, 2003), 233–45.

Chapter 6 was previously published as "Wounds of Repetition in the Age of the Digital: Chris Marker's Cinematic Ghosts," *Cultural Critique* 46 (Fall 2000): 102–23; and was reprinted in *World Memory: Personal Trajectories in Global Time,* ed. Jill Bennett and Roseanne Kennedy (New York: Palgrave Macmillan, 2003), 195–213.

Chapter 8 was published as "Digital Incompossibility: Cruising the Aesthetic Haze of New Media," *CTHEORY* 78 (January 13, 2000). Reprinted with permission.

Chapter 9 appeared as "Debased Projection and Cyberspatial Ping: Chris Marker's Digital Screen," *Parachute* 113 (Winter 2004): 92–99; and as "Scanning Sublimation: The Digital *Pôles* of Performance and Psychoanalysis," in *Psychoanalysis and Performance,* ed. Patrick Campbell and Adrian Kear (London: Routledge, 2001), 47–59.

INDEX

Timothy Murray is professor of comparative literature and English, director of the Society for the Humanities, and curator of the Rose Goldsen Archive of New Media Art at Cornell University. He is the author of *Drama Trauma: Specters of Race and Sexuality in Performance, Video, and Art; Like a Film: Ideological Phantasy on Screen, Camera, and Canvas; Theatrical Legitimation: Allegories of Genius in Seventeenth-Century England and France;* the coeditor of *Repossessions: Psychoanalysis and the Phantasms of Early Modern Culture* (Minnesota, 1998); and editor of *Mimesis, Masochism, and Mime: The Politics of Theatricality in Contemporary French Thought.*

ELECTRONIC MEDIATIONS *(continued from page ii)*